THE STORY OF THE GENERAL THEOLOGICAL SEMINARY

A Sesquicentennial History

1817-1967

The Story of the General Theological Seminary

A SESQUICENTENNIAL HISTORY
1817–1967

POWEL MILLS DAWLEY

Wipf & Stock
PUBLISHERS
Eugene, Oregon

Wipf and Stock Publishers
199 W 8th Ave, Suite 3
Eugene, OR 97401

The Story of the General Theological Seminary
A Sesquicentennial History, 1817-1967
By Dawley, Powel M.

ISBN: 1-57910-306-5
Publication date 11/11/1999
Previously published by Oxford University Press, 1969

To

THE ALUMNI

of

The General Theological Seminary

Preface

When the Board of Trustees invited me to write a history of the General Theological Seminary to mark its Sesquicentennial Anniversary in 1967, I accepted with some hesitancy and chiefly from a sense of duty and obligation. The task, however, speedily became a privilege I have valued greatly. For nearly twenty-five years I have been a professor in the Seminary, and much of that time its subdean. Long ago I sought, however imperfectly, to make the Seminary's intellectual and devotional traditions my own, and to draw upon their strength and vitality to meet the demands of the ministry I have enjoyed in Chelsea Square. If nothing else, therefore, this volume stands as testimony to my profound gratitude for a quarter-century of intimate association with the life of the General Seminary and those who have formed the Chelsea community over the years.

Surprisingly enough, no substantial history of the first and official seminary of the Episcopal Church has heretofore been written. The nearest approach is in the excellent articles by Edward R. Hardy, Jr., E. Clowes Chorley, William W. Manross, and others that appeared more than thirty years ago in a "General Theological Seminary Number" of *The Historical Magazine of the Protestant Episcopal Church* (vol. V, no. 3, September 1936). An admirable summary of the Seminary's first fifty years appeared recently in George L. Blackman's *Faith and Freedom,* a study of theological education in the Episcopal Church with particular reference to the history of the Episcopal Theological School in Cambridge, Massachusetts. Beyond these, there is little more than Dean Hoffman's monograph in the second volume of William Stevens Perry's *American Episcopal Church,* published in 1885; the charming reminiscences of Seminary life before 1860 contained in Professor Turner's *Autobiography;* and a few brief sketches that appeared in copies of *The Seminarian* at the turn of the century, and in several more recent issues of the *G.T.S. Bulletin.*

No lack of source materials has prevented the writing of the Seminary's history. Indeed, the chief problem has been to sift the overwhelming mass of material with as much discrimination as one could muster, exercising a rigorous discipline of selection. Published sources include the numerous volumes of *Proceedings of the Board of Trustees,* containing records of all meetings of the Board, its official acts, reports of committees, and summary financial statistics from 1821 to the present time; the Seminary *Catalogues,* published annually from 1834; the quarterly *Bulletins,* from 1914; publications by the Associate Alumni; issues of *The Seminarian;* collections of chapel sermons and Matriculation and Commencement Addresses; and memorial or occasional booklets of one kind or another. The *Journals of General Convention* contain the triennial reports of the Seminary Trustees, as well as other relevant material, while the journals of a number of early diocesan conventions, notably those of New York and South Carolina, are indispensable to a clear understanding of the events surrounding the Seminary's foundation. Biographies of prominent churchmen of a century and more ago contain points of significant interest, often in the correspondence reproduced in their pages. The Seminary library possesses a unique collection of the many tracts and pamphlets bearing upon the establishment of the institution and the struggles of its early years, and relating to the controversies that troubled different periods of its history. To this list should be added the articles and news reports appearing in issues of *The Church Journal*, *The Churchman*, *The Christian Journal*, *The Episcopal Recorder*, *The Church Advocate*, *The Banner of the Cross*, *The Episcopal Watchman*, *The Protestant Churchman*, and other church newspapers and periodicals of the nineteenth century.

The picture of the one hundred and fifty years of the Seminary's life that may be derived from these printed materials is extended in detail by the considerable mass of letters and documents that are contained in the Seminary's archives or have found their way into the boxes of the library's manuscript collections. For the most part these are virtually unknown, or, at least, there has been little attempt heretofore to make systematic use of them. Providing an intimate glimpse into the character, ideas, and attitudes of men, they tell the story, so to speak, behind the factual and often tantalizingly sparse printed record or report. From them the reconstruction of events during the first seventy-five years of the Seminary's history is considerably enhanced in both accuracy and interest. The Board of Trustees and the Faculty very graciously opened all this material to my use, and, as will be evident from references in the text, I have drawn heavily upon it, permitting men by frequent quotation to speak for themselves, and the reader to draw his conclusions, wherever possible, from contemporary letters and documents.

The most important official records of this character are the minute books of the Standing Committee of the Board of Trustees and of the Faculty of the Seminary. These are illuminated and expanded at many points by the documents to be found in the several series of General Theological Seminary Papers, and by the minute books of various Seminary organizations and subcommittees of the Board of Trustees. Of the numerous collections of letters and papers of bishops, deans, and professors contained among the library's manuscripts, the most useful are the Jarvis Correspondence and the Johnson Papers. The importance of these Seminary collections is matched by that of two others found elsewhere, the Kemper Papers and the Maryland Diocesan Manuscripts, made available to me by the courtesy respectively of the curator of manuscripts of the State Historical Society of Wisconsin and the archivist of the Diocese of Maryland. Jackson Kemper's correspondence with Professor Turner, Bishop Brownell, William Augustus Muhlenberg, and others sheds much light upon the circumstances surrounding the Seminary's move to New Haven in 1820, and its return to New York in the following year to join with Bishop Hobart's Diocesan School. The correspondence of Bishop Kemp in the Maryland Diocesan Manuscripts bears upon the same early years of the Seminary, while that of Bishop Whittingham is useful for a later period. There is much interesting comment, chiefly about personalities, in the letters of John Pintard, some of which may be found in the Seminary's small collection of Pintard Papers, and others in the volumes published by the New-York Historical Society.

All these sources, as well as other letters, documents, and diaries, have been adequately identified by a liberal use of footnotes, enabling the reader easily to determine their importance and locale. If pages sprinkled with references are distracting, I can only plead my own preference for the convenience of ready identification of sources instead of a discouraging search through a mass of footnotes at the back of a book.

In presenting the story of the Seminary, I have given somewhat detailed treatment to the problem of the education of the clergy in the early decades of the nineteenth century, and the circumstances that led to the establishment of a theological school by the General Convention. This is a chapter of importance in the history of the Episcopal Church. Likewise, the first years before and after the settlement of the institution in the downtown west side block of New York, known as Chelsea Square, are described at length, for this is the period of experiment during which there were few precedents to guide the trustees and professors in their undertaking. After that, I have told the story of the ongoing life of the community in Chelsea Square, its students, professors, and trustees, concentrating mainly upon the men and events of those years about which little is now known, and chronicling but briefly that which is within the memory of older graduates. The changes time has brought to the enterprise of theological education are, of course, inseparable from the activity of the Seminary, and they appear in the form in which they were furthered or experienced in Chelsea Square. Significant events and controversies in the history of the Episcopal Church enter the story obliquely through their repercussions in the Seminary or their effects upon its life.

Within the history of the Seminary community, I have been forced to curtail or omit much that deserves greater space or attention. The record of the activity of the Associate Alumni, for example, both in its loyal and generous support of the Seminary and the distinguished service of its members to the Church, is little more than stated with a few illustrations. Similarly, the story of the Seminary's Missionary Society and its close association with the expansion of the Church's work, at least until recent times, has been summarized only in highlights. On the other hand, a number of details of secondary interest have been included, partly because they loomed large in the common life of the Faculty and students, and partly because they answer the inevitable questions about the origins of the Seminary's customs and traditions, or illustrate the character of daily life in the institution at different times. Where were the services held before the Hoffman chapel was built? What was student life like in the old East Building? What were the methods of teaching and the subjects studied a century ago? Answers to many such queries will be found, though I cannot say that I have anticipated all of them. I have provided no answer, for example, to the question that every Junior is taught to ask: Is it true that there is a special endowment to provide ice cream in the refectory? There may be for all I know; perhaps I did not ask the right people. Nor have I offered a solution to the mystery of the fatal shooting, amid the shrubbery of the West Close, of the brother-in-law of Bishop Seymour. It does not appear to have been the deed of a member of the Seminary, and the issues of *The New York Times*, July 5-14, 1879, may satisfy curiosity about the incident.

Undoubtedly some readers will fail to find all the facts they may expect in these pages, while others will be disappointed at the omission of some favorite anecdote that has been passed along from class to class through the years. To the first I can only say that lack of space prevents the recording of every incident or detail, while I must remind the others that many an entertaining anecdote of the oral tradition is revealed to be apocryphal under the scrutiny of historical investigation. It is perhaps better to ignore such a tale than to risk that a denial of its historicity will result in its reappearance as a myth that is supposed to embody some profound truth.

As my chief interest has been in the continuing life of a community of men, students and teachers, candidates and priests, alike striving to fulfill in their generations the vocation God gave them, much of the story is told in biographical vignettes. I am acutely aware that I may have failed to do justice to all who have gone before. The spiritual and intellectual history of the General Seminary is written in the lives of a long line of men, some completely forgotten, others remembered only by the designation of a memorial or the recitation of a name at the annual Commemoration of Benefactors. Among them there is a succession of true greatness—Fosbroke, Hoffman, Johnson, Turner, and others—spanning the century and a half back to the days when the far-sighted vision of Theodore Dehon combined with the vigorous determination of John Henry Hobart to bring into being "for the better education of the candidates for holy orders in this Church, a general Theological Seminary, which may have the united support of the whole Church in these United States." Through the years, in the life of the Seminary there have been times bright with hope, moments darkened by despair, periods of crisis, and days of controversy, but through them all has run the unbreakable thread of the faith of men, united in the fellowship of a believing, worshiping, and witnessing community, finding therein the sustaining presence of the Lord whose ministry they were called to share, and a deeper understanding of the Gospel they were charged to proclaim.

This book could not have been written without the assistance and counsel of a large number of friends, some of whom have read the whole or parts of the work in manuscript. Among them are the Right Reverend Horace W. B. Donegan, chairman of the Board of Trustees; Mr. Andrew Oliver and the Reverend John V. Butler, members of the Trustees' committee to arrange publication; the Right Reverend Robert R. Spears, Jr., chairman of the Seminary's Sesquicentennial Committee; Dr. Lawrence Rose, former dean of the Seminary; Canon Edward N. West, sub-dean of the Cathedral of St. John the Divine, Dr. Robert S. Bosher of the Seminary Faculty, and others among my colleagues, students, and former students. I am immensely indebted to Dr. Niels H. Sonne, librarian of the Seminary, who gave many hours of his time to assist me in locating materials in the Seminary archives and among the library's manuscripts, who secured for me copies of letters and documents in other collections, and who gave invaluable aid in the task of selecting and assembling the illustrations. I wish also to record my great gratitude to Dr. Edward R. Hardy, Jr., who not only shared freely with me his thorough and detailed knowledge of the Seminary's past, but undertook as well a careful review of the entire work, offering many helpful suggestions.

Thanks are due many others, among them the Reverend Gilbert H. Doane, who arranged for the Seminary to secure copies of some of Jackson Kemper's letters, and who kindly permitted me to read the draft of a very enlightening chapter in his projected biography of Bishop Kemper; Mr. F. Garner Ranney, archivist of the Diocese of Maryland, for his assistance with the correspondence contained in the Maryland Diocesan Manuscripts; and Mrs. Gordon Roberts, a friend and neighbor of the Seminary, for permission to make use of and quote from the unpublished journal of her great-grandfather, Francis Praileux Lee of the Class of 1836. Permission to print excerpts from material in manuscript collections has been granted by the State Historical Society of Wisconsin for the Kemper Papers in its Archives and Manuscript Division at Madison, Wisconsin; by the Massachusetts Historical Society for the diaries of Professor Oliver, now in the possession of the society in Boston; and by the archivist of the Diocese of Maryland for the diocesan manuscripts at present on deposit at the Maryland Historical Society in Baltimore. The New-York Historical Society has kindly allowed me to reproduce passages from *The Letters of John Pintard to His Daughter 1816-1833*, published by the society from manuscripts in its possession, while the Church Historical Society has permitted me to quote from some articles in *The Historical Magazine of the Protestant Episcopal Church*. The authorities of the Episcopal Theological School have given permission to make quotations from James Arthur Muller's *Episcopal Theological School*, and the Reverend J. Howard Melish has allowed me to reproduce a passage from his biography of Franklin Spencer Spalding. My gratitude extends to all these, and as well to the publishers who have given permission for brief quotations from *The Diary of George Templeton Strong*, edited by Allen Nevins and Milton Halsey Thomas (The Macmillan Company, New York, 1952); and from *The Last of the Heretics* by A. S. Crapsey (Alfred A. Knopf, Inc., 1924).

Finally, my thanks are due Mr. Herbert D. Thomas, registrar of the Seminary, for his unfailing response to many appeals for assistance; Mrs. Carl W. Peterson and Mrs. Oliver B. Skanse for their faultless typing of my manuscript; Mr. John S. Adams, who has painstakingly checked my references; and to many others of the Seminary community for the stimulation given me by their constant interest and encouragement.

5 Chelsea Square
Christmas 1968

POWEL MILLS DAWLEY

Contents

1 The Want of Ministers, 3

The State of the Church—America on the Move—The Revival of the Church—The Want of Ministers—Reading for Orders—Bishop White and Samuel Turner—The Course of Ecclesiastical Studies—The Diocesan Societies—Bishop Hobart's Conviction

2 Christopher Gadsden's Motion, 27

The South Carolina Convention of 1814—First Proposals for a General Seminary—Hobart's Plans in New York—Meredith's *Brief Remarks*—The General Convention of 1817—The Seminary Established—Activities of the Theological Committee—Professors Jarvis and Turner—The First Sessions at St. Paul's Chapel—Difficulties with Bishop Hobart—The Seminary Languishes

3 Round Trip to New Haven, 56

The Move to New Haven—Bishop Brownell and the New Haven Plan—John Pintard's Support—Dr. Turner and His Students—Bishop Hobart's Diocesan School—Jacob Sherred's Legacy—The General Convention of 1821—The Union of the Seminary and the New York School—Hobart's Satisfaction—Reopening in New York

4 St. John's Park, 82

Old New York and its Churches—The Seminary at St. John's Chapel—Teachers and Students—Early Commencements—The Board of Trustees—Bishop Hobart and the Influence of New York—Dr. Moore's Estate in Chelsea—The East Building Erected—The Move to Chelsea Square

5 Chelsea Square, 111

The Seminary in the East Building—Rigors of Student Life—Organizations and Activities—The West Building—The Chapel and Its Services—The Rotating Deanship—Pastoral Care of the Students—The First Catalogue—Patterns of Study—The Examination Ordeal—Bishop Onderdonk and the Faculty

6 The Little Oxford, 145

Tractarian Influences—Churchmanship Controversy—Bishop Onderdonk and Arthur Carey—A "Little Oxford" in Chelsea Square—Carey's Ordination—The Seminary under Attack—Investigation by the Trustees—The Bishops' Visitation—The Professors Answer Questions—Bishop Onderdonk's Suspension—The Faculty Investigates—Confidence of Churchmen Shaken—Bishop DeLancey's Proposal

7 Mid-Century Troubles, 180

The Aftermath of Controversy—Suspicions of Romanizing—Professors Mahan and Johnson—Agitation for Curriculum Reform—The Professors' Views—Seabury and Eigenbrodt—The Civil War—Dark Days and Financial Troubles—The Kohne Legacy—On the Edge of Disaster—Mr. Pierrepont to the Rescue—Professor Johnson's Faith

8 The Coming of the Deans, 212

Ritualism and Professor Seymour—The New Commons—Changes in the Chapel—John Murray Forbes the First Permanent Dean—Discipline and Dissatisfaction—The Faculty Quarrel and Dr. Seymour's *Defence*—Excitement among the Trustees—Peace Is Restored—Proposals to Move the Seminary—Dr. Seymour's Deanship—The Library in the West Building—The Scheme of Study—New Professors—The First Degrees

9 Our Most Munificent Benefactor, 245

Eugene Augustus Hoffman—Raising the Endowment—The Buildings of the East Quadrangle—The Chapel of the Good Shepherd—The Refectory in the West Building—Hoffman and the Chapel Life—New Customs and Regulations—Increased Enrollment—The Reconstituted Board of Trustees—The Authority of the Dean—The Intellectual Life—Demands for Curriculum Reform—Hoffman's Professors—The Impatience of the Students

10 The Problem of the Curriculum, 281

The Scheme of Study in 1893—Lecture vs. Recitations—New Professors—Seminary Life at the End of the Century—The Bible Collection—The Buildings of the West Quadrangle—Dean Hoffman's Last Commencement—Dean Robbins—Changes in the Faculty—Distinguished Paddock Lecturers—The Problem of the Curriculum—Dean Fosbroke's Revision of 1919

11 The Seminary of Yesterday, 316

Dean Fosbroke and His Influence—A Galaxy of Scholars—The Tutorial System—Seminary Activity Between the Two World Wars—Financial Troubles during the Depression—Theological Education Sunday—The Second World War—The Coming of Dean Rose—Expanding the Faculty—Changes in Chelsea Square—Married Students—The Building Program—St. Mark's Library—The End of an Era

Epilogue, 355

Appendix: Deans, Professors, and Other Members of the Teaching Staff: 1817-1967, 363

Index, 375

THE STORY OF THE GENERAL THEOLOGICAL SEMINARY

A Sesquicentennial History
1817-1967

I

The Want of Ministers

On February 24, 1811, in Bruton Parish Church, Williamsburg, a young man was ordained to the ministry of the Episcopal Church in circumstances so discouraging that it is not surprising that the Church in Virginia was commonly reported "from various causes, so depressed, that there is danger of her total ruin."[1] Forty years later, William Meade recalled the attitude of his acquaintances:

> So low and hopeless was the state of the Church at that time—the time of my ordination—it created surprise and was a matter of much conversation, when it was understood that a young Virginian had entered the ministry of the Episcopal Church.

Only an unquenchable ardor and spiritual courage of a high order could sustain the cheerless ordination Meade describes:

> On arriving at the church we found it in a wretched condition, with broken windows and a gloomy comfortless aspect. The congregation which assembled consisted of two ladies and about fifteen gentlemen, nearly all of whom were relatives or acquaintances. The morning service being over, the ordination and communion were administered, and then I was put into the pulpit to preach, there being no ordination sermon.[2]

1. *Journal of General Convention 1811* (Swords ed.), p. 16.
2. William Meade, *Old Churches, Ministers, and Families of Virginia* (Philadelphia, 1857), I, 29-30.

Meade's experience was matched by that of Christopher Gadsden, who the year before had journeyed from Charleston to be ordained priest at Williamsburg. When it was discovered that the local rector was absent from his church, Bishop Madison with some difficulty persuaded a clergyman who had abandoned the ministry for farming to array himself in borrowed vestments and assist in ordaining the young South Carolinian. Like Meade, Gadsden preached his own ordination sermon.

Two decades of diminishing vigor and declining influence had brought the Episcopal Church in some areas of the United States to this sorry state, the lowest point of vitality in its history. Twenty years earlier, at the end of the American Revolution, the leaders of the Church accomplished a task of heroic proportions. They organized the separate and scattered parishes of the former Church of England into Churches in each of the newly independent states, and this despite prejudice and hostility, the crippling loss of financial grants from the English Society for the Propagation of the Gospel as well as the withdrawal of its missionary clergy, and the emigration of thousands of Loyalist church members to the British colonies in Canada and the West Indies. An episcopate had been secured through the consecration of Samuel Seabury by the bishops of the Scottish Episcopal Church, and that of William White, Samuel Provoost, and James Madison in England.

These achievements were crowned in 1789 by the federation of the separate Churches in the several states into a national body of Episcopalians, bound together by a common order and discipline in their constitution and canons, united in the common faith and practice of their Prayer Book. The successful creation of an independent and self-governing Church, faithful to its Anglican heritage yet adapted to the demands of its mission in the American scene, was an accomplishment that exhausted the resources of Episcopalians in the Revolutionary era. Perhaps more than this could not have been expected of men whose ideas were in large measure shaped by earlier eighteenth-century patterns of thought. To develop effective means of church support, to find ways whereby the national Church might successfully contend with the conflicting claims of regional and local loyalties, to create the agencies necessary for the extension of the Church's work, to devise methods for the education and training of the clergy, and, above all, to meet the challenges brought by the sweeping changes in American life during the early years of the Republic—these were beyond the capacities of the first generation of leaders. They awaited the rise of men reared within the new national life.

The brash strains of "Yankee Doodle" echoed shrilly throughout the land in the days that followed the winning of American independence, until by the second decade of the nineteenth century, it was the dominant music of the age. The United States was stirred by turbulent changes that aroused the pride and quickened the pulse of the citizens. When the War of 1812 brought final freedom from European entanglements, its concomitant was a heady intoxication by what an English visitor described as a national vanity surpassing that of any country. Men saw visions of beckoning promise and vistas of limitless expansion on every national horizon. The smoking ruins in which the British forces left Dolly Madison's White House were soon rebuilt and forgotten. What lasted was the memory of Perry's victorious message from Lake Erie: "We have met the enemy, and they are ours." His words were an appropriate motto for a generation that learned as children Charles Pinckney's defiant cry, "Millions for defence, but not a damned penny for tribute," and lived to echo the bellicose slogan of 1846: "Fifty-four Forty or Fight!"

In this aggressive self-confidence, our forefathers grasped at opportunity on every side. An expanding blanket of cotton promised new wealth to the South; the machinery that began to turn in the mills beside the rivers of New England foreshadowed manufacturing prosperity in the North. Merchantile ventures made the Stars and Stripes an increasingly familiar flag in the harbors of the Far East, while in the west the fur traders began to tap the abundant riches of the endless plains and woods explored by Lewis and Clark.

America was on the move in the new century. A restless and self-reliant spirit was rapidly becoming a characteristic national trait. Hundreds of families migrated from the old farms of the eastern seaboard to start life afresh in the fertile valleys of western Pennsylvania and the lake country of New York State, while others pushed across the mountains to open up the "Old West"—Tennessee, Kentucky, and Ohio.

Movement on this scale placed a premium on rapid means of shipping and transportation, and the newly kindled national feeling gave incentive to improving travel in an effort to bind the states more closely together. In the early years of the nineteenth century, diligences clattered over rebuilt bridges and roads, while the heavy freight wagons of carriers hauled a steadily mounting volume of cargo. But the canal boat soon challenged the turnpike, only itself to give way before the steam engine which rapidly covered America's rivers and harbors with plumes of smoke, and eventually laid the iron rails that would conquer the vast stretches of a continent.

Amid such changes in the old order of life, the foundations of all accepted traditions were shaken. Shackles that bound men to the habits and ideas of the past were loosened, an emancipation nowhere more evident than in the revolt against an earlier orthodoxy or religious conservatism. Terminated or drastically modified in the aftermath of the Revolution, religious establishments once supported by law or social pressures lost much of their hold on a free-thinking folk. This break-up of traditional religious loyalties was accelerated by revolutionary influences from Europe. "Liberty and Equality" was a watchword of the social and political order, but it had religious application as well. Irreligion and agnosticism were widespread. In a day when Thomas Paine's *Age of Reason* was a bestseller, French rationalism and English deism posed a threat to the Churches, which the clergy called "infidelism." William Meade did not find the free-thinking spirit that characterized the College of William and Mary any more to his liking in 1811 than the state of the Church in Williamsburg:

The religious condition of the College may be justly inferred . . . I was informed that not long before this two questions were discussed in a literary society of the College: First, whether there be a God? Secondly, Whether the Christian religion had been injurious or beneficial to mankind? Infidelity, indeed, was then rife in the State, and the College of William and Mary was regarded as the hotbed of French politics and religion.[3]

The extent of these influences may be exaggerated, but it was some years before the evangelical reawakening in Protestantism combined with the rise of Victorian romanticism to diminish their force. In those Churches long identified with the conservative and educated classes, the impact of this "infidelism" was sharply felt—that is, among New England Congregationalists, the Presbyterians of the middle states, and in the Protestant Episcopal Church.

On the other hand, there was no lack of religious enthusiasm among many of America's plain folk—quite the contrary, for the early decades of the nineteenth century witnessed a new "awakening," an outburst of what was later to be called "that old-fashioned Bible religion." It was the enthusiasm of a rough and ready evangelical Christianity, emancipated from the constrictions of sober theological learning, recharged by periodic waves of revivalism, nurtured by the circuit-riding preacher and the camp meeting, and providing both the sustaining faith and emotional release necessary amid the hardships and loneliness of pioneer life. Baptists and Methodists, denominations singularly adapted to reap the harvest of this enthusiasm, increased their membership enormously. The ten thousand Baptists of the end of the colonial period had multiplied tenfold by 1799, and in the next forty years, their number mounted to seven hundred thousand. Methodist growth was even more striking. From about fourteen thousand at the close of the American Revolution, the number of Methodists had risen to nearly a million and a half by 1850. Both Churches shared their success with a proliferation of sects, some born amid theological disputes, some

3. Meade, *Old Churches*, I, 29.

springing from the need of spiritual companionship on the frontier, and others from no more apparent cause than what was called "pure cussedness"—the desire of free Americans to assert their religious independence.

Congregationalists and Presbyterians rallied as best they could, and with some success, to find the resources and flexibility with which to adapt themselves to the changing scene. Most distressed of all was the Episcopal Church, threatened by "infidelism" on the one hand and "fanaticism" on the other, its organization completed, but its vigor on the wane. The sweeping tides of the new era left the Church stranded on the rock of the very Anglican heritage it cherished and expended so much energy to preserve. The repeated assertions of continuity with the Church of England, by which Episcopalians sought to establish their identity among the denominations of the Republic, only returned to roost in the form of suspicion that the Church was still subject to a foreign ecclesiastical jurisdiction. As late as 1814, the *Journal of General Convention* carried a solemn declaration of the Church's "entire independence of the Civil and Ecclesiastical authority of any foreign country," but this availed little, for, as the bishops observed somewhat ruefully in a fine example of understatement in 1817, "the circulation of the Journal is not extensive." In their *Pastoral Letter* of that year, they thought it "expedient to renew the assurance," supporting it with a miniature history of relations with the Church of England since 1785.

If to some men the Episcopal Church seemed more English than American, others viewed it as a vestigial survival of an age they had left behind, a citadel of tradition that now protected no more than the remnant sheltered within its walls. Men sought to discard the established institutions of the eighteenth century, along with the wigs, smallclothes, and winking buckles that remained the property only of the elderly. The Church, with its hierarchical ministry, its inflexible ways, its formal services and prescribed liturgy, seemed to reflect the fading image of a vanishing era. It, too, thought some of William Meade's friends, would disappear with the last of the eighteenth-century generation.

But they were wrong who thought the Church "too far gone ever to be revived." The very year of Meade's ordination marked a turning point in the history of the Episcopal Church. Unmistakable signs of renewed vitality rewarded the labors of a remarkable group of men who assumed the responsibilities of leadership laid down by the passing generation. They were men who grew up with the Republic, and in any partial list of them, there is scarcely one whose work is not known and still venerated in some diocese, institution, or area of the Church's mission: Christopher Gadsden, William Wilmer, Jackson Kemper, John Henry Hobart, Philander Chase, Nathaniel Bowen, Theodore Dehon, Thomas Church Brownell, Alexander Viets Griswold, Richard Channing Moore, and William Meade himself—all of them in spirit and outlook very much men of the new times.

Impatient with the sterility of past Low Church traditions, some, in their piety and ardor, gave witness to the awakening impact of Evangelicalism within the Episcopal Church, while in others the High Churchmanship of seventeenth-century Anglicanism was rekindled with intense conviction. Their common ground was an unswerving devotion to the order, liturgy, and life of their Church. Armed with a resolute sense of unique mission of the Episcopal Church in America, they displayed both tenacious courage in the face of adversity and the imaginative capacity to make use of propitious circumstance. As the years of the second decade of the nineteenth century passed, their infectious zeal spread to a host of younger disciples, such men as John Henshaw, Stephen Tyng, Jonathan Wainwright, and William Augustus Muhlenberg. Slowly but surely, they led the Episcopal Church out of the dark days of despair and decline.

Nothing illustrates the rapid rise of this changing leadership more forcibly than the reinvigoration of the episcopate that took place in the five years between 1811 and 1816. It was hardly a moment too soon, for the fear was common that the episcopal succession might fail, requiring a second recourse to the Church of England. When the House of Bishops assembled at New Haven for the General Convention of 1811, only two of the six bishops appeared: William White of Pennsylvania, and Abraham Jarvis, Seabury's successor in Connecticut. Samuel Provoost of New York, nearly seventy years old, was in retirement; Benjamin Moore, his assistant and successor, was stricken by paralysis. Bishop Madison in Virginia had "engagements which, in his estimation, did not admit of being dispensed with," while Thomas Claggett of Maryland was overcome by illness en route and forced to turn back.[4] Yet it was at the conclusion of this convention that Bishop White and Bishop Jarvis traveled to New York to consecrate two new bishops, determined if necessary to hold the service in Bishop Moore's bedroom. This interesting possibility did not arise, however, for Bishop Provoost was persuaded to emerge from seclusion, and on May 29 in Trinity Church, John Henry Hobart and Alexander Viets Griswold were consecrated. Hobart, a vigorous High Churchman of dynamic spirit and personality, was made Moore's assistant in New York, where already his boundless energy had made itself felt.[5] Griswold was consecrated for the Eastern Diocese, a temporary union whereby four impoverished New England dioceses—Massachusetts, Rhode Island, Vermont, and New Hampshire—might be provided with episcopal ministrations. Griswold brought to his episcopate a strong evangelical fervor that sustained him in all "the hardships and mortifications incident to the office in such an extended territory and under such unpromising circumstances."[6]

In the next year, Theodore Dehon, one of the most attractive

4. *Journal of General Convention 1811* (Swords ed.), p. 19.
5. Hobart was made "Coadjutor," as we would say, "to succeed in case of survivorship" (*Journal of General Convention 1811* [Swords ed.], p. 36). As Hobart was "Acting Bishop" until Moore's death in 1816, in the interests of simplicity he is referred to in these pages as the bishop of New York. Provoost, of course, retained the actual diocesan title until his death in 1815, when Moore became technically the diocesan for a year.
6. See David W. Norton, Jr., *Alexander Viets Griswold of New England* (New York: The National Council, n.d.), p. 8.

Bishop White
Seminary Portrait by Henry Inman

spirits among the new leaders, was made bishop of South Carolina, where there had been no episcopal supervision since the minimal activity of Robert Smith was terminated by his death in 1801. In 1814 Richard Channing Moore succeeded James Madison in Virginia, embarking upon a ministry that was to infuse new life into the Church there, and where William Meade would in turn succeed him. John Croes became the first bishop of New Jersey in 1815, and in the following year James Kemp, who had been consecrated assistant bishop in 1814, succeeded the aged Claggett as bishop of Maryland. When the House of Bishops met in New York for the Convention of 1817, William White alone remained of the earlier group of bishops. He still had nearly twenty years in which to enjoy a seniority that would gradually turn him into a figure of patriarchal aspect, but around him now gathered a group of young men alert to every opportunity for the advance of the Church.

In the Convention of 1811, the dismay caused by the state of the episcopate before the consecration of Hobart and Griswold was somewhat relieved by the encouraging size of the House of Deputies. Forty-seven representatives from nine states met in New Haven. Never before had the deputies numbered more than thirty-three, and in the preceding Convention of 1808, only twenty-seven delegates had appeared. Reports made to the House in 1811 on the state of the Church south of Philadelphia continued to be discouraging. Maryland's Church was "still in a deplorable condition." Delaware sent no deputation, and the prospects there, as reported subsequently, were "truly depressing and gloomy." South Carolina, where twenty-two parishes had been served by twenty ministers at the outbreak of the American Revolution, had suffered the ravages of the war more extensively than any other area. In the aftermath, there were few churches outside Charleston that were not dilapidated, abandoned, or destroyed. Following some sporadic and short-lived attempts at recovery, the Church had fallen into such torpor and isolation that the General Convention had not seen a deputy from South Carolina for sixteen years. Yet word came through to New Haven of new beginnings. Nathaniel Bowen and Theodore Dehon had aroused considerable support for their agency of Church revival, the Society for the Advancement of Christianity, and a reawakened enthusiasm was reported among the dozen clergy in the state.

The news relayed from Virginia, however, was almost uniformly bad, a state of affairs the more discouraging because of the former strength and prosperity of Virginian Anglicanism. After the Revolution, Bishop Madison had tried earnestly to revive a diocese whose clergy had fallen in numbers to few more than half the hundred ministers of 1775. For a while there was hope—an actual increase in the number of clergymen during the last years of the eighteenth century. But the hostility of Baptists and Presbyterians, the loss of the glebe farms in the wake of the Church's disestablishment, the resentful memory of the identification of colonial Anglicanism with wealth and privilege, the disrepute brought upon the Church by an unfortunately large number of unworthy ministers—all combined to extinguish the early signs of promise. By 1811 the Church in Virginia had collapsed. Bishop Madison, then in the last year of his life, virtually abandoned his episcopal duties to devote himself to the presidency of the College of William and Mary. Virginia sent no delegates to general conventions for the eighteen years before 1817, nor were any diocesan conventions held in the state between 1799 and 1803, and after 1805 they lapsed again for seven years. In these circumstances, it is no wonder that William Meade left the Virginia Convention of 1813 so disconsolate that, as he said,

> having just read Scott's "Lay of the Last Minstrel," as I took my solitary way homeward on horseback, I found myself continually saying, in relation to the Church in Virginia, in the words of the elvish page, "Lost . . . lost . . . lost!"[7]

From the northern states, however, clear evidence of recovery was reported. New Jersey's congregations, though not numerous, were "orderly and attentive," and a society, modeled after that of South Carolina, had been formed recently "for the Promotion of Christian Knowledge and Piety." In Pennsylvania, activity among the churches of Philadelphia was on the increase. Rhode Island, Vermont, and New Hampshire had few parishes, but their condition gave good ground for hope. In Massachusetts, though the Church had been without a bishop since the death of Samuel Parker in 1804, the number of clergymen had increased, and some parishes reported growing congregations. Connecticut and New York were the areas of the Church's greatest strength. Both dioceses reported an increase in their clergy, as well as the steady enlargement of existing congregations and the foundation of new ones.

"The want of ministers" was the cry on all sides in the Conven-

7. Meade, *Old Churches*, I, 37-38.

tion of 1811, the need of "a learned and pious ministry." Though exact statistics are difficult to arrive at, chiefly because of the disordered situation in Virginia, there were certainly less than two hundred and twenty-five ministers in the Church, of whom probably no more than a hundred and sixty-five were serving a full parochial ministry, the remainder being employed in educational institutions, retired, or listed simply as "residing" in the several dioceses. Without the recruitment and training of an enlarged body of clergy, sufficient in numbers and armed with the resolution and ability to meet the challenges of the times, the Church's full recovery was impossible, to say nothing of meeting the missionary needs that arose with the westward march of the frontier. The members of the convention were as keenly aware of the urgency of "supplying the congregations of this Church, west of the Allegheny mountains, with the ministrations and worship of the same," as they were of the need of ministers in the settled areas.[8]

How were these clergymen to be provided? Where were they to be trained? No questions appeared more important to the rising group of leaders in the Church. Aware of the deficiencies in their own training and the inadequacy of the conventional methods of preparation for the ministry, theological education was among their primary concerns. The Church had neither colleges nor theological schools, nor was there any institution in the country where a man could obtain a theological education appropriate to the ministry of the Episcopal Church. In their *Pastoral Letter* of 1811, the bishops observed somewhat wistfully: "Our Church is not possessed of any public provisions which will enable learned divines to devote themselves to this department of instruction." In the minds of men like John Henry Hobart and Theodore Dehon, there was a growing determination to make "public provisions," though their precise form had not yet taken shape. In 1811 the bishops could do no more than urge the clergy to greater pains in directing the study of candidates who were "reading for orders"—that is, undertaking the course of private study for ordination that had been customary since the foundation of the Church in America.

8. *Journal of General Convention 1811* (Swords ed.), p. 12.

Before the establishment of theological seminaries, candidates prepared for the ministry in the same fashion as men read law with an attorney or learned medicine from a practicing physician. After graduation from college, preparation for ordination usually extended over a two- or three-year period of private study with a parish priest, who spared what time he could for his pupil and shared with him what books he possessed. Efforts during the colonial period to provide resources for ministerial candidates had been chiefly directed toward the establishment of libraries or the provision of theological textbooks. The Reverend James Blair, commissary of the Bishop of London, had attempted a more ambitious project in the foundation of the College of William and Mary. One aim of its charter in 1693 was "that the Church in Virginia may be furnished with a seminary of ministers of the Gospel," leading to the provision by 1727 for two divinity professors. At best, however, the college educated only a small proportion of the clergy, and the Divinity School was abolished in 1779. Private study remained the path to ordination for most men.

Candidates read with neighboring parsons, clerical relatives, or sometimes traveled considerable distance to stay with or near a clergyman whose learning attracted pupils to him. Dr. Samuel Johnson, for example, who was one of Timothy Cutler's companions among the "Yale Converts" ordained in England in 1723, enjoyed a wide reputation as a supervisor of theological studies, both before and after his term as president of Columbia, then known as King's College. A large number of students found a ready welcome to his study in Stratford, Connecticut. Thomas Bradbury Chandler and Abraham Beach were among Dr. Johnson's students, Chandler in turn guiding the studies of Abraham Jarvis, White's companion in the House of Bishops in 1811. Theodore Dehon and Nathaniel Bowen sought help from Dr. Samuel Parker at Trinity Church, Boston, and Bowen later supervised the preparation of Christopher Gadsden in Charleston. Bishop White's pupils in Philadelphia were numerous. Samuel Turner and Bird Wilson, both destined to become professors in the General Theological Seminary, were White's most promising scholars, though perhaps John Henry

Hobart was the most illustrious churchman to be coached by the Presiding Bishop. Hobart afterwards, as an assistant minister in Trinity Parish, guided the reading of many young men. John McVickar studied for ordination under him, as did Jackson Kemper, and when the latter became an assistant to Bishop White at Christ Church, Philadelphia, William Augustus Muhlenberg and two fellow students "recited regularly to Mr. Kemper."

Often attempts were made to give men more adequate preparation for the exercise of the ministry than a simple review of the accepted theological textbooks. Supervised experience as a lay reader, at least during the final year of study, was frequent, and a few clergymen took seriously the task of introducing their students to the principles of pastoral care and methods of parochial administration. Stephen H. Tyng, later a prominent Evangelical and rector of St. George's Church, New York, and John P. K. Henshaw, who became bishop of Rhode Island when the Church there separated from Griswold's Eastern Diocese, were among the group of candidates for whom Bishop Griswold provided such training at St. Michael's Church, Bristol, Rhode Island.

The weaknesses of this pattern of theological education were less apparent before the American Revolution than afterwards, partly because of the large number of English priests sent out to the colonies by the Society for the Propagation of the Gospel. With the disappearance of this supply of ministers and with reliance upon private preparation alone, it became increasingly clear that a more effective method of theological training was necessary. Reading for orders, at best, had some serious limitations. Preparation for the ministry, for example, was open only to those who could find adequate supervision and, as was often essential, employment to sustain them during the period of study. "Necessitous students," as those less fortunate were called, frequently could find no way to the fulfillment of a vocation to holy orders. Moreover, candidates were subject not only to the intellectual limitations of their mentors, but to their theological idiosyncrasies as well. The result was that for many students, perhaps even for most, preparation was minimal if not woefully inadequate. So able a man as Samuel Turner, ordained in 1811 after finishing his course with Bishop White, found the experience so frustrating that he had little enthusiasm for the system under which he was supposed to have been educated for the ministry:

> My theological studies were pursued under the direction of Bishop White, whom I regularly visited in his study, at first once in two weeks, and afterwards once a month, for upwards of three years. The Bishop never subjected me to any examinations; indeed, I do not recollect that he ever questioned me in reference to any theological point except at my examination for orders. If the plan of stated recitations had been pursued with some regularity, my studies would, no doubt, have been more thorough and my knowledge more accurate. As it was, I read a great deal, but thought and studied little. To use common language, I crammed so fully that I had neither opportunity nor ability to digest anything intellectually.[9]

The Church made some efforts to establish and maintain a standard of theological learning required for ordination, though the first canonical enactment in 1789 was brief. Anyone to be ordained

> shall have satisfied the Bishop and the two Presbyters, by whom he shall be examined, that he is sufficiently acquainted with the New Testament in the original Greek, and can give an account of his faith in the Latin tongue, either in writing or otherwise.[10]

This was speedily amended, for in the troubled times after the Revolution, it was admitted, however reluctantly, that the Church must be content with "a ministry accommodated in some instances rather to the necessities of congregations than to what it were wished to be considered as a standard of sufficiency." The amendment allowed bishops to dispense the requirements of Greek and Latin, if such were recommended by two thirds of the members of a state convention "in consideration of other qualifications for the Gospel ministry."[11]

In 1792 an expansion of the canons required "a competent knowl-

9. *Autobiography of the Rev. Samuel H. Turner, D.D.* (New York, 1863), pp. 22-23.

10. *Journal of General Convention 1789* (July-August), Canon 8.

11. *Journal of General Convention 1789* (September-October), Canon 7.

edge of moral philosophy, church history, and the belles lettres," and also that a candidate "hath paid attention to rhetoric and pulpit eloquence, as the means of giving additional efficacy to his labours."[12] Three years later, the General Convention granted the power of dispensing a man from Greek and Latin to the bishops alone, only to withdraw it entirely in 1799, and finally to restore it in 1801 subject to the consent of the clerical members of standing committees. The fluctuating fortunes of the dispensing power reflect the controversy between those who sought to maintain the highest possible academic requirements and those who felt that much learning was inimical to true piety. By 1808 the canons included a declaration that it was "desirable that every candidate for orders should be acquainted with the Hebrew language," and specified as well that the examination before ordination to the priesthood should be "on those leading books in the course of study prescribed by the House of Bishops."[13]

The reference is to the famous Course of Ecclesiastical Studies, "considered and established" by the House of Bishops in 1804 in response to a request from the House of Deputies for an authorized scheme of theological study to guide men reading for orders. The course was a formidable one, outlining a systematic plan of study covering the whole field of theological learning as it was then understood. Standard textbooks, with some options, were prescribed in each branch of sacred learning. The books on the recommended list have considerable historical interest, though, save for a few that are known as "Anglican classics," most of the works and their authors are unknown to students today. By age alone the majority of them might have been "classics," even in 1804, for most of them had been written at least fifty years earlier, and many were first published in the seventeenth century. Yet it is to the credit of Bishop White, who is probably responsible for drawing up the syllabus, that he included as many contemporary books of genuine worth as possible. The importance of the Course of Ecclesiastical

12. *Journal of General Convention 1792*, Canon 7.
13. *Journal of General Convention 1808*, Canon 11.

Studies lay not only in the provision of an official guide for private study but also in the long shadow that it cast over the curricula of the Church's first theological seminaries. From 1804 until nearly the end of the nineteenth century, the books of the course, or others in harmony with them, occupied a large place in any syllabus of reading for theological students in the Episcopal Church. Attempts to revise the course fifty years after its first publication met with no success. Delays and disagreements prolonged the work of an episcopal committee of revision from 1856 to 1889, and in the end the committee contented itself with reproducing the original as containing books "of permanent utility."[14]

The scheme of the course began with "some books in proof of the divine authority of Christianity." These included Hugo Grotius' *Truth of the Christian Religion*, an early seventeenth-century defense of Christianity by a distinguished Dutch jurist and theologian. Refutations of the writings of the deists followed, Joseph Butler's *Analogy of Religion* being the best-known work in this section. The newest book among these apologetic texts was William Paley's *Christian Evidences*, published in 1794..

Thus armed with arguments in defense of the Christian faith, the student was then directed to "study the Scriptures with the help of approved commentators." Exegetical commentaries and harmonies of the Gospels were recommended, as well as some books on selected topics to which special attention was to be given: the Deluge, the systems of chronology, Old Testament sacrifices, intertestamental "connexions," the Resurrection, and "profane history . . . whenever it mixes with the sacred." Church history was the next subject in the scheme of reading. Eusebius and the Apostolic Fathers were to be studied for the early Church, along with William Cave's *Lives of the Apostles* and *Lives of the Most Eminent Fathers*. Before passing beyond the Council of Nicaea, two topics were to be explored with careful attention: the divinity of Christ,

14. They added a list of more recent books which, though admittedly "of transient value," they thought might assist theological study "for a century to come" (*Journal of General Convention 1889*, pp. 747-762).

AN

EXPOSITION

OF THE

CREED,

BY

JOHN PEARSON.

LONDON,

Printed by ROGER DANIEL, for *John Williams* at the ſign of the *Crown* in St. *Paul's* Church-yard. CIↃ IↃC LIX.

and episcopacy. For the latter, Hooker's *Ecclesiastical Polity* and John Potter's *Defense of Church Government* might be supplemented by Archdeacon Daubeny's *Guide to the Church*, an emphatic defense of apostolic succession published in 1798, the substance of which helped to shape the views of High Churchmen like John Henry Hobart. The standard survey of ecclesiastical history was that of Johann von Mosheim of the University of Göttingen, whose work, published in the middle of the eighteenth century, was marked by a significant advance in objectivity and historical method. Jeremy Collier's *Ecclesiastical History of Great Britain* was recommended for the history of the Church of England, with additional reference to the arguments against papal supremacy in two seventeenth-century works: *The Religion of Protestants* by William Chillingworth, and *A Treatise on the Pope's Supremacy* by Isaac Barrow.

"After these studies, and not before" was the warning that introduced the candidate to his systematic study of theology. The standard works listed were John Pearson's *Exposition of the Creed*, Gilbert Burnet's *Thirty-Nine Articles*, and Thomas Stackhouse's *Complete Body of Divinity*. To these were added "the following modern works": *Elements of Christian Theology* by George Pretyman Tomline, then bishop of Lincoln, and *The Scholar Armed against the Errors of the Time*, a collection of essays and tracts edited by the famous William Jones of Nayland and first published in 1792.

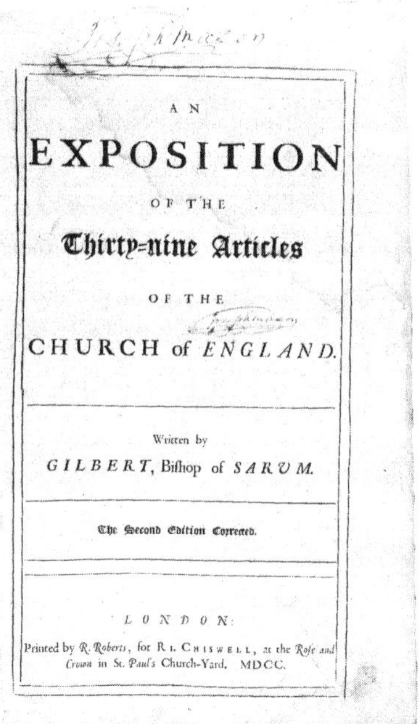

AN
EXPOSITION
OF THE
Thirty-nine Articles
OF THE
CHURCH of *ENGLAND*.

Written by
GILBERT, Biſhop of *SARUM*.

The Second Edition Corrected.

LONDON:
Printed by *R. Roberts*, for Ri. Chiswell, at the *Roſe* and *Crown* in St. *Paul's* Church-Yard. MDCC.

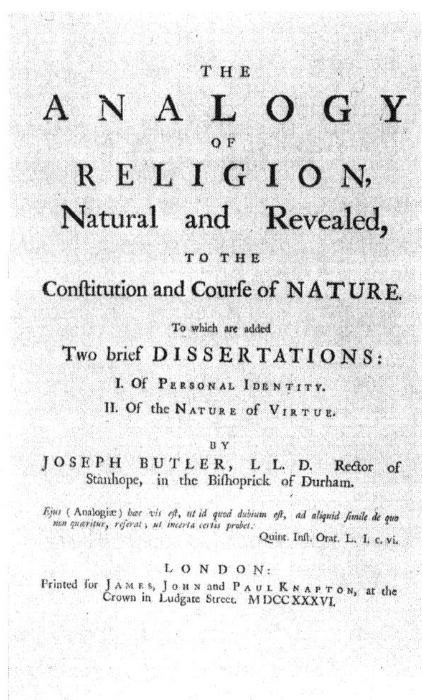

THE
ANALOGY
OF
RELIGION,
Natural and Revealed,
TO THE
Conſtitution and Courſe of NATURE.

To which are added
Two brief DISSERTATIONS:
I. Of Personal Identity.
II. Of the Nature of Virtue.

BY
JOSEPH BUTLER, LL. D. Rector of Stanhope, in the Biſhoprick of Durham.

Ejus (Analogiæ) *hæc vis eſt, ut id quod dubium eſt, ad aliquid ſimile de quo non quæritur, referat; ut incerta certis probet.*
Quint. Inſt. Orat. L. I. c. vi.

LONDON:
Printed for James, John and Paul Knapton, at the Crown in Ludgate Street. MDCCXXXVI.

The reading of sermons by distinguished and eloquent preachers was warmly commended, and a considerable list of these was appended to the course. For Prayer Book study, students were directed to Charles Wheatly's *Rational Illustration of the Book of Common Prayer* and an edition of the Prayer Book with an historical introduction by John Reeves. Books on the pastoral office included St. John Chrysostom's *Christian Priesthood*, Burnet's *Discourse on Pastoral Care*, and the *Parochialia* of Thomas Wilson, an early eighteenth-century bishop of Sodor and Man who had tried diligently to improve the pastoral efficiency of his clergy.

The bishops were well aware that the course would be "disproportioned to the means of some, and fall short of what would be within the compass of others." For the benefit of the latter, a long list of books was appended, drawn chiefly from Bishop Tomline's "Ideal Library of a Parish Minister." Tempering the requirements for the former group—which must have been considerably larger—they set down "what books shall be essential, no student to be ordained without being fully prepared to answer on them." The list was short. Paley's *Evidences*, Mosheim "with a reference to Mr. Hooker for the Episcopacy," Stackhouse's *Body of Divinity*, "Mr. Reeves on the Common Prayer," and the constitution and canons of the Church—these, with a knowledge of the Scriptures and the exegetical facts "in some good commentary," were to be the minimum. The prescription of minimum requirements was obviously necessary, but unfortunately it later gave rise to the idea that there might be two courses of study authorized, a three-year course for men of unusual academic attainments, and a one-year course for others. This distinction was particularly appealing to those bishops who hoped to speed their candidates on to ordination and thence to vacant parishes or new missionary opportunities.

The Course of Ecclasiastical Studies, at least in its "leading books," was widely used to meet the standards of learning set by the canons. Men recited on the books to their preceptors, and a number of ordinands were able to echo Stephen Tyng's remark that he had completed the "course of study as required by the canons."

For others, however, preparation was still sketchy or inadequate. Though the Church had a standard of learning and an authorized syllabus of reading to achieve it, both funds and teachers were lacking. John McVickar, Professor of Moral and Intellectual Philosophy in Columbia College, who was ordained in 1811, summarized the difficulties:

> The divinity student in our Church was, therefore, thrown, necessarily and altogether, upon his own resources, and, mainly, his own judgment. With a few general directions, furnished by the Canons, he was left to grope his way vaguely, if not blindly, through the most voluminous, intricate, and perplexing of all professional studies, without aid or guidance beyond the casual counsel of some friendly parochial minister, who certainly could not have the leisure, and most probably had not the ability to solve the doubts by which the conscientious student must on these subjects be daily arrested, or determine his choice amid conflicting authorities.[15]

Samuel Turner's experience, while reading with Bishop White, bears out the truth of Dr. McVickar's remarks. Confused by the conflicting statements in commentaries on the Bible, he describes a moment of desperation in his studies:

> I got together all the commentators I could procure, had them opened and arranged on a large table, and read one after the other with persevering industry until I became tired and bewildered. The result was a confused jumble of information, often inconsistent, sometimes positively contradictory; and vague, indefinite, unsatisfactory notions of the meaning. I learned by experience that no clear perception of the oracles of God was attainable in this way. I was incompetent to form a judgment respecting the truth among diversified and opposing expositions.[16]

When such was the case with one of the most talented and conscientious students, the condition of the average candidate for holy orders is easily imagined.

15. John McVickar, *The Early Life and Professional Years of Bishop Hobart* (Oxford, 1838), p. 279.
16. *Autobiography*, p. 27.

Serious attempts were made to provide assistance to men reading for orders by the new diocesan societies that were established in increasing numbers during the decade from 1810 to 1820. These organizations aimed at raising the educational and evangelistic thrusts of the Church above the parish level to a coordinated diocesan effort. Attracting the support of those stirred by a reawakened concern for the Church, they speedily became the chief agencies through which the new generation of leaders made their efforts for renewal felt. In many instances, the later structures of diocesan organization for the promotion and extension of the Church's work developed from these early societies. Though commanding slender resources and directed to limited ends, the diocesan societies were patterned after the Society for the Propagation of the Gospel and the Society for the Promotion of Christian Knowledge, both of which had played a vital role in the Church's life during the colonial period.

Typical was the Protestant Episcopal Society for the Advancement of Christianity in South Carolina, formed in 1810 by Nathaniel Bowen and Theodore Dehon. Its aims were (1) to disseminate Christian literature; (2) to further missionary efforts in the state; and (3) to assist in "the education of Young Men of Genius and Piety for the Ministry of the Church," or, as Dehon himself put it:

> to bring youthful genius forward from languishing in obscurity, and under the invigorating influences of a benign patronage to train it up for the service of the temple and the altar.[17]

In 1811 the society began the purchase of books in the Course of Ecclesiastical Studies for the use of candidates, and within the next few years had made financial grants to several students.

The Episcopal Society of New Jersey for the Promotion of Christian Knowledge and Piety, founded a few months after the South Carolina organization, had as one of its purposes, "if the funds of the society should admit, aiding young men of piety and

17. *Historical Magazine of the Protestant Episcopal Church,* XXI (1952), p. 456.

talents, who may need assistance, in the necessary preparation for the Gospel ministry." The Society for the Advancement of Christianity in Pennsylvania, founded in 1812, though its chief efforts were directed to missionary extension in the western parts of the state, maintained a small library for the use of candidates for orders, and in 1813 granted aid to a needy student.

New York's more ample resources permitted the establishment of several societies, each concentrating upon a single objective. The Protestant Episcopal Tract Society published material on the Church's doctrines and practices, the New York Bible and Common Prayer Book Society distributed its books, while missionary work in New York State and the Sunday schools of the diocese were assisted by other organizations. The Protestant Episcopal Society for Promoting Religion and Learning, founded in 1802, the endowments of which were created by grants from Trinity Parish, devoted its attention to numerous projects, among which was the support of theological students. By 1814, the society regularly granted aid to at least four or five candidates each year. In 1806, the New York Protestant Episcopal Theological Society was formed, devoting itself exclusively to assisting ministerial candidates and encouraging younger clergymen to continue their theological studies. From a society that granted assistance to needy students to a society whose funds were ample enough to employ an instructor or a professor to supervise their studies was but a single step. That step was one method of bringing a theological seminary into existence.

The driving force behind all the New York societies was the tireless energy and infectious enthusiasm of John Henry Hobart, who became an assistant minister in Trinity Parish in 1800. Hobart had grown up in Philadelphia in the last decades of the eighteenth century, and after his graduation from Princeton, he abandoned a tutorship at the college to prepare for the ministry under Bishop White. By the time of his ordination in 1798, his views had diverged sharply from the Low Churchmanship of White, and he became an ardent supporter of the High Church principles of seventeenth-century Anglicanism. In Hobart's vigorous ministry, the old-fashioned High Churchmanship of men like his father-in-law, Thomas Bradbury Chandler, or Samuel Seabury of Connecticut, was quickened by a passionate evangelistic concern and an aggressive apologetic for the Episcopal Church. "Evangelical Truth and Apostolic Order" was Hobart's famous watchword.

Bishop Hobart was undoubtedly the most colorful figure among the younger churchmen of the early nineteenth century. From his pen came scores of devotional, doctrinal, and pastoral tracts, while his powerful and persuasive oratory won admiration and support, even from those who found his restless love of excitement unsettling. Under the spell of his charm and immense capacity for friendships, men overlooked his intolerance of opposition and forgave offense when his warmth of spirit led him to make generous amends. Admiring the resourcefulness that made him the ablest episcopal administrator in the Church, men accepted his insistence on retaining a controlling hand over all his ventures.

In no cause was Hobart more fervent or wholehearted than that of the better education of candidates for the ministry, particularly after his consecration in 1811. A man who found two diocesan missionaries in New York in that year and left fifty behind him at his death nineteen years later could never lose sight of the inseparable link between the Church's growth and the adequate provision for the supply and training of the ministry. By 1813, Hobart was convinced that the establishment of a theological college or seminary was essential, but before his plans had become definite a move was made in South Carolina which determined the character of the first seminary of the Episcopal Church. Surprising as it may seem to those who have been accustomed to associate the General Theological Seminary inseparably with New York and, at least in its early years, with Bishop Hobart, the initial step that led to the action of the General Convention of 1817 in establishing a seminary for the whole Church was taken in the Convention of South Carolina in 1814.

2

Christopher Gadsden's Motion

On February 14, 1814, the Reverend Christopher Edwards Gadsden rose in St. Michael's Church, Charleston, to address the Convention of South Carolina on a matter "second in importance to none which has engaged the attention of the Church since its organization after the American Revolution."[1] Gadsden's remarks were directed not only to the need of adequate measures for the education of candidates for the ministry—this was now generally accepted—but to the duty and responsibility of the whole Church to make provision for their training on the widest scale possible.

A grandson of General Christopher Gadsden, Revolutionary patriot and sometime member of the first Continental Congress, Gadsden was a Yale classmate and life-long friend of John C. Calhoun. The youthful Rector of St. Philip's, Charleston, enjoyed an intimacy with many of South Carolina's leading families. While this alone might have assured him a respectful hearing by the convention, his devoted labors for the recovery of the Church in South Carolina had already won him the affection and esteem that would lead members of another convention in Charleston, twenty-five years later, to elect him their bishop. With an eloquence born of the earnest conviction that the training of "a pious and well-informed ministry" lay "at the foundation of all the measures for

1. *Historical Magazine of the Protestant Episcopal Church*, XX (1951), p. 305.

the prosperity of the Church," Gadsden urged that a bold and imaginative step be proposed to the General Convention that was to meet in Philadelphia three months later.[2] He offered a motion that the deputies from South Carolina

> use their endeavours that there may be established in some central situation, under the auspices of the Church in general, a theological seminary, in which young men of genius and piety may be trained for the sacred office.[3]

None followed Gadsden's discourse and its effect upon the convention more intently than the man who presided over this little group of churchmen, Theodore Dehon, second bishop of South Carolina. Gadsden, his admiring disciple, was the spokesman for a scheme long cherished by the Bishop, and one that he was now prepared to present to the Church.

Dehon was not a South Carolinian. The son of a French Huguenot family settled in Boston before the Revolution, he had been educated at Harvard and prepared for the ministry under Dr. Samuel Parker at Trinity Church, Boston. In 1797, while rector of Trinity Church, Newport, Dehon made his first friendships with South Carolinians who traveled between Charleston and the Rhode Island seaport. Never robust, a pastoral ministry of prodigal self-spending combined with the damp and penetrating chill of Newport's winters to take a heavy toll of his health. Some months of recuperation from illness in South Carolina during the winter of 1802-3 strengthened his ties in Charleston, and, after declining a call to St. Philip's in 1804, he finally succumbed to the necessities of health and the entreaties of his friends, accepting the rectorship of St. Michael's Church in 1809 when Dr. Bowen left for Grace Church, New York. Three years later he began his short but notable episcopate in South Carolina.

2. *Reasons in Favour of the General Theological Seminary* (Charleston, 1821), p. 5.
3. *South Carolina Convention Journal 1814*, p. 13.

In his devotion to the distinctive heritage of the Episcopal Church, its historic ministry, ordered liturgy, and emphasis upon the sacramental life, Bishop Dehon, like Hobart, was a High Churchman, though he was more restrained in his advocacy of these principles than the Bishop of New York. The influence of his devotion to the Church, however, was far-reaching. In the year of his consecration, Dehon established the practice that conventions in South Carolina should be opened with a celebration of the Holy Communion, and he was thought to be responsible for the adoption of a similar custom by the General Convention in a resolution of 1814.

Bishop Dehon
Seminary Copy of the Cogdell Portrait

Dehon's proposal was the foundation of a theological institution that belonged to the whole Church. He was convinced that if the diocesan societies that aided candidates for the ministry were to establish local centers of training, the Church's limited resources would be dispersed among a number of small seminaries, few of which could maintain the semblance of a well-established theological college. A single seminary, making use of all available resources and attracting large benefactions, could possess a body of professors and ample library facilities which would compare favorably with those of the institutions established by the Congregationalists in 1808 at Andover or the Presbyterians at Princeton in 1812. Such a seminary would attract, and find means to support, an increased number of promising candidates for the ministry. Moreover, an important by-product of a single national seminary would be its strengthening effect upon the bonds of union among the separate dioceses, both by virtue of their joint responsibility for its maintenance and the intimate association experienced by students from all parts of the Church.

In the view of Dehon and Gadsden, only on the initiative of the General Convention and the readiness of the whole Church to assume responsibility for the education of its candidates could a seminary come into existence that would march with the advance of the Church, providing a steady supply of trained ministers for its expansion. They doubted the effectiveness of timid moves, and in this they were in touch with the spirit that characterized the new era in American life. They were resolved to be content with "no Scheme which is narrow in its first Conception, or not capable of an almost limitless expansion." Any plan narrowly conceived was unsuited "to the temper of the times, or to the circumstances of this Country."[4]

Christopher Gadsden's motion was passed by the South Carolina Convention. Three months later, on Friday, May 20, 1814, Gadsden offered a resolution in the House of Deputies of the General Convention that a joint committee be appointed

4. *Reasons in Favour*, titlepage quotation.

to take into consideration the institution of a theological seminary, and if they should deem the same expedient, to report a plan for the raising of funds, and generally for the accomplishment of the object.[5]

Consideration of the motion was deferred over the week-end, and on Monday, May 23, after a vote to postpone it further was defeated, the motion was voted upon "by States," the phrase then used for a vote by orders in the Deputies. The motion was lost. With the lay vote divided, in the clerical order only the dioceses of Massachusetts, Rhode Island, Virginia, and South Carolina voted in the affirmative.

Gadsden was keenly disappointed. When he attributed defeat to the fact that many deputies opposed any action by the General Convention that might interfere with plans already maturing for the establishment of local seminaries, he was probably overstating the case, or at least arguing from later developments. Many of the deputies were probably not ready to take action on as broad a scale as that contemplated in Gadsden's motion, though active opposition, led by Bishop Hobart's friend Dr. Thomas Y. How, soon to be made assistant rector of Trinity Parish, came from the one diocese where plans for a regional school were assuming some definite shape—New York.[6] Hobart's fertile and restless mind had ranged over a variety of schemes for the foundation of educational institutions under the auspices of the Church, and he had come to the conclusion that a theological school had first claim upon the resources at his disposal in New York. In March of 1813, he wrote to a friend from whom he had hopes of a substantial legacy that might one day support such a venture:

I have long been firmly convinced that a theological school at least, if not a college, is essential to the ultimate prosperity of our Church. The fact that almost all other denominations are establishing and endowing them, and already enjoying the fruits of them, might supersede the

5. *Journal of General Convention 1814* (Inskeep ed.), pp. 8-9, 17-18.
6. Jarvis to White (Draft), December 21, 1819, Jarvis Correspondence, General Theological Seminary Library. Subsequent references to Seminary collections, papers, and publications are identified by the abbreviation G.T.S.

Bishop Hobart
Seminary Portrait by John Paradise

necessity of all argument for the expediency of similar institutions among us.[7]

His pastoral experiences of the same year sharpened his conviction and impressed upon him the urgent priority of this cause. In 1813 he traveled over two thousand miles through New York State, visiting more than thirty parishes and congregations, confirming eleven hundred persons. At every turn he saw opportunities that could be met only by an increase of ministers, and encountered many men who were prevented by lack of means from studying for holy orders.

7. John McVickar, *The Early Life and Professional Years of Bishop Hobart* (Oxford, 1838), p. 336.

Hobart brought the matter forcibly to the attention of the New York Convention in October 1813. He made no definite proposals but asked his convention to consider the possibility "of an establishment for the instruction, for the religious and moral discipline, and, in some cases, for the support of young men designed for holy orders." Hobart was incapable of thinking timidly; he wanted no feeble local seminary. If a theological institution were to be established, it should be capable of serving not only the immediate needs of his own vast diocese, but those of the whole Church as well:

> It is of utmost importance that the plan and situation of this institution should meet the wants and wishes, not merely of the Church in this diocese, but of our Church at large, and thus contribute to advance and preserve those valuable objects, the purity and unity of the Protestant Episcopal Church in these States.

With these sentiments, Bishop Dehon and Christopher Gadsden would have concurred heartily. Where they differed sharply, however, was on the point of responsibility for the seminary and oversight of its operation. Hobart's views on this were quite clear:

> As the responsibility for the admission of persons to Holy Orders ultimately rests on the Bishop . . . it is his duty to exercise a general direction and superintendence of their previous studies.[8]

Bishop Hobart conceived a seminary of far wider usefulness than a school attached only to the needs of New York, but to be satisfactory to him, under whatever remote patronage it might be, it should have the immediate guidance of the bishop of that diocese from which the largest amount of support would inevitably come.

Scarcely a week before the Convention of 1814 opened, Hobart had published a prospectus entitled *Grammar School and Theological Seminary*, incorporating his ideas of the moment. He proposed to establish a preparatory school for boys "as soon as thirty scholars shall offer," to be operated for the support of a theological school.

8. *New York Convention Journals 1785-1819* (Republished, New York, 1844), pp. 257-258.

The boys were to pay an annual tuition of three hundred dollars, a sum which the Bishop calculated would permit "the fees of the students, after the expenses of the institution are defrayed," to be appropriated "to the support and endowment of a Theological Seminary, for the education of young men designed for Holy Orders." Provision would thus be made "for ample instructions and recitations in the course of ecclesiastical study prescribed by the Church." The seminary was to be under the patronage of the General Convention and the immediate care of a board of trustees, of whom all the bishops would be members, together with an equal number of clergy and laymen. The Bishops of New York and New Jersey were to be president and vice-president respectively, as well as "Superintendents of the Theological Seminary." Bishop Hobart recognized that the difficulties brought on by the War of 1812 dimmed the hope of support for the full program, but he hoped that "on a small scale these institutions might be originated" on a tract of land he had already acquired in New Jersey, eighteen miles from New York. The "difficulties of the times" might have made an appeal for funds inopportune, but they did not prevent Hobart from sketching out a large number of details, from the architectural design of the cubicles in which the preparatory school boys would live, to the "occasional participation in the instruction and discipline" of the seminary which the Bishop would not find "incompatible with his other duties."

Bishop Hobart had an inexhaustible fund of ideas, nearly always advocated with impetuous vigor. His most ardent admirers will admit, however, that his ideas were not always well-conceived. There was something faintly preposterous about a seminary that was to derive its support from the surplus income of a boarding school department. Yet the boys' school was no more than a device which the Bishop was quite willing to discard. His real concern was with the structure of authority in a seminary. It is not surprising, therefore, that Hobart's friends in the House of Deputies voted against Christopher Gadsden's motion. The Bishop explained to his diocesan convention in 1814 that the opposition of the New York deputation in General Convention to the establishment of a general Theological Seminary by an *act of that body* did not arise from disaffection to a measure of vital importance to the Church, but from an opinion that the same object could be accomplished on the most correct and enlarged principles and views, by private concert and co-operation among the influential friends of the Church in various parts of the Union, without encountering many difficulties to which the measure would be liable if taken up under present circumstances by the General Convention.[9]

Hobart was torn by a desire to have the best of both worlds, the advantages possessed on the one hand by a general seminary and on the other by an institution under local control. As Professor McVickar put it, he wished a seminary "to possess the influence of the one, and the security of the other." He was certain that it would invite disaster to commit

a power so vital to the Church, as the control of the education of its candidates to a body so fluctuating and irresponsible as the General Convention, at least in its House of Delegates, and of the operation of which the Church had not, at that time, sufficient experience to justify so high a trust.[10]

However the adverse vote in the House of Deputies disappointed Gadsden, Bishop Dehon was not the man to take the defeat of his cherished proposal without a struggle. Fully as determined as Hobart, and armed with arguments that appealed to high principle and aroused an adventurous spirit, Dehon debated the matter with the Bishop of New York in the House of Bishops on the last day of the Convention of 1814. Bishop White, with characteristic caution, held aloof, avoiding "the opening of his mind to the merits of the question" at so late a date in the Convention sessions.[11] Moore of Virginia and Griswold of the Eastern Diocese, however, supported Dehon's motion that inquiry be made throughout the dioceses "concerning the expediency of establishing a Theological Seminary, to be conducted under the general authority of this Church; and to

9. *New York Convention Journals 1785-1819*, p. 274.
10. McVickar, *Hobart*, p. 466.
11. William White, *Memoirs of the Protestant Episcopal Church in the United States of America* (Philadelphia, 1820), p. 296.

report to the next General Convention."[12] The motion passed; Theodore Dehon had saved the day. The Deputies concurred, and the matter was referred to the Church.

During the triennium, the wide discussion of a seminary met with apathy in some areas and hesitancy in others but, wherever the re-awakened spirit of the Church was manifest, there was mounting sentiment in favor of an institution that would belong to the whole Church. South Carolina's Convention of 1815 asserted firmly that "the welfare of the Church imperiously demands the institution of a Theological Seminary under the auspices of the General Convention," a conviction more fully expressed by the same body in 1817 when drafting resolutions to be presented to the forthcoming General Convention.

Pennsylvania was hesitant, reflecting the indecision of Bishop White, who tended to favor local institutions. He put the matter to his Convention of 1816 for study, and a committee reported in the following year with a recommendation to the Church that a fund be raised, the income of which might be applied "to local endeavours, if thought expedient . . . until a general plan be adopted, if that should be hereafter considered more eligible."[13] It was decided that the deputies from Pennsylvania to the General Convention of 1817 "be empowered to concur in whatever the general wisdom of the Church may devise."[14]

William Meredith, a prominent Philadelphia lawyer and banker, and a lay deputy from Pennsylvania, was more forthright. Early in 1817, he published a pamphlet entitled *Brief Remarks on the Importance and Practicability of Instituting a General Theological Seminary* which was widely circulated. Meredith was certain that

> in the intellectual progress of our country . . . an intelligent people must have an intelligent clergy. They must be as well acquainted with their profession, as contemporaries of other professions are with theirs.

12. *Journal of General Convention 1814* (Inskeep ed.), p. 30.
13. White, *Memoirs*, p. 309; see also Bird Wilson, *Memoir of the Life of the Rt. Rev. William White, D.D.* (Philadelphia, 1839), p. 206.
14. *Pennsylvania Convention Journal 1817*, pp. 11-12.

His outline of the requirements of theological education illustrates the intellectual attainments an educated layman hoped to find in his priest:

> Knowledge attracts respect, and thus adds to the influence of a clergyman; and there is no branch of it which might not be made to subserve the great ends of his office. He should be acquainted with metaphysics, for he has to exercise his own mind, and to control the minds of others; with moral philosophy, for it enforces the duties of life, and proves the wisdom of virtue; with natural history and philosophy, for they illustrate the perfections of God; with civil history, geography, and chronology, that he may corroborate the truth of the scriptures; with ecclesiastical history, that he may determine controversies of faith; with natural theology, that he may feel the necessity of revelation; with Christian theology, for it is his duty to explain it; with the original languages of the Bible, that he may not be deceived by translators; with the Latin and the oriental tongues, as assistants to the Greek and Hebrew; with the modern tongues, particularly the German, French, and English, as containing the standard works of protestant divinity. Finally, that these acquirements may be useful, he should be acquainted with the principles of good writing and speaking.[15]

For these heights of education, Meredith felt that "good advice from the house of Bishops respecting the choice of books is not enough . . . a good academy is the best and a sufficient remedy." He feared that the erection of local seminaries would not only scatter the slender resources of the Church, preventing the establishment of a seminary "amply endowed for deep and extensive erudition," but might also incite rivalry where men would

> in the contests of jealousy, depart from truth, disturb the peace of the church, and terminate in schism. In that case, instead of the divinity of Geneva and Augsburgh, we might hear of the doctrine of Massachusetts, Pennsylvania, or Carolina.

Meredith figured that $50,000 would provide "the requisite buildings for fifty students and their instructors"; $200,000 more

15. *Brief Remarks,* pp. 5-6.

would endow it substantially. His calculations may have been realistic, but he was enticed by the horns of Elfland when he asked the question that has appealed with deceiving simplicity to those immersed in the problems of church budgets: "Are there not in the states 250 Episcopalians who could give each $1000 . . . or 2500 persons who would give each $100?" And he was surely naive when he assumed that

> the members of our church would one and all honour the Lord with their substance, and that they who have much would give plenteously. It is only necessary that the measure should come to them recommended by the General Convention.[16]

In New York, sentiment in favor of a general institution rose steadily, and Bishop Hobart trimmed his sails to meet it when it became clear to him that there was wide opinion that the city of New York was "the fittest situation for a General Seminary."[17] In an article signed "An Episcopalian," in *The Christian Journal* in May 1817, the Bishop put the arguments for the local governance of a theological school in their best light, but it is plain that he was ready to support a decision in favor of a general seminary, provided New York was selected for its location.[18] Dated May 21, the day after the sessions of the General Convention opened at Trinity Church, New York, the article was well-timed. Few members of the convention could have been unaffected by an intriguing paragraph which promised a generous benefaction:

> Several Episcopalians in the State of New York have long thought that the Church, there so respectable for numbers and wealth, should establish a Theological Institution. With this in view, a benevolent individual has recently vested in certain persons, land, consisting of above sixty city lots, in trust for the purpose of a Theological Seminary.

16. *Brief Remarks*, pp. 9-10.
17. *An Appeal to the Church in Her Own Behalf Relative to the Education of Her Ministry* (New York, 1817), p. 11.
18. For Hobart's authorship see McVickar, *Hobart*, p. 465; Morgan Dix, *A History of the Parish of Trinity Church* (New York, 1905), III, 240, 499-502.

Consideration of the matter of a seminary began in the Convention of 1817 when the Reverend Charles H. Wharton of New Jersey offered resolutions in the House of Deputies for committee consideration of the best manner of providing for "the better education of candidates for the ministry in the Church."[19] On May 26, the committee reported to the House a series of proposals for a theological seminary governed by a board of trustees elected by the General Convention. Debate on these measures was interrupted by a message from the House of Bishops, communicating to the Deputies four resolutions drafted and proposed by Theodore Dehon. The Bishops had adopted them, and on the following morning, May 27, 1817, the Deputies, abandoning their own proposals, voted concurrence. It was resolved

> that it is expedient to establish, for the better education of the candidates for holy orders in this Church, a general Theological Seminary, which may have the united support of the whole Church in these United States, and be under the superintendence and control of the General Convention.
>
> that this seminary be located in the city of New-York.
>
> that persons be appointed by the House of Bishops to visit the several parts of the United States, and solicit contributions towards funds for founding and endowing such an institution.
>
> that a committee be appointed, to consist of the presiding Bishop, and the Bishops of this Church in New-York and New-Jersey, with three clergymen, and three laymen, to be appointed by the House of Clerical and Lay Deputies; which committee shall be empowered to receive and manage such funds as shall be collected—to devise a plan for establishing and carrying into operation such an institution; which plan shall be communicated to the several Bishops of this Church—and in the event of sufficient funds being obtained, if a majority of the Bishops shall have approved the plan, to carry it into immediate operation.[20]

19. *Journal of General Convention 1817* (Swords ed.), p. 13.
20. *Ibid.*, pp. 34; 45-46. The number of solicitors in the third resolution was originally fixed at three.

These were the resolutions that enabled the foundation of the General Theological Seminary. Although it would be more than a year before the Theological Committee determined "to carry into immediate operation the theological school" and appointed its first professors, and nearly two years before the first small class was assembled for instruction, the date of the convention's resolution has the best claim to be the birthday of the Seminary. "When your Majesty says 'Let a thing be done,' " argues Ko-Ko with characteristic Gilbertian reasoning in *The Mikado*, "practically it *is* done—because your Majesty's will is law." Before the next General Convention in 1820, the will of the meeting of 1817 had been carried out, though the clause bidding the united support of the whole Church never became much more than an expression of hope. General Convention readily assumed superintendence and control over the Church's first theological seminary, but its financial support was left to private benevolence, interested dioceses and parishes, and various religious and philanthropic organizations.

The Theological Committee, in addition to Bishops White, Hobart, and Croes, consisted of Dr. Wharton, Dr. How—Hobart's trusted assistant in Trinity Parish—the Reverend William Harris, president of Columbia College, the Honorable Rufus King of New York, a distinguished statesman, the Honorable Charles F. Mercer of Virginia, and William Meredith, author of *Brief Remarks.* It was in some ways a curious group to be entrusted with a mandate for the Seminary's foundation. While Bishop White was willing to put aside his own preferences in respect for "the general wisdom of the Church," Bishop Croes was not at all sure that any seminary was necessary. President Harris, Mr. King, and Mr. Mercer were unable to attend the important meetings of the committee, and Dr. How was deposed by his Bishop before the committee embarked upon the constructive phase of its task.[21] One concludes that Dr. Wharton and Mr. Meredith were the only active representatives of the House of Deputies.

21. *Letters from John Pintard to His Daughter, 1816-1833* (New-York Hisorical Society, 1940-41), I, 113.

Three solicitors were enlisted to appeal for funds, each responsible for a different area of the country: Daniel Burhans of Newtown, Connecticut, for New England; William H. Wilmer of Alexandria, Virginia, for the southern dioceses; and Dehon's friend, Nathaniel Bowen, then rector of Grace Church, New York, for the middle Atlantic areas. They were equipped with letters from Bishop White to aid them in presenting their cause, and in January 1818, the committee appealed to the Church for a response of "extraordinary liberality," at the same time rebuking those church members who "conceive of the clerical calling as requiring but a slender furniture of intellectual information."[22]

Except in South Carolina and New York, the solicitors met with little success, despite an increase in their number. Burhans was prevented from activity by sickness and death in his family. In the southern area, "some circumstances occurred which prevented Mr. Wilmer's engaging in this work."[23] Whatever the circumstances, Wilmer's loyalties must have been at least strained. Plans were already under discussion for the establishment of a regional or diocesan seminary of which he would soon be honored as a founder. As early as 1815, Dr. John Augustine Smith, president of William and Mary College, had proposed to the Virginia Convention, supported by Bishop Moore, the re-establishment of a divinity professorship in the college. Though no action was then taken, during the winter of 1817-18, Dr. Wilmer was almost certainly contemplating the project that took shape in June 1818, with the formation of the Society for the Education of Pious Young Men for the Ministry, a society that "was indeed the Seminary in embryo; and those who were responsible for its organization were, in reality, the founders of the Theological Seminary in Virginia."[24]

Thomas C. Brownell, then a professor in Union College, Schenectady, and shortly to be elected bishop of Connecticut, took over

22. *Journal of General Convention 1820* (Philadelphia), p. 82.
23. *Ibid.*, p. 64.
24. *History of the Theological Seminary in Virginia*, ed. W. A. R. Goodwin (New York, 1923), I, 122; see also I, 103, 131.

Wilmer's task of solicitation in the South. As might be expected, he had considerable success in South Carolina. A total of \$6246.50 was collected during the triennium 1817-1820, out of which the first year's operation of the Seminary was financed. Of this sum, \$4560.00 came from South Carolina and \$1576.50 from New York. This figure, however, did not represent New York's total interest in the Seminary. Dr. Bowen pursued his solicitation assiduously, backed by an appeal from Bishop Hobart for a liberal response from the diocese. The Bishop informed his Convention of 1817:

> I should fail in my duty, if I neglected to impress upon you, my brethren, and through you, on the Episcopalians of the Dioces, the immense importance of the proposed Theological Establishment. There cannot be an object presented to them which has equal claims on their beneficence. Without a ministry the Church cannot *exist;* and destitute of a *learned* as well as a *pious* ministry, she cannot *flourish* . . .
>
> But a still further and most eminent benefit of the contemplated Theological School will consist in the pecuniary aids which it will furnish to youths of piety, and talents who are destitute of funds to procure the necessary education for the ministry.[25]

In addition to the cash collections in New York, over \$15,000 was raised in pledges, but to be paid only on condition that the total subscription for the Seminary should reach the \$100,000 mark, an arrangement that was shortly a matter of considerable discussion.

Dr. Brownell had secured pledges for future payment of over \$3000, chiefly in South Carolina where the news of the convention's action in 1817 was received with "much satisfaction." It was a satisfaction tempered with sadness, however, for the measure that South Carolina had so persistently supported was now that of "our late honoured Diocesan."[26] Theodore Dehon did not live to see the Seminary he wanted come into operation. In August 1817, he died of yellow fever, contracted during his travels through the diocese. Almost five years to the day after the motion that initiated the events which led to the Seminary's foundation, Christopher Gads-

25. *New York Convention Journal 1817*, p. 19.
26. *South Carolina Convention Journal 1818*, p. 21.

den again addressed the South Carolina Convention. On February 19, 1819, he urged the support of the institution that was to open its sessions within two months, paying a moving tribute to the man whom he always regarded as its chief founder:

> The honor of originating the measure for the proposed Seminary belongs to this Diocese. It was introduced by our delegates to the General Convention in 1814 . . . renewed by our delegates in the Convention of 1817 . . . We are pledged not to permit this institution to die in its birth . . .
>
> May I not be permitted to add that our perseverence is due to the memory of our late Bishop. In this cause he laboured unto death. The resolutions adopted by the General Convention were from his pen. It is generally admitted that what has been done is chiefly owing to his influence and exertions . . .
>
> It is intended to erect a monument to his memory in this Church in which we are now assembled. That monument will be seen by the few only who come within these walls. It will be subject to casualty and the waste of time. But the Theological Seminary will be a memorial of him throughout all generations.[27]

Despite their *Address to the Members of the Church*, issued to pave the way for the solicitors' work, it became evident to the committee by October 1818, that any wide response to the appeal was lacking. Some further stimulation of interest and benefactions was necesary. Accordingly, at a meeting in October, it was resolved "to carry into immediate operation the theological school of the Protestant Episcopal Church."[28] A plan, chiefly devised by Bishop Hobart, was adopted, providing for the establishment of four professorships, the descriptions of which give a sketchy outline of the proposed curriculum. Instruction was to be offered in (1) Biblical Learning, "comprehending the exposition of the Holy Scriptures with whatever relates to the evidences of revealed religion and biblical criticism"; (2) Systematic Theology, "giving correct views of all the doctrines of scripture and of the authorities sustaining them"; (3) Historic Theology—later to be called Ecclesiastical History—

27. *South Carolina Convention Journal 1819*, pp. 49-50.
28. *Journal of General Convention 1820* (Philadelphia), p. 66.

"giving correct information of the state of the Church in all ages, and of the Church of England in particular from the reformation, embracing a view of the constitution of the Christian Church, of the orders of the ministry, and of the nature and duty of Christian unity"; and (4) The Ritual of the Church and of Pulpit Eloquence, "comprehending all the points relative to the liturgy, to the correct and devotional performance of the service of the Church, to the composition and delivery of sermons, and to the duties of the clerical office."

The committee directed that the professors pay particular attention to the progress of the students in the spiritual life, and that their instruction be regulated "by the provisions of the Canons, and the course of study set forth by the House of Bishops," adding a requirement which Samuel Turner later regarded as enjoining an impossible enterprise: "that they conduct the students through all the books prescribed in that course."

Far too ambitious for immediate realization, the scheme was to be implemented in several steps. The professorship of the Ritual of the Church and of Pulpit Eloquence was left vacant, while that of Systematic Theology was to be reserved for the appointment of Dr. Wharton "when the funds of the institution admit." Meanwhile, a modest beginning was to be made by engaging two part-time professors, Samuel Farmar Jarvis in Biblical Learning, and Samuel Hulbeart Turner in Historic Theology. Dividing instruction in the other subjects between them, each would receive a salary of $800 a year "until they can be detached from parochial cures and devoted solely to the objects of the institution."[29]

There was little difficulty in detaching Turner from parochial work. The son of the Reverend Joseph Turner, he had been a student in classics at the University of Pennsylvania, and was ordained in 1811. After six years in the parish in Chestertown, Maryland, where the climate of the eastern shore gave him "agues and intermittent fevers," he had resigned in expectation of a call to Germantown which did not materialize. At the time of the committee's

29. *Journal of General Convention 1820* (Philadelphia), p. 67.

proposals, he was occupied in parochial supply work and in directing the studies of candidates for orders in Philadelphia as "Superintendent of Theological Students." His "youth and inexperience" caused him some misgivings when Jackson Kemper, acting as secretary to Bishop White in the affairs of the Theological Committee, brought him the news of his appointment as professor, but his love of learning and his sense of vocation as a teacher of theological students led him to accept. It was well for the Seminary that he did.

Dr. Jarvis declined to consider a part-time appointment. If the committee wanted him, the only satisfactory arrangement would be one in which he could give himself wholly to teaching. Jarvis was in a position to influence a reconsideration of the proposals, for it was felt that the attachment of a man of his reputation to the Seminary would give it considerable status. The son of Bishop Jarvis of Connecticut, Samuel Jarvis had graduated from Yale in 1805, a class behind Christopher Gadsden, with honors in history and classics. Ordained priest in 1811, he was given charge of St. Michael's, Bloomingdale, and two years later became rector of St. James' Church, New York, as well. At the time of the committee's scheme, he was in his thirty-fourth year, married and with a growing family, and already was widely respected as an effective preacher and a scholar of great erudition. Men reading for orders found Dr. Jarvis an inspiring supervisor, and, in fact, from the group studying under his direction in New York during the winter of 1818-19 came three of the six students enrolled in the first sessions of the Seminary.

Faced with Jarvis' refusal to accept an arrangement which he felt to be unsatisfactory, and doubtless spurred on by the knowledge that he was considering an offer to become assistant minister in Trinity Church, Boston, the committee revised its proposals in February 1819.[30] Jarvis was offered his appointment, together with responsibility for the subjects of the vacant professorships, on a full-time basis at a salary of $3000 a year, $500 of which was intended as a house allowance. By the standards of time, it was a generous

30. Turner to Jarvis, March 8, 1819, Jarvis Correspondence.

stipend, comparable to that paid by large parishes. Turner, younger than Jarvis and unmarried, agreed to accept a full-time professorship at $1000 a year, which the committee offered "in the hope that the funds of the institution will speedily admit a more adequate remuneration."[31]

At this February meeting, Bishop Hobart divulged the news, at which he had already hinted in 1817, that Clement Clarke Moore, son of Bishop Moore of New York and owner of a large estate in Chelsea, then an undeveloped area of Manhattan just north of the city, had offered him a tract of "above sixty lots" on condition that the buildings of a seminary be erected thereon. The committee accepted the offer of the land—the present site of the Seminary—though any building operation was evidently far in the future.

Dr. Jarvis formally accepted the new proposals on March 6, and the two professors were advised to meet their classes in New York as soon as conveniently possible, their salaries to begin from April 1. The committee may have intended Dr. Jarvis to be the chief attraction of the Seminary but, as it turned out, he left his post eighteen months later. It was Samuel Turner's devotion to the Seminary that proved its salvation during the first precarious years. Turner possessed both the capacity for disciplined study and the perceptiveness of mind requisite to genuine scholarship. For over forty years, he was the chief source of intellectual stimulation in the Seminary, particularly in biblical studies. As assiduous in his own research as he was in his teaching, for a long time he was, by later standards, the only professional scholar on the Faculty. He published continuously from 1824 to 1859: notes and commentaries on Hebrews, Romans, Ephesians, Galatians, a *Companion to the Book of Genesis*, translations of Jahn's *An Introduction to the Old Testament* and portions of Planck's *Introduction to Theological Knowledge*, and many articles and sermons.

Judicious in his judgments, the soul of integrity, impatient of deviousness, Turner was at times forthright to the point of tactlessness. He expected and received serious application to study from his

31. *Journal of General Convention 1820* (Philadelphia), p. 69.

Photograph by the Frick Art Reference Library

Professor Turner
Seminary Portrait by Daniel Huntington

students, and with it came a respect and admiration that deepened into affection as the years passed. Trained under Bishop White, he was something of a Low Churchman, though there was no suggestion of sterility in his devotion. His faith, tested by a series of personal tragedies, was a constant source of strength to him and to the students whose lives he touched. The General Seminary is no exception to the rule that any institution owes much of its vitality and spirit to those who have given themselves wholly to its purposes. Dr. Turner was the first of a succession of teachers whose integrity of mind, selfless dedication, and example of genuine Christian concern helped to create the Seminary's finest traditions of priestly ideals. His ministry lasted forty-three years, and to those who gathered at his funeral in St. Peter's Church on Christmas Eve of 1861, it must have seemed truly the end of an era in the life of the Old Seminary.

"Early in the spring of 1819, Dr. Jarvis and I entered upon our duties." Such was Turner's modest description of the opening of the General Seminary.[32] He arrived in New York from Philadelphia on April 2, and the first class met their professors shortly afterward in a small room beyond the north gallery in St. Paul's Chapel of Trinity Parish. Not until after May 1 did Turner secure a sufficient number of books for his students, an example of the complete lack of preparation evident on all sides. No arrangements had been made by the committee for the operation of the Seminary or the regulation of its work beyond the assignment of a room in St. Paul's, and the professors, uncertain of their authority, took little initiative.

Difficulties with Bishop Hobart were encountered even before the classes began. Under the pressure of the urgent need of clergymen in the missionary areas in New York State, the Bishop wanted the professors to supervise two separate courses of study, one designed to prepare men for ordination by completing the essential books in the Course of Ecclesiastical Studies in a single year, and another which might take the more leisurely form of a full three years of study. Dr. Jarvis objected strenuously to a short course, a position in which he was heartily supported by his junior colleague. This was the kind of instruction in which both had been engaged before accepting their new posts. If their energies were to be devoted to such abbreviated cramming, "Where," asked Turner, "is the use of a Theological School at all?"[33] The Bishop did not argue the matter long, for he seems to have sent his one-year candidates elsewhere for supervision.

Six students constituted the Seminary's enrollment in its first academic year. The three who had previously been reading with Dr.

32. *Autobiography*, pp. 83-84; see also Turner's letter to the Trustees, Trustees' Proceedings, June 27-28, 1860.

33. Turner to Jarvis, March 12, 1819, Jarvis Correspondence.

Jarvis were Manton Eastburn, George Washington Doane, and Lawson Carter. The others were Benjamin Dorr, James P. F. Clarke, and William H. Mitchell. As Eastburn temporarily abandoned his study of theology six months after classes began, and Dorr did not enroll until after November, there was a period in which only four students were under instruction, fewer than either professor had anticipated. It is no wonder that a note of discouragement appeared in the correspondence of Turner with his friend Jackson Kemper.[34]

The committee had made no public notice of the establishment of the Seminary's operation, and Bishop Hobart virtually ignored it. Though he had spoken vigorously to the New York Conventions of 1817 and 1818 on the importance of a theological school, in the Convention of 1819, when Turner and Jarvis were meeting their students, he was silent on the subject. When Dr. Jarvis complained of the lack of notice, the Bishop countered with the argument that Jarvis himself should have given an inaugural address. So little knowledge was had of the Seminary by New York churchmen that when Samuel Turner met some old friends in Grace Church as late as December 1819, they were surprised to find him in New York and enquired how long he would remain there.[35]

The professors closed their sessions on August 1 for a summer vacation, intending to resume classes on October 1. In the late summer, however, yellow fever was epidemic in the city, and fear of the disease was such that "the public mind is fairly unhinged."[36] After discussing the possibility of a temporary move to Burlington, New Jersey, Jarvis and Turner decided to await "till the abatement of the sickness should render it safe and proper to re-assemble the students."[37] By mid-October the worst was over, and Dr. Jarvis advertised the reopening on October 25 in the New York newspa-

34. Turner to Kemper, November 8, 1819, Kemper Papers 5 G 111, Manuscript Division, State Historical Society of Wisconsin.

35. Turner to Kemper, December 24, 1819, Kemper Papers 5 G 112.

36. Pintard, *Letters,* I, 218.

37. Turner to Jarvis, September 25, 1819; see also Jarvis to Hobart (Draft), October 12, 1819, Jarvis Correspondence.

pers, informing Bishop White with some asperity that his advertisement was the first intimation the public had received of the existence of a theological school.[38]

In the fall, an even less hospitable atmosphere surrounded the Seminary. Cold weather soon drove the group from their unheated

St. Paul's Chapel

room in St. Paul's to St. John's Chapel in Varick Street, where, recalled Turner,

> sometimes in the vestry-room, which lay then contiguous to the chancel . . . and sometimes in the adjoining part of the church which contained one of the stoves, we continued our attendance on the class.[39]

38. Jarvis to White (Draft), October 19, 1819, Jarvis Correspondence.
39. *Autobiography*, p. 87.

From this refuge, they were soon locked out by a sexton who refused to supply their fuel, an action which Turner suspected to have been directed by someone with more authority than the caretaker of St. John's. Fortunately, Lawson Carter, one of the students, provided a room for use in the afternoons in the second story of a house on the corner of Broadway and Cedar Street where he held a girl's school in the mornings. It was this move that gave rise to the recollection of George Washington Doane in later years, when he had become bishop of New Jersey:

> I was one of those who studied and recited when the whole Seminary was accommodated in a second story room over a saddler's shop down town.[40]

Samuel Turner had little doubt as to the cause of what Jackson Kemper called "the languishing state of the school." Bishop Hobart

> treated it with comparative indifference; and it is not to be questioned that, with the great proportion of Churchmen in his diocese, his word and practice were equivalent to law.[41]

Hobart had little interest in a Seminary that so inadequately approximated his ideas of a theological school. A few students reciting to Jarvis and Turner under the uncertain auspices of the General Convention offered no assurance that the resources of New York would be wisely spent on its continuance. He had, moreover, a sharp difference of opinion with Samuel Turner over his favorite principle, the necessity of episcopacy to the constitution of the Church.[42] So strongly did the Bishop feel on this matter that he sent some of his candidates to recite to Benjamin Onderdonk, then an assistant minister in Trinity Parish, whose views on ecclesiastical polity he felt to be more sound than those of Professor Turner.

The Bishop's difficulties with Dr. Jarvis evidently sprang from the clash of two strong personalities. Jarvis had little respect for

40. W. C. Doane, *The Life and Writings of George Washington Doane, D.D., LL.D.* (New York, 1860), I, 27.
41. *Autobiography*, pp. 86-87; see also Turner to Tilghman, September 26, 1821, Maryland Diocesan Manuscripts, Maryland Historical Society, Baltimore—hereafter cited as Md. Dio. Ms.
42. *Autobiography*, pp. 95-98.

Hobart and complained bitterly of his attitude toward the Seminary. Drafting a letter to Bishop White in December, Jarvis described his early hopes that the Seminary

> like the Temple of Jerusalem, would blend the tribes of our Israel in the most harmonious concord. I imagined that it would become a lofty monument of our learning, piety and zeal; that by being subject to the entire control of the General Convention, it would effectively preclude the undue influence of local interests.

But, he continued,

> these bright anticipations were soon clouded, when I perceived that I had the misfortune to differ in opinion from the active and enterprising assistant Bishop of this diocese. It is well known that he disapproved of a General Seminary from the very moment it was first mentioned.

Professor Jarvis waxed eloquent in his conviction that Bishop Hobart's ambitious desire for power seemed

> to warrant the fear that at some future day the liberties of the American Church might be prostrated at the feet of a Victor or a Hildebrand.[43]

Before the Seminary had been more than a few weeks in session, Bishop Hobart found a cause for a quarrel with Dr. Jarvis that brought his quick temper to the surface. Early in June, the Bishop learned to his astonishment that Jarvis had already decided to resign his professorship as soon as the first academic year was over. He had been asked by his Boston friends to become rector of their new church there, the present St. Paul's Cathedral, then being built. By May 6, Dr. Jarvis had agreed to take the post as soon as the church was completed, that is, in the following summer.[44] Hobart angrily accused Jarvis of destroying the prospects for the success of the Seminary by proposing to desert his professorship.[45] Dr. Jarvis

43. Jarvis to White (Draft), December 21, 1819, Jarvis Correspondence.
44. Turner to Kemper, May 17, 1819, Kemper Papers 5 G 104.
45. Turner to Kemper, July 7, 1819, Kemper Papers 5 G 106; 117; see also Jarvis to Gadsden (Draft), January 29, 1820, Jarvis Correspondence.

maintained that he was going to Boston because he had become convinced that the Seminary could not succeed in the conditions under which it operated in New York. He put his case to Bishop White, explaining his decision to resign as of the following August:

> By that time a fair opportunity will have been given to try the experiment of establishing a General Theological Seminary. If funds are collected, and it receives the cordial and unanimous support of the Bishops and Clergy throughout the Union, it must succeed, and my vacating the chair which I hold will, I trust, produce no other effect than making room for one who will be more able than I am to discharge its duties. If on the other hand, from conflicting interests and an open or secret opposition to the measure, the Seminary should unhappily fail, and I think I had ample reason to believe that it will fail, it will be evident that it was my duty as well as my right to make that provision for a permanent support of which I have been deprived by accepting the professorship.[46]

Even Samuel Turner, sympathetic and friendly with Dr. Jarvis, could not defend his conviction that the Seminary would fail after so short a time in operation.[47] It is not difficult to understand Dr. Jarvis' mind. He had relinquished the activities of a busy parochial life, enticed by his own academic interests and a somewhat unreal estimate of the difficulty of creating a theological institution. He waked to find himself in an insecure position, with even fewer students than he had attracted at St. James' Church, tucked away in obscurity in a corner of New York, under the indifference and disapprobation of Bishop Hobart. For this he had not only given up his parish but also declined the first opportunity to go to Boston. Now that a second chance had come, Dr. Jarvis was determined to extricate himself from a position that gave little scope to his talents and less security to his family.

His quarrel with Hobart was past repair when the Bishop refused to authorize the committee's treasurer to pay his salary. Jarvis bombarded Hobart and Bishop White with letters of complaint, and finally, on November 6, he wrote angrily to Rufus King:

46. Jarvis to White (Draft), October 19, 1819, Jarvis Correspondence.
47. *Autobiography,* pp. 93-94.

> No one seems to think himself authorized, at least no one is willing to take a step which only carries into effect a previous resolution of the Committee. They were competent to stipulate with the professor that a certain sum should be paid, but are not competent to order the Treasurer to pay it. They have suffered me to resign a permanent living which was punctually paid, every three months, and then permit me to remain nearly eight months without receiving a cent.[48]

Bishop Hobart claimed that Jarvis had voided a contract to remain with the Seminary as long as the committee had funds to pay his salary, but there is no evidence that these were the terms on which he had accepted his professorship. Samuel Turner defended him. Jarvis may have been hasty in assuming that the Seminary would fail and even treated his obligations irresponsibly, but he had not broken his word.[49]

In these circumstances, the Seminary truly languished, though Turner often forgot his discouragement as he diligently led his students through Potter on church government, Hooker's *Ecclesiastical Polity*, Mosheim's history, and Daubeny on the Church.[50] In the Church there was much correspondence about the future of the school. Had the experiment failed? A number of churchmen thought so, and interest in diocesan institutions grew stronger. Dr. Wilmer and the supporters of Virginia's Society for the Education of Pious Young Men for the Ministry were raising money in 1819-20 to finance candidates who were to be placed for study and an apprenticeship with some competent clergyman. Dr. Wilmer's letter, issued before the General Seminary opened in 1819, explained:

> In this view it will be perceived that the Society does not design to supersede or interfere with the General Seminary intended to be established by the Church, but to reach those local cases to which the nature of the General Institution would not be adapted.[51]

48. Jarvis to King (Draft), November 6, 1819, Jarvis Correspondence.
49. Turner to Kemper, November 8, 1819, Kemper Papers 5 G 111.
50. Turner to Kemper, December 24, 1819, Kemper Papers 5 G 112.
51. Goodwin, *Theological Seminary in Virginia,* I, 129; see also Wilmer to Kemp, April 26, 1819, Md. Dio. Ms.

Whatever this meant, it is certain that Wilmer and his friends did not intend to support a seminary in New York—nor, indeed, as events proved, anywhere apart from "the southern district."

The dissolution of the General Seminary was widely anticipated, even by its friends. Jackson Kemper, who had been in close touch with the situation in New York, moved a resolution in the Pennsylvania Diocesan Convention in early May of 1820 which made it plain that Pennsylvania was prepared to act should the Seminary be abandoned. It was resolved

> that the deputies from this body, to the general convention to sit in this city on the 16th of the present month are hereby instructed to use their best endeavours for the immediate and permanent establishment of a general Theological Seminary; But if the plan of such a Seminary should be abandoned by the general convention, it shall be the duty of the standing committee of this diocess to make the most strenuous exertions, with the approbation of the bishop, to raise a fund for the support of a Theological professor, and to adopt all such measures as shall appear to them expedient, to insure to the Church a ministry of pious and learned men.[52]

The Theological Committee had no suggestions to offer. In their report to the General Convention of 1820, they confessed "that some new excitement is necessary in favour of the contemplated institution."[53] The General Convention provided that excitement by transferring Professor Turner and his pupils from New York to New Haven, thus bringing to the rescue of the Seminary the interest and capabilities of Thomas Church Brownell, the bishop of Connecticut.

52. *Pennsylvania Convention Journal 1820*, p. 19.
53. *Journal of General Convention 1820* (Philadelphia), p. 69.

3
Round Trip to New Haven

When the General Convention assembled in Philadelphia on May 16, 1820, the report of the Theological Committee placed the fate of the Seminary in the hands of the convention. A committee of the House of Deputies, headed by the Honorable Duncan Cameron of North Carolina, one of the Seminary's firmest supporters, and including Gadsden among its members, reported to the House on May 22. Lamenting that the effort to establish the Seminary in New York had met with difficulties, the committee nevertheless refused to abandon the enterprise. Instead, they proposed to move the school to a place

> where the professors and students can have access to public libraries, enjoying the benefits resulting from literary society, and live comfortably at moderate expense.[1]

These inducements were offered, in the opinion of the committee, by New Haven, where the Seminary would be situated far from "the scene of bustle and wickedness," amid "the habits of order, industry, and good morals, by which the people of New-England are characterized."[2] Two days later, after considerable

1. *Journal of General Convention 1820* (Philadelphia), p. 18.
2. *Reasons in Favour of the General Theological Seminary* (Charleston, 1821), pp. 11-12.

debate and some attempts to change the proposed location, the House of Deputies authorized the move to New Haven, vesting the management of the Seminary in a board of trustees consisting of all the bishops, together with twelve clergymen and twelve laymen, elected at each General Convention. The debate in the House of Bishops on the resolutions of the Deputies can only be conjectured, but it is clear that Bishop Brownell of Connecticut brought his concern for the Seminary decisively to bear upon its future.

A zealous solicitor in behalf of the Seminary in 1817-18, Brownell shared the enthusiasm of Theodore Dehon for an institution which would command the support of the whole Church, and was determined that any "intention to annihilate" it would not succeed.[3] A former professor at Union College, Brownell was an educator of some experience. He offered to move from Hartford to New Haven, and subsequently did so, to undertake both the supervision of the Seminary and a share in the instruction of students. It was Bishop Brownell who was chiefly responsible for the New Haven regulations that provided a basis for the Seminary's later statutes, and which gave the somewhat unstructured tutoring school of Samuel Turner and his pupils the character of a true theological institution.

The bishops were divided in opinion, if not in debate, on the issue of the move. Griswold, Bowen, and Brownell favored it, while Bishop White still preferred diocesan schools.[4] James Kemp and Philander Chase were absent from the House, a fact which made little difference, for the latter would soon manifest an energy in the foundation of a local school which matched the former's support of a general seminary. Hobart, Croes, and Moore, all favoring diocesan institutions, though on a more ambitious scale than Bishop White, finally agreed to concur with the resolutions of the House of Deputies. It is probable that the price exacted for their agreement was the "Declaration" which the bishops attached to their concurrence:

3. Brownell to Kemper, November 22, 1820, Kemper Papers 5 G 147.
4. White to Kemp, September 7, 1820, Md. Dio. Ms.

The house of bishops inform the house of clerical and lay deputies that in concurring with the resolutions relative to the theological seminary, and in its removal from the city of New York, they deem it proper to declare that they do not mean by this concurrence to interfere with any plan now contemplated, or that may hereafter be contemplated, in any diocese or dioceses for the establishment of theological institutions or professorships; and further they deem it their duty to express the opinion that the various sums subscribed, having been thus subscribed under an act of the convention establishing the seminary in New York, the subscribers who have not paid are not now bound, except they think proper, to pay their subscription, the institution being moved to a different city.[5]

The Seminary would go to New Haven, but the bishops now opened the way for the establishment of other schools where local interest dictated and to which local support could be diverted. A "Declaration" that released men from any sense of obligation to a seminary for which the resolutions of 1817 had asked "the united support of the whole Church" was of critical importance to Bishop Hobart. Over $15,000 remained on unpaid subscriptions in New York. But it was of equal interest to Dr. Wilmer, president of the House of Deputies in this convention. He had recently informed the Virginia Convention that a theological professor might soon be located in the diocese. Within six months, he was urging contributions to support "a theological professorship to be located at William and Mary College or elsewhere," for he expected

the public will give more liberally and cheerfully to an object thus brought home to them, and identified with their local interests and associations, than to the remote though equally important institution at New Haven.[6]

On the last day of the convention, the House of Deputies elected the clergymen and laymen to serve with the bishops on the new Board of Trustees, among them a large number of stalwart friends of the General Seminary: Dr. Wharton, Jackson Kemper, William

5. *Journal of General Convention 1820* (Philadelphia), p. 57.
6. See *History of the Theological Seminary in Virginia*, ed. W. A. P. Goodwin (New York, 1923), I, 130-131, 133.

Meredith, Dr. Jarvis—shortly to move to Boston—Mr. Isaac Lawrence of New York, Judge Cameron, Christopher Gadsden, and seven trustees from Connecticut.

Scarcely had Bishop Hobart returned from Philadelphia to New York than he revived his plans for a diocesan school, stimulated by what he had heard of projects afoot in Virginia and eager to capture the unpaid New York subscriptions for his own proposals.[7] Rumors filled the spate of correspondence evoked by Hobart's activity. Letters in the New York newspapers debated the relative merits of New York and New Haven as locations for a seminary and discussed the meaning and application of the "Declaration" of the House of Bishops. On June 22, Professor Turner informed Jackson Kemper that Bishop Hobart was seeking to form a faculty for a New York school. Two days later Bishop Brownell also had news for Kemper:

> I hear that Bishop Hobart has been making great exertions for the establishment of a local institution in New-York. With this I can find no fault if he has not (though I am informed that he has) endeavoured to persuade those who have subscribed to the General Seminary to withdraw their subscriptions and devote them to the City Institution. I could have wished, however, that as much zeal had been manifested for the General Seminary for the three years past. It would not then have been necessary to effect its removal.[8]

Hobart was astute. He knew that his efforts to stir public excitement would ensure wide interest in his next move. This was the publication in July of a *Pastoral Letter*, summarizing the events from 1817 and implying that Dr. Jarvis' resignation was the major cause of lack of confidence in the Seminary during its first year in New York. Describing his impressions of the recent General Convention, Bishop Hobart warned his diocese of the possibility that New York would be bereft of means of educating its candidates:

> There was every reason to believe, however, that diocesan institutions would ultimately be established—that a general institution would rather

7. Muhlenberg to Kemper, June 12, 1820, Kemper Papers 5 G 123.
8. Kemper Papers 5 G 127.

be acquiesced in by many than cordially supported—and thus, while the principal part of the funds of the general institution would be raised in New York, she might ultimately be one of the few dioceses that had not a theological seminary subject to her own control.[9]

Hobart was overcome by the fear that his candidates might be prepared for the ministry under influences he could not respect. Convinced that each diocese had a clear right to make provisions for training its men and that it was expedient for New York to do so, especially when "our brethren in a southern diocese have set us the example," he continued:

other dioceses have made, or will make such provision. Shall, then, New York relinquish the resources which she preeminently possesses for making ample provision . . . What would be the consequence? Other dioceses would have their establishments for theological education, and New York, who has every claim to one, having bestowed her resources elsewhere, would be destitute.[10]

He then proposes that, with the approval of the New York Convention in October, there be formed a Protestant Episcopal Theological Education Society of the State of New York for the support of divinity professors in the city and the establishment of a branch school to train candidates in the northern or western part of the diocese. Bishop Hobart was as shrewd as he was energetic. He knew that the arguments of the *Pastoral Letter* would appeal to New Yorkers, and that a few months' discussion of his general proposals would prepare the way for the more specific plans in his mind.

Meanwhile, on July 14 Bishop Brownell and the Board of Trustees published a set of regulations for the governance of the Seminary in New Haven. The "New Haven Plan" constituted the first statutes of the institution. Provision was made for the future endowment of professorships, the care of funds and scholarships, and for a committee of the Board to superintend the operation of the Seminary. The three-year course was to be in five departments of

9. *A Pastoral Letter Relative to Measures for the Theological Education of Candidates for Orders* (New York, 1820), p. 16.
10. *Pastoral Letter*, pp. 19-20.

theological learning: Biblical Literature, Systematic Theology, Ecclesiastical History, the Ministry, Polity and Ritual of the Church, and Homiletics and Pastoral Care. The two terms were fixed to run from the first Thursday in September to the second Thursday in December, and from the second Thursday in March to the first Thursday in July. The professors, constituting a Faculty, were to make regulations for the work and discipline of the students, who were enjoined to be "assiduous in the cultivation of a sound practical piety—neither . . . with mere formality, on one hand, nor running into fanaticism on the other"—sober Connecticut churchmanship.

The regulations of the plan were brief and workable, though two provisions were the target of much criticism. While no Episcopalian student was to be admitted without being a candidate for holy orders, or producing other satisfactory credentials, nor without being considered a probationer during his first term, the Seminary opened its classes to men of other denominations, though no one "while a member of the Institution shall be permitted to promulgate opinions tending to disturb the harmony of the Protestant Episcopal Church." Also, any student who received scholarship aid in the amount of one hundred dollars a year

> shall on his receiving Holy Orders, officiate, if required by the Trustees, as a Missionary under the direction of the Board of Directors of "The Foreign and Domestic Missionary Society of the Protestant Episcopal Church" . . . for the term of from one to three years, according to the discretion of the said Board—provided a suitable provision be made for his support, and the consent of his Diocesan be obtained.[11]

The last qualification was added in the second edition of the New Haven Plan as a result of the accusation that the Trustees were interfering with episcopal prerogatives. The attachment of the requirement of missionary service to scholarship aid, a reflection of the growing awareness of the urgent need for men on the frontiers,

11. *Plan of the Theological Seminary of the Protestant Episcopal Church, Second Edition* (Hartford, 1820), p. 14.

was bitterly attacked by the anonymous author of *An Address to the Episcopalians of the United States*, a tendentious pamphlet published in the late summer of 1820, which raised the question of the propriety of supporting an institution said now to be a local school, managed by Connecticut churchmen, and no longer a seminary of the whole Church. Its strictures were petty and frivolous. The admission of students of other denominations was deplored. The "contiguity of Yale College," advertised by the Trustees as an advantage, was thought by the author of the *Address* to expose the students to the influence of men whose doctrines were opposed to those of the Episcopal Church.

The pamphlet attracted more attention than it deserved, largely because of the suspicion that its author was the Bishop of New York. Jackson Kemper, who had just returned to New Haven from a trip through the Mohawk Valley, appealing for support of the General Seminary in Hobart's own territory, heard from William Augustus Muhlenberg in September that it was said that Hobart had written the tract. "I hope for the honour of the Mitre," wrote Muhlenberg, "that John Henry can wash his hands in innocency."[12] Kemper was not sure, perhaps because the *Address* was signed "An Episcopalian," a favorite pseudonym of the Bishop. Suspicion shifted, however, to John Churchill Rudd, rector of St. John's Church, Elizabethtown, New Jersey, and perhaps with more reason.[13] While Hobart may have shared some of the sentiments of the pamphlet, the style was not his, nor is it likely that he would have made the personal remarks about Bishop Brownell contained in it, though he always suspected that Brownell was not a wholehearted supporter of "sound church principles."[14]

The friends of the Seminary sprang to its defense. *The Christian Herald* published a "Review of Pamphlets on the Theological Seminary," and Christopher Gadsden produced his *Reasons in Favour of the General Theological Seminary*. Samuel Turner, indignant at

12. Kemper Papers 5 G 134.
13. Muhlenberg to Kemper, September 12, 1820, Kemper Papers 5 G 136.
14. Hobart to Kemp, January 24, 1821, Md. Dio. Ms.

the "impertinent intemperance" of the *Address*, was chiefly aroused by the objections to the ecumenical spirit of the Seminary's regulations and the idea that the Seminary should not be a place where any man could study theology. He wrote to Dr. Jarvis:

> Why should we not allow young men to study theology with us, even if they do not belong to our Church? If they prefer our course of studies and it is more convenient for them to come to us, it would be ill-natured to refuse. It may be the means of making them Episcopalians. Or, supposing a young man to wish to study theology, without intending to enter the ministry, why should his wish be objected to?[15]

Few defenders of the Seminary were more ardent in their loyalty or generous in their patronage than John Pintard, a distinguished citizen of New York. Banker, merchant, and philanthropist, sometime assistant alderman in the city and a member of the state assembly, Pintard was involved in much of the civic, economic, and cultural life of New York. The shrewd and perceptive comments on current affairs with which his voluminous correspondence sparkles make a fascinating contribution to the social history of the times. One of the founders of the New-York Historical Society and a lifelong patron of the American Bible Society, Pintard's interests were many-sided. A staunch Episcopalian, he was as well read in theology as in literature or the classics. Books were Pintard's first love, and the favorite project to which he devoted time and money unstintingly was the establishment of a theological library of distinction at the Seminary. The magnificent collections which the library possesses today had their origins in both Pintard's personal gifts and his enlistment of the interest and enthusiasm of others. The procession of founders of the General Seminary is not wholly a clerical one, nor were donors of large benefactions like Clement Clarke Moore and Jacob Sherred the only ones to whom the Seminary is indebted. A significant role was played by the sagacity of Judge Cameron, the firm support of Isaac Lawrence and John Pintard, and the wisdom of William Meredith.

15. Turner to Jarvis, August 29, 1820, Jarvis Correspondence.

When the Seminary moved to New Haven, Pintard's interest went with it. Bishop Hobart tried in vain to attach his support to the projected diocesan school. "The Bishop wrote me a candid letter," Pintard told his daughter in the summer of 1820, "dehorting me from having anything to do with the General Seminary." Pintard was not to be moved:

I confess that I feel all the delicacy possible in acting against the Bishops judgment. But I have deliberately reflected . . . & am too old a Bird to learn to whistle a new tune . . . Episcopalians generally trouble themselves very little about dogmas or Church matters, their duty is prescribed and they follow implicitly the Bell weather of the Flock. A few restive old rams however choose to look before they leap, of whom I am one.[16]

He wrote the Bishop on September 15 a firm refusal, "I have," he said

given your pastoral as well as private letter my most deliberate consideration. The result is that I regard it most expedient and to the best of my judgment most for the unity, character and interest of our Church to render my feeble services in support of the general Theological Seminary.[17]

Bishop Hobart was displeased, nor was his annoyance lessened by the news of Kemper's invasion of the western parts of his diocese, seeking support for the Seminary. The Bishop would not be satisfied with less than complete support for his plans in New York. While his *Pastoral Letter* had detached many of the former subscribers to the General Seminary, there remained a small group of influential men who could not be shaken, among them Pintard, Isaac Lawrence, and James Milnor, rector of St. George's Church.

On September 13, 1820, the sessions of the Seminary opened in New Haven. Professor Turner, armed with an inaugural address, boarded the steamboat in New York the day before, with Mr. Law-

16. *Letters from John Pintard to His Daughter, 1816-1833* (New-York Historical Society, 1940-41), I, 319.

17. Morgan Dix, *A History of the Parish of Trinity Church* (New York, 1905), III, 259.

rence, Mr. Pintard, "and several other gentlemen who had showed great interest in the Seminary."[18] The opening ceremonies in Trinity Church were described by Pintard:

At 11 Divine Service was performed by the Rev. Doctor Jarvis, now of Boston, after which Professor Turner delivered an appropriate inaugural address of an hour & a quarter . . . After service we returned to the Hotel, where the clergy of N Haven, together with the President & Professors of Yale College, were invited to dine with us. With the ladies, our party was nearly 50.

The occasion had its amusing side, for Jarvis and Pintard discovered that the New Englanders expected abstemiousness of their clergy.

On entering the hall Dr. Jarvis whispered that this was not like a New York dinner party, *no wine*. I replied that it was not my fault, that some had been ordered, & enquired of Mr. Lawrence who sat at the head of the table, why it had not been called for. He said that Bishop Brownell & the clergy had declined it. The fact turned out, that at the last meeting of the Trustees Wine was circulated, & a remark had been made that the Episcopal clergy could not convene & dine without wine.[19]

Pintard thoroughly enjoyed his day in New Haven, and upon his return to New York he shipped a surprise to be delivered on Dr. Turner's doorstep. Turner described it to Jackson Kemper on September 18:

This morning I received a letter from Dr. Milnor, & another from Mr. Pintard, informing me that on Saturday at 9 o'clock a subscription was opened for the purchase of a set of the Fathers at Eastburn's in 55 folios with the addition of Luther's works in 4; at 12 it was filled up to the amount of 325 dollars including Eastburn's 50 and Milnor's 50, the rest of 25. The books were immediately purchased, before sunset were shipped and are now in one large box safely deposited at my residence, a present to the Seminary from the subscribers. What think you of this?

18. *Autobiography of the Rev. Samuel H. Turner, D.D.* (New York, 1863), p. 101.
19. Pintard, *Letters*, I, 323-324.

Courtesy of the New-York Historical Society, New York City

John Pintard
Portrait by John Trumbull

Furthermore—Mr. Pintard has redeemed his hundred dollars' worth pledge. He has sent in another larger box 165 vols., worth (says Dr. Milnor) from 4 to 500 dollars.[20]

Samuel Turner settled down in New Haven to what might have been his happiest winter. He met his students in rooms over the post office, teaching all the more academic subjects, while Bishop Brownell "attended to the delivery of sermons, and to the department of Pastoral Theology." The seminarians found living quarters where they could, Turner staying at Mrs. Blagge's, "perhaps the best boarding house in town." Two of his ablest pupils were there with him, Frederick Schroeder and Manton Eastburn, the latter having

20. Kemper Papers 5 G 137.

returned to the study of theology after a brief interest in law. Eastburn, later bishop of Massachusetts, was a favorite with the friends of the Seminary. A few years later in New York, Pintard found him "decidedly the first Episcopal clergyman, for his years, in this diocese," though "not high toned enough for his Bishop."[21] Turner, in the New Haven days, thought him "learned for his age, clear-headed and discriminating, serious and judicious."[22] But Dr. Turner was delighted with all his students:

> I can truly say that, during the whole period of my connection with the Institution, I have never known more attentive, studious, thorough, and in every respect decorous young men . . . We lived together in

21. Pintard, *Letters,* II, 347.
22. Turner to Jarvis, April 23, 1821, Jarvis Correspondence.

Rooms "Over the Postoffice" in New Haven
Engraving from *Middlebrook's Almanac*

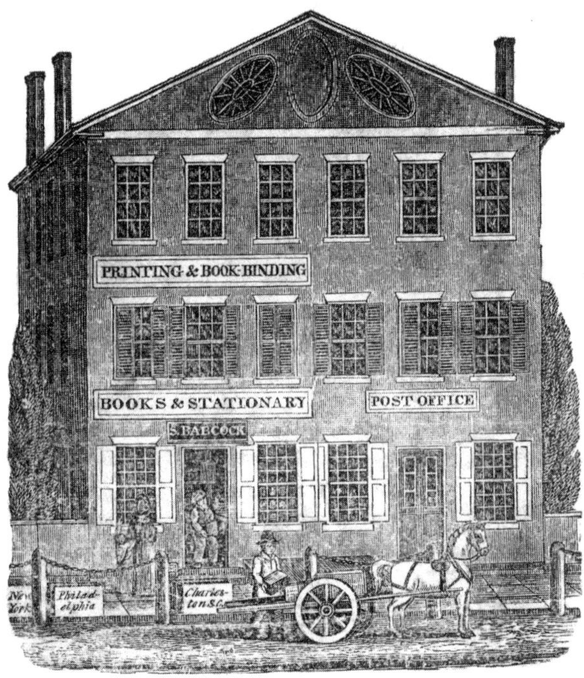

Courtesy of the Yale University Library

great harmony, and my feelings were like those of an elder brother helping the young members of the family.[23]

The recollections of the Reverend Samuel Roosevelt Johnson, then a student and later a professor in the Seminary, were equally pleasant:

> The students, although they had of course some occasional disputes, were as a band of brothers . . . The recreations were in the agreeable society of the place . . . in the waters and on the shore of the Sound . . . in expeditions to West Rock and the Judges' Cave, to East Rock and the Hermit's Cell, to the Arsenal or the quarries. Converse's celebrated Bookstore was their literary and theological exchange, and the ladies' parish sewing circle their most grateful entertainment.[24]

The "band of brothers" in New Haven was surprisingly large. Ten students assembled for the first sessions, and four others were soon added. By the middle of the third term of the Seminary's interlude in New Haven, that is, in November 1821, there were twenty-two students, and Turner happily forgot the discouragements of the first year in New York.

While Turner diligently led his students through their biblical studies and heard them recite from Pearson on the Creed, the Bishop of New York took measures to bring his diocesan school into existence. He had Mr. Moore's gift of the land in Chelsea and the larger amount of New York pledges formerly made to the Seminary. At the New York Convention in October 1820, Hobart asked for the establishment of the organization he had proposed in his *Pastoral Letter* of the previous July, the Protestant Episcopal Theological Education Society, through which the diocese could apply her extensive resources for theological education "in a way in which she would have reasonable control of them." He reiterated his favorite point:

> According to the organization of the General Institution, the Dioccss of New-York, which if her resources were liberally applied to this purpose, would certainly have the largest interest in the funds collected, has but three members in the Board of Trustees, in which sev-

23. *Autobiography*, pp. 103-105.
24. *The Church Journal*, July 24, 1856.

eral other Diocesses has the same number, and one Diocess eight members . . . The influence of the various parts of our Church, in the direction of a general institution, ought, obviously, in some degree, to be proportioned to the amount of their benefactions to it.[25]

Arguing persuasively the advantages of New York as a location for a theological school, he pointed to the association it might have with Columbia College, where the religious influences, in contrast to Yale, would be Episcopalian, and to the benefits of preparation for the ministry in a diocese so large in numbers of clergy and congregations. Hobart was willing—indeed, eager—that his local school should attract students from all parts of the Church. "Shall it be said," he asked,

that an institution in this Diocess would be unfriendly to the authority and unity of the Church? While this institution is subject, as it must be, to the general regulations of the General Convention—while its discipline and instructions must be in accordance with the prescriptions of the canons of that Convention, and with the course of study prescribed by its Bishops, there can be no danger of its unfriendly operation on the authority and unity of the Church. Let the institution be as general as the Episcopalians elsewhere may be disposed to make it. Let it invite students from all quarters.[26]

The convention established the society, "to provide for theological education by the establishment of theological schools in this diocese." The Bishop's proposal, Kemper heard, was adopted, "with astonishing unanimity in the fullest and most respectable convention ever assembled in this diocese."[27] Only Dr. Milnor rose to oppose it "in a most eloquent, luminous and conducive speech of about 1½ hours."[28] But Milnor's eloquence could muster no more than eight opposing votes. Kemper's nephew may have been right when he reported to his uncle from New York:

The Clergy here oppose the General Seminary because they believe some of the distinctive principles of the Church will be lost in it. They

25. *New York Convention Journal 1820,* pp. 17-18.
26. *Ibid.,* pp. 21-22.
27. Clark to Kemper, November 6, 1820, Kemper Papers 5 G 139.
28. Lacey to Kemper, October 19, 1820, Kemper Papers 5 G 138.

say they see it to be quite low church or evangelical. This Diocese has shown itself to be more unanimous than was at first supposed.[29]

The supporters of the Seminary were disheartened by the news that Bishop Hobart's project was going forward. With Dr. Wilmer and his friends busy in Virginia with their own plans, it began to look as though the institution at New Haven might soon belong to everybody in general and only Connecticut in particular.

Hobart's society, as established by the convention on October 19, 1820, was organized with a speed that revealed careful planning. Consisting of a large membership of contributors, its powers were vested in a group of trustees who chose its board of managers. Bishop Hobart strove to enlist the interest of every influential New York churchman, though there were a few like Rufus King who declined to regard the supporters of the General Seminary as guilty of a plot against the Bishop of New York or his church principles. Hobart wrote King on October 23:

I remember being much struck with the wisdom of a remark which several years since you made to me, that the resources of the Church in this City . . . ought to be carefully cherished and guarded. In accordance with this sentiment it has always appeared to me that the unrivalled resources and advantages which we here enjoy for theological education . . . ought not to be placed beyond our control. For the General Convention, organized on the principles of the old confederation, admitting a vote by States, the vote of N. Y. in that body is no more than the vote of Maine or Delaware, where our Church scarcely exists . . . a general institution, to which N. Y. would most largely contribute, might not only ultimately be placed under the influence of others . . . but under the control of those, who, in the fanatical spirit of superior sanctity, aim to destroy, or to alloy, those antient and sober features of our Church . . . by which she traces her origin to the Church of the first ages.

Then the Bishop came to the point:

A meeting of the Trustees in order to take preparatory measures is to be held in Trinity Church tomorrow afternoon . . . The Trustees

29. Sitgreaves to Kemper, November 6, 1820, Kemper Papers 5 G 140.

consist of some of the most influential or active Episcopalians, and it is all important at the outset a strong impression should be made. Addresses to them at the time by laymen of elevated character and commanding influence will operate incalculably more . . . than all the pastoral letters or addresses which I could make . . . Your presence on this occasion, and even a single expression of your favorable wishes are of more importance than can be attached to any other person . . .

The Milnors of N. Y. and the Hawleys and Henshaws and Keys of the South are rallying around the institution at New Haven, because they have reason to think that it will be favorable to their views, and will break down New York. Even from personal and official considerations I should wish to prevent their triumph—but I should lament its fatal influence on higher interests . . .

We only want your presence this once, with such remarks as you may think proper, approving the leading objects of the plan. We promise not to trouble you again on the subject.[30]

Rufus King was not to be drawn. He declined to serve as a trustee, but Bishop Hobart need not have been worried. The meeting on October 24 was well-attended, the plans of the Bishop went smoothly, and regulations were adopted that would soon bring into being a theological school in the city with a branch in western New York. It was arranged that an annual grant from Trinity Parish should be transferred from the Fairfield Academy to the "Interior School of Geneva," where three professorships were established for the education of candidates in the distant parts of the diocese. Four professorships were to be fixed in New York, though until funds allowed more permanent arrangements, the clergymen appointed to two of them were to retain their other ministerial duties. By February 1821, plans for both schools were complete. In the New York Diocesan School, Hobart himself was to teach Systematic Divinity and Pastoral Theology. Benjamin T. Onderdonk, later Hobart's successor as bishop of New York, was appointed Professor of the Nature, Ministry, and Polity of the Church, with "the department of Ecclesiastical History annexed." Clement Clarke Moore, as much distinguished for his learning as his wealth, an accomplished linguist

30. Charles R. King, *The Life and Correspondence of Rufus King* (New York, 1900), VI, 351-352.

and Hebrew scholar whose famous *Hebrew Lexicon* was published in 1809, undertook instruction in Biblical Learning. A gifted and eccentric New York lawyer and member of the state assembly, Gulian C. Verplanck, who combined his political activity with an interest in Shakespearean studies, gave his services to teach the Evidences of Revealed Religion and of Moral Science in its relation to Theology. At the Branch or Interior School at Geneva, the faculty consisted of John Reed, rector of Christ Church, Poughkeepsie; Orin Clark, rector of Trinity Church, Geneva; and Daniel McDonald, rector of Christ Church, Fairfield, and principal of the Fairfield Academy.[31]

On May 18, 1821, classes began in the New York Diocesan School with four students, the most notable being Samuel Seabury, grandson of the Bishop and later a professor in the General Seminary. By October there were eight students. At the Branch School, nine students appeared for the opening on June 11 in Trinity Church, Geneva. By this time, however, an unexpected event had occurred which drastically altered the future course of both the Seminary at New Haven and the New York schools. On March 30, New Yorkers opened their newspapers to read of the sudden death of Jacob Sherred, a prominent builder and contractor of the city, who, as John Pintard wrote his daughter,

> dies affluent, probably worth $200,000 or more, all the fruits of his own industry. A German by descent, he came from the country to this city, before the revolutionary war, & served his apprenticeship to the painter & glazier's trade, which he prosecuted till within 3 years with unparalleled industry and success . . . Of good sound plain sense, he was . . . an eminently useful vestryman of Trinity.[32]

A few days later, Pintard, and a great many others, were "all agitation," for on April 3, Sherred's will, dated January 28, 1820, was published. John Pintard discovered that his earnest request to Mr. Sherred to leave some money for theological education had been

31. *New York Convention Journal 1821*, pp. 29-37.
32. Pintard, *Letters*, II, 19.

heeded, and in a fashion far exceeding his fondest expectations. The whole of Sherred's residuary estate, estimated to be at least $60,000, was to be paid over by his executors when

> there shall be established within the state of New-York, under the direction or by the authority of the General Convention of the Protestant Episcopal Church in the United States of America, or of the Convention of the Protestant Episcopal Church in the State of New-York, a College, Academy, School or Seminary, for the education of young men designed for holy orders in the Protestant Episcopal Church.[33]

Bishop Hobart had no doubt that the legacy would come to the Diocesan School. On April 4, the *New York Evening Post* carried his public gratitude for "this elevated act of munificence," for which Sherred's memory "will long be cherished by the friends of religion and learning," and which "puts beyond all hazard" the theological schools in New York and Geneva. One hazard, however, Hobart ignored—the possible claim of the General Seminary to this legacy should its location be transferred back to New York.

Authenticated copies of Sherred's will were enclosed in the frenzied correspondence on which the friends of the General Seminary embarked. Pintard was virtually certain that if the General Convention should move the location of its seminary back to New York, the money would come to it. Dr. Milnor was hopeful, but not sure. On April 9 he wrote to his friend Charles P. McIlvaine:

> Mr Tyng can give you information, if you have not before had it, respecting a splendid testamentary benefaction to Bishop Hobart's seminary. May the great Head of the Church overrule its application to the promotion of his own glory and the salvation of sinners. If the General Seminary had remained in New York the legacy would have been theirs. Some think, if it be brought back into this state, they may yet claim it. But Bishop Hobart's lawyers say it is a clear case for him.[34]

33. *Proceedings Relating to the Organization of the General Theological Seminary* (New York, 1854), p. 68.
34. John S. Stone, *A Memoir of the Life of James Milnor, D.D.* (New York, 1848), p. 238.

Photograph by the Frick Art Reference Library

Jacob Sherred
Seminary Portrait by Samuel Waldo

Photograph by the Frick Art Reference Library

William L. Johnson, the
Seminary's First Graduate
Seminary Portrait by
Rembrandt Peale

Five days later, Dr. Milnor and others had raised the question of a special session of the General Convention to move the Seminary once more in order to pursue "a rightful and honorable claim" to the legacy, and before the month was out, Bishop Brownell had summoned the trustees to New Haven to consider the matter. On May 25 they petitioned the bishops to call a special meeting of the General Convention "for the purpose of ascertaining whether any, and what measures shall be taken in relation to the bequest of the late Jacob Sherred, Esq."[35]

During the early summer, threat of a dispute over the legacy subsided. In its place rose the happy solution of a union of the two seminaries. Amalgamation was the popular topic of discussion, but the New Yorkers were firm on one point. Onderdonk put it plainly to Kemper on June 19:

35. Circular Letter to the Bishops, May 25, 1821. See *Foundation*, G.T.S. Library.

When we shall be in the full possession of our rights, if the peace of the Church, its unity, or harmony be still thought to demand an amalgamation of the two seminaries, we shall be willing to meet the question in a fair and Christian spirit. But shall most assuredly deem it essential to the former and perfectly compatible with the latter to require that the great institution thus formed be established in the only equitable mode of proportioning the influence of each diocese by the extent of its patronage.[36]

Upon the request of Kemp, Bowen, Griswold, Moore, and Brownell, Bishop White issued a summons for a special session of the General Convention to meet in Philadelphia at the end of October. Most of the Seminary's friends had come to the conclusion that union with the New York school was inevitable, and even desirable. For Jackson Kemper, however, it was simply a case of unite or perish. He shared his gloomy views with Turner on September 27:

You will know that all the lawyers here think our case hopeless . . . I think it probable therefore that the proposition of claiming the legacy will be rejected . . . Then we unite & N. Y. has all in her own power, or else the General S. continues or is broken up to make room for Diocesan ones.

He was writing from Philadelphia, and if the General Seminary should be abandoned, and

only Diocesan ones are to exist, the general welfare of the Church calls upon us to have one here . . . All steady churchmen will want a medium not only of doctrine but of place between N. Y. & Virginia . . . I still think the ambition & views of Bp. H. must be firmly met and steadily opposed.[37]

A fortnight before the General Convention was to meet, Bishop Hobart persuaded his diocesan convention to take preparatory steps to implement a speedy amalgamation, should it be offered on favorable terms. The New York deputies were empowered to concur in any plan that would preserve "all the essential provisions and

36. Kemper Papers 6 G 32; see also Hobart to Kemp, January 24, 1821, Md. Dio. Ms.
37. Kemper Papers 6 G 42.

regulations of the seminary now established, under the authority of the Convention of this State," as long as "a just influence in the management and control of the general institution" was secured "to each diocese within which contributions may be obtained." Said the Bishop:

> Should they propose the course of compromise on correct principles, I trust we shall be prepared to meet it in the spirit of conciliation and candour.[38]

Conciliation was the spirit in which the special session of the General Convention assembled.[39] On November 1, a joint committee, headed by Judge Cameron of the House of Deputies and including Bishops Hobart and Kemp, reported a constitution for the General Theological Seminary. By its provisions, the Seminary was reestablished in New York, its trustees having power to set up branch schools elsewhere. Management was invested in a group of trustees to be elected at the next stated meeting of the convention, until which time the twenty-four trustees of the Seminary were to be joined by fourteen chosen by the New York society. The funds or claims to funds, and the properties of both institutions were to be transferred to the reconstituted Seminary, and the professors in both were to form its Faculty.

Bishop Hobart's demand for an influence in the Seminary's governance proportioned in accordance with the relative importance and amount of support of the several dioceses was met by the regulations fixing the composition of the future Board of Trustees. All the bishops were to be trustees *ex officio*. In addition, each diocese was to have one clerical or lay trustee; one additional trustee for every eight clergymen in the diocese; another additional trustee for each $2000 in any way given or contributed to the Seminary, up to $10,000; and one more trustee for every $10,000 thereafter. The

38. *New York Convention Journal 1821*, pp. 25-26, 69.

39. To preserve harmony in the Church, Brownell was ready to see the Seminary moved back to New York, and, if necessary, placed "under the controlling direction of the Bishop of that Diocese" (Brownell to Kemp, June 25, 1821, Md. Dio. Ms.).

Board was always to meet in New York, eleven members being a quorum. Provision was made for the trustees to vote, upon demand, in the fashion of the two houses of the General Convention, the concurrence of a majority among the bishops and among the clerical and lay trustees being necessary to any act.

There was general satisfaction when the houses of the convention concurred in action upon the constitution, despite the murmurings of the Virginia deputies that a general seminary ought to be "placed under more favorable auspices for the promotion of what we believed to be sound views of the Gospel and the Church, than it would be in New York."[40] Most churchmen applauded the sentiments of Bishop White as he closed the sessions with praise for

> the harmony with which we are concluding the present session; after having met with diversity of sentiment on some important points; on which, in consequence of mutual concession, and the merging of local attachments in the great object of general good, we are now separating with confirmed zeal for the great cause in which we are engaged.[41]

Bishop Hobart was entirely satisfied; Brownell was pleased with the outcome.[42] Bishop Bowen "contemplated the result with great satisfaction," for despite the "fidelity of our Brother Brownell," he had been apprehensive of the kind of religious influence Yale might have had upon the Seminary.[43] The chief credit for the spirit in which the union was achieved belongs to Duncan Cameron. His irenic efforts overcame the doubts of many who disliked the influence of New York. William Meade, a deputy from Virginia in this convention, recalled Cameron's convictions:

> He believed, or at least hoped, that the evil of the undue influence

40. William Meade, *Old Churches, Ministers and Families of Virginia* (Philadelphia, 1857), II, 373.
41. *Journals of General Conventions 1785-1835*, ed. W. S. Perry (New York, 1874), I, 619.
42. Brownell to Hobart, November 23, 1821, Brownell Papers, G.T.S. Library (Robbins Collection); see also Brownell to Kemp, November 21, 1821, Md. Dio. Ms.
43. Bowen to Hobart, February 7, 1822, Bowen Papers, G.T.S. Library (Robbins Collection).

of New York in the General Seminary, under the constitution as agreed upon by the committee, would be chiefly at the beginning, and would be decreasing every year. In glowing prophetic vision, he saw the Church extending itself over the land; new dioceses rising up in every part and rapidly filling themselves with ministers and churches,—sending their funds to the treasury of the General Seminary, and, on their account, as well as on account of the ministers, having the right to regulate the seminary; by which means the power of the General Church would be increasing, and that of New York proportionally decreasing . . . I well remember how he applied the prophetic words of the Patriarch Jacob, that "*the sceptre should not depart from Judah until Shiloh come; and unto him should be the gathering of the nations.*" I do not say that the scriptural application was correct, but his meaning was plain. The dioceses were to be the gathering together of the nations to take the sceptre from New York in the management of the General Seminary.[44]

But twenty-five years later, when Meade wrote those words, Cameron's hopes had not been realized. "The sceptre," said Meade, "has not yet departed from Judah . . . the gathering together of the nations (dioceses) has not yet been, and never will be." Sectional loyalties—and there were few stronger than those of William Meade—reinforced by differing theological emphases, dimmed Judge Cameron's vision. The move to establish local seminaries gained ground rapidly. The Virginia Convention of 1821, appealing to the Bishops' earlier "Declaration," set in motion the steps that led to the opening of the Theological Seminary at Alexandria in October 1823.[45] An attempt to found a seminary in Maryland during the winter of 1822-23 was brought to an abrupt end by Bishop Kemp, but in 1824, Philander Chase had persuaded the Ohio legislature to charter the Theological Seminary of the Protestant Episcopal Church in the diocese of Ohio, and four years later his school, first established at Worthington, moved to Gambier. In 1831 the Convention of Massachusetts, encouraged by Bishop Griswold, resolved to establish a diocesan school at Cambridge, and the Reverend John Henry Hopkins moved from Pittsburgh to become its chief professor. His

44. Meade, *Old Churches*, II, 372.
45. *Virginia Convention Journals 1821*, pp. 19-20; *1824*, p. 17.

election as Bishop of Vermont in 1832 ended this attempt to start a seminary in Massachusetts. Two years later, Benjamin Bosworth Smith, bishop of Kentucky, chartered a diocesan institution there. Amid this sectional activity, the "sceptre" remained in New York. Fifty years later, when new dioceses had spread over the land, and by the provisions of the Seminary's constitution the Board of Trustees numbered no less than four hundred and sixty, few were interested in the management of the General Seminary, and still fewer in sending their funds to its treasury.

The temporary trustees met to take the first steps in the effective amalgamation of the two schools on December 18, 1821, in order that the Seminary might reopen without delay. Arrangements were made for the consolidation of funds and properties, and a Standing Committee was chosen to manage the business of the trustees between their meetings. John Henry Hobart displayed his attractive streak of magnanimity in the union of the two faculties. He offered Dr. Turner his choice of the professorships, and Turner's love of biblical studies led him to take that of Biblical Learning and the Interpretation of Scripture, at a salary of $1500 a year. The Bishop yielded Systematic Divinity, at the same salary, to Bird Wilson, who had been appointed to that chair by the New Haven trustees shortly before the union. The son of James Wilson, a signer of the Declaration of Independence, he had been a Pennsylvania lawyer and judge before his admission to holy orders in 1819. A careful, if not an inspiring scholar, well read in the Fathers and the seventeenth-century Anglican divines, Dr. Wilson's devotion and unassuming modesty earned him the respect of all who knew him.

Mr. Moore became Professor of Hebrew and Greek Literature at a salary of $750 a year. Offering their services without compensation, Mr. Verplanck continued to teach Christian Evidences, and Benjamin Onderdonk, the Nature, Ministry and Polity of the Church, with Ecclesiastical History, though he relinquished the latter in 1822 when Turner and Wilson divided it temporarily between them. Bishop Hobart took the chair of Pastoral Theology and Pulpit Eloquence, and at the Branch School in Geneva, the three instructors were reappointed with appropriate compensation.

February 13, 1822, was "the day appointed by the Board of Trustees of the General Theological Seminary . . . for the commencing of the first session of the said Seminary." So runs the first entry in the minutes of the Faculty, recorded in Onderdonk's sprawling hand. Twenty-three students were admitted to the classes that assembled in the vestry room of St. John's Chapel until quarters in the adjacent building of Trinity's school had been prepared for them. Five others appeared before the end of June. The students included William L. Johnson, who finished his studies that summer, becoming the Seminary's first graduate; Samuel Roosevelt Johnson, William's younger brother; Robert Croes, son of Bishop Croes; Philip Gadsden; Henry J. Whitehouse, later bishop of Illinois; and Levi Silliman Ives, who thirty years afterwards resigned as bishop of North Carolina to make his submission to the Church of Rome.

Trinity Church was the scene of a solemn service of inauguration on the evening of March 11. John Pintard arranged the ceremonies, a responsibility he took very seriously on such occasions, while Dr. Milnor said the evening office. Trinity was crowded with clergy and trustees, professors and students, and a large congregation. Bishop Hobart addressed them at length—an hour and twenty minutes to be exact. "I have hardly room to give you an account of the address which the Bishop delivered," wrote Turner to Dr. Jarvis:

> It was given in Trinity Church last Monday to a crowded audience. It did him great credit . . . He took a view of the objects, principles, results, and means of the Seminary. Its objects he considered in reference to the preparing of a *learned*, *orthodox*, *pious*, and *practical* ministry.[46]

Bishop Hobart was at his best. He set forth succinctly and admirably his ideals of the ministry, challenged the professors and students with their realization, appealed to churchmen for understanding and support, and concluded his charge to the entire congregation with the Seminary's prayer:

MOST Gracious Father, who by thy blessed Son our Saviour Jesus

46. Turner to Jarvis, March 13, 1822, Jarvis Correspondence.

Christ, didst commission thy holy Apostles, and through them a succession of Pastors, to the end of time, to proclaim to the world the knowledge of salvation through a Redeemer; we implore thy blessing on this Seminary, instituted with a view to the same ministry of the Gospel. May the hearts and hands of thy people be open with supplies for the carrying of the design into effect. May the Trustees and the Professors be endued with fidelity and wisdom; and sustained by thy Providence in the discharge of the duties respectively committed to them. May the pupils be favoured with health for the prosecution of their studies; and preserved, by thy grace, from all temptation to relaxation from industry in the pursuit of knowledge. Strengthen in them the good desires which have been excited in them by the inspiration of thy holy Spirit; and impress on their minds a sense of the high origin, of the salutory tendency, and of the rich rewards of the Gospel Ministry. Endue them with humility in the pursuit of truth, and with zeal and steadfastness in the profession of it. Preserve them from prejudices, and from whatever else may betray their understandings into error, or their hearts into sin. May they be useful in their generation to the increase of thy glory and the edification of thy Church; and may they at last receive the commendation of faithful servants from the great Shepherd and Bishop of souls, thy Son Jesus Christ our Lord; in whose name, and through whose prevailing merits, we offer up these our imperfect prayers. *Amen.*[47]

47. John Henry Hobart, *An Introductory Address on the Occasion of the Opening of the General Theological Seminary* (New York, 1822), pp. 39-40.

4
St. John's Park

In 1820, when Professor Turner and his pupils moved to New Haven, the population of New York was approximately 123,000. Five years later, after the Seminary settled back into operation in the city, the number of inhabitants had risen to 166,000. Four fifths of the citizens lived in lower Manhattan, most of them south of Houston and Rivington Streets, though the advancing houses were already spreading northwards toward the village of Greenwich on the west side and the open fields between the Bowery and the river to the east.

The city was small enough for the families of its leading bankers, merchants, and professional men to share an intimate social life still marked by simplicity. Few people kept carriages for daily use, and the omnibuses or accommodation stages that jammed the streets a decade later had not yet appeared in great numbers. Drays served the purposes of commerce; gangs of porters clustered on busy corners to offer the services of their handcarts. One could conveniently walk to almost any point in the compact city, from the promenade at the Battery up past the banking houses in the vicinity of Wall Street, over to the docks where dozens of ships and sloops were moored in the East and North Rivers, around the new City Hall and old Columbia College in nearby Park Place, and along Broadway past the city's most imposing residences. On such a stroll one might still see the vagrant pigs that scavenged the streets, stand aside to let pass a shouting crowd of volunteer firemen rushing their hand engine to a blaze—and perhaps a brawl as well with a rival company —or step over the chain with which some churches still closed their streets against the rumble of wagons during service time on Sundays.

Above Fourteenth Street was the rural countryside, dotted with farms and estates, with occasional groups of summer cottages overlooking both rivers. John Randel's survey of 1807 had laid out the gridiron plan for the future development of New York's avenues and streets, but as yet little construction appeared beyond Fourteenth Street. The old thoroughfares to the north still meandered along the ridges of the island. The extension of Broadway known as the Bloomingdale Road ran toward the village of Bloomingdale, which lay along the Hudson a little south of the present site of Columbia University. It was linked at intervals with roads on the east side of Manhattan by lanes that wandered through wooded stretches of the countryside, over the brooks, and across the common lands. This was the area familiar to Dr. Jarvis before his brief term as one of the Seminary's original professors. He had been rector of St. Michael's Church, Bloomingdale Village, and also in charge of St. James' Church, then a summer chapel across the island near Hamilton Square.

In the mid-eighteen twenties, the greater number of New York's Episcopal churches were located in the heavily populated wards of the city within a radius of a mile from City Hall. Trinity's congregation worshiped in their second building at the present site. Close by on Broadway rose the squat tower of Grace Church, and two blocks away in Pine Street was the former Huguenot Church of St. Esprit, where John Pintard, once a pewholder and vestryman, had helped to adapt the French translation of the Prayer Book of the Church of England to accord with the American liturgy. On Beekman Street, east of St. Paul's Chapel, was Dr. Milnor's St. George's Church, near the old Brooklyn ferry slips.

Another group of parishes lay north of the City Hall. Christ Church had recently moved from Ann Street to a more central location in Anthony Street near Broadway. This was a favorite place of worship for Columbia students; Thomas Lyell was its rector, and the incomparable Manton Eastburn its assistant minister, until he became rector of the Church of the Ascension in 1827. Adjacent, also in Anthony Street, was the Negro congregation of St. Philip's, a parish destined one day to become one of the largest congregations in the Episcopal Church. To the east, at Cross and Mott Streets, stood Zion Church, its people having been Lutherans until 1810. St. Stephen's Church, organized by a distinguished group of citizens that included Cornelius Schuyler, William Rhinelander, Rufus King, and DeWitt Clinton, was located in the Bowery near Broome Street. Henry Feltus, the first librarian of the Seminary, had succeeded Richard Channing Moore as its rector when the latter became bishop of Virginia in 1814. Much further east, at the junction of Division and Grand Streets, was All Saints' Church, erected in 1824.

On the northern edge of the city, at the corner of Broadway and Houston Street, was the new Gothic edifice of St. Thomas' Church, harbinger of an architectural style that soon changed the character of Episcopal church buildings. Beyond St. Thomas', in the open stretches around Stuyvesant Street, was St. Mark's-in-the-Bowery. Across the island from St. Mark's, on the western edge of Greenwich Village, was St. Luke's Church, now St. Luke's Chapel of Trinity Parish, at its present location on Hudson Street. It was organized by Clement Clarke Moore and a group of his friends in 1820. With the Amos farm on the river side and the Old State Prison in the fields to the north, St. Luke's was still in rural surroundings, though houses were springing up rapidly as people moved from the crowded quarters of the lower city to escape the intermittant epidemics of yellow fever.

Below St. Luke's, a short distance south of Canal Street and about halfway back to City Hall, was St. John's Chapel of Trinity Parish. Here the life of the Seminary was centered after the return from New Haven. Erected in 1807 on the east side of Varick Street, between Laight and Beech Streets, and backed by St. John's Lane—

along which one may still walk—the church was a large sandstone building, architecturally similar in many ways to Trinity's older chapel, St. Paul's. It was fronted with a broad portico under a pediment supported by four graceful Corinthian columns. Above the porch rose the clock tower and ornate steeple, the tallest in the city except for Trinity's spire. The beauty of St. John's lay partly in its setting, for across Varick Street was St. John's Park, extending to Hudson Street. The ornamental shrubs and specimen trees made it one of the loveliest of New York's old squares. Around the park were the substantial homes of some of the wealthiest and most prominent citizens, for this section of the city was enjoying its few years as a fashionable area. A short distance northwards on Varick Street was the new and spacious school building of Trinity Parish. Two rooms on its lower floor were leased by the Seminary, and here classes were held from 1822 until 1827.

Both church and park have long since disappeared, the beauty of the latter destroyed in 1867 to make room for Commodore Vander-

St. John's Chapel and Park

bilt's vast New York Central freight depot, and the former torn down in 1919 when Varick Street was widened and the subway excavated below. Today, however, from the doorway of the office building at 50 Varick Street, once the site of the chapel portico, one looks out again on a broad open space. Vanderbilt's ugly structure has vanished, and the old park is now the traffic plaza for exit roads from the Holland Tunnel.

The Seminary's first full academic year at St. John's was 1822-23. Having secured an act of incorporation from the New York legislature on April 5, 1822, the Trustees met in July to complete the organization begun the previous December. After receiving a report of assets of the combined seminaries which, thanks to the Sherred legacy, totaled nearly $70,000, plus the "sixty-two lots in Greenwich," the Board enacted a set of statutes governing the Seminary in ample detail. The committee of the General Convention in 1819 may have left the professors too much to their own devices during the first New York period. If so, the situation was corrected by the Trustees to whom the new constitution gave the Seminary's management. The statutes, amended and expanded as the experience of the years at St. John's dictated, controlled virtually every aspect of the life of the institution.[1] Still today the statutes regulate the operation of the General Seminary, in somewhat less detail but in every significant phase of its governance.

The Trustees prescribed a course of study in eight departments: Oriental and Greek Literature, Biblical Learning, the Interpretation of the Scriptures, the Evidences of Revealed Religion, Systematic Divinity, Ecclesiastical History, the Nature, Ministry and Polity of the Church, and Pastoral Theology and Pulpit Eloquence. The Faculty was required annually to report on the pursuit of these subjects, and in time it became customary for individual professors to submit summaries of each year's work in their several departments.

1. *The Constitution, Act of Incorporation and Statutes of the General Theological Seminary* (New York, 1822), pp. 9-19.

The students were distributed into First, Second, and Third Classes, nomenclature that was altered in 1832 to the familiar designation of Senior, Middle, and Junior years. The statutes fixed the basic curriculum for each class. In the first year, students in the Third Class embarked chiefly upon biblical studies, including Hebrew and Greek texts, and the study of Christian evidences. In the next year, church history, theology, and polity were added, and the First Class spent the greater amount of its time on theological and historical topics. All classes met one day a week for practice in the composition and delivery of sermons, the performance of the liturgy, and the study of principles of pastoral care. There were usually two periods of class exercises a day, each of an hour or an hour and a half, consisting mainly of recitations on assigned reading. By order of the statutes, the books prescribed were those included in the authorized Course of Ecclesiastical Studies of 1804, unless substitute texts were approved by vote of the Faculty. Each term the professors drew up a schedule of daily recitation hours from Tuesday through Saturday. Monday was normally reserved for the Professor of Pastoral Theology and Pulpit Eloquence, an office for which Bishop Hobart volunteered his services until his death in 1830.

This simple scheme of recitation periods with the individual professors was continued for more than fifty years. It was not until after the middle of the century that the Seminary catalogues described the curriculum of the three classes by subject matter rather than with the direction "attends the professor," and it was many years after that before course listings were set out in the fashion familiar in seminary catalogues today.

Little instruction was given by lecture in these early days, though the professors expanded their examination of students on the reading, as Dr. Wilson reported to the Trustees in 1831, by "such explanatory and additional remarks as appear suitable." Gulian Verplanck seems to have used in lecture form some of the material he published in 1824 as *Essays on the Nature and Uses of the Various Evidences of Revealed Religion.* He was by no means an inconsid-

Professor Wilson
Seminary Portrait by Daniel Huntington

erable scholar, as Pintard, with whom he was no favorite, admitted.[2] Philip Hone, the famous diarist and sometime mayor of New York, thought Verplanck's learning exceeded his political acumen, especially in the fields of literature and the fine arts.[3] Mr. Verplanck, however, preferred his political activities, and when he found it impossible to meet his classroom engagements with regularity, he resigned his professorship in 1825, leaving the teaching of Christian evidences to be added to the burdens of Professor Wilson.

Samuel Turner seems to have made tentative experiments with the lecture method, largely because of his growing dissatisfaction

2. *Letters from John Pintard to His Daughter, 1816-1833* (New-York Historical Society, 1940-41), II, 160.

3. *The Diary of Philip Hone, 1818-1851*, ed. Allan Nevins (New York, 1927), I, 120.

with the textbooks available for Old Testament study. Bird Wilson, on the other hand, seldom went further than "explanatory remarks" supplementing the recitation exercise. The recollection of an alumnus in later years that he was an "eccentric old bachelor . . . as unable to communicate his stores of learning to his pupils as a dumb man is to sing an aria from an oratorio" is an unduly harsh judgment, at least upon Wilson's capacity as a teacher in the early days.[4] His custom, however, of drawing names from a little packet to determine who would recite on Burnet, Pearson, or Stackhouse must have given his students plenty of scope to calculate their chances of escaping a class recitation.

Opportunity for theological discussion was provided by the monthly meetings of the Theological Society, in which all students were expected to participate.[5] Essays were read, an occasional sermon heard, but the chief feature was a prepared debate, with one of the professors as chairman, on a significant or controversial question.[6] Is the division of Christians into different sects favorable to Christianity? Should the American Bible Society receive the patronage of Episcopalians? Was the flood in the time of Noah universal? Can the existence of God be made evident by reason alone? Does the subscribing to a "regula fidei" retard the advancement of truth? Did Moses in writing the Book of Genesis make use of pre-existent documents? Should members of the Church engage in support of foreign missions? Such questions were often heatedly discussed, though unfortunately the minute books of the Theological Society do not always record the decision with which an evening's debate concluded. It is noted, however, that the negative prevailed on the question, "Was the introduction of Philosophy into the Church during the first three centuries beneficial to Christianity," and the debate over "Do we derive our moral principles from nature or education?" was decided in favor of man's possession of a natural moral sense.

4. G.T.S. *Seminarian* (1901), p. 56.
5. Faculty Minutes, March 3, 1823.
6. Minutes of the Theological Society 1820-1828, G.T.S. Library.

Through the years, the books of the Course of Ecclesiastical Studies appear as the hardiest of perennials, though a few new titles were added or substituted from time to time, duly approved in the minutes of the Faculty. Burnet's classic on the Thirty-Nine Articles yielded first place to Browne's *Exposition* after the latter's appearance in the mid-'fifties. Verplanck's *Essays* supplemented Paley's *Evidences;* Trench on miracles and Hurd on prophesy won places in the list. But Pearson, Leslie, Butler, Magee, and Waterland were as prominent in the last quarter of the century as they were in the early years. In ecclesiastical history, Mosheim was gradually supplemented with Neander, Milman, and Neale, though Collier on the English Church and Burnet on the Reformation remain, while in polity Hooker, Potter, and Barrow were recited upon as often in 1875 as they were in 1825. Perceval on the apostolic succession was the only notable addition in this department.

At the end of the academic year, while the Board of Trustees was holding its stated meeting during the few days before commencement, the statutes prescribed an oral examination for the students in each class. This ordeal, occupying the better part of two and a half days, was conducted by the professors in the presence of an Examination Committee appointed by the trustees. The examiners, of course, not only observed the proficiency of the students, but formed as well an impression of the ability of their instructors and the thoroughness with which the studies had been pursued.[7] Members of the First Class who sustained the examination successfully, and were recommended by the Faculty, were awarded diplomas or "Testimonials," as they were called. The Seminary granted no degrees in theology for many years, and the Testimonial, signed by the professors and representative trustees, certified that the graduating student

has completed the full Course of Study and satisfactorily sustained the

7. In 1834 an "intermediate examination" before members of the Trustees' Standing Committee was added at the end of the first term. The Faculty disliked this interruption of the year's work, however, and the practice was abandoned before the middle of the century (see the Faculty Minutes, June 28, 1849).

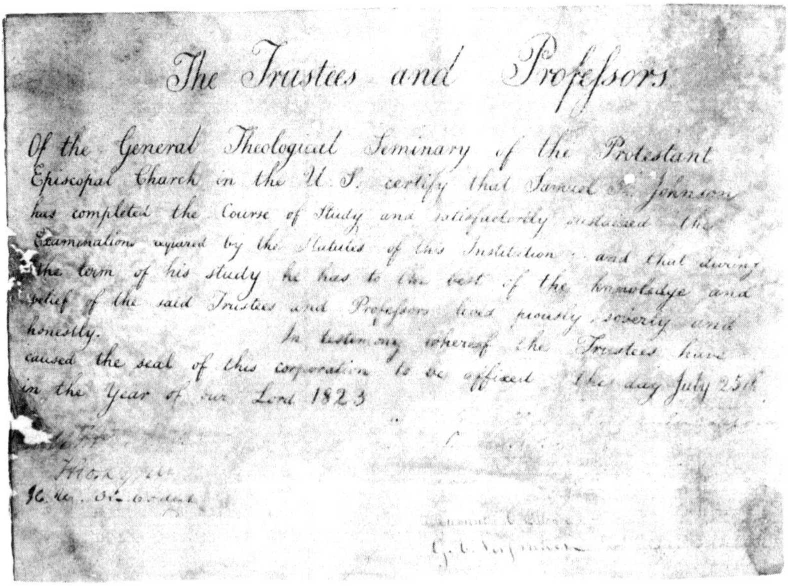

The Trustees and Professors

Of the General Theological Seminary of the Protestant Episcopal Church in the U. S. certify that Samuel R. Johnson has completed the Course of Study and satisfactorily sustained the Examinations required by the Statutes of this Institution and that during the term of his study he has to the best of the knowledge and belief of the said Trustees and Professors lived piously, soberly and honestly. In testimony whereof the Trustees have caused the seal of this corporation to be affixed the day July 25th in the Year of our Lord 1823

The Testimonial of 1823

THE

Trustees AND Professors

of the

General THEOLOGICAL Seminary

of the

Protestant Episcopal Church

IN THE

UNITED STATES

Certify that Edward Ballard has completed the full course of study and satisfactorily sustained the examinations required by the statutes of this Institution, and that during the term of his studies he has, to the best of the knowledge and belief of the said Trustees & Professors, lived soberly, piously, & honestly. In Testimony whereof, the Trustees have caused the seal of this Corporation to be affixed, this Twenty Sixth day of June in the Year of our Lord One Thousand Eight hundred & Twenty Nine

TRUSTEES. PROFESSORS.

The Testimonial as Used for Fifty Years

Examinations required by the Statutes of this Institution, and that during the term of his studies he has, to the best of the knowledge and belief of the said Trustees and Professors, lived soberly, piously, and honestly. In Testimony whereof the Trustees have caused the seal of this corporation to be affixed.

The seal, adopted in 1823, depicted an open Bible, surmounted by a large mitre, and across the pages of which lay a Prayer Book. Around it a riband bore the words of 1 Corinthians 3:11: ΘΕΜΕΛΙΟΝ ΓΑΡ ΑΛΛΟΝ ΟΥΔΕΙϹ ΔΥΝΑΤΑΙ ΘΕΙΝΑΙ.

After some experiments with the dates of the academic year, during which it was found that hot weather made a July commencement in New York unbearable, the Board of Trustees in 1828 fixed the terms to run from the first Monday in October to early February, and from that time until the Saturday after the fourth Tuesday in June. Vacations were provided in the Christmas season and during Holy Week, with a suspension of classes on Ash Wednesday, Easter Monday and Tuesday, Ascension Day, Whit Monday and Tuesday, and on any "days of thanksgiving or fasting appointed by the ecclesiastical or civil authority."

Under the statutes, the admission of students required evidence of candidacy for holy orders "with full qualifications, according to the Canons of the Protestant Episcopal Church." Those who lacked "full qualifications" might be admitted if they gave

> satisfactory evidence of religious and moral character and of classical and scientific attainments, and in general of such dispositions and habits as may render them apt and meet to exercise the ministry.

The Faculty interpreted the academic admissions requirements to be fulfilled by the possession of a college diploma, or by the passing of an examination on the general principles of natural and moral philosophy, rhetoric, and in the Latin and Greek languages.[8]

Students were matriculated at a special service in December, usually on an Advent Ember Day or on St. Thomas' Day, one of the rare occasions in these early years on which there was a Seminary

8. Faculty Minutes, December 2, 1822.

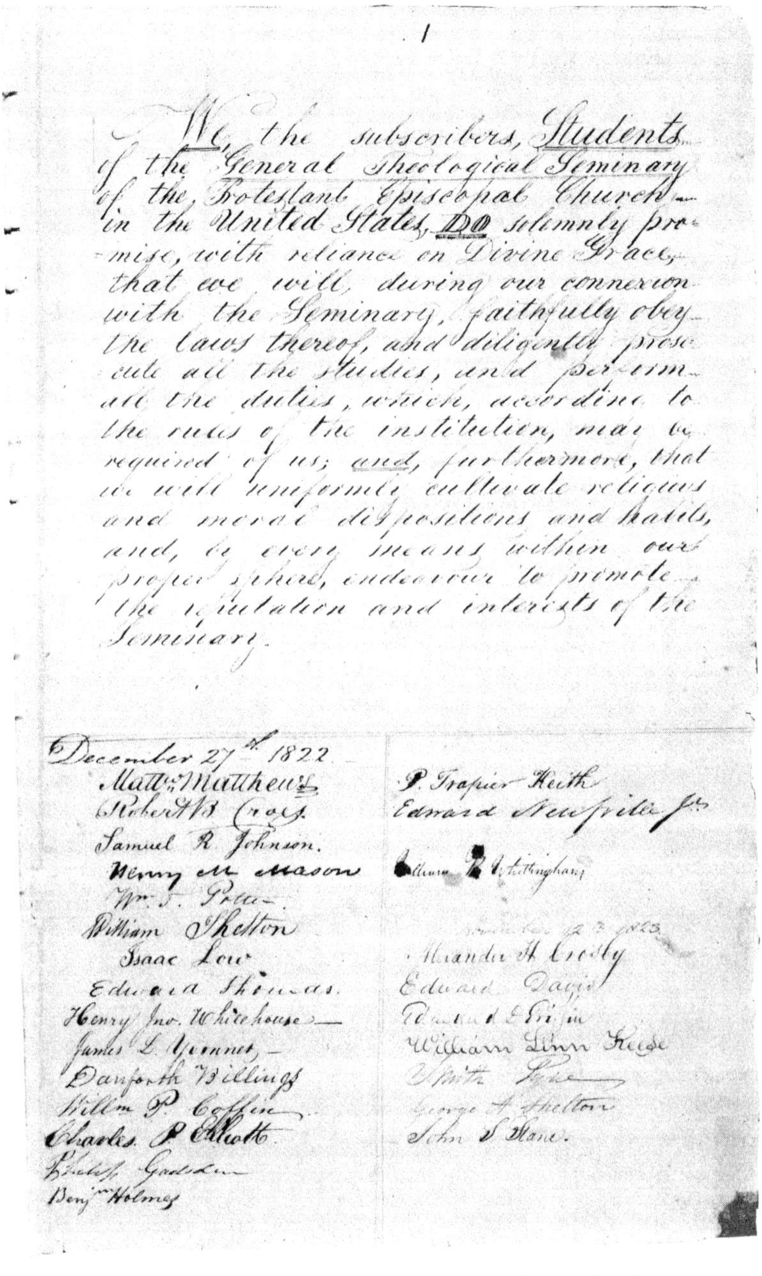
1

We, the subscribers, Students of the General Theological Seminary of the Protestant Episcopal Church in the United States, DO solemnly promise, with reliance on Divine Grace, that we will, during our connexion with the Seminary, faithfully obey the laws thereof, and diligently prosecute all the studies, and perform all the duties, which, according to the rules of the institution, may be required of us; and, furthermore, that we will uniformly cultivate religious and moral dispositions and habits, and, by every means within our proper sphere, endeavour to promote the reputation and interests of the Seminary.

December 27th 1822.
Matthew Matthews
Robert B. Croes
Samuel R. Johnson.
Henry M. Mason
Wm. S. Potter
William Shelton
Isaac Low
Edward Thomas.
Henry Jno. Whitehouse
James L. Yvonnet
Danforth Billings
Willm P. Coffin
Charles P. Elliott
Philip Gadsden
Benjm Holmes

P. Trapier Keith
Edward Neufville Jr.
William R. Whittingham
Alexander H. Crosby
Edward Davis
Edward [illegible]
William Linn Keese
Smith Pyne
George A. Shelton
John S. Kane

The First Page of the Matriculation Book

celebration of the Holy Communion, and at which time a special address was given by one of the professors. The entering students subscribed the solemn promise in the Matriculation Book, affirming

> with reliance on Divine Grace, that we will, during our connexion with the Seminary, faithfully obey the laws thereof, and diligently prosecute all the studies, and perform all the duties which, according to the rules of the institution, may be required of us; and, furthermore, that we will uniformly cultivate religious and moral dispositions and habits, and, by every means within our proper sphere, endeavour to promote the reputation and interests of the Seminary.

The first subscriptions were made in 1822, and since that time all members of the Seminary have signed the same Matriculation Book. Years later, Dean Hoffman moved the matriculation ceremony to All Saints' Day, and in 1914 the phrases of the original promise were somewhat shortened, though without substantial change.

Students were enjoined by the statutes, in words borrowed from the earlier New Haven Plan, to "humble reliance on Divine Grace," and to be assiduous in "the cultivation of evangelical faith and a sound practical piety." They were warned against the extremes of "mere formality" in spiritual exercises on one hand, or "running into fanaticism" on the other. Members of the Seminary met for brief daily prayers in St. John's Chapel. This was the extent of their corporate religious exercises, it being assumed that students would associate themselves with one of the nearby parish churches for their regular church life. The statutes exhorted them to supplement their participation in the public worship of the Church with daily periods of private devotion and meditation, and the professors were expected to guide them in the cultivation of the life of prayer.

Little initiation or independence was left to the members of the Faculty in matters of Seminary policy or governance. They had the authority to admit students and grant dismissions, to arrange the conduct of the studies, to exercise discipline when necessary, and to regulate the daily schedule of Seminary activities. For many years, therefore, the minutes of the monthly Faculty meetings contained little beyond routine entries relating to these arrangements. Now and then a stated Faculty meeting was abandoned for lack of a quorum, and surprisingly often the minutes contained one terse entry: "No business offering, the Faculty adjourned." Far more information about the developing life of the institution appears in the minute books of the Standing Committee of the Trustees. This was the body that managed the operation of the Seminary for the Board, and it consisted of the Bishop of New York, "such other Bishop or Bishops as may be in the city of New-York at any meeting of the Committee," the secretary and treasurer of the Board, six clerical and six lay trustees elected annually. Its powers were virtually unlimited, and its directives to the Faculty touched upon nearly every phase of Seminary life. In short, the Standing Committee was the seat of Seminary authority and remained so until an effective deanship was established a half-century later. Even then, the long years of superintendance by the committee led to a division of authority that is characteristic of the administration of the Seminary today.

The statutes provided that if there were a bishop among the professors, he should preside at Faculty meetings. For a long time, John Henry Hobart and Benjamin Onderdonk, his successor as bishop of New York, did so, unless absent on episcopal visitations or other business. In that event, the Faculty chose a chairman *pro tem*, generally Dr. Turner.

Such were the basic patterns inaugurated at St. John's, establishing practices and precedents that were followed for many years. These administrative arrangements sufficed as long as the Seminary remained an institution without much corporate life, its members meeting daily for the recitations in the Trinity School building. Complexities presented themselves when the Seminary became a residential college at Chelsea in 1827. Then the Standing Committee and the Faculty embarked upon the new and sometimes painful task of learning how to manage a theological institution in the full sense of that term. It was an uncharted course, for there were no clear patterns for the operation of an Anglican seminary in the early years of the nineteenth century. The expanding responsibilities were met by the method of trial and error, and experiment, with its attendant experience of success or failure, by men who were pioneers in a system of theological education.

Seminary life during the five years in downtown New York could not have been very different from that in New Haven. Twenty-four students was the average number in an academic year, about a third of whom were New Yorkers. Many of these lived at home, and the others boarded in a house rented by the Trustees. During the first years, Samuel Turner lived with his sisters at the southwest corner of Franklin and Church Streets, less than five minutes' walk from St. John's and at the present site of the Department of Welfare Building of the City of New York. After his marriage in 1826, he moved to a house in the more open area near Washington Square, just south of Bleeker Street where the premises of 633 Broadway now stand. There he remained until the Seminary moved to Chelsea, spending most of his spare time writing New Testament commentaries and, in company with Manton Eastburn, learning German in order that he might become better acquainted with continental Old Testament scholarship.

Though there were two dozen students under instruction each year, there was a wide discrepancy between the number who matriculated annually and those who graduated with the Testimonial. In 1824, for example, 15 men entered the Third Class, but only 2 were left to graduate in the First Class. Five men received Testimonials in 1823, 2 in 1825, 6 in 1826, and the same number in 1827. By the end of a decade, the Seminary had matriculated 135 men since its foundation, but its alumni—those who had completed the full course—numbered only 44. "Young men," complained Turner to Dr. Jarvis,

> will not remain in the institution 3 years if they can get into holy orders after pursuing their studies 18 months.[9]

Among the students, and among some of the bishops as well, it was a long time before it was assumed that all candidates would remain for the full three years. To many, the Seminary was simply a place where a man could conveniently read for orders in the company of others and under qualified supervision. Why remain longer if he could prepare for ordination in eighteen months? It was not until

9. Turner to Jarvis, March 16, 1824, Jarvis Correspondence.

the full benefits of life in a residential institution were felt, and after the canons of the Church in 1826 extended the normal period of candidacy to three years, that most students began to remain for the complete course of study. Even then, it was some time before the canons were enforced with few exceptions.

The gradual increase in the number of men who remained to graduate caused some adjustments to be made in the ceremonies of commencement. The original order for the graduation exercises was devised by the Trustees for the first formal commencement on July 26, 1823. The service was in Christ Church, and the order, with some slight elaborations, was followed for nearly twenty years. A procession, accompanied by organ music, took the bishops present to the chancel, the Faculty and students to seats near them, and the Trustees and visiting clergy to the front pews of the nave. Bishop White, who was usually present to preside at early commencements, opened the exercises with prayer. An appropriate psalm followed, and then each member of the graduating class read a dissertation in turn, with "music between." After awarding Testimonials to the students presented to him, the Bishop delivered the Commencement Address, a formal discourse that was afterward printed and distributed in pamphlet form. A hymn and some final prayers concluded the ceremonies.

As the number of candidates for the Testimonial increased, the service became something of an endurance test. One might, without flagging interest, listen to two dissertations, as in 1824—on "The Propriety of Giving a Figurative Interpretation to Passages of Scripture Ascribing Personality to the Holy Ghost" and "An Examination of the Charge Brought Against Christianity that the Motives it Holds Out for the Good Conduct of Life are Selfish and Mercenary"—and still have an ear for Bishop White's address. But when there were eleven graduates, as in 1833, each armed with an erudite oration, considerable fortitude must have been required, even on the part of folk accustomed to long-windedness in their clergy. At the exercises in 1833, a few years after the Seminary had moved to Chelsea, Bishop Brownell had come from Connecticut to preside, and John Henry Hopkins, the new bishop of Vermont, was prepared to address the assemblage. He must have listened with increasing dismay as one dissertation followed another inexorably, until all eleven members of the Senior Class had displayed their learning on such topics as "The Prospects of the Heathen in Reference to their Eternal Destiny," "The Inability of Unaided Reason to Establish the Doctrine of a Future State," or "The Necessity of Piety as a Qualification for the Interpretation of the Scriptures." Even the musical refreshment of the congregation by four verses of a hymn and the Doxology between the sixth and seventh orations could have brought only temporary relief. By the time Brownell had awarded the Testimonials, Bishop Hopkins' chronometer warned him that nearly four hours had passed. He put aside the manuscript of his prepared discourse and uttered what *The Churchman* described as a few "brief and impressive words." There is no printed Commencement Address for 1833, mute testimony to the mercy of the Bishop of Vermont on a warm New York day in late June.

Warm it must have been, for the congregation at the exercises in 1833 was crowded into the small building then known as St. Peter's Chapel, just east of Ninth Avenue on Twentieth Street, that served the newly established parish of Chelsea until its church was completed next door. Until 1826, Seminary commencements were held in Christ Church, and after that, at St. John's Chapel, where Columbia College also held its graduation ceremonies. The move to St. Peter's Chapel was an experiment, soon abandoned either because of inadequate facilities or in response to the complaint that this "remote corner of our city" was too far for the friends of the Seminary to attend without serious inconvenience.[10] The exercises, therefore, returned to St. John's until 1838. By that time, St. Peter's Church had been erected, and the graduation services were normally held there every year thereafter, until the Seminary's present chapel was built more than forty years later.

The reading of dissertations by seniors at commencement was curtailed in 1836, when only selected orations were heard, and after 1842 the custom was abandoned altogether. At that time, chiefly through the influence of Bishop Onderdonk, the old order of com-

10. *The Churchman*, July 6, 1833.

mencement was changed in favor of the regular divine service of the Church: Morning Prayer, Litany, and Holy Communion.[11] Bishop Onderdonk was greatly pleased at the decision of the Trustees that "the commencement exercises shall be less of an academic, and more of an ecclesiastical character." He delighted in this evidence of "the growing attachment of the age to Catholic principles and feelings," and when the new order was first used in 1843 he waxed eloquent in praise of

> the administration of the Lord's Supper, furnishing a fitting close to the academic year, a Christian parting with the young brethren . . . and a delightful season of solemn communion between bishops, clergy, and people . . . and of commendation to God's mercy, through the great sacrifice then commemorated, of this blessed institution.[12]

All those who listened to the Bishop's praise of the Seminary were by no means as delighted as he, for a swelling tide of suspicion and criticism was rising against the same "growing attachment to Catholic principles and feelings"; however, the new order of commencement was to outlive the storm that broke over Chelsea Square shortly afterwards.

After the amalgamation of the General Seminary and Hobart's Diocesan School, a new Board of Trustees was elected at the General Convention of 1823 in accordance with the complicated provisions of the Constitution of 1821. Each diocese nominated to the House of Deputies the number of trustees to which it was entitled by the size of its clergy and the amount of its contributions. In addition to the bishops, all of whom were *ex officio* members of the Board, 66 clerical and lay trustees were elected in 1823. Twenty-one were from New York and 8 from South Carolina. Maryland had 7, Connecticut and Pennsylvania 6 each, Virginia and Massachusetts 5, and the remaining dioceses 1 or 2. Three years later, when the process was repeated, New Yorkers numbered 31 out of 83 trustees. By 1838, when the Board included 138 clerical and lay members in addition to the bishops, 57 represented the diocese of New York.

11. Onderdonk to Whittingham, April 7, 1842, Md. Dio. Ms.
12. *New York Convention Journal 1842*, p. 59; *1843*, p. 71.

At meetings of the Board in the 'twenties and 'thirties the usual number in attendance was between twenty-five and thirty, a third of whom were New Yorkers. The all-important Standing Committee was composed almost entirely of clergymen and laymen from the city. In such circumstances, the influence of New York was decisive in the affairs of the Seminary, as Bishop Hobart had hoped. It was not to the liking of John Pintard, who was inclined to blame any reverse in the Seminary's fortunes, perhaps unfairly, on the "deleterious atmosphere in this Diocese . . . which paralyzes our Seminary."[13] Mr. Pintard's mood fluctuated. At times he lamented bitterly the paramount influence of New York, reproaching the trustees from other dioceses for their failure to attend Board meetings and counterbalance "the whole phalanx of Bp. H.'s Trustees." If they do not come, he wrote to Dr. Jarvis, and "therefore N.Y. Diocesan influence prevails, who is to blame?"[14] At other times he felt better about the Seminary, perhaps because Dr. Turner assured him that Bishop Hobart did not exercise any undue personal influence in its affairs. Pintard, however, was reluctant to believe it. He was convinced that if the Bishop withheld his "intriguing, managing hand," it was only because of his greater interest in the Branch School at Geneva. "Cardinal Wolsey's College," fumed Pintard, sure that the Bishop's "affections are set towards Geneva—that tail to our kite, that prevents it soaring."[15] Pintard never overcame his prejudice against John Henry Hobart, and he was seldom just to the gifted bishop. Even when Hobart's untimely death in 1830 deprived the Church of its ablest and most dynamic leader, Pintard reported to his daughter, that

> he died on Sunday morning . . . an active, ambitious High Church prelate, & will be canonized by his party as such. I could not nor did not go all lengths with him, especially in his . . . indifference to our Gen. Theol. Seminary which he did all in his power to degenerate into a Diocesan School. He has however gone to his account & let him rest. I hope he is better off as I trust our Diocese will be.[16]

13. Pintard to Jarvis, June 13, 1822, Pintard Papers, G.T.S. Library.
14. Pintard Papers, July 23, 1823; see also June 24, 1822.
15. Pintard to Jarvis, June 13, 1822, Pintard Papers.
16. Pintard, *Letters*, III, 175.

In the long run, Hobart won the only victory in the Seminary he cared about. Nearly forty years after his death at the meeting of the Board of Trustees in June 1867, the Examination Committee reported that in a searching three-day examination they detected "not the slightest appearance of a leaning towards Ultraism, either as lax and indifferent, or in astute and fanciful Churchmanship." On the contrary, they were pleased to observe that "the course of teaching had evidently been of the plain, straightforward Bishop Hobart School."[17] Surely that was the immortality John Henry Hobart desired.

It is true that Bishop Hobart shifted his concern to Geneva once the Seminary was securely founded in New York. His attention there, however, centered upon the eight men enrolled in a pre-theological collegiate course rather than upon the four candidates for orders studying at the academy. His ambition, as he told Clement Clarke Moore, was to build up a stronghold for the Church in the west by converting Geneva Academy into a college under Church auspices. Few of the Trustees shared this enthusiasm, and the members of the Faculty cared even less. "As to the Geneva Branch," wrote Turner to Jarvis,

> I declare to you that I do not know anything about it, nor do I believe that a single man among the Trustees who is not under influence or bias, is much in favor of it. But no one lifts up his voice against it . . . Our friend Pintard calls it the *incubus*. I wish the Trustees would get rid of it.[18]

Samuel Turner got his wish sooner than he expected. In 1824 the Trustees took the first steps toward the abolition of the Branch Theological School, and two years later the separation of the two institutions was completed. The Seminary discharged its financial obligations to the Geneva trustees by a grant of $8,000, a sum advanced by the Society for Promoting Religion and Learning in return for "four scholarships in this Seminary, with all the rights and privileges given and granted . . . to the founders of Scholar-

17. Trustees' Proceedings, June 26, 1867 (IV, 77). Subsequent references to the Trustees' Proceedings are identified by the abbreviation Tr P.
18. Jarvis Correspondence, December 30, 1822.

ships."[19] Bishop Hobart had raised sufficient money to launch his college successfully, and the academy was incorporated as Geneva College in 1825.[20] Thirty years later, its name was changed to Hobart College, a tribute to the unswerving determination and persistent efforts of the Bishop to establish both a seminary and a Church college in New York State.

John Pintard's irritation with Bishop Hobart did not diminish his interest in the Seminary library. During the years at St. John's, he made some of his most notable efforts on its behalf, and his personal gifts included a splendid copy of the Complutensian Polyglot Bible of 1514-17, presented to the library in 1827. He had already donated a copy of the LeJay or Paris Polyglot and headed the subscription list of those who purchased a Walton or London Polyglot for the Seminary. But in Pintard's judgment, the Complutensian Polyglot was his crowning benefaction. He inscribed it in 1827 "Festo Sancti Bartholemaei Apostoli," and remembering his Huguenot ancestors, "Die insigni tristique, in Annalibus Ecclesiae Reformatae Gallicane . . . Academicae Theologicae Generalis, Ecclesiae Episcopalis Reformatae in Republica Americana, ex dono Joannis Pintard."

The sparse records for the five years the Seminary spent at St. John's give only a few indications of the activities of the students outside the classroom. Bishop Hobart held occasional receptions for them at his house in Varick Street, their instructors introduced them to friends in the city, and they were welcomed to the neighboring rectories, particularly when the clerical family, as in the case of Dr. Lyell at Christ Church, included a marriageable daughter or two. The local students shared with their out-of-town classmates whatever pleasures New York offered theological students. Musical evenings, picnics at estates and cottages on the island, and Hudson River trips are, at least, the recorded diversions. On Sundays, the students attended the churches of their choice or parochial connection, and nearly all taught in the city's flourishing Sunday schools.

Some men must have shared the excitement that attended the ar-

19. Tr P, June 30, 1826 (I, 248).
20. Turner to Jarvis, February 6, 1823, Jarvis Correspondence.

rival of the Marquis de LaFayette on his famous return trip to America. Thousands cheered him at Castle Garden, while the bells of the city rang wildly and the cannon of all the batteries banged their welcome to "this distinguished Guest of the Nation." Similarly, few students could have missed the orgy of patriotism and self-congratulation in which New York indulged on November 4, 1825, to mark the opening of the Grand Erie Canal. They may have had only a distant view of the "Wedding of the Waters," when Governor Clinton poured a keg of Erie water into the Atlantic, but they could hardly have missed a detail of the flamboyant parade that later escorted the notables from the Battery through the city. Craftsmen of nearly every trade proudly marched with their decorated cars and floats, many of them dramatically portraying their work in operation. Five hundred butchers, for example, escorted their six-horse car on which, in a bower of branches, stood a steer, dressed for the slaughter. The printers, unlike the butchers, carried their activity to its conclusion. Their float bore a press that clanked away busily, distributing thousands of copies of Samuel Wentworth's *Ode for the Canal Celebration*, scattering its noble sentiments in fresh ink to the crowds that lined the streets:

> 'Tis done! 'Tis done! The mighty chain
> Which joins bright Erie to the Main,
> For ages, shall perpetuate
> The glory of our native State.[21]

The Erie marchers were seemingly endless: the Governor and the Lieutenant Governor, their guards, suites, and guests, the Corporation and other city officials, eight fire companies with resplendent engines, officers of the Army and Navy, the members of the Masonic Grand Lodge in full regalia, and among the many others, the students of Columbia College in their gowns.

On quieter days the seminarians walked in the rural country above Fourteenth Street. At Chelsea they were entertained by Pro-

21. James Hardie, *The Description of the City of New-York* (New York, 1827), p. 349.

fessor Moore, whose manor house stood on high ground just south of the present Twenty-third Street and a little west of Ninth Avenue. There they could stroll through the orchard that marked the land where the Seminary's permanent home was to be.

Chelsea was a little over two miles from City Hall, reached by the stage which ran hourly from Pine Street to Greenwich Village, and thence by a walk up the newly opened Ninth Avenue that prolonged Hudson Street to the north. Within a few years the stage line would run from South Ferry up Ninth Avenue to Twenty-third Street, giving quicker access to the Seminary site. Earlier, before the avenues beyond Fourteenth Street were laid out, the Chelsea area could be reached by the old Fitzroy Road, following approximately the line of the later Eighth Avenue. At Twenty-first Street, a wandering lane, called Abingdon Road or Love Lane, crossed the Fitzroy Road, leading westward to the estate of Captain Thomas Clarke on the shores of the Hudson. Captain Clarke's daughter, Charity, became the wife of Benjamin Moore, rector of Trinity Parish and Hobart's predecessor as bishop of New York. Thus the old Chelsea estate, from the south side of Twenty-fourth Street to the north side of Nineteenth Street, and from Eighth Avenue to the river, came to be the inheritance of their son, Clement Clarke Moore.

By the time the Seminary was in operation at St. John's, Dr. Moore, like other owners of large tracts adjacent to the expanding city, had begun to open the streets and survey his lots for possible sale. Ninth Avenue, cutting through the estate, gave ready access to the eastern lots in Moore's holdings as well as to the Seminary block and the manor house north of it. The land donated by Dr. Moore at the time of the Seminary's foundation lay between Twentieth and Twenty-first Streets, from Ninth Avenue to the Hudson River. It contained about fifty-five usable city lots, for the high water mark of the river ran in a northwesterly direction across the property about a hundred feet east of the present Tenth Avenue. In time the process of bulkheading and filling these marshy tracts along the river's edge increased the number of lots to sixty-four, and later, as additional "water-lots" were recovered, the Seminary's property in-

Professor Moore
Seminary Portrait by Daniel Huntington

cluded a long stretch of filled-in ground west of Tenth Avenue. In 1825, however, the erection of the bulkheads, destined to become a crippling drain upon the finances of the Seminary, was still some years in the future.

Professor Moore used his Chelsea mansion chiefly as a summer residence in these early days, maintaining a town house on Broadway between Maiden Lane and John Street. As the Chelsea area became increasingly populous in the eighteen thirties and forties, he prolonged his stay in the old manor house, finally making it his winter home and spending the summers, as did so many other New Yorkers with ample means, in a villa at Newport, Rhode Island. It was at the old Chelsea house, however, that Dr. Moore in 1822 composed for his children the poem on which his fame and memory rest today—*A Visit from St. Nicholas:*

'Twas the night before Christmas,
When all through the house
Not a creature was stirring,
Not even a mouse . . .

In the spring of 1824 there was much discussion of the project that had been uppermost in the minds of many of the Seminary's supporters since the return from New Haven, the erection of the Seminary's own buildings on its Chelsea property. On July 7, the Standing Committee resolved to recommend immediate action to the Board of Trustees, and at the July Trustees' meeting a similar recommendation was made in a message from Nathaniel Bowen, Christopher Gadsden, and other members of the Board in South Carolina. They argued that the erection of suitable buildings would not only save the charge of renting student accommodations, but also generally lower the costs to students. More important, a residence building would further the common life desirable for candidates for holy orders and would be such a venture of confidence as to proclaim the stability of the Seminary and bring it forcibly to the notice of the Church, thereby attracting more students and larger benefactions. Faith in the Seminary's future was still strong among the South Carolinians, though some of their detailed suggestions were hardly practicable. The idea was put forward, for example, that clergymen might be invited to contribute to the building program in return for

> the use of a room, rent free, at the institution. This might be an object to those who would pass the summer from their parish, and to those who would make provision for old age.[22]

Fortunately, this suggestion went no further, and the Seminary was mercifully spared a group of retired clergymen whose presence and influence might have earned for them the name of "Chelsea corrodians."

Bishop Brownell, seconded by Jackson Kemper, moved a resolution on July 28, 1824, that set in motion plans for erecting the Seminary's first building. A building fund was established, and the Standing Committee was authorized "to proceed in the erection of

22. Tr P, July 27, 1824 (I, 208).

said buildings" when the amount subscribed reached $10,000, using at that time a similar sum taken from the general funds of the Seminary. Exactly a year later, on July 28, 1825, the Trustees interrupted their meeting to attend the laying of the cornerstone of the Seminary building. "Yesterday afternoon at a little after 6 o'clock," reported *The New-York American* on July 29,

> the ceremony of laying the foundation stone of the General Theological Seminary of the Protestant Episcopal Church in the United States was performed with all accustomed solemnities . . .
>
> The numerous clergymen of the Episcopal Church now here, the trustees, professors and students of the Seminary, together with deputations from the vestries of several Episcopal churches in the city, all assembled at the residence of Mr. Moore, immediately adjoining the land granted by him to the Institution; and thence forming a procession led by the junior students, and closed by the bishops, proceeded to the foundation, where the procession halted, and opening inwards, the Rt. Rev. Bishops White, Croes, Kemp and Brownell passed through . . . to the spot where the cornerstone was to be laid.

Bishop White prefaced his prayers with a brief address, stressing the advantages possessed by a seminary over private instruction of candidates for ordination. He uttered a solemn warning—speaking of himself, as was his quaint habit, in the third person—that

> he would deprecate the laying of one stone on another, and would withdraw his hand from the laying of the first stone, if he could foresee, that in the instruction to be given in the building, there would at any future time—at present there is no danger of it—be a departure from those properties of our system, in doctrine, in discipline, and in worship, which in the sixteenth century were cleared from superstition by the leaders in the English Reformation . . .
>
> These principles will be in the mind of him who now presides, when, agreeably to the office committed to him by the trustees, he shall lay his hand on the stone before him, accompanying this gesture with the saying of Scripture—"Other foundation can no man lay, than that is laid, which is Jesus Christ."[23]

The Bishop not only laid his hand on the stone but also, according to *The New-York American*, received from the architect

23. Tr P, July 28, 1825 (I, 228).

a hammer with which he thrice struck the stone, and dedicated it in the name of the three persons of the Trinity. The same ceremony was repeated by the other bishops . . . and the company separated, well satisfied by the work in which they had been engaged.

Though the cornerstone was laid, there was considerable delay before construction began, apparently owing to some differences of opinion over the architectural design. On September 9, 1825, the Standing Committee, in Hobart's absence, approved plans for the building which evidently did not satisfy the Bishop. Consequently, on January 24, 1826, when Bishop Hobart was present at the Standing Committee meeting, the original design was altered. "When the Bishop returned," Samuel Turner informed Dr. Jarvis, "he persuaded the committee to change their Grecian plan for a Gothic."[24] The Seminary's old East Building might thus have been in a classical style instead of "a three story stone building 104 by about 52 feet in the plain Gothic Style of architecture," affording

accommodation for two professors & families, & forty students, & one large room for a temporary chapel & library, two lecture rooms, & the necessary accommodation for boarding and lodging the Students.[25]

Watching the progress of construction provided new diversion for the students who journeyed out to Chelsea to inspect it regularly.

We found the edifice in a beautifully-sheltered and secluded spot, within a stone's throw of the North River. It is built of irregular stone, and shows through the trees like a genuine antique; turrets, buttresses, battlements, heavy Gothic casements, and all that sort of thing.[26]

By the time the stark rectangular pile of stone had been finished, the romantic appeal of its "genuine antique" appearance was lost on Professor Turner. "The edifice," he wrote,

is rather unsightly. A rude attempt was made to give it something of a

24. Jarvis Correspondence, February 3, 1826.
25. Standing Committee Minutes, June 26, 1826.
26. Harry Croswell, *Memoir of the Late William Croswell, D.D.* (New York, 1853), p. 33.

Gothic appearance by supplying it with eight rough buttresses, and attaching wooden fixtures like mullions outside of very plain window-sashes with square angles. The shingled roof was surrounded by a wooden parapet, and the eight buttresses terminated by wooden conical turrets.[27]

Bishop Hobart, who had been abroad, did not see his Gothic building until after it was completed. He must have then regretted either his action or his absence, for Dr. Turner recalled that when the Bishop saw the turretted structure, he "expressed in my hearing his feelings of disappointment in brief but most marked language."

On October 1, 1827, the new academic year opened at Chelsea Square. The only shadow upon the Seminary's bright future was cast by a threatening cloud of financial insolvency. The building costs were far greater than had been anticipated. In June 1828, the Trustees heard that the expenditures totaled $32,449.99. This included the furnishings, the erection of stables, coal sheds, and other outbuildings, and an estimated cost between $500 and $1000 was

27. *Autobiography of the Rev. Samuel H. Turner, D.D.* (New York, 1863), p. 122.

The Seminary Building
From *The Church Register* 1826

yet to be paid for leveling the grounds. By the end of another year, $33,520 had been spent, and the financial drain still continued. Three years later, when some of the low-lying lots had been filled in and city assessments for the opening of the streets had been paid, the Chelsea property had cost the Seminary $44,440; by 1835 this figure had exceeded $50,000.

The response to the building fund appeal had been disappointing, a perennial experience in the history of the Seminary except during the affluent years of Dean Hoffman. Consequently, the depletion of the general funds to meet the property costs caused a serious diminution of capital. But the Trustees were optimistic in their report to the General Convention of 1829, thanks to the anticipation of a large and totally unexpected legacy:

> The state of the finances, as exhibited in the present report, might have excited in the minds of the General Convention some degree of anxiety, but for the seasonable and munificent bequest of the late Frederick Kohne, Esq., of Pennsylvania.[28]

Mr. Kohne, who died on May 26, 1829, left religious and charitable benefactions totaling nearly $400,000.[29] For the Seminary, he designated the magnificent sum of $100,000, to be paid upon the death of his wife. Unfortunately, the wide publicity given this legacy by the church press created the impression that the Seminary was safely beyond any financial difficulty, with a consequent decline in contributions throughout the Church. Even more unfortunately, the bequest proved to be anything but what the Trustees called "seasonable," for it was nearly twenty-five years before a compromise with the testator's widow actually brought the money to the Seminary. By that time, the financial condition of the institution was such that the Kohne legacy, even had it been wisely invested, could not wholly repair the Seminary's fortunes. These dark days, however, lay long in the future as the Seminary community settled into its new home in the fall of 1827. Immediately ahead were fifteen years of growth and flourishing development in every aspect of the life of the Old Seminary.

28. *Journal of General Convention 1829* (P. E. Press ed.), p. 97.
29. *The Gospel Messenger*, June 13, 1829.

5

Chelsea Square

Samuel Turner, writing a few years before the Civil War, gives a vivid picture of Seminary Square, as it was called, in the days when the Seminary first moved to its new building in Chelsea:[1]

> Those who are acquainted with the present site and appearance of the Seminary, will be surprised to learn that the building lay in a hollow. The carriage-entrance thereto, almost halfway between Twentieth and Twenty-first streets, was about fifteen feet higher than the spot on which the edifice stood, and in some places the ground was eighteen feet above it. We drove down the short hill through a small apple-orchard, and riding behind the building came around in front of the west entrance.[2]

In 1827, rising ground surrounded the Seminary building. A gentle slope led northwards toward Twenty-first Street, while a little

1. The name "Chelsea Square" was in unofficial use by 1835. See A. H. Cornish to J. H. Cornish, August 15, 1835, and thereafter, the Cornish Papers, Southern Historical Collection, University of North Carolina Library. The Standing Committee's Minutes of December 21, 1836, indicate that the committee, after consultation with Clement Clarke Moore, adopted the suggestion of adjacent property owners and designated the Seminary block by its present name. By 1841 "Chelsea Square" was in common use as a postal address. The Aldermen of New York made it a legal designation in 1886 (Standing Committee Minutes, April 12, 1886).
2. *Autobiography of the Rev. Samuel H. Turner, D.D.* (New York, 1863), pp. 122-123.

rugged hill rose where the apartments for married students now stand on Twentieth Street. The west side of the property was, of course, bordered by the Hudson River, the tidal marshes reaching to the site of the present tennis court. The front of the Seminary building was its long south side. There, from a central door, as well as from the professors' entrances on either end, paths ran out to Twentieth Street, the grading of which down to its present level was completed in 1830. The location was low-lying, damp, and watery. "The Hudson River," Dr. Turner recalled,

> at high tide washed what is now the Tenth Avenue, and even a portion of the lot east of it. During the winter the water was sometimes ankle deep in front of the house, so that in order to have a dry access to the lecture-room . . . I had a door cut through the garret partition. One winter the mud was so deep immediately behind the building as to make it almost inaccessible, except on horseback or in a carriage.

Turner lived in the three-story faculty residence on the west end of the building, Dr. Wilson occupying the corresponding house on the opposite end. If spring tides and storms occasionally made Professor Turner's front steps unusable, at least he had the pleasant prospect of the sparkling Hudson and the wooded Jersey shore from his front windows. Extensive leveling and filling in the so-called "water-lots" changed the face of the land, and in time

> the grounds were reduced to the present level, which is considerably above that of the adjoining streets; the low lots on the river, and even a considerable distance into it, were filled in, and the whole block beautifully ornamented with trees and shrubbery.[3]

Though the recovery of the water-lots on the west side of Tenth Avenue brought the Seminary considerable additional ground, the city assessments for development and the cost of erecting bulkheads and filling in the land made a constant and serious demand upon the Seminary's resources. In 1833 Clement Clarke Moore, whose property bordered the Hudson both north and south of the Seminary block, offered to meet a considerable part of the reclamation costs

3. Turner, *Autobiography*, pp. 123-124.

by erecting the second set of bulkheads along the Seminary's waterfront, in consequence of a grant from the city extending the property line into the river about halfway between the present Tenth and Eleventh Avenues.[4] The Trustees accepted Dr. Moore's "new act of munificence" with alacrity, though it was not entirely altruistic. His own bulkheads on either side of the Seminary's property would be both more expensive to construct and seriously imperiled by the tidal wash if they were not joined across the intervening space. Moore's offer was

> upon condition that this Board will execute to him a bond for the cost thereof, estimated at about $7320, with legal interest, to be secured by a mortgage on the block of ground on which the Seminary buildings now stand.[5]

4. A final grant in 1849 carried the property line beyond Eleventh Avenue to the present line of the river, and the Seminary completed its last bulkheads in 1859. The successive steps in extending the property are shown on a map attached to the Trustees' Proceedings, September 27, 1859 (III, 296).
5. Tr P, June 27, 1833 (I, 432).

Pencil Sketch of the East Building
Labeled 'W. d. Feb 7th 1835'

It was stipulated, however, that neither the principal nor the interest should become due "so long as the said block of ground, and the buildings thereon, shall be used for the Seminary exclusively." If the Seminary property were sold or used for purposes other than a theological institution, the bond and mortgage would immediately come due and be payable with compound interest. This transaction was the origin of the later erroneous belief that Dr. Moore had attached such conditions to his original gift of the Chelsea site as to make it impossible for the Seminary to move away without loss of the land. In 1860, when the Trustees were exploring the feasibility of moving the Seminary, Dr. Moore's "act of munificence" then appeared a "heavy and unjust incumbrance" from which equitable relief should be sought, if necessary at the hands of the law courts.[6] The mortgage by that time, with compound interest, had grown to over $40,000. But Moore's liberality toward the Seminary was as great as it had been forty years before. He canceled the bond and mortage on July 31, 1860, freeing the Trustees from all legal obli-

6. Tr P, June 27, 1860 (III, 329-330).

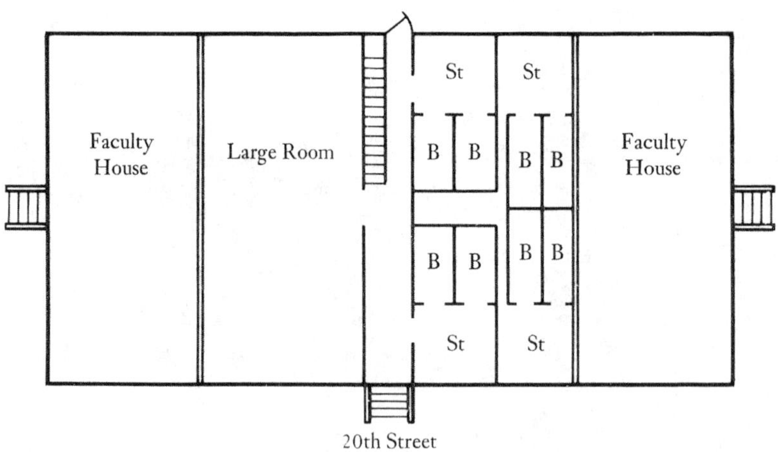

gation, and they acknowledged their gratitude by resolving to attach his name to a professorship of Hebrew.[7]

If the surroundings of the Seminary's new building were improved by grading and landscaping, its exterior appearance was certainly enhanced by the eventual removal of much of the pseudo-Gothic ornamentation. Unfortunately, little could be done to improve its interior design. The students' living quarters were dark, uncomfortable, and poorly ventilated. Above the basement, the windows of which were at ground level, there were three stories, the first of which was laid out as in the accompanying sketch. The second and third floors of the central portion were entirely occupied by students' apartments, similar to those opposite the Large Room or library. In the basement were two recitation rooms, kitchen and dining room, and accommodations for the domestic staff. The lack of a proper cellar necessitated the erection of a string of coal sheds and other outbuildings which rambled in an unsightly fashion along the north side of the building.

Each student study had a window, but the bedrooms were little more than dark elongated closets. In a circular in 1831, the Trustees described the Seminary as "possessing all the advantages of the country in point of health and the foundation of pastoral habits." The latter might have been induced by this remote corner of Manhattan, but the former were certainly not obvious to the students. The building was bitterly cold in the winter, and its occupants fed their Lackawanna coals to the little stoves and grates, and nailed strips around their doors in a losing battle against the penetrating chill that swept in from the river. Their suffering must have been acute in January 1835 when the thermometer stood at one time at 20° below zero.[8]

Coal gas was the insidious ally of the frigid dampness, for the defective flues and inadequate draft of the low chimneys filled the rooms with an atmosphere that seriously menaced the students' health. Cases of typhus, smallpox, diphtheria, and scarlet fever, some

7. Tr P, October 15, 1860 (III, 379-381).
8. Journal of Francis P. Lee, January 5, 1835.

of which were fatal, were perhaps unavoidable, but the living conditions were largely responsible for the constant suffering from colds, sore throats, fevers, "disordered bowels," and unbearable headaches. To combat these ills, the students dosed themselves with sage tea, or a solution of alum, or, in desperation, secured from the apothecary some calomel or a dram of laudanum. In such circumstances it must have been difficult for them to take seriously a description of their accommodations as "airy, healthful, convenient and pleasant," adjectives that were often used in the church press. For years no entries in the Faculty minutes appear more frequently than those granting excuses from classes or absence from the Seminary because of sickness.

One is tempted to say that theological students of a century and a half ago were made of sterner stuff than the present generation, but it probably would be more accurate to observe that they had greater opportunity to display their fortitude amid the circumstances of daily life. There were limits, however, and one was the narrow wooden shelf, equipped with a straw pallet, that was provided as a bed. Despite rules to the contrary, a large number of enterprising students succeeded in surreptitiously replacing these uncomfortable bunks with cots.[9] From these they rose early, for the first regulation of student life in Chelsea Square fixed the rising bell at 6:30 A.M. during the fall and winter, and a half-hour earlier in the spring. At 7:00 A.M. they gathered for Family Prayers in the Large Room and breakfasted afterwards. Recitation hours occupied the late morning; dinner was at 2:30 P.M., with tea or supper at 6:00 P.M. The day concluded with evening Family Prayers at 10:00 P.M., the students being required to attend, as they were in the morning, and the doors of the building were closed an hour later.[10]

After a few months at Chelsea Square, the service of Morning Prayer was substituted for the informal Family Prayers on Wednesdays, Fridays, Holy Days, and Sundays, accompanied on the last by a sermon. In 1835, Family Prayers disappeared entirely from the

9. Standing Committee Minutes, December 5, 1836.
10. Faculty Minutes, November 17, 1828.

schedule, for the Faculty granted the petition of the students to have "the stated services of the Church" daily. Morning Prayer was recited after breakfast and Evening Prayer after tea. Thus began the recitation of the Daily Offices which for more than a hundred and thirty years has structured the spiritual life of the Seminary community. Celebrations of the Holy Communion were not held in the Seminary building in these early years. Matriculation Day and, after 1842, Commencement Day were the only regular occasions of the administration of the Sacrament under Seminary auspices. It was assumed that the members of the Seminary had both the opportunity and the duty to participate in the Eucharist in the regular course of services at the parish churches where they worked or with which they were connected. It was not until the academic year 1849-50 that monthly celebrations of the Holy Communion in the Seminary chapel were instituted.[11]

The social life of the students differed little in the eighteen thirties from that in the earlier years at St. John's, though a common residence enabled a closer companionship of students with each other and with their teachers. Dr. Moore's hospitality at Chelsea House was close by, and while relations with Dr. Wilson were nearly always somewhat distant, Samuel Turner welcomed the students to evenings of music and conversation, and Bishop Onderdonk continued Hobart's custom of being often at home to them. A walk downtown led the students back to suppers, as well as parties of singing and dancing, chiefly with friends among the clerical families, at which time there might even be a bit of champagne, and from which they could escort the young ladies home. Now and then they heard oratorios, a diversion more respectable than attending the theater.[12] For those who loved the open countryside, a popular pastime was a hike along the shores of the Hudson. Others, fascinated by the enticements of the crowded city, indulged in a variety of pleasures, on occasion even those inappropriate to theological stu-

11. Tr P, June 28, 1849 (II, 581), and June 26, 1850 (II, 602); see also Faculty Minutes, July 5, 1849.
12. Lee's Journal, June 3, 1834.

dents.[13] Incidents, however, that merited stern disciplinary action were rare in the Old Seminary; students were generally content with a visit to the museums or a trip to the Zoological Institute to look at the hyena and to see a man put his head in the lion's mouth.[14]

Organized activities among the students were more numerous after the move to Chelsea. Societies and informal clubs proliferated in the Seminary, rising and dying as interest quickened and waned. Literary groups read Shakespeare together; a Rhetorical Association encouraged practice in composition and oratory. Students often met informally to hear and criticize each other's sermons. The Society of Inquiry, founded, while the Seminary was at St. John's, to seek information about the missionary activity of the Church and promote its progress, gave way in 1831 to a Missionary Association, formed as an auxiliary to the Church's Domestic and Foreign Missionary Society, with "a view to gain missionary intelligence, to excite in our bosoms a spirit of missionary zeal, and to contribute our mite toward the promotion of the Gospel." The members of the society met regularly to hear papers on missions, to receive news of missionary progress, often from letters sent by missionaries in the field, and to welcome visiting speakers.[15] Jackson Kemper was one of the frequent visitors, and it was in 1840 that Kemper, then missionary bishop in the Old Northwest, made his famous appeal at the Seminary. "Bishop Kemper was here," noted James Lloyd Breck,

> and addressed us on Friday night. He gave great satisfaction, and made us more proud of our Missionary Bishop than ever before. His two chief wants at the west are *means* and *men*: the first, to found seminaries of learning to be under the control of the Church; the second, laborers to assist him in preaching the Gospel. The good bishop spoke very plainly respecting the kind of men he wanted, the burthen of which was–self-denying men, men willing to go there and endure every species of hardship for the sake of Christ and his Church.[16]

13. Faculty Minutes, November 1, 1842.
14. Lee's Journal, March 8, 1834; March 28, 1835.
15. See the Minute Book of the Missionary Association 1835-1847, G.T.S. Library.
16. *The Life of the Reverend James Lloyd Breck, D.D.*, ed. Charles Breck (New York, 1886), pp. 7-8.

This was the challenge that took James Lloyd Breck, William Adams, and John Henry Hobart, Jr., all graduates in the Class of 1841, out to Wisconsin to establish the famous missionary center at Nashotah. Missionary zeal ran high in the Old Seminary, and its graduates felt a strong attraction to a ministry on the expanding western frontiers.

The seminary community manifested early a concern for the people of Chelsea. One of the most successful activities of the students in their new location was the formation of Sunday school classes under the auspices of a Sunday School Society that was organized in 1827. The classes met first in the Seminary library, and later, after the organization of St. Peter's Parish, were transferred to a basement room in the new St. Peter's Chapel. Wrote one student in 1828:

> The grounds about here are literally thronged with idlers from the city [on Sundays], who profane the day with the most boisterous merriment. Such is the state of moral degredation in this neighborhood. We are doing, however, what we can to check these things. A Sunday School has been established, and we have already gathered in 258 scholars (148 boys and 110 girls), being an increase of 81 since the report made in April.[17]

Five years later, there were over four hundred children in the classes, testimony to the rapidity with which the Chelsea area was built up during the thirties. The Sunday School continued under the direction of the students' society until St. Peter's Church could assume responsibility for the Christian nurture of many of the neighborhood children.[18] Meanwhile, a number of students assisted in the organization of the Eighth Avenue Sunday School in 1836, out of which grew the parish of the Holy Apostles, a little north of Twenty-third Street.

Morale was high in the Seminary family in this decade. Graduates

17. *The Episcopal Watchman*, June 21, 1828.
18. The students revived their neighborhood work in 1851 with the older boys in Chelsea who could not be reached by the Sunday School (Tr P, June 23, 1852 (II, 751).

looked back upon their years in Chelsea Square with affection, and with the intent of advancing the Seminary's interests formed themselves into the Associate Alumni on June 29, 1832. The avowed object of the association was

> to cherish a spirit of mutual interest and union among its members; to advance the cause of Theological learning and evangelic truth and piety; and to promote the advantage of the Institution with which it is connected.[19]

To these ends the Seminary's graduates have faithfully and loyally devoted their concerted effort for nearly a hundred and forty years. A strong sense of fellowship has not only been a bond among the alumni but also united the members of the Seminary family in Chelsea Square with the many others serving the Church in every area of its mission.

In 1832, when the Alumni Association was formed, about fifty men had completed the full course and received the Testimonial of the General Seminary—full-fledged alumni. Many more had prepared for ordination in the institution and were numbered among the "sometime students." By 1840, the rise in student enrollment had brought the total graduates to more than four times that number. On every side, as the Seminary flourished in Chelsea Square, its circle of friends and supporters widened. Professor McVickar of Columbia was a staunch promoter of the institution, constantly attempting to convince churchmen of the need for a learned ministry. He was tireless in his effort to arouse interest in the Seminary library and elicit contributions to its enlargement. In 1835, he and his friends, with the help of a legacy of $1000 from Margaret Pendleton, and a generous gift of $4000 from the Corporation of Trinity Parish, succeeded in raising $10,000, of which $6000 was to be set aside for a library endowment fund, while the remainder was to be expended in immediate purchases. In June 1834, the library possessed 3880 volumes; in June 1837, largely as a result of McVickar's

19. *Constitution of the Associate Alumni, 1832* (Alumni Publications, 1842), Article 3.

activity, the number of books had increased to more than 6000.

An associate of McVickar in these efforts, and a firm supporter of the Seminary, was George Washington Doane, a sometime student of the year 1824 who succeeded John Croes as bishop of New Jersey in 1832. Doane's tall, spare figure, "hook-nosed and shark-faced," was frequently seen in Chelsea Square where he was a favorite with the students.[20] John Pintard, as one might expect, deplored Doane's influence. "The Rev. Mr. Doane of Boston," he noted,

> has been elected Bishop of N. Jersey. He is an accomplished Divine of our Church. I regret to add an Ultra high Church, who out-Hobarts Hobart. It is supposed he will accept, as he married a lady of fortune $300,000 & will not depend on a salary.[21]

From 1835 to 1845, Doane seconded and strengthened the influence of Bishop Onderdonk's High Church convictions. After that, when Onderdonk was no longer active in Seminary affairs, Bishop Doane was the chief leader among the strong churchmen on the Board of Trustees.

The Seminary attracted the admiration and affection of the youthful George Templeton Strong, later to become one of New York's most prominent laymen and an important figure in civic and national affairs. Strong had friends among the students and was a frequent visitor in these days.[22] Twenty years later, when Mr. Strong as a trustee bore his share of the worry over the Seminary's financial difficulties, his enthusiasm was more restrained, but he never abandoned his sincere concern for its welfare.

The Seminary's circle of visitors in the 'thirties soon included the traveling Englishman, who was frequently seen in Chelsea Square as the years went by. He might have been brought by the "high commendation in foreign journals," which Bishop Onderdonk boasted in 1832 had enhanced the Seminary's repute, but he did not

20. Lee's Journal, March 12, 1835.

21. *Letters from John Pintard to His Daughter, 1816-1833* (New-York Historical Society, 1940-41), IV, 97.

22. *The Diary of George Templeton Strong*, ed. Allan Nevins and Milton Halsey Thomas (New York: Macmillan, 1952), I, 167-168, 187.

always return home to add to those tributes. If visiting Anglican clerics have often been critical of American seminaries, it is at least a habit with considerable history, for in 1835 a student found a visiting Englishman "too ready to find fault with the state of affairs with us."[23]

The hope of the South Carolina trustees that the move to Chelsea would attract more students and wider support was speedily fulfilled in the former, if not wholly in the latter respect. Five years after the first building had been erected, the student body had outgrown it. During the academic year 1833-34, there were sixty-four men enrolled, two dozen of whom were lodged in tenements rented for them on Eighth Avenue. While the expense of housing men outside the Square was not excessive at first, the rapid suburban development of Chelsea brought both rising costs and increasing difficulty in procuring suitable quarters for students. It was, moreover, an arrangement that threatened the common life of the institution.

Confronted in 1834 with an anticipated student body of eighty men in the following year, the Trustees determined to erect a second building on Twentieth Street, just west of the first one. The building was to be

> correspondent in its exterior to the present one, and erected on the same block of ground, at the same distance from the Tenth as the present is from the Ninth Avenue, or as nearly so as may be practicable.[24]

To meet the major part of the expected cost, $20,000 was borrowed on the strength of a legacy in that amount bequeathed to the Seminary by Mr. George Lorillard in 1832. The legacy was not, in fact, paid over until 1836, but in the confidence that the Kohne bequest ensured future security, the Trustees did not consider the risk excessive. When it became evident that the cost would be considerably greater than anticipated, the Standing Committee was authorized to expend up to $32,000, raising the additional funds by lease

23. Lee's Journal, January 12, 1835.
24. Tr P, June 25, 1834 (I, 460).

or mortgage of the recovered water-lots west of Tenth Avenue. The cost was actually slightly more than $32,000.

Completed in the spring of 1836, the West Building, as it was soon called, was designed to provide accommodations for sixty students in double rooms in its central portion.[25] Two rooms, however, were set aside for use as an infirmary. With other rooms used for reception and administrative purposes, as well as a robing room for the Faculty, ninety students was the comfortable maximum in both buildings of the Old Seminary. This number was reached in the academic year 1835-36, but then not again until 1879-80, Dean Hoffman's first year. During the 'thirties, the number averaged annually between seventy-five and eighty, approximately one third of whom were from the Diocese of New York. Of the other dioceses, Western New York, Pennsylvania, Connecticut, Massachusetts, Rhode Island, and New Jersey had substantial representation, with a sprinkling of one or two men from each more distant area. The average number declined to sixty-five amid the violent controversies of the next decade, and in the 'fifties, when the Seminary was the object of sharp criticism and beset by a disastrous financial crisis, forty-four men was the usual yearly average. Only nine Juniors entered in the fall of 1855, and the same number in the following year. This brought the enrollment to its lowest point in 1857-58, when there were only thirty-six men, scarcely enough to fill the East Building. Two thirds of them were from the dioceses of New York and Western New York. The upward turn came, however, after the Civil War. In the years of gradual recovery following the war, the numbers climbed to sixty-five or seventy, where they remained until the Hoffman era brought a substantial increase.

In general appearance, the West Building resembled its earlier companion, though it was more soundly constructed and its Gothic adornment more restrained. Improvements in interior design provided a full cellar, eliminating the ugly out buildings that clung to the north side of the East Building. The students' quarters were

25. The names "West" and "East" were immediately applied to the two buildings (*G.T.S. Catalogue, 1836-37*, pp. 12-13).

lighter and pleasanter than those in the older building. The West Building still stands amid the Seminary's modern quadrangles, now an architectural landmark of New York. Except for the one faculty residence that was provided on its eastern end—and into which Samuel Turner immediately moved from the East Building—its interior has been extensively altered and successively remodeled. It is difficult now to picture its arrangement during most of the nineteenth century. The few rooms still used by students seem unusually spacious. Originally there were cubicle partitions in them, separating the sleeping space at the corridor end from the study area near the window. Students were housed in the basement below the three upper floors, a location that was found so damp that when the Faculty met for the first time in the new building in one of the ground-floor classrooms, they hastily adjourned to a room in St. Peter's Chapel.

The west end of the building was planned to serve a number of purposes. In the basement were two recitation rooms, their windows at ground level, adjacent to the present tennis court. Entrance steps, similar to those of the faculty house in the east wing of the building, gave access to the first floor area where the infirmary and seminar room are now located. Here, stretching the full width of the building, was a hall known as the Long Room. It was used for special lectures, missionary meetings, practice preaching sessions, meetings of the Trustees, and on occasions when considerable space was required. Here, too, were held the daily chapel services of Morning and Evening Prayer, moved from the crowded library in the East Building. When the West Building was first occupied, the two floors above the Long Room were left unfinished, but the disadvantages of holding chapel services in a hall that was in use for other purposes soon caused considerable complaint. In 1843 the Board of Trustees was informed that the location was

> every way unfitted to promote the great object of the sacred services celebrated therein. It is in every respect utterly at variance with that decency and order, which pre-eminently characterize the services of the Church, and which are especially called for in a place where the

future Ministers of the Church are daily training their spirits for the service of Christ. Their devotion and their taste must needs be impaired by daily frequenting a place in which so little of the beauty of holiness is visible. But it is needless to detail the many arguments in favor of the exclusive appropriation to Divine Worship, and of the seemly arrangement of the Seminary Chapel; although it will be superseded at some future time, by a consecrated edifice.[26]

The "consecrated edifice" had to await Dean Hoffman's building program a half-century later, but by the fall of 1845, when the upper floors of the west wing of the West Building had been finished, the chapel was moved from the Long Room to the corresponding space on the floor above.[27] Here, like the Long Room, the chapel ran the full width of the building, its little chancel at the north end. It was not a place where "the beauty of holiness" was overwhelming, and the students later remembered their West Building chapel as a

long, low room, very stuffy and very crowded. At one end was a little chancel, raised a step, with a plain altar. No cross and no flowers. At the other end was a little wheezy organ which we took turns in blowing, although sometimes very proud and haughty students refused to do it, saying it was menial work.[28]

Nevertheless, it was the Seminary's first "exclusive appropriation" of a place for its worship, and as such it marked a significant change in the concept of the character of a seminary community. The prevailing notion of a quarter-century earlier, that the institution was a hostel for resident study, the advantage of which was chiefly convenient and companionable proximity, had slowly given way to a

26. Tr P, June 28, 1843 (II, 362).

27. *Ibid.*, June 24, 1846 (II, 466); see also the Missionary Association Minute Book, November 10, 1845. The third, or top floor, still open to the roof beams, was fitted up as a gymnasium, for the trustees had long expressed a concern that the students have opportunity for "regular and cheerful exercise, judiciously prosecuted."

28. G.T.S. *Seminarian* (1895-96), p. 11; see also G.T.S. *Seminarian* (1901), p. 54. The Seminary chapel remained in this location until the academic year 1873-74 when the library was moved into this wing of the West Building and the Large Room of the East Building redecorated as a chapel.

concept of the Seminary as primarily a community of men whose common life and vocation should find its empowering center in their regular corporate worship. A gradual shift had come about in the spiritual orientation of the students, from the parish churches with which they were connected to the community in which they lived and studied.

Undoubtedly this changing concept of the place of the Seminary chapel in the life of the student body inspired the Trustees in June 1849 to make two new regulations governing the chapel services. The first was that, in addition to the regular daily services,

> there shall be held two services in the Chapel each Lord's Day, and at least one on each of the Great Festivals and Fasts of the Church . . . at such services there shall be preaching.[29]

For nearly eight years the professors dutifully preached in rotation at these services, but the attempt to make Sunday a day of corporate worship in Chelsea Square failed.[30] Far too many students had to be excused from attendance in order to teach in the Sunday schools and do other work in the parishes.

More significant was the second order of the Trustees. The Holy Communion, which hitherto had been celebrated only twice a year under Seminary auspices—on Matriculation Day and at Commencement—was now to be administered "as often as once in each month" in the chapel. Agitation for frequent celebrations of the Sacrament had appeared earlier in the 'forties. In 1842, for example, a large group of students, most of whom were enthusiastic adherents of the principles of the Oxford Movement, had petitioned the Faculty "to receive from their hands the weekly communion."[31] The professors had then thought it inexpedient to grant the petitioners their request.[32] Now, nine years later, the practice of administering the

29. Tr P, June 28, 1849 (II, 580); see also *G.T.S. Catalogue, 1849-50*. There is a description of the new Sunday schedule in Hoffman's Journal. See Theodore M. Riley, *A Memorial Biography of Eugene Augustus Hoffman* (New York, 1904), I, 231-232.

30. Faculty Minutes, April 9, 1857.

31. G.T.S. Papers, 1842.

32. Faculty Minutes, March 1, 1842.

Holy Communion on "first Sundays" was established, and very shortly thereafter the Sacrament was also celebrated on major Festivals that fell in term-time. By 1867, weekly celebrations of the Holy Communion were held every Sunday at "the early service," in response to student petitions, as well as on Saints' Days, and a decade later each Thursday was added in the gradual progress towards a daily Eucharist in the Seminary chapel.[33]

The rapid expansion of the Seminary after the move from St. John's Park to Chelsea Square soon made it apparent that the daily affairs of the institution could not be efficiently governed by the Standing Committee of the Trustees. Local and continuous representation of the committee's authority was necessary if the custodial and administrative responsibilities of a residential community were adequately to be met. In 1832, therefore, the Board of Trustees created the office of dean, to be held "in annual rotation by the resident professors." The chief duties of the dean were to be "generally responsible for the internal arrangements" of the Seminary, to preside in meetings of the Faculty, and to see that the statutes of the Trustees and the directives of the Standing Committee were enforced.[34] As he was also "invested with the general charge and superintendance of the buildings and premises," it has sometimes been remarked, and with some justice, that the only independent authority entrusted to the dean was over the janitor, who was to be "subject to his orders and make report to him." Even this freedom was sharply curtailed by the amount of money he might order spent on care and repairs.[35]

Custodial oversight of the buildings and grounds, as well as periodic inspection of the students' rooms, was a chore which the professors discharged faithfully, though with little enthusiasm, as their

33. *G.T.S. Catalogue, 1878-79*, p. 28.
34. Standing Committee Minutes, December 5, 1836.
35. The dean was allowed "to draw upon the Treasurer for such minute needful expenditures as may be presently necessary . . . within such limits as the Standing Committee may from time to time deem expedient, to which body he shall report quarterly his expenditures" (*Constitution and Statutes* [New York, 1832], p. 15).

turns as dean came around. Samuel Turner was conscientious in a task plainly distasteful to him, while Bird Wilson took few pains to conceal his lack of interest in it. Annually their reports called the Trustees' attention to leaky roofs, broken locks, inadequate flues, peeling paint, and cracked plaster—all of which the Committee on the State of the Seminary solemnly inspected, though often with little resulting action. A perusal of the reports in the Trustees' Proceedings leads one to think that the committee was less alarmed by deficiencies in the fabric of the buildings than by faults in their occupants. Considerable indignation was expressed, for example, when members of the committee discovered

> that the floors of the rooms of some of the students, and the passages of the buildings, are very much stained, it is presumed by the use of tobacco, a practice of which they cannot speak in terms of too decided reprehension.[36]

There was little in the Seminary that escaped the committee's annual investigation. They probed into the number of chapel and class absences, and found fault with the professors for failing to give marks at each recitation or submit their notations on the students' progress to the Committee on the Examination. They were disturbed at learning that an occasional class exercise had been omitted. But a report to the Trustees generally satisfied their zeal, and when the meeting of the Board adjourned, Seminary life continued much as before. Gradually the administrative chores of the rotating deanship grew more burdensome as the Seminary increased in numbers. The "internal arrangements" for which the dean was responsible included the conduct of all official correspondence, the assignment of rooms to students, matters dealing with admissions and the granting of scholarships, and much of the work that in later years would increase so greatly as to require the services of a registrar and a bursar.

In 1837, however, the Committee on the State of the Seminary discovered another area of responsibility in the common life of the

36. Tr P, June 29, 1838 (I, 660).

institution to which little or no attention had been given in any formal way. They addressed the Trustees passionately in questions that were obviously compounded of the Evangelical idiom of Dr. Milnor of St. George's Church and the High Church vocabulary of Bishop Doane, two active members of the committee:

> Where is the pastoral care of the students of the General Theological Seminary? They are a Christian family. But who exercises towards them the paternal influence? Who officiates in the devotions of the family altar? Again, they are a Christian congregation. But who exercises towards them the pastoral relation? Who offers their common prayers before the throne of grace? Who labors among them in the word and doctrine, for their edification in truth and holiness? Who breaks for them the bread of life, for their growth in grace and spiritual communion with the Divine Head and Saviour of the Church?[37]

The Trustees promptly responded to this challenging peroration by adding to the statutory duties of the dean "the public instruction and the pastoral care of the students of the Seminary."

Professor Turner, to whom it fell to act as dean in the ensuing academic year, firmly declined to exercise pastoral responsibility for his students.[38] As he understood the meaning of "the pastoral care of the students," and the other professors agreed with him, it was a responsibility that properly belonged to the rectors of the New York parishes with which students were identified by membership or work. Faced with the intransigence of Dr. Turner on this point, the Trustees dropped the matter for some years. By 1848, however, they were again seeking some plan "by which the students of the Seminary can be placed under proper pastoral care within the walls of the Institution." At the end of that academic year, a committee report, presented to the Trustees by Bishop Alonzo Potter of Pennsylvania, recommended the creation of the office of President or Rector of the Seminary to act as "the authorized agent of the several Bishops," and who should

> exercise such authority over their candidates while in the Seminary, as

37. Tr P, June 29, 1837 (I, 617).
38. *Autobiography*, pp. 239-240.

might be necessary to secure diligence in study, a blameless Christian walk and conversation, and due loyalty to the principles and authority of the Church.[39]

It is perhaps fortunate that there were no funds at the time to provide for the appointment of a Seminary head who would make the office of dean an "authorized agent of the several Bishops." The committee, as a temporary measure, therefore, proposed that the responsibility which Dr. Turner and his colleagues refused to accept a decade before be transferred from the dean to one of the professors, who should be designated each year by the Faculty as "Chaplain of the Seminary, and to whom shall be entrusted the whole pastoral care of the students." The Faculty adjusted themselves to the idea of an annual rotating chaplaincy as well as a similar deanship, but their adjustment was perhaps made easier by the fact that Dr. Turner was the first to serve as "Chaplain for the Year." He reported to the Trustees in 1850 that the arrangements for the Seminary's chapel services, sermons, and addresses had been duly carried out, a task that was assigned to the chaplain, but as for the "whole pastoral care"—he has not undertaken it nor will he do so, for the same reasons given by him a dozen years before. Turner elaborated more fully his conviction on this point in his decanal report of 1855:

> The chief reason of my unwillingness to be regarded as the Students' Pastor, I will state with that frankness which ought to characterize every right-minded man, and which a long connection with the Seminary may the rather justify me in employing. The ordinary pastoral duties, those namely of religious service and instruction, of attention and consolation, also in occasional sickness, I am quite willing to perform . . .
>
> But there is another duty incumbent on a Pastor, which, if it is fully exercised in all cases, might bring a Dean into collision with some Rectors, and it may be, Standing Committees and Bishops. The Pastor is expected to recommend the Candidate for Holy Orders, as "worthy to be admitted thereto"—Canon XV of 1832. I cannot pledge myself to do this for every student, whose testimonial of having properly attended to the prescribed course of study in the Seminary, I may be

39. Tr P, June 28, 1849 (II, 579).

fully authorized to sign. On the contrary, it may happen, that as Pastor, I should sometimes be obliged to discourage a Student from taking upon him the Ministerial Office.[40]

In the end the Faculty simply added the duty of arranging for the Seminary's religious services and activities to the existing responsibilities of the dean. From 1852 to 1869, the Seminary's catalogues describe the office which the resident professors held in rotation as "Dean and Chaplain." Meanwhile, through the years the Trustees, Faculty, and alumni continued to explore the question of the necessity of a "Pastoral Head."[41] What would be his duties and authority? What should be his relation to the Faculty and to the Board of Trustees? The questions remained unresolved until the first dean, in the modern sense, was elected in 1869.

The first of the Seminary's annual catalogues was published in November 1834, a slight twenty-page pamphlet, bearing on the cover an engraving of the Seminary building nestling among the trees, with the white sails of a sloop on the Hudson River in the background. Professors and students were listed, the latter with their colleges. Twenty-eight of the eighty students were not university graduates. Presumably they had satisfied the Faculty by examination that they had sufficient education in "the general principles of Natural and Moral Philosophy and Rhetoric, and in the Latin and Greek languages" to do the work of the Seminary. Among those with degrees, Washington (Trinity) College stood first with twelve graduates; Columbia and Union College next, with six and five respectively. Yale and the University of Pennsylvania had four each; three were graduates of Harvard and a like number of Brown. Dartmouth, Flushing Institute, the West Point Military Academy, and Amherst provided two men each, and a single graduate was listed from Jefferson College, St. Mary's College, Williams, Geneva (Hobart) College, Western University of

40. Tr P, June 27, 1855 (III, 15).

41. Coxe to Whittingham, February 27, 1851; Johnson to Whittingham, April 1, 1865, Md. Dio. Ms. See also Tr P, June 25, 1856 (III, 84-87); June 24, 1857 (III, 163 ff.); October 15, 1860 (III, 376).

From *The Churchman's Almanac* 1832

The Seminary Building as It Appeared on the Cover of the Catalogue of 1834

Pennsylvania, The College of South Carolina, and St. John's College. A glance at the catalogues for the two decades following 1834 reveals that the proportionate number of nongraduates declined from approximately one third of the total to less than one quarter, while Washington (Trinity) College, Columbia, Yale, Union College, the University of Pennsylvania, and New York University provided by far the largest number of Seminary students during that period.

It is evident from these early catalogues, as well as from the annual reports of the Committee on the State of the Seminary, that one aim of those who advocated the move to Chelsea Square has been achieved—low cost to the student. No charge was made for tuition and rooms in the Seminary, and in 1830 a student's expenditures for board, fuel, and laundry were estimated at $70. Slowly rising prices marked the passage of years, but in the middle of the century the cost of these necessities was still below $130. A student fortunate enough to be nominated to one of the dozen or more scholarships received from its endowment between $105 and $150 annually to help pay his expenses. Most scholarships, by the terms of their foundation, were in the gift of bishops or parish rectors. Some imposed special requirements, but few had such precautionary conditions as the William C. Rhinelander Scholarship, founded 1834, the recipient of which was required to "declare it to be *bona fide* his intention to go through the whole three years' course of study." The founder took no chances on the possible defection of the Seminary from the Church's doctrine, for he provided:

> Should it ever happen from any cause hereafter (which God forbid) that the General Seminary should depart from the doctrines now held by the Protestant Episcopal Church and hold or inculcate especially either Roman Catholic or Unitarian doctrines, then it is understood that the two thousand dollars hereby given shall be paid back.[42]

The largest item in a student's expenses was the cost of board. During the first few years at Chelsea, this was provided at two dollars a week in the commons maintained in the East Building basement. The dining room, conducted under the supervision of a student committee, was intended as a convenience; there was little or no feeling that fellowship in a refectory was an aspect of the students' common life. When it proved a financial burden, often accumulating debts, and too exacting a responsibility for management by students, it was temporarily abandoned. A good many years passed before the idea that the refectory should be operated by the Seminary won acceptance. Meanwhile, the dining room appeared and disappeared at intervals. When there was no commons, stu-

42. Standing Committee Minutes, December 18, 1834.

dents took their main meals in the numerous boarding houses that opened in the neighborhood as the Chelsea area grew more populous. Shortly after the middle of the century, a dining room with some permanence was established in the form of a "Boarding Club," maintained by its student members, but with a steward—generally the Seminary janitor assisted by his wife—in direct charge of its operation. Meals could be had in the "Boarding Club" for four dollars a week, after payment of a ten-dollar membership fee. Students were free to choose between eating in the basement refectory or patronizing, at slightly higher cost, one of the nearby boarding houses. This remained the custom in the Old Seminary even into the first years of Dean Hoffman.

The early catalogues of the Seminary do not describe the course of instruction in detail. Instead, they simply note which professors the students of the three classes attend each year in the two recitation periods that were scheduled daily except Saturdays. It is plain, however, that the scheme of study in the academic year 1864-65, for example, did not differ materially from that laid out sixty years before by Bishop White in the Course of Ecclesiastical Studies. Nor did the list of textbooks assigned for recitation or recommended for reference differ very much from the titles attached to the authorized course. The books of 1834 were still basically those of 1804. In the twenty years between 1835 and 1855, less than a half-dozen books were discarded and a like number added, except in the area of ecclesiastical history, whose Mosheim was augmented by a number of reference books for particular periods.

The General Seminary was not unique in clinging to the old patterns of theological study. Until after the Civil War, the same conservatism was shown in the diocesan schools and in the Virginia Theological Seminary. Eugene Augustus Hoffman, while a student at Chelsea Square, visited Alexandria during the Christmas vacation in 1849. His description of the Virginia curriculum in his Journal suggests that the students there, whom he thought were "mostly rank Calvinists," used a selection of books from the authorized course of 1804 that was even more meager than that recommended in the General Seminary's classes. However sagacious he may have later become, the youthful Hoffman seems to have been as fiercely partisan as many others in the mid-century quarrels that disturbed the Episcopal Church. "On asking a middleman," noted Hoffman,

> whether he had ever read the "Apostolic Fathers," he said, "we don't think much of the Fathers here." Possibly they might have returned the compliment. I must say that my visit of three days to Alexandria had a tendency to make me, if anything, a Higher Churchman than I have been.[43]

The partisanship was on both sides, of course. Clinton Locke recalled that when, in the early fifties,

> I told my Rector in Virginia that I was going to the New York Seminary as soon as my school engagement there was over, he rose to his feet and said solemnly, "Young man, I consider that you are placing your immortal soul in peril."[44]

Details of the Seminary's curriculum emerge more clearly from a study of the annual reports of the professors and those of the Examining Committee of the Trustees. Despite growing dissatisfaction with the practice of examining men in the three classes at the end of each academic year, the committee still sat for some hours on two or three days, just before commencement, listening to the answers of students to their professors' questions. The examination had always been regarded by the students with considerable trepidation, and it appears to have become an increasing source of anxiety as the years passed. Students were sometimes too ill to attend, suffering perhaps from nerves and vapors, and more than one collapsed in despair. "I am too sick and disheartened to try to pass the examinations this year," wrote one man to the dean.[45] Perhaps it was the

43. Riley, *Hoffman*, I, 235.

44. G.T.S. *Seminarian* (1895-96), p. 13.

45. Samuel Roosevelt Johnson Papers, June 1856, G.T.S. Library. The reports of the Examining Committee appeared each June in the Trustees' Proceedings. See the description of a Senior's examination, A. H. Cornish to J. H. Cornish, June 26, 1838, Cornish Papers.

approach of examination time that stripped Francis Lee of his usual ebullient spirits and inspired a rhyme of tedium:

> I must confess that I am very
> tired of the Seminary
> tired of streets with muddy gutters
> tired of cries the coal man utters
> tired of the spicy breezes
> wafted from the rotten pieces
> of catskin lining every sidewalk . . .
> tired of theologic lore
> which we have voted quite a bore
> tired of Wilson, tired of Moore,
> & of the Bp's papal roar
> tired of Whittingham & Turner
> (a hard word that for poet's corner)
> tired of them altogether
> and tired lastly of the weather.[46]

The examination ordeal could not have been as severe as anticipation sometimes made it. The professors, after all, asked the questions of students whom they had drilled in the subject matter. Even if a man had neglected the topics he knew might be mentioned, a quick wit and a ready tongue might save him. There is the case of the student who, when asked a question concerning the Scottish Reformation on which he was totally unprepared, earned the admiration of the examiners by a fluent discourse of ten minutes, entirely drawn from his recollection of two of Sir Walter Scott's novels.[47] Few students failed to pass the examinations. At worst, the examiners censured their deficiency in some subjects, usually Greek or Hebrew, though once in a while they found them with "no clear apprehension of the current of events" in church history.[48] It will be no surprise to anyone who examines theological students today to learn that the lack of familiarity with the English Bible was lamented in reports to the Trustees, and from time to time it was proposed to have a special examination on its contents.

46. Journal, June 1, 1836.
47. G.T.S. *Seminarian* (1901), p. 58.
48. Tr P, June 25, 1856 (III, 82).

The examinations reveal that the Juniors read in Hebrew the early chapters of Genesis, a number of Psalms, and a dozen or more chapters of "the Evangelical Prophet Isaiah." In the New Testament, they studied the Gospels, with special emphasis on St. John, and at least half of the Book of Acts, using, of course, the Greek text. Biblical study in the Middle year included the Pauline Epistles, further reading in the Hebrew Psalter, and the remainder of Isaiah, as well as Jeremiah and selected minor prophets, Seniors invariably studied the Book of Job, and occasionally portions of Judges.

Evidences of Christianity was a subject of the Junior year, studied chiefly in the works of Paley, Leslie, Hurd, and Trench. Systematic divinity was begun by the Middlers in the second term, with Pearson on the Creed and Waterland on Regeneration and Justification as the principal textbooks for recitation. The theology course continued throughout the Senior year, covering the whole range of Christian doctrine. Burnet or Browne on the Thirty-Nine Articles was the basic text. Both Middlers and Seniors attended the classes of the Professor of the Nature, Polity and Ministry of the Church, reciting upon readings in the doctrine and constitution of the Church, Perceval on apostolic succession, and Potter on church government.

Ecclesiastical history was studied in each year. The Juniors concentrated upon the Church to 325 A.D., while the Middlers carried this survey down to the period of Charlemagne, though in some years they progressed as far as Pope Gregory VII. The Seniors continued the study of church history through the Reformation to the Council of Trent, and at the same time read English church history from the Norman Conquest to Elizabeth I. Homiletics was also practiced in each year, all classes demonstrating in the examination the proficiency they had acquired in sermon construction under the Professor of Pastoral Theology and Pulpit Eloquence. The Seniors were also questioned by him on their knowledge of the liturgy and the principles of pastoral care.

The subjects of the curriculum, then, at least during the lifetime of Dr. Turner, did not change in any basic particular from the course of study he pursued in the days when he reported to Bishop White.

Nor is it surprising that little alteration occurred in the methods of the Seminary's instruction in the first half of the nineteenth century. For nearly thirty years after the union of the General Seminary and the New York Diocesan School, the teaching remained in the hands of a surviving nucleus of the original Faculty. Samuel Turner gave a lifetime to his Seminary duties—over forty years—and Bird Wilson, the other continuing full-time resident professor, held his chair for thirty years. Dr. Moore, their Chelsea neighbor and for many years secretary of the Faculty, served the Seminary for a span equal to Dr. Wilson's tenure. Verplanck's early resignation and Hobart's death in 1830 left Benjamin Onderdonk as the fourth surviving member of the original group. As Professor of the Nature, Polity and Ministry of the Church, he gave such time to the students as his duties as Bishop of New York would allow. This was generally one day a week for formal classes, the usual practice of clergymen who served without pay as part-time professors in the Old Seminary.

Bishop Onderdonk was not a man of exceptional ability, but he was immensely hard-working, single-minded in his devotion to the Church, and tireless in his efforts to extend its influence and defend its traditions. Though not an inspiring teacher, he won the devotion of his students, setting before them a pattern of industry and strong church convictions that many of them were to emulate. John Pintard did not like him, chiefly because Bishop Onderdonk succeeded not only to Hobart's episcopate but also to his position as the leading champion of High Church principles, and advanced them with less tact than his predecessor. "The Bishop of this Diocese," wrote Pintard to his daughter,

> is perhaps as a Divine, below mediocrity. His excellence consisted in being the satellite of Bp. Hobart, whose bigotry he follows without his talents.[49]

49. Pintard, *Letters*, IV, 90; see also III, 178.

Mr. Pintard's prejudices increased with his age, and he was as unfair to Onderdonk as he had been to Bishop Hobart. Benjamin Onderdonk's influence upon the Seminary students over the years far exceeded Hobart's, and if his talents were fewer, he had the same remarkable capacity to arouse respect for his ability and win admirers who were steadfast in their loyalty and affection. The time came when Bishop Onderdonk stood sorely in need of his friends, for his capacity to make bitter enemies by his reckless espousal of the Oxford Movement in the 'forties exposed him to an attack upon his personal character which resulted in his disgrace and suspension from the bishopric of New York.

Shortly after the move to Chelsea, the flourishing state of the Seminary stimulated efforts to secure a third resident professor to supervise the study of ecclesiastical history. After Turner and Wilson had carried the historical studies in addition to their own subjects for a decade, the Standing Committee in 1834 enlisted the part-time services of Francis Lister Hawks, the popular rector of St. Thomas' Church and one of the most colorful figures among the New York clergy. With stability, Hawks might have become a notable leader of the time, for he was captivatingly charming, an effective orator, a successful rector, and his astonishing versatility included genuine ability in historical studies. But Hawks was restless. One term of the humdrum task at the Seminary and his interest waned. He hankered for a wider sphere of action, although he declined an election as bishop of the new Missionary District of the Southwest.[50]

Hawks' chief contribution to the Seminary was the interest he aroused in one of his admirers, Mr. Peter G. Stuyvesant of St. Mark's Church. In 1835 Mr. Stuyvesant established an endowment of $25,000 for a chair to be known as the St. Mark's Church-in-the-Bowery Professorship of Ecclesiastical History. At six per cent, this sum yielded $1,500 a year, the salary that was then paid the resident professors, with the use of a house in addition. The Trustees accepted a stipulation that gave the founder of the pro-

50. Strong, *Diary*, I, 200.

fessorship the right to nominate an incumbent for the Board's approval, twice if necessary, though after a second declination or rejection the Trustees were free to elect. Dr. Hawks declined his immediate nomination by Stuyvesant, and the South Carolina trustees suggested the return of the former professor, Samuel Farmar Jarvis, should the founder's second nomination fail. Dr. Jarvis' career since he left the Seminary was such as to find him, they said, "at present comparatively unemployed."[51] But Mr. Stuyvesant named William Rollinson Whittingham, who was duly elected in January 1836.[52] With his move into Dr. Turner's former apartments in the East Building, the resident professors were increased to three.

Though frail in health, Whittingham, just turned thirty, brought a brilliant mind and an inspiring personality to the Faculty. He had graduated from the Seminary in 1825, universally admired for both his scholarship and character, and he was one of the few proponents of High Church principles who won Pintard's admiration. "Yesterday," wrote Mr. Pintard on March 12, 1827,

> I attended the ordination as Deacon, of one of our Theological Students, Mr. R. Whittingham, who, if his life and health be spared will become eminent in our Church . . . I staid to join the Communion. At my period, an aged believing Christian ought never to turn his back on the Lord's Table.[53]

Made a Fellow of the Seminary upon his graduation, and librarian in succession to Henry Feltus, Whittingham's youth and pastoral concern speedily made him the friend and counselor of the students. In 1831, after a year of missionary work in New Jersey, he became rector of St. Luke's, Hudson Street, resigning in 1834 when the doctors sent him to the Mediterranean to regain his health. From abroad he returned to the professorship until 1840, when he was elected bishop of Maryland.

51. Tr P, November 25, 1835 (I, 532).
52. On December 1, 1835, the Standing Committee had appointed him to temporary charge of the departments of Ecclesiastical History and Pastoral Theology (G.T.S. Dean's Papers, December 9, 1835).
53. Pintard, *Letters,* II, 336.

Whittingham's influence upon the Seminary and its students was very marked. His devotion to the best traditions of High Churchmanship was strong and infectious, his standards of scholarship were high, and his personal life exemplified the finest spiritual and pastoral ideals of the priesthood. If he on occasion betrayed a streak of harshness and severity, it only served to kindle a deeper sense of seriousness in his admiring students. Whittingham's intimate association with Chelsea Square was relatively brief, but his influence far out-lasted his residence. He never lost his interest in the Seminary, and he was active in the affairs of the Board of Trustees until his death.

Upon Whittingham's resignation, Mr. Stuyvesant nominated John D. Ogilby, an eloquent, somewhat quick-tempered Irishman whose distinguished record in classical studies at Columbia was rewarded by appointment as Professor of Ancient Languages at Rutgers at the age of twenty-three. Church history was not his first love, but he brought to the chair the same genuine scholarship his predecessor possessed. Ogilby was a staunch Anglican of the Hobart type, equally hostile to Romanism and Protestantism. Like Whittingham, however, in contrast to an older generation of High Churchmen, he was young enough to be receptive to the Catholic influences of the Oxford Movement. Energetic and vivacious, Ogilby might have replaced his predecessor in the affections of the student body had he not been stubbornly opinionated. He maintained nearly all his views with uncompromising rigidity, impatient if not intolerant of opposition. His health failed him early, and sent abroad to regain his strength, he died in Paris in 1851.

The problem of instruction in pastoral theology proved more difficult to solve than that of ecclesiastical history. After Hobart's death, Bishop Onderdonk, with Professors Turner and Wilson, shared the responsibilities of supervision in this department. Efforts were made to arouse interest in an endowment of a resident professorship, but the heavy losses in New York's fire of 1835 and the chaos that accompanied the financial panic in 1837 postponed hope of successful response. The customary voluntary assistance of parochial clergymen was therefore sought at intervals, the first of these part-time instructors being Henry Anthon in 1834-35. Anthon, a brother of the famous Columbia Professor Charles Anthon, had been an advocate of strong church principles in his younger days, probably under the spell of Bishop Hobart's personality and influence. He had changed his views by 1836, when he became rector of St. Mark's Church, and was destined to become one of the leading Evangelical partisans in the churchmanship quarrels that divided Episcopalians in the 'forties. Violently hostile to the influences of the Oxford Movement and the implacable enemy of Bishop Onderdonk, Anthon's bigotry reached distressing proportions shortly after his service as an instructor at the Seminary.

Dr. Anthon was zealous in his attention to his classes in homiletics. Each Monday he met the Juniors and Middlers in the morning and the Seniors in the afternoon, listening critically to a half-dozen sermons and coaching the men in proper reading of the Prayer Book services. During the academic year 1834-35 Anthon heard over a hundred sermons and read nearly two hundred more that were handed in for his comments. Great stress was placed upon the careful preparation of written sermons, and the advisability of assembling a well-stocked barrel of discourses for future use. "Bp. Onderdonk says we must have 50 sermons when we graduate," wrote one student.[54]

At the conclusion of his year of part-time teaching, Anthon urged vigorously upon the Trustees the need of the appointment of a resident professor in this department:

> The course of theological learning in this Seminary must be viewed as incomplete until this appointment is made. The champions preparing to take their stand upon the battlements of Zion, have in this department *to prove* the armor which their other guides have put upon them with so much ability and skill. All the proficiency that is acquired in other departments is to be *exemplified* in this. The exercises, moreover, of the desk and pulpit are the *only* standard by which, at the present day, a large majority are disposed to estimate the value of an education for the sacred calling.[55]

54. Lee's Journal, May 26, 1834.
55. Tr P, June 24, 1835 (I, 500).

Even after more than a century and a quarter, Anthon's remarks have considerable bite. Pastoral theology was supervised in the following year by Professor Whittingham, and for 1836-37 the Trustees appointed Anthon's close friend and fellow-Evangelical, Hugh Smith, at the time rector of St. Peter's Church near the Seminary.

For the next year, the Trustees secured the services of the rector of All Saints' Church, Benjamin I. Haight, a graduate in the Class of 1831 who had been the organizing minister of St. Peter's Parish. He was elected Professor of Pastoral Theology and Pulpit Eloquence in 1841, holding the professorship in combination with his parochial work for fifteen years, though he resigned All Saints' later to accept a post on the staff of Trinity Church. Haight had considerable administrative ability, and his turn as dean in rotation was welcomed by those who cared about the efficient operation of the Seminary. Affable, enjoying a wide circle of friends, and active in the affairs of both the New York diocese and the Church, he was prominent enough to be elected bishop of Massachusetts in 1872 in succession to Manton Eastburn. He declined this honor and ended his days as assistant rector of Trinity Parish. Haight was as much a figure in New York's world of fashion as he was in its church life. One of his famous receptions invited from George Templeton Strong the comment:

> Haight's big ball the other night, the town talk, nine rooms open . . . and a hose company privately entertained in the cellar to interfere in case of a conflagration.[56]

Unfortunately, Dr. Haight was not very inspiring as a teacher of homiletics. His somewhat dry and old-fashioned High Churchmanship lacked Anthon's fiery evangelical zeal. For a number of years, the students had modeled their sermons after those of Bishop Sherlock, which they preferred to Tillotson's sermons, using as their textbook an English translation of Jean Claude's *Essay on the Composition of a Sermon*, the late seventeenth-century work of a French Huguenot. Professor Haight brought them up on his edition of William Gresley's *Ecclesiasticus Anglicanus*, a treatise

56. Strong, *Diary*, II, 35.

on preaching first published in 1835. They cordially detested recitations on Gresley. The book was, as an alumnus later recalled,

> almost a prodigy of the commonplace. One would read carefully a chapter and be able to remember scarcely a thing in it. There was nothing in it for the memory to catch hold of and retain. All was smooth, trite, flat, and slipped through the mind as wet soap does through the fingers.[57]

Here, then, was the roll of teachers in the first period of the Old Seminary—Turner, Wilson, Moore and Onderdonk remaining from the earliest years; a succession in Ecclesiastical History: Hawks temporarily, then Whittingham and Ogilby as professors; Anthon and Smith giving place to Haight in Pastoral Theology. This original group of professors began to break up as the decade of the 'forties drew to an end. Bishop Onderdonk ceased to teach after his suspension from episcopal office in 1845, though he was retained in the nominal professorship, the later catalogues of the Seminary merely noting that "This Professor does not now attend the classes." Bird Wilson and Clement Clarke Moore retired in 1850, Dr. Ogilby died a year later, and Professor Haight resigned in 1855. Only Samuel Turner, stout and bewigged, testy and eccentric with advancing age, remained as a link between the old Faculty and the new professors who began to make their appearance in the years just before the Civil War. Before the original group dissolved, however, they had to sustain the shattering crisis through which the Seminary passed in the 'forties when violent partisan controversy, aroused by the impact of the Oxford Movement, affected the repute and the fortunes of the institution for the next thirty years.

57. G.T.S. *Seminarian* (1901), p. 57. This was in the 'fifties. Twenty years later, student opinion of Gresley was much the same; see A. S. Crapsey, *The Last of the Heretics* (New York: Alfred A. Knopf, 1924), p. 85.

6

The Little Oxford

On July 2, 1843, St. Stephen's Church in New York was the scene of a dramatic incident that precipitated a crisis in both the Episcopal Church and in the affairs of the General Seminary. The churchmanship controversy between the High Churchmen and the Evangelicals, which had been smouldering with increasing intensity for a half-dozen years, was suddenly fanned into a flame of partisan strife that had disastrous effects upon the welfare of the Seminary. On that Sunday morning, Bishop Onderdonk, assisted by Bishop Ives of North Carolina, was conducting an ordination to the diaconate. With them in the chancel were Professor Haight, who presented the candidates, Dr. William Berrian of Trinity Church, and Joseph Price, the rector of St. Stephen's. The Bishop had reached the challenge:

> Brethren, if there be any of you, who knoweth any impediment or notable crime in any of these Persons presented to be ordered Deacons, for the which he ought not to be admitted to that Office, let him come forth in the Name of God, and show what the crime or impediment is.

At that moment the congregation was astonished by the sight of the Rector of St. Peter's Church standing in the aisle, arrayed in his gown, and reading solemnly:

> I, Hugh Smith, Doctor in Divinity . . . come forth, in the name of God, to declare, before Him and this congregation, my solemn conviction and belief, that there is a most serious and weighty impediment to the ordination of Mr. Arthur Carey . . . founded upon his holding sentiments not conformable to the doctrines of the Protestant Episcopal Church . . . and in too close conformity with those of the Church of Rome.[1]

The instant he finished, Dr. Anthon of St. Mark's-in-the-Bowery stepped beside him to utter a similar protest.

Clarence Walworth, a Seminary student and friend of Carey, described the effect of this unprecedented interruption of the service:

> The sensation that followed was something fearful, though the silence was profound. My father, who sat beside me, trembled from head to foot, and turned to me with a look of awe and wonder which I can never forget. "The bishop will ordain him all the same," said I.[2]

Walworth was right. The Bishop rose, "majestic, indignant and determined," and read his own statement:

> The accusation now brought against one of the persons presented to be ordered deacons has been fully investigated by me with the knowledge and in the presence of his accusers, and with the advantage of the valuable aid and counsel of six of the worthiest, wisest, and most learned of the presbyters of this diocese, including the three who are assisting in the present solemnities. The result was that there was no just ground for rejecting the candidate's application for holy orders. There is consequently no reason for any change in the solemn service of the day, and therefore all these persons, being found meet to be ordered, are recommended to the prayers of the congregation.[3]

1. Hugh Smith and Henry Anthon, *The True Issue for the True Churchman: A Statement of Facts in Relation to the Recent Ordination* (New York, 1843), p. 35.
2. C. A. Walworth, *Reminiscences of Edgar P. Wadhams* (New York, 1893), pp. 17-18.
3. *A Full and True Statement of the Examination and Ordination of Mr. Arthur Carey* (New York, 1843), pp. 5-6. This is a reprint of the articles that appeared weekly in *The Churchman* during July and August 1843.

Bishop Ives at once began the ordination litany, and the two protesting clergymen strode out of the church. Before nightfall, the incident was the talk of New York churchmen. Within a few days, it was a topic of acrimonious discussion in the press, and shortly a hurricane of pamphlets provided fuel for the fires of controversy over the Carey ordination.

Arthur Carey was the object of the bitter Evangelical hostility and the equally intemperate High Church support that had been aroused in some quarters by the appearance of the *Tracts for the Times.* The first of these challenging pamphlets that launched the Oxford Movement in England was circulated in 1833. The last, the famous *Tract 90,* was published in 1841. During those eight years, John Henry Newman, Edward Bouverie Pusey, John Keble, and others of their circle in the University of Oxford sounded their revolutionary recall of the Church of England to the knowledge and recovery of her essentially Catholic heritage of doctrine and spirituality. At first the *Tracts* created little stir among Episcopalians in this country, largely because their emphasis upon a high doctrine of the Church and its sacraments, the necessity of apostolic succession, the appeal to the ancient Church Fathers and the authority of tradition had long been familiar principles to old-fashioned High Churchmen. There was thought to be little in them that Bishop Seabury had not bequeathed to Connecticut churchmen, or that Bishop Hobart had not maintained throughout his ministry. Bishop Onderdonk, for example, praised the doctrine of the *Tracts* as "being the same with that which he has taught for many years, even long before the movement in Great Britain."[4]

In 1839, however, when an American edition of the *Tracts* received the enthusiastic support of Onderdonk and his friend the Reverend Samuel Seabury, talented grandson of Bishop Seabury and a man who at that time wielded a powerful influence from the editor's desk of *The Churchman,* those who viewed the Episcopal Church as thoroughly wedded to the Protestant heritage of the

4. John S. Stone, *A Memoir of the Life of James Milnor, D.D.* (New York, 1848), p. 546.

Photograph by the Frick Art Reference Library

Samuel Seabury
Seminary Portrait by
W. S. Mount

Arthur Carey
Seminary Portrait

Reformation were filled with alarm. The maintenance of traditional High Church doctrines in a somewhat dry and academic form, reminiscent of the teaching of seventeenth-century divines, was one thing; the advocacy of those same principles with the revolutionary demand that the Church conform to their implications for Catholic faith, worship, and life was quite another. The Evangelicals had long maintained their views to be the only authentic Gospel. A plea for the Catholic heritage of Anglicanism conjured up the dread specter of Popery, a repudiation of the gains of the Reformation, and an inescapable confrontation with the same heritage as it was embodied in the dogmas of the Church of Rome.

The support of the *Tracts* by the bishop of the strongest diocese in the Church filled extreme Evangelicals with dismay. Dr. Milnor of St. George's, who deplored "the baneful influence of Tractarianism," retailed to his friend Charles P. McIlvaine, Chase's successor as bishop of Ohio, the latest story of Onderdonk's approval:

In answer to a clergyman who said that he could go halfway with the authors of the tracts, the bishop told him to read and study them more attentively, and he would be prepared, like himself, to go the whole.[5]

Bishop McIlvaine, a violent opponent of Tractarian principles, was not surprised. It was what he might have expected from a man whose influence he had long deplored.[6] That summer, McIlvaine informed his diocesan convention that he was preparing a book to confute the teachings of the *Tracts* as "thoroughly unscriptural, thoroughly contradictory to our Articles and Homilies . . . thoroughly Popish in principle."[7]

When McIlvaine's *Oxford Divinity* was ridiculed in a scathing review in *The Churchman*, the Bishop was furious. Brushing aside the editor scornfully, he vented his wrath on Bishop Onderdonk, whose mouthpiece he believed Seabury to be:

It is the Bishop of New-York whom the Bishop of Ohio must consider as thus speaking . . . it is not merely Dr. Seabury who is responsible, but it is his endorser and patron and director and supervisor, his protector in these things; it is the Bishop of New-York, who is just so much the more responsible for these expressions and charges, as his influence in giving them weight is greater; and so will he be held by the church as well as myself.[8]

The appearance of *Tract 90*, with its contention that the Thirty-Nine Articles did not exclude Catholic doctrines from Anglican theology but only the Romish perversion of them, brought even shriller accusations of Popery from the leaders of the Evangelical party. Bishop Meade of Virginia spoke warningly of "those erroneous and strange doctrines . . . which Bishops are solemnly sworn to banish and drive away."[9] McIlvaine, smarting with re-

5. Stone, *Milnor*, pp. 543-544.
6. McIlvaine to Whittingham, June 23, 1838, Md. Dio. Ms.
7. *Ohio Convention Journal 1840*, pp. 17-18.
8. *The Episcopal Recorder*, March 6, 1841. For Onderdonk's reply see *Obsequies and Obituary Notices of the Late Right Reverend Benj. Tredwell Onderdonk . . . and Other Documents* (New York, 1862), pp. 49-50.
9. J. Johns, *A Memoir of the Life of William Meade, D.D.* (Baltimore, 1867), p. 263.

sentment, repeated his condemnation to the Ohio Convention. Bishop Griswold in the Eastern Diocese warned his people against

> a new sect lately sprung up among us, called Puseyites or Low Papists, who have, chiefly in England, written, and preached, and published much against the Reformation, and are endeavoring to bring back into the Church of England many of those superstitious mummeries, and idolatrous practices, for protesting against which so many of her pious Bishops and other ministers have been burnt at the stake.[10]

Among the High Church bishops, few, perhaps only Doane of New Jersey and Ives of North Carolina, were as fulsome in their praise of the *Tracts* as Bishop Onderdonk, whose enthusiasm led him into utterances which, however courageous, were at least ill-timed in this explosive atmosphere of controversy. Warmly commending the Oxford theology to the New York Convention in 1841, he asked:

> Ought not Christians to be brought to see . . . that the true blessings of the Reformation are not to be found in departure from Rome, but in return to Christ—to the principles, faith, and order of His One Holy Catholic and Apostolic Church? So thought the brethren who have been termed the "Oxford Divines."

He pleaded, not for an undiscriminating acceptance of all the ideas of the *Tracts*, but for "a patient and unbiased hearing." Recommending that the clergy study "the points of difference between the catholic and the Romish systems," the Bishop expressed his satisfaction that the Oxford writings had arrested the attention of some of the most intelligent and serious-minded of his laymen. "I would," he told them, "that it were more so."[11]

Bishop Onderdonk's reasonable arguments had themselves little chance of an unbiased hearing from those who disagreed with him, for he accompanied them with a sweeping denunciation of Protestantism, describing it to this same convention as

10. John S. Stone, *Memoir of the Life of the Rt. Rev. Alexander Viets Griswold, D.D.* (Northampton, 1854), p. 442.
11. *New York Convention Journal 1841*, pp. 82-83.

> Riven to its very centre with internal dissension; covering with its name every variety of schism, and every bold and wicked innovation of heresy; forming an unholy alliance with the veriest infidelity . . . For we must remember that protestantism is but a negative term. It implies no principle but that of dissent . . . the rejection of Christ's priesthood, the rejection of His sacraments.

On the other side, Dr. Milnor, older and less passionate than some of his partisan friends, revealed to Bishop Smith of Kentucky the misgivings of a thoughtful Evangelical:

> Recent developments here afford reason to believe, that to a greater extent than we had imagined, the Oxford heresy has invaded this diocese . . . corrupted the minds of our younger clergy and candidates for orders . . . When I speak thus I do not mean that they are prepared to *go over* to the "mother of abominations."

His basic concern was the peril that he saw threatening the Gospel:

> The danger lies in the exaltation of the Church above Christ, the Great Head; making her, not Him, the dispenser of renewing and sanctifying grace, and giving to external sacraments and ordinances the inherent efficacy which constitutes so much of the superstition of the papacy. They do not mean—until a great many impediments are removed—to unite with Rome; but on the principles of Tract No. Ninety, they adopt, as the means of allaying such a desire, the expedient of giving an aspect to our doctrines and observances, that should approximate them as nearly as possible to hers.

Milnor put the Evangelical theological opposition to the *Tracts* clearly and succinctly. He continued,

> The evangelical doctrines . . . are now to be superseded by the dogmas of the school at Oxford. The great principle of justification by faith is by many virtually abandoned . . . God is impiously confined . . . to the channel of the sacraments; and a most unwarrantable denial of covenanted mercy to all but the members of a church enjoying Episcopal succession, is insisted on. The Reformation is now found to have been fraught with evils . . . we are to condemn its authors for having taken dangerous liberties; and, as far as possible, to unprotestantize the Church.[12]

12. Stone, *Milnor*, pp. 571-572.

The Evangelical convictions of Dr. Hugh Smith of St. Peter's Church were such that he could not, in good conscience, sign the canonical certificate required for Arthur Carey's ordination. He was well aware that Carey was among the students in the Seminary who "embraced the doctrines of the Oxford school." Searching conversations with him led Dr. Smith to believe that the young man's views were such that were he ordained, he would come to his people "with a double creed—with the Thirty-nine Articles and the Creed of Pius IV, with the Prayer Book and the Missal."[13]

Agitation over the spread of Oxford doctrines in the Seminary had already begun. Judge John Duer, one of Dr. Anthon's laymen at St. Mark's, sought to rouse the New York Convention by a violent speech, lamenting that Tractarian teachings

> have become a favorite study of the youth in our seminary, the future candidates for orders, and by many of the younger clergy who have issued from the seminary they have been passionately embraced and are now zealously propagated.[14]

Dr. Anthon, at the Trustees' meeting in 1843, on the very day Hugh Smith informed Bishop Onderdonk that he could not give Arthur Carey the required testimonial, attempted to have the Examination Committee instructed to examine the students with "particular regard to the points in controversy between us and the Church of Rome."[15] Like most of Anthon's motions, it was tabled. He and Dr. Smith were added to the committee, only to dissent three days later from its favorable report on the ground "that it contains in their judgment an incorrect view of the true authority of the Fathers."

The suspicions of the Evangelicals in respect to the Seminary were well-founded. The imagination and enthusiasm of a considerable number of students had been kindled by the bold and ringing challenge of the *Tracts*. Here were the dusty principles of old-fash-

13. *The True Issue*, pp. 5-6, 8-12, 42.
14. Clarence A. Walworth, *The Oxford Movement in America; or Glimpses of Life in an Anglican Seminary* (New York, 1895), pp. 123-124.
15. Tr P, June 26, 1843 (II, 360).

ioned High Churchmen clothed in dynamic splendor and fraught with daring implications that promised change and renewal in the Church's life. Nor were the *Tracts* their only source of stimulation. Froude's *Remains* excited them with its outright repudiation of Protestantism. The new translations of the Fathers, edited by the Oxford scholars, gave them easy access to the patristic writings to which the *Tracts* appealed. Newman's *Lyra Apostolica* and Keble's *Christian Year* stirred a warmth of poetic piety. The reading room tables in the Seminary bore well-thumbed copies of *The British Critic*, an organ of the Oxford Movement, *The True Catholic*, and *The Ecclesiologist*, while Breck's letters describing life in the monastic and missionary settlement at Nashotah gave students a vision of spiritual accomplishment through the power of Catholic revival.[16] If the men in Chelsea Square could not hear the persuasive sermons through which John Henry Newman enthralled Oxford undergraduates, at least they could read them and rejoice that, as one of them put it,

> we had, in truth, a little Oxford on this side of the Atlantic. It was located in a little suburban appendix to New York City, known as Chelsea. Its name was the General Theological Seminary of the Protestant Episcopal Church.[17]

Clarence Walworth, from whose recollections these words are taken, was among the dozen or more students whose aggressive promotion of Tractarian doctrines won them mention in contemporary records or later reminiscences. Most of them were candidates from the Diocese of New York, including the studious Edgar Wadhams, the erudite William Everett, Walworth himself, the brash Benjamin McMaster, and Henry McVickar, son of the Columbia professor. Few possessed qualities to match the intellectual brilliance and personal charm of Arthur Carey. Scarcely anyone failed to be attracted by the rare beauty of spirit he displayed. Even Dr. Smith testified to "the purity and excellence of his Christian

16. Missionary Association Minutes, January 24, and May 9, 1843.
17. Walworth, *Oxford Movement*, p. 119.

character, his quiet and studious habits, and his love for truth."[18] His friends were even more fulsome in their praises, and Walworth, who lived across the hall from him in the East Building, admired him enormously.

Faced with Dr. Smith's refusal to certify Carey less than a week before the ordination service, Bishop Onderdonk speedily arranged to examine the young man before himself and six of his clergy—Professor Haight of the Seminary, Professor McVickar of Columbia, Dr. Price, Dr. Berrian, Dr. Higbee, one of Trinity's assistant ministers, and Dr. Seabury of *The Churchman*. Smith and his friend Anthon were invited to participate in the investigation of the charge that Carey held opinions "contrary to the doctrine and discipline of the Protestant Episcopal Church."

The examination of Arthur Carey was held in the shadow of the Articles of Religion, for the American version of the Thirty-Nine Articles then received much popular veneration. Men took seriously their establishment by the General Convention in 1801, and to the Evangelicals, the Articles were the chief protection of the true Gospel against the perversions of Roman Catholicism. The new High Churchmen of the Oxford school took the Articles equally seriously. The Prayer Book, they believed, gave ample support to the claim of catholicity for the Church of England. But the Articles, framed amid the controversies of the Reformation, were more difficult. Newman's aim in *Tract 90* was to show that a Catholic heritage was embodied in both the Anglican articles and the Roman decrees of the Council of Trent, though their points of kinship were obscured by the exclusive Protestant interpretation riveted on the one, and the errors which were taught and received in the Romish system surrounding the other. This was strange and dangerous doctrine to men for whom there was no Catholicism except that displayed in the dogmas and practices of Rome. Smith and Anthon put this point on trial in their examination of Carey. "Do you hold to, and receive the decrees of the Council of Trent?" asked Dr. Smith. "I do not deny them—I would not positively affirm them."

18. *The True Issue*, p. 6.

Carey's answer was thus reported in *The True Issue* in which the two clergymen described the proceedings. When the other examiners, however, led Carey to express his meaning more fully, it emerged that

> in what he might say favorably of the decrees of Trent, he took the decrees in the mere letter, and not as interpreted by the Romish system, and the concurrent sense of the Roman divines . . . he held the Roman Church responsible for the errors of her system, and the teaching of her doctors.[19]

When asked if the Romish doctrine of purgatory was "in any respects maintained by our Standards," the reply was "that he considered our Standards as condemning the doctrine *popularly* held to be the Roman doctrine." No amount of adroit questioning by Dr. Seabury could erase from the minds of the two Evangelicals the impression that Carey's answers, far from being candid and honest, were full of "cobweb distinctions and scholastic subtleties." While he would not embrace the articles of the Creed of Pius IV, he would receive them "so far as they are repetitions of the decrees of the Council of Trent," a statement which it took Dr. Seabury a lengthy discussion to clarify.[20]

Despite the numerous pamphlets and articles that subsequently described the examination, the reports of what Carey "was *understood* to say" leave considerable confusion as to some of the answers and discussion. It is clear, however, that the candidate did not hold "that doctrine of transubstantiation which I suppose our Article condemns," though he conceived himself "at liberty to confess ignorance on the mode of the Presence." He refused to admit that the denial of the cup to the laity in the Eucharist was "an unwarrantable change in a sacrament of Christ's own institution," preferring to term it "a severe act of discipline." The sin of schism, in consequence of the English Reformation, he maintained, "in some respects rests on both sides."

19. *Full and True Statement*, p. 34.
20. *The Churchman*, July 29, 1843.

Hypothetical questions did not assist in reducing the suspicions of the two chief examiners. "Supposing," asked Dr. Anthon,

> entrance into the ministry of the Protestant Episcopal Church in this country were not open to you, would you, or would you not, have recourse, in such case, to the ministry of the Church of Rome?

Dr. Seabury objected vigorously to this question, and Professor McVickar remarked "that they might as well ask Mr. C. whether if he had lived at the time of the patriarchs he would have had two wives." Carey, however, willingly answered:

> Possibly I might, after due deliberation, but think that I should more likely remain in our own communion, as I have no special leaning towards the joining of theirs at present.

The upshot of the examination was what might have been expected. Six of the presbyters were satisfied with Arthur Carey's answers, and the Rector of Trinity Parish provided the credentials necessary for ordination. Anthon and Smith, of course, dissented, confirmed in their "previous impressions as to his unsoundness." On the day before the ordination, Saturday, July 1, they each sent the Bishop a written protest, warning him that they might be forced "to take, if needful, the last and most painful step pointed out by the Church."[21] All the elements of melodrama were played out to the end. Early Sunday morning, Dr. Smith dispatched his sexton from St. Peter's to the Bishop's house in Franklin Street, asking what he planned to do. Bishop Onderdonk, having already that morning declined to inform Dr. Anthon of his decision, refused to reply to Dr. Smith's inquiry. The two clergymen hastened downtown to St. Stephen's Church and accosted the Bishop in the Sunday School room. When they learned that the ordination would proceed, they took their places in the congregation, ready to see the "great issue between the Church and Romanism joined."

The church press speedily spread the circumstances attending Carey's ordination throughout the Church. Seabury's defense of

21. *The True Issue*, p. 29.

Bishop Onderdonk in *The Churchman* was seconded in *The Banner of the Cross,* whose readers were flatly informed that Dr. Anthon and Dr. Smith had "wantonly defamed their Bishop and brother presbyters" in their *True Issue for the True Churchmen.*[22] *The Gospel Messenger* was more cautious, while *The Christian Witness and Church Advocate* leaned to the Evangelical side of the controversy. *The Episcopal Recorder* sprang to the defense of the protesting clergymen, as did *The Protestant Churchman,* a new publication founded in New York to combat the influence of Seabury's paper. Its first issue appeared within six weeks of the ordination, and thereafter its columns were filled with anti-Tractarian polemic and diatribes against "Puseyism."

Evangelical leaders everywhere rose in arms against Bishop Onderdonk's action. "We have reached a fearful crisis," wrote Bishop Meade to Dr. Milnor. "I had not supposed it possible that Romanism had so far regained its power among us, as recent events in your city . . . would indicate."[23] His hope that Smith and Anthon would find strong support in New York was vain. There were sharp words at the New York Convention in 1843, but the Bishop was sustained by an overwhelming vote. The convention ended, however, in a tumultuous scene when Bishop Onderdonk overruled the attempt of Judge Duer to censure him for his approbation of *The Churchman.* Vehement protests against the ordination were published by Philander Chase in Illinois, McIlvaine in Ohio, and, to the delight of the Evangelicals, by that unpredictable High Churchman, Bishop Hopkins of Vermont. Meade joined in their outburst.[24] Bishop Onderdonk, supported by the prestige and influence of the Diocese of New York, was not easily intimidated. His reply was as belligerent as their protest.[25] McIlvaine might inform his convention that he conceived it his duty "to protect the ministry of the whole Church from the introduction into it of false doctrine or evil life

22. *The Banner of the Cross,* August 26, 1843.
23. Stone, *Milnor,* p. 566.
24. *The Christian Witness and Church Advocate,* February 23, 1844.
25. *Pastoral Letter,* January 27, 1844; see *Obsequies,* pp. 51-70.

by the Bishop of any part of it," but his words had little effect upon the churchmen of New York. A far more vulnerable target of Evangelical wrath was the General Seminary and the professors under whose influence Arthur Carey had studied. The Bishop of Ohio shared with his convention his misgivings about

> the character of our General Theological Seminary in the city of New York. The Bishop who ordained is not only President of the Faculty of that Seminary, but Professor also of the Nature, Ministry and Polity of the Church. One of the clergy who assisted in the examination of Mr. Carey, and advised his being ordained is Professor in the same, of pastoral theology.[26]

The very claim of the Seminary to belong to the whole Church, so long ignored when its appeals for support were presented, now laid the institution open to the brunt of Evangelical attack. Wild rumors of Popery in Chelsea Square spread everywhere, and the professors were charged with indoctrinating their students with Puseyite views.[27] The story had gone about, for example, that Professor Haight had received a sermon from the student McMaster in which the adoration of the Virgin Mary was advocated. No explanation by Dr. Haight could quiet the agitation caused by such a useful piece of evidence of Romish tendencies in Chelsea Square, not even when Haight was armed with McMaster's own statement that in his discourse on the "blessedness among women" of the Mother of Jesus, no adoration of her was commended or excused.[28]

Even wider publicity was given to the incident that occurred on Christmas Eve in 1843 in the West Building. Dr. Turner, then acting as dean of the Faculty, described it in response to a demand made by Bishop McIlvaine during the later episcopal visitation of the Seminary:

> On the afternoon of the 24th of December last, my attention was arrested by a wooden cross about two feet high, placed on the front

26. *Ohio Convention Journal 1843*, p. 22.
27. *The Protestant Churchman*, August 26, 1843.
28. Haight Papers, August 14, 1843, G.T.S. Library; see also *The Churchman*, August 26, 1843.

railing of the chancel in the Seminary chapel, ornamented partly by natural greens, and partly by artificial flowers, and intended as a portion of the customary adorning of the chapel for the festival of Christmas. As rumors of certain practices accordant with those of the Church of Rome being in use by some students, had already been considerably circulated, and in very exaggerated form . . . I thought it highly inexpedient to suffer a novelty like this to pass unnoticed . . . I required the cross to be removed.

On Christmas Day, Dr. Turner rebuked the students, not only for this objectionable adornment of the chapel, but even more firmly because, as he said,

I have heard also, with the same feelings, that the bell was rung last night about midnight (and not by the Janitor), and that a service was held immediately after in the Chapel, which must have been entered (as by a *mere chance* the key happened to be with me) by "some other way" than the regular one . . . a midnight service in the Chapel, whether called a vigil with the Romanists and others, or a watch-night service with the Methodists, is not to be allowed.[29]

The students replied with an apology for their unauthorized midnight devotions on Christmas Eve, and it seems plain that the actions of Clarence Walworth and his friends sprang as much from their rebellious temper as from feelings of piety at the Nativity season.[30]

A move to investigate conditions in the Seminary came hard upon the heels of the increasing rumors. Bishop Eastburn of Massachusetts, who had retained a concern for the Seminary lacking among many of his Evangelical friends, addressed his convention with firm determination:

If anything should be wrong in it [G. T. S.], this wrong will be made right, through that supervision of the whole Church which was contemplated when the Seminary was first set on foot.[31]

His words were echoed in the South Carolina Convention. The friends of the Seminary in Christopher Gadsden's diocese, ever

29. *Journal of General Convention 1844* (Sparks ed.), pp. 248-249.
30. Walworth, *Oxford Movement*, p. 28.
31. *Massachusetts Convention Journal 1843*, p. 32.

watchful of its welfare and good name, were much disturbed. The leader of the South Carolina trustees, the Reverend Paul Trapier of Charleston, wrote Professor Haight shortly before the Board was to assemble for its June meeting:

> I have come most reluctantly to the conclusion that, though to my mind there is no sufficient ground for these reports, & no reason whatever to distrust any of the Professors, yet such an investigation is advisable, if only to silence gainsayers, & to prove that the friends of the Seminary have no wish to silence inquiry. In fact, in our Diocese, where we are unhappily much divided in conscientious opinion, these impressions respecting the Seminary have been gaining ground, & are now so general & strong as to keep from it almost all candidates for orders.[32]

Trapier's letter was the unwelcome warning that the long and intimate association between the General Seminary and the Diocese of South Carolina was nearing an end. When the Board of Trustees assembled a fortnight later, with the unprecedented number of more than sixty members present, one of the South Carolinians prsented a resolution calling for an investigation of the grounds "for the rumor that the instruction imparted in the Seminary deviates from the standards of the Protestant Episcopal Church."[33] Two bishops, William Heathcote DeLancey of Western New York and Manton Eastburn; three priests, one of whom was Mr. Trapier; and two laymen were named a committee to conduct the investigation. Bishop Gadsden, asked to join them later, declined to serve.

The committee diligently collected and recorded each "rumor" called to their attention. Among others were the allegations that Professor Onderdonk had endorsed "the whole series of the Tracts for the Times, without any reservation or exception," and that Professor Haight "had stated in a printed letter, that the Decrees of the Council of Trent (the damnatory clauses excepted) can be

32. Haight Papers, June 12, 1844.
33. Tr P, June 26, 1844 (II, 393).

made consistent with Catholic truth."[34] Professor Ogilby was noted to have said "that the Roman Church may not be declared heretical, because no General Council has so decided," as well as to have made "slurs and sneers at various things which many members of our communion reverence and love"—this latter in his lectures, reports on which Bishop Eastburn had received from students.[35]

When the Board met in September to prepare its triennial report to the General Convention, the committee submitted to the professors four "Heads of Inquiry," with a request for written answers within forty-eight hours. Their attention, of course, was concentrated upon Onderdonk, Haight, and Ogilby. They were the offenders. No one suspected Dr. Turner or Dr. Wilson of what were called "ultra views," and no one thought of Clement Clarke Moore in this connection at all. Therefore, when the inquiries were dispatched to the professors, the three High Churchmen were requested to

> attend this Committee on Saturday next at 10 o'clock A.M., in the lower Sunday-School room of St. John's Chapel, for the purpose of answering to such interrogatories as may then be proposed to them.

The "Heads of Inquiry" were:

> 1st Whether in the instructions of the Professors to the Students of the Seminary, any or what text books, other than those duly authorized or recommended, are used; whether the writings called the "Oxford Tracts," or any of them, have been adopted or used as text books; and whether in any other and what particulars the course of instruction prescribed by the standards of the Church has been deviated from;
>
> 2nd Whether any & what books, other than those so authorized and recommended, & especially whether the writings called the "Oxford Tracts," are, or have been, recommended to the approbation or perusal of the Students, & by what Professor, & under what limitations or circumstances;

34. See the attack on Haight in *The Protestant Churchman*, September 2, 1843. The basis of the charge against Haight were statements in his *Letter to a Parishioner* (New York, 1843), a pamphlet he had written in defense of Carey's ordination.
35. Minute Book of the Committee, G.T.S. Papers, 1844.

3rd Whether in the intercourse between the Professors, or any of them & the Students, either in the Seminary apartments or elsewhere, any influence, direct or indirect, is exerted with a view to inculcate any errors of the Romish Church, or any doctrines inconsistent with the articles of the Prot: Episc: Church, or having a tendency to encourage or palliate any such errors or doctrines;

4th Do the teachings of the Professors inculcate that Holy Scripture is the Supreme Rule of Faith, as taught in the 6th Article of the 39?[36]

The Seminary in 1841 from West 22nd Street
Lithograph by C. Bartlett

The committee received little satisfaction from the professors. Dr. Moore curtly informed them that he knew no ground for the questions asked him "other than what I consider idle and malicious rumors." Samuel Turner and Bird Wilson had not recommended the *Tracts*, nor did they know that any of their colleagues had done so. Turner, with some asperity, informed the committee that he did not understand what was meant by the phrase "the supreme rule of faith." He regarded the Scriptures, "properly speaking, the only

36. Trapier to Haight, September 26, 1844, Haight Papers.

rule of faith," and so, he said, did his brethren on the Faculty. Bishop Onderdonk and Dr. Haight acknowledged that the *Tracts* had been recommended to students as "books of reference," in order that they might become "thoroughly informed as to various opinions." Both denied that any influence was exerted to inculcate Romish errors or doctrines contrary to those of the Episcopal Church. Both also made it perfectly clear that they considered the committee's actions to be usurping the constitutional right of the bishops of the Church to act as Visitors under the statutes. Dr. Haight declined to appear personally before the committee, objecting to "the restriction of such request to two of my colleagues and myself," while Bishop Onderdonk firmly rebuked the members of the committee for assuming a right "to sit in judgment upon my episcopal acts and counsels." John Ogilby's quick temper displayed itself in a tart answer. Informing them that "my position as a Presbyter of the Church, is proof that I am not conscious of teaching . . . anything contrary to any of the 39 Articles," he wrote:

> I regard the invidious designation of *three* out of *six* members of the Faculty, as evidence that the *effect* of the resolution (whatever its design) would be, if possible, to make the parties incriminate themselves . . . I must respectfully, but peremptorily, decline being a party to so injurious a precedent.[37]

Balked by this encounter with the professors, the committee relinquished its task. On September 30, they laid their minutes before the Board of Trustees with the recommendation that the whole matter be referred to the House of Bishops. The affair might thus have been ended in an inclusive debate in that House had not the Trustees seen fit to include in the draft of their report to General Convention a fatal final paragraph:

> In conclusion, the Trustees feel assured that the General Theological Seminary has never been in a more healthful condition than it is at the present time.

37. For the full correspondence, see Tr P, September 30, 1844, App. E. (II, 427-435).

Paul Trapier moved to strike these words from the report. When the count was taken, they were retained by only one vote: twenty-six to twenty-five.

Two days later, General Convention assembled in Philadelphia. The atmosphere was tense with partisan feeling, and the debates were occasionally acrimonious. Amid scenes of considerable excitement, the House of Deputies, after prolonged wrangling, declined to condemn the doctrines of the Oxford *Tracts*, affirming instead

> that the House of Clerical and Lay Deputies consider the Liturgy, Offices, and Articles of the Church sufficient exponents of her sense of the essential doctrine of Holy Scripture; and that the Canons of the Church afford ample means of discipline and correction for all who depart from her Standards.[38]

Meanwhile, the House of Bishops, which had just adopted new canons for the resignation and trial of bishops, accepted the resignation of Henry Ustick Onderdonk, bishop of Pennsylvania and brother of New York's Onderdonk. Charges of drunkenness had so damaged his reputation as to destroy the effectiveness of his ministry. Onderdonk confessed his addiction to "the habitual use of spirituous liquor as a remedy for disease," after following a physician's advice to relieve a chronic digestive complaint with alcoholic stimulants. He had broken the habit, however, and his penitent resignation gave opportunity for the exercise of such mercy as might have allowed him to retire into obscurity. Unfortunately, Henry Onderdonk had been the object of ill-will in some quarters ever since his bitterly contested election in 1827. What part in his disgrace this feeling played is hard to say, but the atmosphere of this convention was not one in which the quality of mercy was unstrained. A sentence of suspension from the exercise of the ministry was pronounced upon him as the "administration of discipline in the premises."[39]

The harbinger of a more tragic personal catastrophe, and one that

38. *Journal of General Convention 1844* (Sparks ed.), p. 64.
39. *Ibid.*, pp. 171-172.

was to do immense harm to the repute of the General Seminary, appeared behind the scenes of the convention in the form of a letter entrusted to Bishop Meade for his use among the Bishops. Signed by Paul Trapier and four other South Carolinians, the paper reported that Mr. Trapier had, during the Trustees' investigation of the Seminary professors in New York, confirmed his previous knowledge

> that many rumors are in circulation among the public charging unchaste conduct and intemperance against the Right Rev. B. T. Onderdonk.

The signers expressed themselves deeply grieved at the scandal such rumors bring upon the Church, and "the injury which they inflict upon the General Seminary, in which Bishop O. is a Professor."[40] The bishops, informed by Philander Chase, the Presiding Bishop, of the nature of the letter, refused to receive it, and it was returned unopened to Mr. Trapier.[41] Within a week after the House of Bishops closed its sessions, however, three of its members, Meade of Virginia, Otey of Tennessee, and Elliott of Georgia, were prepared to present the Bishop of New York for trial.

When the triennial report of the Trustees of the General Seminary was received by the House of Deputies, it was accompanied by a "Memorial" from seven members of the Board—a minority report, in effect, objecting to the confident pronouncement about the "healthful condition" of the Seminary. Bishops Hopkins, McIlvaine, and Eastburn signed the "Memorial," together with Dr. Anthon, William Barnwell of South Carolina, Edward Neufville of Georgia, and Mr. Stuyvesant of New York.

In the House of Bishops, however, the High Churchmen had already taken steps to retain control of the situation. On October 2,

40. Paul Trapier, *A Narrative of the Facts Which Led to the Presentment* (New York, 1845), pp. 15-16.

41. Benjamin T. Onderdonk, *A Statement of Facts and Circumstances* (New York, 1845), p. 7. Trapier accepted its return, understanding that Bishop Elliott would be willing to receive "affidavits in proof of Bp. O's misconduct" (Trapier, *Narrative*, p. 17).

the House passed a resolution offered by Bishop Doane and seconded by Bishop Ives:

> Whereas the Bishops, by the Second Article of the Constitution of the General Theological Seminary, are individually and collectively Visitors thereof, to see that the instruction and discipline be duly carried out,
>
> *Resolved*, That they will proceed, with all convenient dispatch, to discharge their office as such Visitors; and that to this end, Bishops Hopkins, DeLancey, and Gadsden, be a Committee to prepare a plan of proceedings in the premises, and a suitable list of questions, which together with such as may be suggested by the Bishops individually, shall be addressed to the Professors of the Seminary severally; and to report the same on Friday next, at 12 o'clock.[42]

Bishop McIlvaine made sure that a full report of the Trustees' investigating committee was provided the Bishops, and for a week the episcopal committee gathered suitable questions to put to the professors. By October 19, forty-three questions had been dispatched to New York from Philadelphia, each professor being requested to return his answers as speedily as possible.

When Dr. Turner opened his communication from Bishop Chase, he was astounded. As he read the questions,

> occasionally the thought occurred to me that the document could not be genuine. Some of the questions appeared irrelevant; others to imply what was wholly improbable; others, again, to have been proposed simply in order to counterbalance what had been previously admitted, so that one class might neutralize the other. I was hardly able to persuade myself that they could have originated with such a body.[43]

Dr. Seabury's derisive remarks in *The Churchman* of November 23 had much justification, for these are a fair sample of the Bishops' questions:[44]

42. *Journal of General Convention 1844* (Sparks ed), p. 120.
43. *Autobiography of the Rev. Samuel H. Turner, D.D.* (New York, 1863), pp. 192-193.
44. The complete list of questions is printed in Appendix F (III) of the *Journal of General Convention 1844*.

1. What have you taught concerning the Church of Rome, as being in error in matters of faith?

5. What concerning the consistency of a clergyman's receiving at the same time, the doctrines of this Church and the doctrinal decrees of the Council of Trent, or any of them, the damnatory clauses excepted?

6. What concerning the obligation of a clergyman of this Church to be conformed in doctrine to the 39 Articles *in their literal and grammatical sense*, as well as concerning any liberty of *reservation?*

9. What have you taught concerning the difference between the doctrine of the decrees of Trent and the popular doctrine of Rome, and of the compatibility of the doctrine of this Church with either?

10. In what manner is the doctrine of the real presence in the administration of the Eucharist, taught in the Seminary?

12. Are the works of the Rev. Dr. Pusey, Messrs. Newman, Keble, Palmer, Ward and Massingberd, or any of them, used as Text Books, or publicly or privately recommended in the Seminary?

14. Has it been publicly or privately taught in the Seminary, that any portion of the sacred narrative in the Book of Genesis, is in the nature of a myth, or is merely or principally allegorical?

15. Has it been publicly or privately taught in the Seminary, that any portions of the Historical Books of the Old Testament are of uninspired originals?

17. What is taught in the Seminary, either publicly or privately, respecting the large body of English divinity, which is called the Calvinistic view of the 39 Articles?

21. Are the Holy Scriptures publicly and privately taught in the Seminary, as containing all things necessary to salvation?

27. Are the students publicly or privately taught to regard the English Reformation of the 16th century, as a useless or unjustifiable proceeding?

28. Are the Oxford Tracts adopted as Text Books in the Seminary?

29. Are the Oxford Tracts publicly or privately recommended to the students in the Seminary?

31. Is Calvinism, comprehending what are known as "the Five Points," publicly or privately taught or recommended in the Seminary?

33. Is the doctrine of Transubstantiation, as repudiated by the 33rd article of the Church, publicly or privately taught or recommended in the Seminary?

35. Are the doctrinal and other errors of the Romish Church, as referred to in the 39 Articles, duly exposed in the instructions of the Seminary?

36. Are any superstitious practices of the Romish Church, such as the use or worship of the crucifix, of images of saints, and the invocation of the Blessed Virgin and other saints, adopted, or publicly or privately recommended in the Seminary?

37. Is the German system of rationalism, i.e., of rejecting everything mysterious in the doctrines and institutions of the Gospel and making human reason the sole umpire in Theology, adopted, or publicly or privately recommended in the Seminary?

39. What are the deviations, if any, from the course of study prescribed by the House of Bishops?

Bird Wilson's answer to the Bishops' question was a brief and dignified reproof. "After having held a professorship in the Seminary for nearly twenty-three years," he wrote,

> and so often conducted examinations in the presence of the Trustees, and reported to them my course of instruction, the principles maintained by me cannot be unknown personally, to at least the greater number of the Bishops. Approbation of them has been several times expressed; and I have not heard that they have been thought at variance with those of our Church, or to have a leaning to the peculiarities of any of the systems mentioned in the questions; *viz.* the Roman Catholic, that of the Oxford Tracts, Rationalism, or Calvinism.[45]

Dr. Moore's letter was almost as brief as his note to the Trustees' committee. His answer to two questions plainly applied to them all: "I have never heard of anything in the Seminary which could prompt such inquiries."

45. The professors answers are printed in full in the *Journal of General Convention 1844,* Appendix F (IV).

Samuel Turner knew nothing of the use of the Oxford *Tracts*, nor did he suppose that the theological questions applied to his department. He was nettled by the questions on "the German system of Rationalism," which he took as applying to himself, and said with some indignation;

> If there be any one thing for which I feel conscious that I merit the approval of the Trustees and the Church, it is for the uniform opposition, which I have made to the whole system referred to, whether appearing in Germany, England or America.

No one thought seriously that there was "a rationalistic tendency in Professor Turner's department." The irrepressible Dr. Seabury stirred up the only trouble over this by his review of the Bishops' questions in *The Churchman*.[46]

Professor Haight was "not aware of any important deviations from the course of study prescribed by the House of Bishops," though he defended the recommendation of other writings, including the *Tracts*, as enabling the students "to understand the past and present state of Theological Science." The condition of the institution he believed to be good, though "I fear," he said, "that it has been somewhat injured by the late controversies in the Church and the attacks upon the Seminary."

Bishop Onderdonk elaborated at three points. Concerning the Church of Rome, he had uniformly represented it

> as so much in error, by mutilations of the true faith, and additions thereto, that a Christian man ought to be prevented, *in conscience*, from joining her communion . . . I have frequently referred to the fact of there being many popular errors in the Roman Church, not essentially growing out of the decrees of Trent; but for which I consider its priesthood responsible.

As to the Oxford *Tracts:*

> Many years ago, when but a portion of the Oxford Tracts had been published, and long before the appearance of No. 90 . . . I recom-

46. November 23, 1844. Turner answered him in a pamphlet entitled *Remarks on a Late Editorial Article in The Churchman* (New York, 1845).

mended the reading of the Tracts as likely to have an important influence on the theological character of the age, which I thought should be well understood by theological students.

He informed the bishops that he invariably taught the students

that the Liturgy, Creeds, Catechism, Articles, and other contents of the "Prayer-Book" are the doctrinal standards of this Church, and are to be understood in their literal and grammatical sense . . . I am accustomed to instruct the students diligently to study Holy Scripture, as containing all things necessary to salvation, and primitive catholic tradition as a rule for the right understanding of Scripture.

Professor Ogilby wrote at greater length than his colleagues, clearly on the defensive. While he would not say that the decrees of Trent contained no truths, he regarded them as "artfully contrived to deceive and beguile the simple and unwary," though less "offensive to the eye and ear than the popular doctrine of Rome." As to the Fathers, personally or individually, they had no "peculiar authority of their own as interpreters of Holy Scripture, but as collectively witnesses to the sense in which the Church from the beginning understood the Word of God." He was explicit about the English Reformation. It was

a singular instance of God's favor and mercy to his Church; whereby he was pleased to deliver a part of it at least, from a grievous tyranny, and from very many corruptions of doctrine and practice; although *some* of the agents, and *some* of the means instrumental in accomplishing it, cannot escape the severe censure of the impartial historian.

What offended Ogilby was the reception of twenty-four additional questions from Bishop McIlvaine, addressed to him alone among the professors. He answered them "under special protest, as unsuitable in themselves, and entirely inapplicable to my department." A number of them probed Ogilby's views on the mode of Christ's presence in the Sacrament of the Supper, to which the professor replied:

With the Church, I wholly avoid entertaining, in a *positive* way, the question touching the *mode* of the Presence. It is enough for me, that, to the *faithful* receivers of the consecrated elements, Christ's promise is made good: "This is my Body"—"This is my Blood."

One question gave him opportunity to triumph over McIlvaine:

> Are any outward or bodily expressions of reverence towards the communion-table, either at the communion, or otherwise, except such as are common in our churches, practised in the Seminary, or inculcated privately or publicly among the students?

"I am sorry to say," replied Professor Ogilby, "that the Seminary has no 'communion-table.' "

After the sessions of the General Convention closed at Philadelphia, the Bishops continued to meet to consider the answers to their queries. On October 30, they moved to New York, assembling in the hall of the West Building to conclude their visitation. The next day they adopted a number of resolutions, among them one expressing the conviction that the Seminary should have a pastoral head appointed by the House of Bishops, and another recommending that the Board of Trustees take measures to erect a suitable Seminary chapel. Two resolutions terminated the investigation, declaring

> that the Bishops, as Visitors, have visited the Seminary and inspected the same, do not find in any of its interior arrangements any evidences that superstitious or Romish practices are allowed or encouraged in the Institution.
>
> that the Bishops deem the publication of the questions of the Bishops and the answers of the Professors the most appropriate reply to the current rumors respecting the doctrinal teaching of the Seminary.[47]

Dr. Turner had a few caustic words on the whole proceeding in his comments on the two resolutions:

> With regard to the latter, I am compelled to say, that such questions, with the answers which they would naturally produce, appear to me to afford a very *insufficient* reply to the rumors alluded to. As to the

47. *Journal of General Convention 1844* (Sparks ed.), p. 188. The visitation proceedings were published in *Episcopal Visitation of the General Theological Seminary* (New York, 1844).

Photograph by Lawrence Thornton

Bishop Onderdonk
Engraving by W. L. Ormsby

Professor Ogilby
Seminary Portrait by
Daniel Huntington

former, I never heard of the private rooms of the students having been inspected by the Right Reverend visitors. I presume, therefore, that the "interior arrangements" mentioned, relate to those of the Chapel, Library, and Lecture-rooms. A short time after the "Episcopal visitation," I heard, from a source to be entirely relied on, of it having been said by one student, that "if they had come into his room he could have shown them a crucifix." It will be evident from what is yet to be narrated in this connection that the inquiries and the visitation were practically of little or no benefit. And indeed this might have been expected from the character of both.[48]

The Bishops had scarcely disbanded before they were summoned to sit as judges in the trial court before which Benjamin Onderdonk was presented by three of his brethren "as being guilty of immorality and impurity." Amid assertions that "he is of evil report in the diocese, and in other parts of the Protestant Episcopal Church,"

48. *Autobiography,* p. 202.

were the allegations that he has been "improperly excited by vinous or spirituous liquors," and that "at sundry other times he had impurely and unchastely laid his hands upon the bodies of other virtuous and respectable ladies." The half-dozen specific offenses laid against the Bishop dated back to a period before the canon under which he was tried had been enacted, the oldest being seven years earlier and the most recent two years before. The charges were so tenuously supported by direct evidence as to make the trial a travesty of justice. Possibly Bishop Onderdonk had at times taken too much to drink, and it is certain that his characteristically affectionate and indiscreet familiarity of manner had been imprudent and perhaps offensive, but this is far from "immorality with a deliberately impure intent." On January 2, 1845, however, the episcopal court found him guilty by a vote of eleven to six, the Evangelical bishops, joined by Hopkins and Brownell, condemning him, and the High Church bishops voting "not guilty."

Three votes were taken before the Bishops reached a majority decision upon the sentence to be inflicted upon Bishop Onderdonk. On the first, Bishops Whittingham, Doane, Ives, Kemper, DeLancey, and Gadsden, all of whom had voted him innocent, declared for a sentence of admonition, "in the lightest degree," added Whittingham, a request with which Ives and Doane concurred. The other eleven bishops, however, voted for suspension from office or deposition from the ministry. On the third ballot, Bishop Onderdonk's supporters, unable to gain adherents to a sentence of admonition, reluctantly agreed to suspend him in order to ward off the threatened deposition.[49]

The Bishop of New York, maintaining his innocence, returned home to live in quiet seclusion, exhibiting a spirit of Christian charity and submission that won the admiration of all save his most vengeful enemies, until the day of his death fifteen years later. To try to estimate the part played in Onderdonk's disgrace by the pas-

49. See *The Proceedings of the Court Convened Under the Third Canon of 1844 . . . for the Trial of the Right Rev. Benjamin T. Onderdonk, etc.* (New York, 1845), p. 256-333.

sions of controversy is now almost useless. That ecclesiastical partisanship was an important element in the sad affair has long been admitted.[50] It is with singular appropriateness that the serpent of slander is depicted under the feet of the effigy of the Bishop that lies in Trinity Church. A cruel vindictiveness, which William Whittingham deplored, followed him even after his suspension. It is not pleasant to read Dr. Anthon's letter to Bishop Hopkins in February 1845, after Bishop Onderdonk's influence had been destroyed: "What shall we say of New Jersey and Maryland? Thorns and thistles will yet spring up in their path."[51] Small wonder that Bishop Whittingham, on the day after the Onderdonk trial closed, wrote to his wife:

> Never have I so desponded with regard to the Church as I do now . . . What is to become of us who are set as marks for everybody to shoot at, God only knows. Mere innocence can no longer be any man's protection; malice and deceit can break any man down if allowed to work as they have in the case of poor Bishop Onderdonk.[52]

The disgrace of Bishop Onderdonk was a stunning blow to the diocese of New York and scarcely less to the Seminary in which he had been the most influential professor. Only the most loyal friends of the institution believed it to be free from "Romish errors and superstitious practices," despite the episcopal visitation. Within a few weeks after the publication of the Bishops' resolutions new rumors were spreading throughout the Church. "You have not heard," Professor Sparrow of the Virginia Seminary wrote to a friend early in January 1845,

> of the regular conspiracy in the General Seminary to Romanize the Church. The students had formed a society, secret, with the watchword "C.U.," Catholic Unity, and have been in communication with

50. See the admirable discussion by E. Clowes Chorley in *Historical Magazine of the Protestant Episcopal Church*, IX (1940), pp. 1-51.
51. John Henry Hopkins, Jr., *The Life of the Right Reverend John Henry Hopkins* (New York, 1873), p. 233.
52. W. F. Brand, *The Life of William Rollinson Whittingham* (New York, 1886), I, 361.

the Romish Bishop . . . It is curious enough that this should have come out after they had, by resolution, just whitewashed the Seminary.[53]

Dr. Sparrow's information, however exaggerated, was correct in one respect. "The subject," he said, "is now before the Faculty in New York."

Shortly before Christmas in 1844, Professor Ogilby heard reports that a group of students were advocating the adoration of the Virgin and the invocation of saints, promoting belief in the doctrines of purgatory, transubstantiation, and the papal supremacy, and maintaining as well the authority of the Tridentine decrees. They were reported to have disparaged the Seminary's course of instruction, scorned its textbooks, and sought to subvert "new and inexperienced members of the Seminary." Ogilby, in a fever of excitement, roused the Faculty to action with specific charges against two students.[54] The ensuing investigation did little to quiet the rumors that there were "a number of Jesuit students in disguise here at the General."[55] The reconstitution of the Jesuit Order by the Pope, after its dissolution in 1773, had taken place only thirty years before, and the mounting Roman Catholic ultramontanism that was to lead to the First Vatican Council filled Protestants everywhere with fear and dismay. The secret activities of "Jesuits" were suspected in the most improbable places. Greatly upset, the Faculty met for many hours each day from January 7 to January 13, interrogating students and seeking to smoke out the "secret Romanists." Few weeks in the Seminary's history can have been so disruptive of its peace or disastrous to its morale. Dr. Wilson, dean for that academic year, became "haggard, careworn, utterly heartsick," and the strain under which he labored led to the slight stroke a few months later with which the decline of his health began.[56] Even

53. Cornelius Walker, *The Life and Correspondence of Rev. William Sparrow, D.D.* (Philadelphia, 1876), p. 159.
54. Faculty Minutes, December 21, 1844.
55. Walworth, *Oxford Movement*, p. 137.
56. W. White Bronson, *A Memorial of the Rev. Bird Wilson, D.D., LL.D.* (Philadelphia, 1864), pp. 113-116.

Samuel Turner believed that the rumors of conspiracy had some foundation.

> The evidence showed that there were students whose views at some points were Romish, and whose intention was, after entering upon parochial duties within our Church, to endeavour gradually to lead their congregations along with themselves to the Church of Rome . . . so deeply had unsound, jesuitical principles insinuated themselves into the mind, in defiance of morality and commonsense.[57]

The investigation resulted in the expulsion of two students and the solemn admonition of two others by Dr. Wilson, both of whom withdrew from the Seminary shortly afterwards. The Faculty action was not based on the fact that the students had embraced "theological errors," for the professors were careful to point out that this was primarily the concern of their bishops. They explained:

> The principle on which the Faculty have proceeded is that the students charged have acted contrary to their duties and engagements to this Institution . . . this conduct tended to create parties among the students with excitement of feeling, thus disturbing the harmony of the Seminary . . . it exposed the Institution itself to the imputation of maintaining and instilling erroneous doctrines and encouraging superstitious practices, and thus injured its reputation and usefulness . . . These were the reasons which persuaded the Faculty that their interposition was necessary to preserve the order, harmony, and usefulness of the Institution.[58]

The conspirators who were expelled or admonished, however, proved to be more akin to those followers of the Tractarian doctrines whom Dr. Turner described as "ready to affirm statements of doctrine, of the meaning of which they had no idea" than disguised Jesuits. All four of them were later ordained, and none of them left the Episcopal Church to join the Roman fold. A half-dozen defections to Roman Catholicism, however, were enough to satisfy those who believed every rumor to be true, particularly as the majority of

57. *Autobiography*, pp. 208-209.
58. Faculty Minutes, June 26, 1845.

them were from Arthur Carey's circle of friends or classmates. Carey himself did not live to see the end of the storm his ordination had precipitated. After a few months as Dr. Seabury's assistant at the Church of the Annunciation, his health broke completely. Racked with tuberculosis, he was sent south by his physicians and died at sea on the vessel that was taking him to Havana.

These events of the mid-'forties virtually destroyed the confidence many churchmen had in the Seminary as an institution of the whole Church. Inside Chelsea Square, morale crumbled; outside, the repute of the Seminary declined sharply. In vain Dr. Turner protested against judging the institution by a few men noted for "ultra views."[59] The Evangelical bishops turned their backs on the Seminary. Manton Eastburn, who had been determined in 1843 to set right anything wrong in Chelsea Square, came to the conclusion that "a young student's residence in our General Seminary, notwithstanding some great advantages enjoyed there, [is] at present a matter of doubtful expediency."[60] Even some of the High Churchmen questioned the wisdom of continuing to operate a seminary of such anomalous constitution that it lost what strength a diocesan school might possess without securing the advantages of a truly general institution. When the Board of Trustees met in 1846, Bishop DeLancey of Western New York startled the members with a resolution he had been considering for some time. He moved

> that the next General Convention be respectfully and earnestly requested to consider and decide upon the expediency of *dissolving* the General Theological Seminary as a general institution of the Church, and if deemed expedient, then to dissolve the said Seminary, returning the funds and other property of the said Seminary to the respective dioceses from which they were derived, for use, or for distribution to the donors, and dividing all other property, if there be any, equitably among the dioceses.[61]

DeLancey was ready to settle for a New York diocesan school. The

59. *Autobiography*, p. 211.
60. *Massachusetts Convention Journal 1846*, p. 29.
61. Tr P, June 24, 1846 (II, 468).

Board, unprepared to debate such a radical proposal, postponed consideration until its next annual meeting, and the matter was given wide attention in the church press.

DeLancey's arguments were those of a realist interested primarily in securing effective theological training for the candidates of those dioceses which supported the General Seminary. He appealed for a frank recognition that the Seminary was "general" in name only. It educated little more than one third of the Church's candidates and received significant financial support from only a very few dioceses. Yet its anomalous constitution, born of compromise and bearing the seeds of constant discord, prevented it from achieving the strength that was possible in a well-governed diocesan school. Periodic interference from without and lack of firm authority within made it impossible for the Seminary to free itself from the mistrust and suspicion that recent events had aroused. The institution was, DeLancey concluded with regret and pain, a source of disquiet in the Church, disruptive of the very unity and harmony that it was hoped the Seminary's existence would further. Give the New York diocese, he pleaded, the opportunity to restore peace, order, and usefulness to a theological institution that might then achieve the influence that the existing diocesan schools enjoyed. The Virginia Seminary, the Bishop pointed out, had "the kind of reputation it desired; those who approved it, favored it; those who did not, could stand aloof."[62] If the experiment of "a general Theological Seminary, which may have the united support of the whole Church" had failed after a trial of nearly forty years, then DeLancey was ready to see the institution reconstituted in the interests of its own welfare.

Bishop DeLancey's proposal had few supporters. Men were not ready to abandon the vision of Dehon, Gadsden, and other founders of the General Seminary, however much it had been clouded by partisan controversy. A good many churchmen sincerely believed that the existence of an institution for which, at least in some way, the whole Church was responsible provided one of the few links that bound the separate dioceses into a national Church. The Gen-

62. See *The Churchman*, July 4, 1846, and July 3, 1847.

eral Convention, the Board of Missions, and the General Theological Seminary—these were cherished as the only organizational instruments of union possessed by a federation of dioceses that had not yet fully grown to the stature of a national Episcopal Church.

More than eighty trustees—the extreme Evangelical bishops notable by their absence—assembled for the Board meeting on June 23, 1847. They listened to a powerful speech against Bishop DeLancey's proposal, made by John Henry Hopkins of Vermont. Bishop Whittingham strongly seconded his arguments, and when the vote was taken, late in the evening after some hours of debate, it was overwhelmingly lost. The Trustees, however, had no alternative to DeLancey's plan for the rehabilitation of the Seminary's morale and repute. The institution was left to face its time of troubles as best it could.

7
Mid-Century Troubles

The bitterest time of troubles in the Seminary's history came in mid-century. The enrollment declined with discouraging rapidity, until from 1854 to 1858 the average number was less than half the eighty-five students of twenty years earlier. At the same time, financial support from the Church diminished to the vanishing point, and the gap between the Seminary's income and the costs of operation and property maintenance opened so wide as to endanger the very survival of the institution.

The Seminary's friends were worried by the reduction in numbers and the eclipse of prosperity, for in these circumstances the morale of the community was hard to sustain. Some argued that applicants were discouraged by the high standards for admission and the difficult language requirements. The professors, however, preferred to think that the increasing number of diocesan schools drew men away from the General Seminary, a view shared by the editors of *The Church Journal.* Undoubtedly both these factors contributed to the loss of students, but so also did the damaged repute with which the Seminary emerged from the controversy over the Oxford *Tracts* and the Onderdonk affair.[1] The attitude of

1. *The Diary of George Templeton Strong,* ed. Allan Nevins and Milton Halsey Thomas (New York: Macmillan, 1952), III, 384; see also Hemen Dyer, *Records of an Active Life* (New York, 1886), p. 268.

"Evangelical men" toward the General Seminary varied from indifference to open hostility, and even moderate churchmen felt misgivings at the frequent charges of "romanizing influences."[2] The annual examination of the students, always a strain and now sometimes more forensic than academic, brought a new form of anxiety when one or more of the examiners undertook a penetrating search for traces of Romish doctrines. The students dreaded the examination period so much that one of them begged pathetically to be excused, even if it meant the sacrifice of his Testimonial. "My brain," he wrote, "is too much enfeebled" to sustain the ordeal.[3] His nerves were likely as much shattered as his brain enfeebled, and the examination prayer must have been offered with earnest fervency:

> Almighty God, the Fountain of all wisdom, we ask Thy especial presence on the occasion of this Examination of the Pupils of this Seminary, now about to be held; that they may be endued with presence of mind for the manifestation of their respective proficiency, and that the Professors may judge the same without prejudice or partiality; through Jesus Christ our Lord. Amen.[4]

Occasional conversions to Roman Catholicism appeared to give substance to the charge of "romanizing influences." Only a small number of men informed the Faculty, as one Junior did in 1855, of their "submission to the Holy Catholic Church of which His Holiness Pius IX is the visible head here on the earth," but such incidents occurred with sufficient regularity to fan the smoldering embers of mistrust.[5] If the fire burned too low, fuel was available in the pages of *The Protestant Churchman*, which on November 10, 1855, described the General Theological Seminary and the Church of the Advent in Boston as "offices for the sale of through tickets for Rome."

2. Johnson to Kemper, March 27, 1851, Johnson Papers.
3. G.T.S. Papers, 1849; see also Johnson to Kemper, June 16, 1852, Johnson Papers.
4. *Proceedings of the Board of Trustees* (New York, 1866), III, iii.
5. Faculty Minutes, October 30, 1855.

The baleful influence of Chelsea Square was usually blamed for the defection of students, and few men apologized to the Faculty with the candor of Bishop Chase of New Hampshire. When informed that one of his candidates had joined the Roman Church, he wrote Professor Haight:

> It is somewhat mortifying for me to have troubled the Faculty with an introduction to so foolish and giddy a youth. I shall in future endeavor to understand my men better.[6]

Today's ecumenical climate makes it hard to imagine the intensity of Protestant prejudices against Catholicism a century ago. Even the most sensible men behaved in odd ways when confronted by the specter of Rome's attraction. In 1862, four students, apparently in the habit of escorting young ladies of their acquaintance to services of the Roman Church, were severely admonished and warned of possible ecclesiastical penalties as well as the loss of their scholarships if they persisted in this practice.[7] Thirty years later, the Faculty, informed of the conversion of two students to Roman Catholicism, passed a regulation forbidding students "to attend any place of worship except that of the P. E. Church without having obtained the permission of the Dean."[8]

Despite the declining support given the Seminary, the two dioceses of New York State remained firmly loyal. In these troubled years, they frequently supplied two thirds of the student body, and as nearly half the graduates were serving in one diocese or the other, there was considerable point to the remark that

> the New York and Alexandria institutions, in fact, are the converse of each other; the one being a Diocesan institution under a general title; the other a general institution under a Diocesan title.[9]

The New York trustees, who invariably dominated the Board meetings, paid little attention to the Seminary's critics, and measures to curb the decisive New York influence proved impossible to se-

6. G.T.S. Dean's Papers, November 8, 1855.
7. "Allocution to the Four Students," May 3, 1862, Johnson Papers (Misc.).
8. Faculty Minutes, May 1, 1891.
9. G.T.S. Clippings, Box 4; see also *The Episcopal Recorder*, March 8, 1851.

cure. In 1850, for example, the General Convention proposed changes in the Seminary's constitution that would allow absent trustees to vote by proxy in the elections of professors, as well as providing for a meeting of the Board at the time and place of each convention. The reaction of the New Yorkers was plainly put in *The Churchman* on July 5, 1851—an attempt "to despoil this Diocese of the vested rights secured to her." The Trustees, whose assent was necessary to constitutional changes, voted down the proposals by a substantial majority, and when similar changes were again passed by the Convention of 1856, they were defeated by the unanimous vote of the Board. The two New York dioceses were entitled to 65 board members in 1850, a number that rose to 85 in 1860, and represented about one quarter of the total number of trustees. As the average attendance at meetings varied from 60 to 80, it is not difficult to understand the dominance of New York in the Trustee's affairs.

Repeated outbursts of Evangelical indignation were provoked by the refusal of the New Yorkers to terminate Bishop Onderdonk's nominal professorship. Efforts to remove him were invariably defeated or tabled. Dr. Anthon repeatedly offered motions that a successor be elected to Onderdonk's professorship, and as late as a dozen years after the Bishop's suspension, Paul Trapier was still seeking to deprive him of his title or abolish the professorship itself. The New York trustees declined to take action against a man whose suspension might be lifted by the House of Bishops, and who, in any case, many believed to have been unjustly condemned. Bishop Onderdonk no longer came to Chelsea Square, but the students were welcome at his house to share his pastoral wisdom and experience. Philander Chase fulminated against receiving instruction from one who had been "suspended for immorality and impurity," and he was fond of describing "the skulking student from the General Seminary" who crept through the streets to visit Bishop Onderdonk "when the shades of night appear."[10] Professor Turner, when called upon to see this practice halted, informed

10. *The Banner of the Cross*, June 13, 1846.

Bishop Chase that the Faculty had no power to interfere, being but "the servants of the Trustees."[11] This was not the first, nor would it be the last time a complaint would be heard from the Faculty about the respective responsibilities of the professors and the Trustees in the life of the Seminary. Shortly after he came to Chelsea Square, for example, Professor Johnson discovered that

> the trustees & Professors have but little intercommunication—nor do we have any more influence than what we would have individually.[12]

Though the situation that irritated the Faculty more than a century ago has slowly changed, the voices of Turner and Johnson long echoed through the Seminary's structures of authority, encrusted as they were with statutory regulations and traditional practices.

The suspension of Bishop Onderdonk deprived the diocese of New York of episcopal authority, and as Onderdonk was still technically the diocesan, there was great uncertainty as to the canonical remedy in such a case. After much discussion, Dr. Wainwright of Grace Church was elected "Provisional Bishop" in 1852. Two years later, he was succeeded by Horatio Potter, who became the diocesan on the death of Bishop Onderdonk in 1861. The uncertainty of episcopal authority affected the Seminary as well as the diocese, perhaps even more intensely. For many years the decisive influence of the Bishop of New York as *ex officio* chairman of the Faculty had compensated for the lack of a permanent dean. After 1845, the Seminary lost the oversight which both Hobart and Onderdonk had exercised through their professorships, a significant factor in the seminary's deterioration during the mid-century years. No bishop on the Faculty could have altered some of the causes of the Seminary's decline, but vigorous leadership of the kind given by Hobart might well have rallied forces to cope with some of the difficulties. A titular deanship that rotated among the resident professors was a totally inadequate form of administration with which to meet the problems of the times.

11. *The Banner of the Cross*, July 18, 1846.
12. Johnson to Kemper, August 30, 1851, Johnson Papers.

The changes in the Faculty at this time convinced many that the Trustees were as determined to maintain Bishop Onderdonk's church principles in the classroom as they were to retain his name in the catalogue. George H. Houghton, founder and first rector of the Church of the Transfiguration, undertook to teach Hebrew classes upon the retirement of Dr. Moore in 1850. Houghton's beauty of spirit and remarkable skill as pastor and confessor were later to win him widespread admiration and affection, but at this time what seemed most evident and alarming was that he was "a believer in the Oxford revival." Nor did the two new resident professors who replaced Wilson and Ogilby bring reassurance to those who were sensitive to Catholic influences in the Seminary. Samuel Roosevelt Johnson was a churchman of what the Trustees called approvingly "the Bishop Hobart School," and his election as Professor of Systematic Divinity in 1850 was in accord with their devotion to "the cause of Evangelic Truth and Apostolic Order."[13] Milo Mahan, successor to Ogilby in Ecclesiastical History, was more venturesome than Johnson, combining the theological views of Bishop Onderdonk with the colorful versatility of his earlier predecessor, Dr. Hawks. Mahan was not only a strong Tractarian churchman; he showed as well considerable sympathy with the rising Ritualist Movement, and his successor in the chair of history, George Franklin Seymour, was a notable leader among the Ritualists.

Dr. Mahan was a Virginian who at an impressionable age had come under the influence of William Augustus Muhlenberg at St. Paul's College, Flushing. Accomplished in classical studies, he was persuaded by Bishop Meade to join the teaching staff at the Virginia High School in Alexandria. Meade is said to have regretted his action when he discovered copies of the Oxford *Tracts* on his protégé's bookshelves, and Mahan returned to St. Paul's to teach and to prepare for ordination. After some years in the parish ministry, including an assistantship with Seabury at the Church of the Annunciation, Dr. Mahan came to the Seminary in 1851. Seven ballots

13. Tr P, September 30, 1862 (III, 535).

Photograph by Lawrence Thornton

Professor Mahan
Seminary Portrait

Photograph by the Frick Art Reference Library

Professor Johnson
Seminary Portrait by F. W. Herring

were taken before he received a majority in his election to the professorship, and the final choice of the Trustees was much lamented by *The Protestant Churchman.* Mahan was not a notable scholar. Johnson's verdict came closer to the mark—"an accomplished fellow, a beautiful writer, & an agreeable man."[14] The author of his biographical memoir admits that Mahan "had no special preparation to the subject of Ecclesiastical History," but he admired the exuberant zeal with which the new professor attacked his subject, "wrapping the warm flesh and blood of present life around the dry bones of past ages."[15] Despite the fact that Mahan "used to say that his professorship gave him abundant opportunity to teach all the other departments as well"—an enthusiasm that might have been somewhat irksome to his colleagues—Chelsea Square did not absorb all his restless energy. He wrote a *Church History of the First Three Cen-*

14. Johnson to Shelton, May 17, 1852, Johnson Papers.
15. *The Collected Works of the Late Milo Mahan, D.D.*, ed. John Henry Hopkins (New York, 1875), III, xii.

turies, numerous poems and essays, served on the editorial staff of *The Church Journal*, sat as a deputy in General Conventions, and won a wide reputation as a gifted speaker and preacher. Dr. Mahan brought a touch of irrepressible wit to most things he did. A visit to England, for example, took him not only to the new Anglican religious communities at Cowley and East Grinstead but also to the ritualistic services in London. He loved them all. "The more advanced movement, in this country," he wrote from abroad, "is enough to make one's hair stand on end; but as I am rather deficient in hair, I do not suffer much from it."[16]

Criticism of the professors' views was somewhat unfair, for the whole spectrum of Episcopalian churchmanship was covered by the three resident teachers. On the other hand, dissatisfaction with the Seminary's course of studies was amply justified. No important change had taken place in the Seminary's curriculum since its earliest days. As far as possible the Course of Ecclesiastical Studies of 1804 was still followed, with the occasional substitution of a new textbook. The report of the Examining Committee in 1855 reveals that the students had achieved proficiency in precisely the same studies in which the examiners had been drilled in their time–and some of them had graduated from the Seminary more than thirty years before.

Dissatisfaction with the training of candidates for the ministry was not directed against the General Seminary alone. During the 'fifties, problems of theological education engaged the attention of a number of thoughtful churchmen. There was a growing recognition that a theological training appropriate to the needs of an earlier time was no longer an adequate preparation for clergymen in the mid-nineteenth century. The rapid expansion of the country, for example, that left the Old Northwest a populous area and pushed out to include the "Route to Oregon and California" in Jackson Kemper's jurisdiction, required men trained to preach effectively and minister resourcefully in frontier conditions. On the other hand, the ministry needed as well a superior intellectual training, for

16. Hopkins, *Mahan*, III, xlii.

advances in scientific knowledge and a widespread revolution in thought and education offered challenges to traditional forms of Christian belief that could be met successfully only by a revitalized and redirected Christian apologetic.

Awareness of the inadequacy of the old scheme of seminary education was undoubtedly quickened by "The Muhlenberg Memorial," a paper presented to the House of Bishops in 1853 by Dr. Muhlenberg and a group of memorialists that included Professors Turner and Johnson. Their aim was to raise forcibly the question of the competence of the Episcopal Church, as then constituted, "to do the work of the Lord in this land and in this age," a starting-point for the Church in any age of renewal. The now famous advocacy of ecumenical experiment and liturgical flexibility in the "Memorial" was accompanied by a plea that "a wider door must be opened for admission to the Gospel ministry than that through which candidates for holy orders are now obliged to enter."[17] Reform in theological education was one topic debated by the members of a committee that reported on the "Memorial" at the following General Convention. They advocated the cultivation by the clergy of forceful extemporaneous preaching, a better understanding of the intellectual climate of the times, and more thorough training in the principles of religious education and methods of reaching young people. Candidates for holy orders should acquire "more robust intellectual habits by a more thorough and severe mental discipline," as well as forming "better established habits of systematic study after ordination."[18]

The effect of these recommendations was slight, and in any case they were not radical enough to satisfy those younger clergymen who were painfully aware of the deficiencies in their seminary training. Two years after his graduation, William A. Johnson complained to Bishop Whittingham that the Seminary's course of study "does *not* arm the student to meet *any* of the practical *issues* of the day." Except for its intriguing illustration, his letter might well have

17. *Journal of General Convention 1853*, p. 182.
18. *Journal of General Convention 1856*, p. 348.

been written today to voice the familiar criticism that the seminaries prepare men to minister in an age already past. He wrote:

> The real doubts & difficulties which agitate men's minds, which the mechanic is discussing at his bench & the farmer at his work, the graduate of the Seminary knows nothing of 'till he finds them out for himself by bitter experience . . .
>
> You will remember, that at Braddocks defeat it was the best trained troops in Europe who were so utterly routed; why was it? Because they were not trained to battle with the foe they actually had to meet.[19]

Moved by this agitation, the Trustees of the Seminary appointed a committee to consider changes in the curriculum. Inviting comments and suggestions from the professors, they received lengthy replies.[20] The members of the Faculty agreed with Dr. Turner's "Dean's Report" of 1855. The curiculum was already overcrowded, and if lectures were to be given on topics of contemporary concern, an idea to which they were favorable, time should be taken from the subjects of lesser importance. They admitted, for example, that two years of Hebrew would suffice; its study in the Senior year might be abandoned. Time given to other studies could be shortened as well, though they were not wholly in agreement as to what might be cut down. Turner would allow liturgics only what attention could be afforded it in the general course of ecclesiastical history, while homiletics and pastoral care might be made subjects for the last year only.

Dr. Mahan was not sure that drill in sermon preparation should be reduced, but he was quite definite about pastoral care. This subject was

> an excellent theme for reading, observation, and quiet reflection; but like most subjects of an immediately practical character, not exactly fitted for the class-room.

He did not believe that what he called "ministerial or spiritual tact" could be taught. "Such things," he said,

19. Johnson to Whittingham, June 27, 1859, Md. Dio. Ms.
20. Tr P, June 24, 1857 (II, 159-184).

are learned and not taught. At the same time, a few carefully prepared Lectures, not by a Professor, but by some able and experienced Pastor, or Bishop, who should come before the students with the odor of the hay-fields, as it were, breathing fresh and sweet around him, would have the effect—which is all that is needed prior to experience—of awakening the minds of young men to the importance and sacredness of the subject.

Recitations and Lectures; 1855–56.

	Monday	Tuesday	Wednesday	Thursday	Friday.
Senior Class.					
First Hour 10 to 11.	Prof. Haight	Pr. Turner	Pr. Johnson	Pr. Haight	Pr. Johnson
Second Hour 11 to 12	Mr. Houghton	Pr. Johnson	Pr. Mahan	Pr. Johnson	Prof. Mahan
Middle Class.					
First Hour 10 to 11.	Pr. Turner.	Pr. Mahan	Pr. Turner	Pr. Johnson	Prof. Mahan
Second Hour 11 to 12	Prof. Johnson	Mr. Houghton	Mr. Houghton	Pr. Haight	Pr. Turner
Junior Class.					
First Hour 10 to 11.	Mr. Houghton	Mr. Houghton	Mr. Houghton	Pr. Turner	Prof. Turner
Second Hour 11 to 12	Prof. Haight	Pr. Mahan	Pr. Turner	Pr. Mahan	Pr. Johnson

The Senior and Middle Classes will attend the Prof. of Pastoral Theology for the Delivery of Sermons, &c, Friday Afternoons, at 3 O'clock.

Theological Seminary, October 1. 1855.

By Order of the Faculty:

The Mid-Century Recitation Schedule 1855-56

The professors' replies provided interesting glimpses into their capacities of mind and views on theological education. Faithful to the drudgery of the daily routine, Dr. Johnson had neither the experience nor the imagination to suggest any significant alteration in "our existing excellent arrangements." He thought that more precise assignments for recitations would give students closer direction in their study, while greater flexibility in the use of textbooks might help stimulate their interest. His main objection to adding to the course of study rose from his sympathetic sensitivity to the amount of time students were forced to spend in "quasi ministerial labors" to eke out their slender financial resources.

Dr. Turner, whose long years of teaching and study made him the only professional scholar among them, had two suggestions to make, both of which would one day become part of the Seminary's program. The first was the possibility of two distinct courses of study, one for ordinary students and embodied in the curriculum as it was, the other a shorter course, far simpler in scope. He had changed his mind since the days when he and Dr. Jarvis opposed Hobart's "short course," and he felt that "practical and sensible men of religion and piety might be trained as effective laborers in the Lord's vineyard" with an abbreviated course of study. His second suggestion was the expression of his hope

> that the time will come when the General Theological Seminary will be able to afford facilities for carrying on a Divinity Course to some high degree of excellence . . . In this way a class of Divines might be raised, competent to fill . . . any position which may require more than ordinary talent and learning.

It was a hope that in later years was realized in the Seminary's provision for graduate study.

Dr. Mahan's reply was the most interesting. He looked at the whole enterprise of theological education with more objectivity than Turner and more originality than Johnson. "No school," he was convinced, "can possibly furnish all that a clergyman ought to know. Something must be left for after study." Some of the studies necesary to "the outfit of an accomplished ministry" are "things *necessary to be taught*," while others are "things *necessary to be learned.*" This distinction was an important one. The traditional theological disciplines belonged to the first category and required the drill of the classroom—they "must be *taught*, line upon line, and precept upon precept." Those necessary to be *learned* were

> more juicy, more attractive, more immediately and obviously useful, more easily picked up in the course of reading, experience, or conversation; and for that reason may be safely left to the enlightened industry and ambition of after-life. To introduce such studies into the Class-room savors more of quackery than of solid education.

Some of these subjects—pastoral theology, apologetics, ethics, canon law, music—Mahan thought might best be introduced into the Seminary by an enlivening course of popular lectures

> extending over three years, embracing three or four subjects, numbering from six to twelve or twenty lectures each Seminary year, attended by the Students and open to the public . . . The course should be entertaining as well as instructive. For that, to my mind, is a matter of no little importance. Of regular routine work the Students have enough . . . Without Class-Room drill, which is not only hard work, but often somewhat of a bore, no solid foundation can be laid. Still "all work and no play" is as bad for Students of Divinity as it is for others . . . a little more diversion of a healthy kind is precisely the thing most needed.

When in later years the lecture method finally supplemented the deadly monotony of learning by recitation, Mahan might have felt that some essential part of the educational process had been lost, but at least he was aware of the force of a resolution which was debated at this time in the students' Rhetorical Society: "That for the instruction of educated men the system of voluntary lectures with written examinations is preferable to the recitation system."

The Trustees accepted the recommendations made to them in 1857: the reduction in the study of Hebrew, an entrance examination in the contents of the English Bible, written examinations to supplement the annual orals, and the expediency of providing lectureships in Christian Evidences, Ethics, and the Connection of Science and Religion "so soon as the finances of the Seminary will warrant any additional expenditures."[21] The significant outcome of the agitation for curriculum reform was a revised outline of the course of study, as the Standing Committee reported in 1860,

> to be carried into effect by degrees as circumstances may warrant, and to be placed on record for consideration and improvement as wisdom and experience may suggest.[22]

The effect of the new scheme was not felt until it was incorporated in a slightly changed form into the revision of the statutes in 1867. Then it became the harbinger of the eventual break away from an educational process based upon the mastery of prescribed textbooks to one devoted more freely to the study of the disciplines of theology.[23]

Little was changed in the mid-century years. The Trustees, in whose hands lay complete control of the course of study, were too preoccupied with the Seminary's financial state to give their attention to much else. Student interest in Mahan's "more juicy" subjects had to be sustained by the activities of the Rhetorical Society, which met regularly, like the old Theological Society, to hear sermons and listen to debates. Is Baptism by Dissenters valid? Is it advisable for the Priesthood to marry? Are the chasuble and other eucharistic vestments allowed by the American Book of Common Prayer? Has more hurt than good resulted from the Oxford Tractarianism? These were some of the questions debated, and if they had their trivial aspect, they were at least topics of vehement controversy in the Church.[24] Other questions revealed the concerns brought by the changing times. Should politics be entirely excluded from the pulpit? Is the system of renting pews as practiced in our churches contrary to the spirit of Christianity? Should street preaching in large

21. Tr P, June 24, 1857 (III, 147-148).
22. *Ibid.*, October 15, 1860 (III, 370).
23. See G. L. Blackman's *Faith and Freedom* (New York, 1967), a centenary history of the Episcopal Theological School, in which the story of the development of theological education in the Episcopal Church is admirably told.
24. Minutes of the Rhetorical Society 1864-1869, G.T.S. Library.

cities be encouraged? Does the existence of pre-Adamic man contradict the origins of the human race? The outcome of few of these debates is known, but it is on record that the question of the verbal inspiration of the Holy Scriptures was decided in the negative.

Even had the Seminary's resources permitted some enlargement of the Faculty, it is doubtful that the professors could have adjusted themselves to any very radical changes, or indeed, possessed the skill and learning necessary to introduce them effectively. Dr. Turner died in 1861, and his successor in Biblical Learning was Samuel Seabury. Then sixty years old and in precarious health, Dr. Seabury was no longer the zealous controversialist of earlier years. Never a Ritualist, he maintained his old-fashioned High Churchmanship to the end, though even that mellowed enough to allow one of his students to describe him as "an old man, ripe with the wisdom of age, never dogmatic, always delightful, always instructive."[25] Seabury's only compensation at the outset was Turner's house, and he retained the rectorship of the Church of the Annunciation for a number of years, dividing his attention between Chelsea Square and his parish church on Fourteenth Street.

With Seabury came a new Professor of Pastoral Theology and Pulpit Eloquence.[26] Dr. Haight, the former professor in this department, had moved out of the Seminary in 1855, relinquishing much of his work in favor of a closer association with Trinity Parish. Johnson, who promptly exchanged his house on the western end of the East Building for Haight's on the other end, took some of Dr. Haight's classes, and Mahan, who moved from outside into Johnson's quarters, was assigned work in this department as well. For the rest, Bishop Potter was invited by the Faculty to come over from his residence at 33 West Twenty-fourth Street for weekly lectures on the nature and duties of the ministry. When Haight resigned, the Trustees in 1862 elected William Ernest Eigenbrodt, associate rector of Calvary Church, to the chair. Eigenbrodt, the son of a distin-

25. A. S. Crapsey, *The Last of the Heretics* (New York: Alfred A. Knopf, 1924), p. 86.

26. "Pulpit Eloquence" was dropped from the title in 1864.

guished German scholar and schoolmaster, was a gracious and kindly man of punctilious courtesy, unimaginative, humorless, and possessed of a passion for the tasks of detail and routine that few men wanted. Secretaryships seem to have been his forte, and for many years he undertook the duties of that office for the New York Convention, the Standing Committee of the diocese, and the trustees of Trinity School. With very considerable independent means, Dr. Eigenbrodt could well afford to concentrate upon activities that interested him, yet he was never oblivious to the demands that good fortune made upon his charity and generosity. When he died in 1894, he left the Seminary his library, $10,000 to endow a fellowship, and over $250,000 for the permanent endowment funds. Eigenbrodt's classes in homiletics, liturgics, and pastoral care might have been uniformly dull and uninspiring, but at least his students could count upon a teacher who gave meticulous attention to his subject and had a sincere, if somewhat distant, concern for their welfare.

These were the years of the Civil War, and the outbreak of hostilities between North and South inevitably diverted attention from the problems of theological education. Each night in the spring of 1861, as the threat of actual war drew closer, the students of the Seminary met in the chapel to pray for the return of peace—"Why at that late hour," asked *The Calendar*, "when they ought to be retiring to rest?"[27] The alumni in the South sought to maintain communication with their friends at the Seminary, despite the gulf of sectional loyalty that divided them. In 1861 Aldert Smedes, rector of St. Mary's School, North Carolina, was forced to decline an invitation to be an examiner at commencement time. Fort Sumter had been fired on, and the gathering of armies made the journey impossible. He wrote to explain the reasons for his refusal, and continued:

> I, of course take the Southern view of the question, and wonder at the madness of the government in not letting us secede quietly. If they conquer us we shall be no more a united people . . . But they can-

27. May 18, 1861. The hour was 10:00 p.m.

not conquer us . . . a treaty will be made conceding all that we ask . . .

Happily I don't find my affection for my old friends in the least diminished by this national disruption . . . I hope you don't mean to avail yourself of the laws, or rather of the lawlessness of a state of war, to evade paying me that $1,000 which would be very acceptable just at this time.[28]

The Seminary showed few visible effects of the war. Some Southern students left for home in June 1861, but the number of men in the Seminary actually increased until the last year of the war. Five students volunteered for service with the U. S. Sanitary Commission, while a small number of others joined the Union Army. The Faculty granted those who enlisted an honorable dismission, though they thought that military service was not "consistent with the sacred office or its Candidateship."[29] The Seminary came in for some sharp criticism during the war, however, when objections were raised to the views of two professors, Mahan and Seabury. Both were Southern sympathizers.[30] Neither was disloyal to the Union, but Dr. Mahan, who had vehemently opposed the strong pro-Union resolution which was debated in the General Convention of 1862, consistently refused to glory in the righteousness of the Northern cause, and the worst possible construction was probably placed upon his objection to flying the flag over the Seminary buildings.[31] Dr. Seabury, who had published a defense of slavery in 1861—ill-timed if nothing more—was, as always, outspoken in his views.[32] Even the gentle Dr. Johnson had strong feelings about his colleagues, for he wrote Jackson Kemper:

Drs. Seabury & Mahan are rather on the Southern side in Politics (disloyal as I view the matter) and are both great friends of slavery, at least justifying it, and deeming it best.[33]

28. G.T.S. Papers, May 13, 1861.
29. Johnson to Kemper, May 1 and July 12, 1862, Johnson Papers.
30. Strong, *Diary*, III, 384.
31. Mahan to Johnson, G.T.S. Dean's Papers, 1861.
32. Coxe to Whittingham, October 3, 1864, Md. Dio. Ms.
33. Johnson Papers, July 12, 1862.

But, then, Johnson was, in his own words, "a strong Union man."[34]

If a number of circumstances combined to inhibit change in the curriculum of the Seminary during these troublesome years—the inflexibility of the administrative structure, the lack of interest on the part of most of the Trustees, the limited abilities of the professors, the coming of the Civil War—one certain cause of stagnation was contained in the qualification the Trustees placed upon their curriculum recommendations of 1857: "as soon as the finances of the Seminary will warrant any additional expenditures." The financial crisis became so severe that far from finding funds for new ventures in theological education, the constant quest was for enough money to enable the institution to survive. There were times when even the most optimistic believed that the Seminary might, at least temporarily, be forced to close its doors.

In 1850 the new treasurer, Mr. Abel T. Anderson, who had taken over the office from William H. Harison, and with it the accumulated problems of twenty years of injudicious management on the part of the Finance Committee, found no way to check a steady drift toward financial disaster. His first report to the Trustees was a sad one. The annual deficit had risen to $5500, the cash endowments were alarmingly depleted, and the Seminary had received that year only one contribution from a parish church—$17.16.

The clouds of financial insolvency had been gathering over the Seminary for long time. Twenty-five years earlier, when the students were still in the neighborhood of St. John's Park and the East Building under construction, the invested funds amounted in round figures to about $100,000, of which $20,000 represented endowments for specific purposes. From the remainder came an annual income of $5000 to defray operating expenses. At that time, and for many years afterwards, the small deficit of each year was readily covered by contributions received from the Church at large. After the move to Chelsea, however, the total income proved insufficient to meet the increasingly heavy expenses. These were not, in fact, the costs of operating the institution, but chiefly those imposed by

34. Johnson to Kemper, June 18, 1861, Johnson Papers.

the erection of the two buildings and the maintenance and improvement of the real estate. Dr. Moore's gift of all the land from Ninth Avenue to the river was a magnificent, but expensive benefaction, for the property levied a continuous drain upon the Seminary's resources. The repeated costs of bulkheading and filling the river lots as the western side of the land was gradually extended, expenses of construction, taxes on the real estate, municipal assessments for sewers, grading, opening streets, and paving—all made deep inroads into capital funds. Each year in the 'thirties the deficit was far beyond what could be made up by contributions; each year the Finance Committee paid the difference from the Seminary's "personal estate" of cash and securities. By 1838 the available capital for operating expenses, apart from that set aside for the endowments of scholarships, the library, and the professorship of Ecclesiastical History, had shrunk from approximately $80,000 to less than $28,000. That year the Trustees heard the dismal news:

> The small remaining capital of this whole institution is in danger of being spent in a few years. The ordinary expenses of the Seminary exceed the income arising from its funds by more than $4,000 . . . How shall we arrest the downward tendency of the Seminary's funds?[35]

The obvious answer of a vigorous campaign to raise a large capital sum from friends of the Seminary does not seem to have occurred to the Trustees. The Seminary belonged to the Church; the Church must be reminded of its responsibility. The recourse of the Trustees was to appeal, somewhat plaintively, to the Church for assistance, a procedure that had been adopted several times since 1828, when the first version of what is now called "Theological Education Sunday" was devised. The members of the Board, therefore, discharged their consciences by circularizing the clergy in accordance with their resolution

> that the ministers of our Church throughout our country be again earnestly solicited to have collections made in their several parishes, in aid of the funds of the Seminary.

35. Tr P, June 25, 1838 (I, 663).

Though the response to this appeal was momentarily encouraging, contributions were not sustained at a very generous level. Most church people believed the General Seminary to be amply endowed. Aside from the valuable real estate, the legacies of Jacob Sherred and George Lorillard, together with Stuyvesant's endowment of a professorship seemed vast and quite adequate sums—and if not, the prospect of the $100,000 Kohne bequest, which would come to the Seminary in time, made it difficult to persuade people that the institution could be in urgent need.

Contributions fell off after the $5000 that was brought by the appeal in 1838, and during the 'forties the theological controversies and partisan quarrels caused a rapid decrease in gifts. The antagonism of Evangelicals and the misgivings of moderate churchmen affected the Seminary's income as well as its repute. The $1400 received in 1842 fell to less than half that amount by 1845, and the annual contributions thereafter steadily diminished to the point of Anderson's statement in 1850. Simultaneously, the capital funds which were used to make up the deficits disappeared so fast that less than $2000 remained for general purposes in that year. Anderson, on behalf of the Finance Committee, informed the Trustees that to make up the deficiencies, each year the Standing Committee

> have appropriated from funds for general purposes sufficient for such objects until, as *cash or money investments*, those funds are now exhausted; but it must not be supposed that the whole has thus been expended—that is to say, in *ordinary current expenses;* water-grants and interest, assessments for sewers, paving streets, laying side-walks, Professors' houses, and numerous other expenses . . . largely contributed to this result. In principle, your Committee consider most of these expenses to be rather a *change of investment* than a destruction of capital, causing perhaps for the time being a curtailment of income, but adding eventually to the means of the Seminary.[36]

The Trustees could not shake off their fascination with the potential value of the real estate west of Tenth Avenue. They were confident that the "Central Block" between Tenth and Eleventh Ave-

36. Tr P, September 18, 1850 (II, 658).

nues would yield a handsome income when all the land could be leased, while the "Wharf Block" from Eleventh Avenue to the river promised to become an asset of dazzling proportions as the city's docks and shipping moved northward along the Hudson. Easily persuading themselves that it was "rather a change of investment than a destruction of capital," and with the Kohne legacy in nearer prospect each year, they gambled against time, believing that the increased value of the real estate would more than repay the capital invested in it.

The fact seems to be that the relatively few trustees who displayed genuine interest in the Seminary's affairs regarded their primary responsibilities as the preservation and development of the real estate. The successful operation of the educational enterprise was a secondary consideration. The theological school trained the Church's clergymen. The Church, therefore, should support an institution established by General Convention. Its failure to do so lay at the root of the difficulties. The Trustees were learning the hard way—and so were the professors and students on whom the real inconveniences and deprivations of penury fell—that a seminary that belonged in a vague way to the whole Church was likely to be the first concern of few churchmen. Diocesan seminaries commanded enthusiastic local or regional support. The General Seminary, except for the loyalty of groups within the two New York dioceses, had no coherent and organized body of supporters, closely identified with its fortunes and welfare. The General Convention's Committee on the General Seminary put the whole matter succinctly to the convention in 1865:

> The Dioceses are now so numerous, and the residences of most of the Bishops and Trustees are so remote from the city of New York, that four-fifths of them never think of attending the meetings of the Board . . . When founded the General Theological Seminary was the only institution of the kind among us. But now, many of the Dioceses have seminaries of their own; and others are looking forward to the same means of supplying their local wants. Virginia was the first to take this step; and the Bishop of Virginia has never since then attended

a meeting of the Board . . . Similar feelings will naturally prevail more or less in the case of every Diocesan seminary; its friends being conscious that they cannot fairly claim the right to control the operations of a general institution which has no longer the first place in their affections or their support . . . The fact that other Dioceses have a potential share in the management deadens the interest of New York . . . the fact that New York preponderates so strongly in the Board as well as in the benefits derived from the Seminary deadens still more the interest of all Dioceses outside of New York.[37]

Five months after Mr. Anderson's melancholy report of 1850, the long-anticipated Kohne legacy came in. A compromise was made, and the Seminary's capital funds were increased by $97,500 worth of Pennsylvania stocks, bearing five per cent interest. It was just in time, for the Trustees faced a forced expenditure of nearly $60,000 for the final extension of the Wharf Block by bulkhead and fill along the river. There was no choice. Either the Seminary complied with the ordinance or the City Corporation would have caused the work to be done and assessed the cost on the Seminary property. This was no moment to exercise poor judgment or embark upon a questionable risk, but the Finance Committee was lured by the attraction of an investment that promised a seven per cent return on the Kohne bequest. The stocks were sold for $94,433.17 and $90,000 was invested in loans to a real estate promoter and builder, secured by mortgages on half-finished houses and tenements in a Brooklyn development scheme.[38] The investment was a costly mistake. The builder failed, the interest was not paid, and eventually the Seminary was forced to take over the houses under foreclosures and complete their construction in the hope that the property would produce some income. The unpalatable truth was that the Finance Committee had put $90,000 into a property that was a source of added expense, and which, when finally sold, brought little more than $50,000.

Each year after 1850 deficits were made up from such capital as was available, and as the general funds were then exhausted, the

37. *Journal of General Convention 1865*, p. 290.
38. Tr P, June 29, 1853 (II, 795).

specific endowments were also subjected to a "change of investment." By 1858 these, too, had almost vanished, though the Trustees regarded their obligation to them as faithfully met by making an amount equal to their income a charge upon monies received from leases and rents. Soon the endowments for specific purposes were listed as liabilities in the sums of their former interest.[39] As borrowing was the only means of relief, mortgages and other debts quickly rose to nearly $55,000. The edge of disaster had been reached, or so it appeared to George Templeton Strong, who was elected a trustee in 1859.[40]

Investments of the kind that beguiled the Trustees to risk the Kohne legacy were common at a time when both sober businessmen and reckless speculators grasped at the golden opportunities offered by skyrocketing property values in the rapidly growing city. Only the most conservative could resist a venture that might double their investment within a few years. Unfortunately the Trustees' excursion into the real estate market was overtaken by the financial panic of 1857, in which all but the soundest investments were affected. Banks suspended specie payments in October of that year, and prosperous merchantile houses failed. "Wall Street," noted Mr. Strong gloomily, is "blue with collapse."[41] During the hard winter of 1857-58, thousands were unemployed, while property was in a condition of stagnation. Income from leases and rents fell sharply in the prolonged months of depression that followed, when even Trinity Church was forced to practice measures of rigid economy to keep down a deficit.[42]

The year 1859-60 was the darkest period in the Seminary's crisis. Delancy's old proposal to make the institution a diocesan seminary was revived, though it met with little support from members of the Board of Trustees. They were much more attracted by the idea of moving the Seminary out of the city to a less expensive location, re-

39. Tr P, June 26, 1861 (III, 411); see also Johnson to Kemper, June 18, 1861, Johnson Papers.
40. Strong, *Diary,* III, 37.
41. *Ibid.,* II, 363.
42. *Ibid.,* p. 434.

taining the Chelsea real estate as source of income. Nothing came of the proposal to move at this time, save that the Trustees found Clement Clark Moore willing to cancel the bond and mortgage executed to him in 1833 when he constructed the Seminary's second set of river bulkheads. As this represented a debt of nearly $43,000 that would immediately become due if the institution left Chelsea Square, Moore's generous act of cancellation in 1860 was his crowning gift to the Seminary.[43]

At this juncture, Mr. Anderson resigned as treasurer. After two unsuccessful attempts to fill the office, the Standing Committee on July 19, 1860, elected Mr. Henry E. Pierrepont, a member of a prominent and wealthy family long associated with the spacious splendor of old Brooklyn Heights. Mr. Pierrepont, informed of his election at his summer cottage in Newport, was reluctant to take on the task, but "in a spirit of self-sacrifice for the good of the Church" he accepted "for the year." Fortunately for the Seminary, he remained its treasurer for twenty-three years. Pierrepont at once integrated the old Finance Committee and a new Real Estate Committee into the Standing Committee, creating a more efficient system of managing financial affairs. He loaned the Seminary $17,000 to pay up back taxes and accumulated interest due on mortgages. As income from the real estate was barely enough to pay the charges of its maintenance, the costs of operating the Seminary were pared down to the absolute minimum. The brunt of this economy fell upon the professors, for their salaries were the largest item in the expenses of operation.

The professors were already accustomed to hardship. Their salaries had frequently gone unpaid for months.[44] Two thousand dollars was the stipend of resident members of the Faculty at this time, though Dr. Turner received an additional $500 in recognition of his long years of service.[45] During the late 'fifties, salaries were so much

43. Standing Committee Minutes, July 26, 1860.

44. Johnson to Shelton, February 25, 1860, Johnson Papers.

45. Columbia professors at this time usually received $4000 of which $1000 was intended as a rent allowance.

in arrears that the professors could hardly have continued their work except for the aid of friends. In 1856 Dr. Johnson put their plight plainly to the Standing Committee in "a private communication":

> The Professors of the Seminary have very moderate means of their own—they are chiefly dependent upon their salaries. They occupy expensive positions . . . surrounded by beloved students, frequently in necessitous conditions . . .
>
> Now it does happen, & we have had this experience for several years, & nothing that the Committee has thus far done, has given us the slightest relief; it does happen that our salaries are largely & regularly behindhand. Months pass, when we are put to all the turns which an honorable & conscientious person can take to make arrangements for passing expenses. We have bills at the grocers, at the tailors, at the butchers, with the milkman, with our poor domestics unpaid . . . As matters are going on now, it is simply a cruelty.[46]

Characteristically, Johnson said nothing about his own dire straits. He had often "lived on tic," as he put it, but a few months after he had written the Standing Committee, he was forced to close his house in the East Building, send his wife to live with their daughter and son-in-law in Connecticut, while he moved into a vacant basement room of the West Building, taking his meals at a nearby boardinghouse. The academic year 1859-60 found him able to be reunited with Mrs. Johnson in their house, just in time to receive the blow of Mr. Pierrepont's drastic economies. The salaries of the resident professors were cut in half, though Dr. Mahan could not be reduced below the $1250 considered to be the income of the vanished endowment of the chair of Ecclesiastical History. Houghton relinquished the compensation paid for instruction in Hebrew, and Dr. Turner died in 1861, relieving the budget of one salary, small though it was. When the Trustees elected his successor, they voted Dr. Seabury a salary of $2000 "to commence whenever the Income of the Corporation shall warrant the same, in the judgment of this Board."[47]

46. G.T.S. Papers, April 7, 1856.

47. Tr P, June 26, 1862 (III, 518). The same qualification was added to Dr. Eigenbrodt's election on September 30, 1862.

Desperate appeals to raise money for the reduced operating expenses were made to bishops, alumni, and, inevitably, to the Vestry of Trinity Parish. A committee of the Trustees was sent, as Bishop Potter phrased it, "to knock on the door of Trinity Corporation with the whole weight of that Board.[48] Much to the irritation of the Trustees, the Vestry declined to help without even giving the committee a hearing.[49] Temporary relief came, however, in the form of some private gifts, new scholarship endowments, and the prompt action of the Society for Promoting Religion and Learning, the Seminary's staunch friend and benefactor. The society, which had already made its customary scholarship grants for the academic year 1860-61 to forty-six students in an amount of nearly $6000, as well as contributing $800 to purchase their textbooks, pledged an annual payment of $1000 "to avert so great a calamity from the Church at large as the closed Doors of this noble Institution," and "for the special purpose of paying the existing salaries of the present Professors."[50] Professor Johnson's reduced salary was paid by the society for a half-dozen years, and by taking a couple to board with them, he and Mrs. Johnson were able to remain in their house. How relief was had when the Seminary's janitor, attempting to buy candles for the chapel, was refused credit until an old bill for $52.39 had been paid, is not known.[51]

In 1863 the Trustees issued a "Solemn Appeal for Aid," seeking to raise $20,000 at once, though "it were better," they added tentatively, "to raise $100,000." Proclaiming that "the Great School," which "has been to the Church what West Point has been to the nation . . . is in imminent peril," the sixty signers pledged $50 apiece, the sum asked of each trustee and alumnus. The "Appeal" had little capacity to arouse enthusiastic response, except from the Seminary's warmest friends. There was a defensive note in the an-

48. *The Church Journal*, July 3 and October 23, 1861.

49. A similar appeal was made to Trinity Church in 1863. After prolonged discussion, the Vestry again refused assistance (Strong, *Diary*, III, 295).

50. Minutes of the Society for Promoting Religion and Learning, June 6, 1861, G.T.S. Library.

51. G.T.S. Papers, March 13, 1860.

nouncement of indebtedness of nearly $145,000, with no capital assets beyond real estate which yielded less than $11,000 and cost $18,800 to maintain. As the operating expense was $6200, this brought the expected deficit for 1863-64 to $14,000. No amount of pious exhortation could overcome the belief that somewhere there had been reprehensible mismanagement.[52] Funds came in all too slowly for Mr. Pierrepont. With the aid of Bishop Potter, who was determined to save the Seminary, the treasurer and some of his friends planned to launch a personal campaign. Two dozen prominent clergy and laymen, including Bishop Chase of New Hampshire, Bishop Odenheimer of New Jersey, and a delegation from Western New York, met at Potter's house in January of 1864 to plan their strategy.[53] They aimed at $150,000, and in the months that followed, a strenuous effort was made to arouse wide and informed support for the Seminary. Perhaps the results could hardly have been other than disappointing at a time when the burden of the Civil War was heaviest, but about $15,000 was received before September, enough to raise hopes that some change might alter the discouraging outlook.

The tide turned, in fact, before the year was out. The real estate market began to stir with the anticipated end of the national conflict, and the Trustees authorized the sale of some of the property. When Pierrepont had an offer for the sixty-six lots in the Central Block, he held off the prospective purchaser, convinced that real estate would command a higher price when the war was over. In June 1865 he had good news for the Trustees. The Brooklyn property had been sold for $51,750, and the mortgage of $45,000 on the Central Block was paid off from the proceeds of the sale. In the following February, Mr. Pierrepont shared with Professor Johnson his

52. Controversy over the investment of the Kohne legacy had occupied the church press for some time. See *The Church Journal*, June 6, 13, and 20, 1860; and November 6, 13, and 20, 1861. Abel Anderson replied to his critics in *A Letter to the Trustees of the General Theological Seminary from the Late Treasurer* (New York, 1862). See *The Church Journal*, March 26, 1862, and *Some Facts Touching the Kohne Legacy* (New York, 1862).

53. Strong, *Diary*, III, 398.

jubilant conviction that "the financial crisis in our affairs is past and a good time coming."[54] He had sold the western half of the Central Block for $90,900. The endowment funds were restored in "good bonds and mortgages," the remaining indebtedness retired, and the professors' full salaries paid. With some smugness, the Standing Committee hailed the "great and happy changes" as

> the dawn of that future prosperity which, even in the darkest hours of the past, has been with confidence predicted as certain to come.[55]

Annual deficits would again appear, sometimes in substantial amounts, but never in sums that could not be safely financed or overcome by measures of strict economy. With the financial recovery that came with the end of the Civil War, there was an increasing demand for leases in the remainder of the Central Block and the lots of the Wharf Block. The real estate was gradually transformed from a liability into an asset.

Mr. Pierrepont's realistic and efficient management, the timely assistance of the Society for Promoting Religion and Learning, the response of friends and alumni to successive appeals, and the fortuitous circumstances that improved the real estate market—all combined to preserve the General Seminary from extinction. Yet without the self-denying example and devoted labors of Professor Johnson within Chelsea Square, there might have been little worth saving. At all events, it is probable that Dr. Johnson's influence, more than anything else, saved the Seminary community from a spiritual impoverishment as great as that of the financial debacle.

A younger brother of William L. Johnson, the Seminary's first graduate, Samuel Roosevelt Johnson—"Rosy" to his intimate friends—was educated at Columbia and in the Seminary during the New Haven days. A parish ministry in St. James' Church, Hyde Park, and St. George's Church, Flushing, matured his unusual pastoral gifts, and ten years as a missionary in Indiana brought him a concern for the mission of the Church and a close friendship with Jackson

54. Pierrepont to Johnson, February 6, 1866, G.T.S. Papers.
55. Tr P, June 27, 1866 (IV, 10).

Kemper, neither of which he ever allowed to diminish. When he came to the Seminary from St. John's Church, Brooklyn, in 1850, he was deeply involved in the wreckage of a sizable family inheritance which had been submerged in a tangle of debts, mortgages, and property that could not readily be liquidated. His remaining small independent income was little enough with which to meet the financial strain placed upon the professors by the reduction of salaries. Yet there is never a trace of self-pity in Johnson's correspondence with his friends. His only complaint was that straitened circumstances denied him the privilege of helping others to the extent that his generous nature prompted. He could not endure the plight of students, alumni, or friends in need, and the appeals that were constantly made to him stirred him to repeated acts of self-denial. In 1865, for example, he received a moving letter from an alumnus who had been made homeless and destitute by a destructive explosion that rocked Charleston, South Carolina, after its fall to the federal troops in 1865. Assisted by Houghton of the Transfiguration, Johnson helped to raise $500 for his immediate relief, contributing himself a sum that he could hardly afford.[56] It was Johnson, again, who collected some money to help supply chapel vestments for the faculty of the Virginia Seminary when that institution opened its doors after the war.[57] These are instances of special occasions of generosity; relief of his "necessitous" students was a constant occurrence.

The burden of the Seminary's internal affairs fell upon Dr. Johnson, even when he was not taking his turn as dean, for he served for twelve years as secretary of the Faculty. Schedules of chapel services, recitations and lectures, lists of preachers, and all the paper work of administration crossed his desk. As a letter deserved a prompt answer in Professor Johnson's concept of courtesy, the pressures of correspondence kept him at work at all hours. An exchange of notes with an applicant for admission is both entertaining and revealing. The young man wrote:

56. Phillips to Johnson, February 25, 1865, G.T.S. Papers.
57. Johnson to W. L. Johnson, February 14, 1866, Johnson Papers (Misc.).

Rev. Dean of General Sem'y, P.E.C.:—

I wrote perhaps two weeks since for certain information about the studies of the Junior class as I had some idea of entering that class next spring and desired to make some preparation. I have not received any answer. Through forgetfulness I omitted to enclose stamp for return postage. I now enclose a stamped envelope and most respectfully request a reply.

Dr. Johnson replied:

My dear young friend,

Your note of Nov. 26th wounded me. It intimated that my delay to answer your letter might be influenced by the absence of a three cent stamp. Never do so again. Imagine 40 letters unanswered ahead of your own; imagine a pressure in the professional work and the old man toiling away at 2 o'clock in the morning while you were sleeping; imagine him engaged in securing scholarships for 50 young men, and working against time that no one should fail; Imagine absence, sickness, peevishness, idleness—anything, my boy, but meanness! Never do so again.[58]

One letter Johnson declined to answer—a proposal from a book agent that the students should earn some extra money by selling copies of a lurid publication entitled *The Escaped Nun.*

Though he often agonized over problems and was inclined to be highly emotional, Johnson's sense of humor never failed to help him keep the little storms that swept through the Seminary in proper perspective. In the academic year 1855-56, John Henry Hopkins, Jr., gifted and artistic son of the Bishop of Vermont and just as pugnacious as his father, was appointed Instructor in Vocal Sacred Music. He immediately destroyed the peace of Chelsea Square by introducing plainsong for the chanting of the Psalms, stirring up that kind of tempest that has often agitated seminary students and professors. Dr. Turner refused to tolerate a setting of the Psalter which he thought neither "agreeable to a musical ear or devotional in its expression." He would not have the new music when he officiated. As Hopkins promptly refused to play on those days, "some

58. G.T.S. Papers, November 26, 1866.

anti-plain-song student presided at the organ" when Dr. Turner read prayers.[59] The students plunged into the row with delight, circulating petitions against "the Hopkins book," and making lists of those for and against Gregorian chant. They stayed away from Hopkin's classes in music, explaining that they thought attendance optional, and absented themselves from chapel on the ground that they preferred "the Anglican Music," an excuse the Faculty declined to accept.[60] Dr. Johnson was serious when he reminded them that

> the talent for agitation is a gift from God given for honorable and useful purposes . . . Be careful, beloved, where God has imparted this talent, to use it in strengthening . . . the Institution, or Parish, or Diocese . . . never the contrary. So shall a dangerous talent become a very special grace . . . and a blessing to others and yourself.[61]

But he enjoyed describing the flurry to Bishop Kemper:

> We have had a grand excitement in our Seminary among the boys, & a private correspondence on the part of Dr. Turner & Hopkins, the Instructor of Music and Organist, about Plain Song. It is a simple pleasing tune—not worthy of 5 minutes controversy, but how could we live without something to dispute about. I hear that in Nashotah you have been quarrelling about bread and butter.[62]

Such are glimpses of "Rosy"—self-denying in all things, sensitive and affectionate to others, indefatigable in his labors, bearing all his burdens with a heart lightened by an unshakeable faith in God. He was no scholar, and his guidance in the study of theology was scarcely more than any well-read clergyman might have provided. But his students adored him, meeting his trust and affection with the best that was in them, making his ideal of the priestly vocation their own. There are other glimpses of Johnson—watching all night

59. *Autobiography of the Rev. Samuel H. Turner, D.D.* (New York, 1863), pp. 237-238.

60. Faculty Minutes, March 20, 1856.

61. Samuel R. Johnson, *A Lent Lecture Delivered in the Chapel, etc.* (New York, 1856), p. 11.

62. Johnson Papers, May 13, 1856.

with some students by the body of Bishop Onderdonk in Trinity Church, braving the disapproval of the City Attorney to plead for a student who had been arrested, quietly interceding with their bishop for those whom he admonished for attending Roman Catholic services, sleeping on a mattress on the floor when his hospitality filled his house to overflowing, encouraging students to read to the inmates of the Blind Asylum, stimulating the renewed missionary interest that seized upon the Seminary in the 'fifties, and at every turn revealing a spirituality so pure and guileless that few could resist its spell. It is no wonder that Professor Seymour and Bishop Potter saw more than a little of the spirit of George Herbert and John Keble in Dr. Johnson. His own claim would have been far more modest. It is the Seminary's loss that no visible memorial keeps his name or memory alive today, for Samuel Roosevelt Johnson preserved through the time of troubles all that was finest in the ideals of the Christian life and ministry that were cherished in Chelsea Square.

8

The Coming of the Deans

The allegiance of High Churchmen in the 'forties to the teachings of the Oxford *Tracts* was won by their fresh and forceful vindication of the Catholic heritage of Anglicanism. Largely theological and historical in its orientation, however, this phase of the Oxford Movement had less effect upon the devotional practices of Episcopalians or the conduct of public worship than is sometimes imagined. Church services were invested with greater dignity and orderliness, the use of the black preaching gown was abandoned, and here and there stone altars appeared, occasionally adorned with a cross, candles, and flowers. But such changes were not widespread. Tractarian churchmen laid claims to the rightful possession of doctrines that had been supposed to belong almost exclusively to Roman Catholicism, but they made few efforts to introduce practices or ceremonies that gave visual expression to the devotional and liturgical life of a Catholic Church. Young men in the succeeding generation, however, were not content with theoretical or academic claims to Catholicism. Practices that were called "ritualistic," especially in the celebration of the Holy Communion, were increasingly common in the 'sixties when men became convinced that both the Church's public worship and the churchman's private devotions should manifest plainly the Catholic doctrines which lay behind them. Shortly after the Civil War, usages appeared that many thought shockingly Popish—the wearing of eucharistic vestments, the adoption of liturgical colors to mark the seasons of the Church's year, the use of incense, sacring bells, signs of the cross, genuflections—much of the ceremonial panoply of Catholicism. These were accompanied by teachings that advocated the desirability of sacramental confession and fasting communion, the use of prayers for the dead, the importance of daily celebrations of the Holy Communion, with accompanying adoration of the Presence of Christ in the Sacrament, and the appropriateness of offering a Choral Eucharist or Sung Mass as the chief act of Sunday worship in the parish.

Here was Anglo-Catholicism, known a century ago as the Ritual Movement. It produced an even bitterer conflict in the Episcopal Church than the earlier controversy over the Oxford *Tracts*, largely because the laity were far more sensitive to alterations in public worship than they had been to the intellectual excitements of theological essays. What their clergyman thought about the Catholic heritage of Anglicanism was one thing; what he did in the chancel on Sunday morning was quite another. A storm of outrage often greeted the enriched ceremonial and the Catholic sacramental instruction, yet a growing list of churches became known for their "advanced ritual": St. Clement's, Philadelphia, the Church of the Advent in Boston, and in New York, St. Alban's, St. Ignatius', the Church of St. Mary the Virgin, and Houghton's Transfiguration. Elsewhere others followed their lead, precipitating disputes, parochial schisms, and passionate ecclesiastical conflict. Sharp as it was, however, the controversy in its full intensity was brief, lasting scarcely more than a decade from 1868, when the first move was made in General Convention to curb the Ritualists, to 1878, when it became evident that the canon passed in 1874 to prohibit ritualistic usages was a dead letter.

The controversy found the older conservative High Churchmen confused, divided in their opinions about Ritualism. Some were content to tolerate the changes introduced by their younger disciples. Others, perhaps the majority, ranged themselves in opposition, alongside their former Evangelical opponents. It was no help to

The East Building in the Last Century

them when Bishop Hopkins in Vermont, unpredictable to the end, published his *Law of Ritualism*, defending the practices as canonically permissible for Anglicans and predicting that

> this Ritualism will grow into favor, by degrees, until it becomes the prevailing system. The old, the fixed, and the fearful will resist it. But the young, the ardent, and the impressible will follow it more and more . . . And the opposition arising from its resemblance to Romanism will die away, as men learn to understand that Popery does not consist in the Ritualism which it pleased the Lord to order for His own chosen people . . . I have little doubt that my children will behold the "glory and the beauty" of our public worship brought back to the first stage in the Reformation.[1]

Just as the Low Churchmen of nearly a century earlier had seen their greater number swept up into the vigorous Evangelical Movement, so now the churchmen of the old "high and dry" school

1. John Henry Hopkins, *Law of Ritualism* (New York, 1867), pp. 94-98.

watched with dismay what was made of their principles by the new Anglo-Catholicism.

Like all controversies that disturbed the peace of the Church, the disputes over Ritualism were echoed in Chelsea Square. There they were the background of the troubles that accompanied the coming of the first permanent deans. The champion of Ritualism among the professors was George Franklin Seymour, successor to Milo Mahan when the latter resigned the history chair in 1864 to become rector of St. Paul's Church, Baltimore.[2] Seymour, then rector of St. John's, Brooklyn, was a young man, ten years out of the Seminary where his roommate had been James Dekoven, later president of Racine College and the most eminent defender of the Ritual Movement in the Church. Seymour had done notable parish work at Annandale-on-Hudson, and with the support of Bishop Potter and Dr. John McVickar, he had been chosen as first warden of the new St. Stephen's College. A Columbia honors graduate and an assiduous student at the Seminary, Seymour's scholarship won the tribute of Bishop Potter's respect.[3] The love of a pastoral ministry, which Seymour combined with his zest for learning, was evident in his long service as chaplain at the House of Mercy, a girls' reformatory in New York City.

An enthusiastic and stimulating teacher, Dr. Seymour won a large following among the students. Perhaps some of his popularity was due to the fact that as a bachelor he shared their daily life more fully than either Seabury or Johnson, the other resident professors. Certainly the students appreciated his indefatigable efforts to improve conditions of daily life in the Seminary community. Dr. Seymour had his faults. He bridled under criticism and often took offense where none was intended. His provocative defense of his own convictions was not always marked by charity, nor was his partisan activity wholly free from intrigue. Yet these are perhaps understandable characteristics in a man who suffered much at the hands

2. An attempt was made to persuade Bishop Whittingham to return to the Seminary. He was elected as Mahan's successor in 1864, but he felt constrained to decline.

3. Potter to Whittingham, November 3, 1864, Md. Dio. Ms.

of opponents who did not hesitate to spread baseless rumors about him.[4] Dr. Seymour was not intolerant. He honestly believed that the General Seminary should welcome candidates from every diocese, and he was willing to respect all views "within the limits which the Church allows as to doctrine and practice." He was in entire agreement with a remark he quoted from Bishop Burgess concerning the Seminary's influence:

> I hope that my young friends . . . will come out with Church views in harmony with my own; but I want them to understand themselves, and to be clear and free for just and manly decision.[5]

What aroused Seymour's anger was the attempt to exclude his own Anglo-Catholic views from "within the limits which the Church allows." Once, however, he had won a victory for a comprehensiveness that included his own position, he readily accorded to others the same toleration he expected to receive. He had no hesitancy, for example, in extending a cordial invitation to prominent Evangelical clergymen to join those who gave occasional lectures to the students in Chelsea Square.

Assuming the responsibilities of the rotating deanship in his first year, Professor Seymour at once began his improvement of the students' community life. He revived the commons, establishing a refectory in the basement floor of the East Building. The dining room was refurbished, and the basement rebuilt to provide adequate Matron's quarters, storage cellars, and the building's water closet and bathroom.[6] Known as the "Boarding Club," the refectory offered food at $4 per week to students who wished to find meals somewhat more cheaply than they could be had in neighboring boarding houses. The majority of students ate together in the new commons, assisted by the generosity of the Society for Promoting Religion and Learning, which not only paid from six to seven thousand dollars a year for students' refectory charges, but also stood the cost of re-

4. Seymour to Whittingham, November 21, 1864; December 6, 1864, Md. Dio. Ms.
5. Tr P, June 24, 1875 (IV, 730).
6. See the Minute Book of the Committee of Supplies and Repairs 1867-1883, G.T.S. Library.

fitting the kitchen with new appliances. Four dollars a week seems a small charge, but Park & Tilford supplied groceries at wholesale prices, and these were the days when potatoes cost $6 a barrel and apples $3.50, while steak was had at 18 cents a pound and stew beef at 12 cents. Milk appears in the kitchen book at 6 cents a quart, eggs at 26 cents a dozen. Dr. Seymour was proud of his refectory. "The viands," he reported,

> are abundant in quantity and of the best quality, and under the able management of the excellent Janitor and his wife, are admirably prepared and served. In large and expensive boarding houses . . . greater variety would be found on the table, but . . . in the substantial articles of diet which the Seminary Refectory furnishes its guests, it need fear comparison with no competitor.[7]

Seymour personally raised considerable sums of money to make other domestic improvements for the comfort and convenience of the students, including structural alterations in the double bedrooms of the East Building which eliminated the elongated airless cells that had been designed as sleeping quarters. His interests naturally extended to the chapel and its services. The drab surroundings of the West Building chapel had already been relieved by changes made by Dr. Johnson and Dr. Mahan. By 1858 the room had "a comely altar," and a few years later $500 was raised, mostly through student concerts, to redecorate it throughout. A new carpet was laid, pine seats and kneelers replaced the old benches, and hangings of green velvet, embroidered by the sister of one of the students, added a touch of color. The walls were painted grey and the ceiling given a churchly touch by wooden ribs and bosses. Early in 1864, Dr. Mahan gave public lectures to help raise $850 for a new organ, installed behind a gauze-filled butternut wood screen.

When in 1867, three quarters of the students petitioned for an early Communion every Sunday to supplement the "first Sunday" late celebration, it was clear that Professor Seymour's influence had been felt. He supported the request in the Faculty meeting on Octo-

7. Tr P, June 26, 1873 (IV, 584).

ber 30, and it was carried over Dr. Eigenbrodt's negative vote. Anxious to improve the poor attendance at daily Morning Prayer, Seymour persauded the Faculty to change the hour of the service from 6:30 to 9:00 A.M. The attendance improved markedly, convincing him, as he said to the Trustees, that

> early hours for service as a rule are inconsistent with city habits. Even in secular colleges in the rural districts the custom that almost universally prevailed in former years of hurrying Students from their beds in a condition of mind and body neither fit to appear before God, nor prepared to engage profitably in their religious duties, has been in many instances abandoned, as highly pernicious in its influence upon the spiritual life.[8]

Professor Seabury's ill health and Eigenbrodt's nonresidence left the

8. Tr P, June 27, 1866 (IV, 19).

The West Building in the Last Century

new weekly celebrations to Seymour and Johnson. For a year or so all was quiet, and Professor Johnson could write his old friend and classmate William Shelton:

> In our Seminary we go on in our old traditional way. One of our students bows slightly at the name of the Saviour, as my old English labourers Darby and Gripton did in Indiana . . . We have too little love for our ritual and attendance too slender . . . I think our service would please even Dr. Tyng or Dyer, for simplicity.[9]

By 1869, however, the simplicity had evidently yielded to Seymour's ritualistic influence. In the winter term, the Faculty received a petition, signed by more than half the Seniors, objecting to certain practices which "have been engrafted" onto the Sunday service. The petitioners instanced the celebrant facing the altar for the Ante-communion, the occasional appearance of candles on the Holy Table, and the pause made in the course of the prayer for the Church Militant, "apparently to give opportunity to pray for the dead, thus teaching by example doctrine not taught in the standards of our Church." Rinsing the chalice was said to be made "a ceremony," and objection was raised to the administration of the Sacrament to some students in the mouth instead of upon the hands.[10] The protesting Seniors blamed the professors' example for the habits of some of their fellow students:

> We cannot fail to trace a connection between these practices within the chancel and certain practices which obtain without the chancel rails, frequent crossings, reverences to the altar, eucharistic adoration, standing during the presentation of the alms . . . The oratories and crucifixes with candles, in different rooms, suggest themselves as possibly encouraged by the same departures from the regulated order of the service.[11]

The petition aroused mixed feelings among the Faculty. Obviously Seymour and Johnson had offended, but Seabury and the

9. Johnson Papers, January 12, 1867.
10. G.T.S. Dean's Papers, 1869.
11. Faculty Minutes, February 25, 1869.

others could not bring themselves to express their disapproval of Ritualism by accepting from the students what they regarded as a piece of outrageous impertinence. This aspect of the affair aroused the ire of Dr. Francis Vinton, attending his first Faculty meeting as the newest professor. A year earlier Miss Elizabeth Ludlow had given $25,000 in trust to establish a professorship of Ecclesiastical Polity and Law in memory of her father and mother, and her nomination of Francis Vinton to the chair had been ratified by the Trustees.[12] Upon Vinton's motion—Dr. Eigenbrodt alone dissenting—the Faculty rejected the students' petition as "being both disrespectful towards their Ecclesiastical superiors and inconsistent with their relations as pupils of the Seminary." The issue, however, brought the division among the professors into the open. Dr. Vinton shared with Dr. Seabury the distrust which the new Anglo-Catholicism aroused among the old High Churchmen, and together they ranged themselves against Professor Seymour. Though not an ardent Ritualist, Dr. Johnson was prepared to look with tolerant sympathy upon the changes time had brought. He expressed his convictions on Ritualism to Shelton in one of his revealing letters:

> The puritans saw it in the surplice of old; & even in the academic gown. We do not find the one robe Romanizing;—why should one of our old Anglican robes such as our Martyrs used, be Romanizing now, because revived and restored? And why should the expressed idea "let your lights be burning" involve any objectionable thing . . . it is no more of an innovation to make some such changes *now*, than to make the changes you and I have seen in our day . . .
>
> Why should we, *who have had our day*, now interfere with stern censure upon those who act on our principles and tread in our footsteps? Why should it kill my devotion more to have the choir boys in white, than to have a fashionable choir in gay worldly dress . . . Why should it shock to have a robe for the Eucharist, more than one for the prayers?

12. Tr P, February 3, 1869 (IV, 172). On April 7, the Trustees elected the Reverend William Walton, who had been teaching Hebrew since Dr. Houghton's resignation in 1863, as Clement Clarke Moore Professor of the Hebrew and Greek Languages. Walton died shortly thereafter, and took no significant part in the controversies of these years.

> The great reason of Ritual advance is simply our improved knowledge and culture . . . American Society has gone on handsomely in culture, in architecture, in music, in art, in cultivated tastes. The tide has risen all around us in all institutions, in associations, in homes. Torchlight Ritual is in the political rejoicings, Carols of Children sweetly greet our approval, processions and banners, Christmas trees, and costly fairs, masonic and oddfellow ritual—everywhere beauty and taste are creative. And now when Christ's Church feel the ocean swell, and declines to be bald & cold and inexpressive . . . is it not a mistake to be timid, and more than a mistake to be cruel . . .
>
> You will see that I stand with you on the same high Church principles, which you have ever claimed to be the truth, with old Launcelot Andrewes . . . and with the noble great Anglican Divines of renown. Only I am not so fearful of the things which *they did* and which . . . some earnest minds are now reproducing. Fear not for the Church—Our Lord is in the boat, we are but passengers. Soon I hope to leave the Seminary & have a younger man succeed me.[13]

Johnson's irenic spirit, unfortunately, had little influence upon the actions of the Faculty. He resigned his professorship in 1868, continuing to teach, however, until the Trustees could find a successor. Despite Seymour's pleas, the other professors somewhat ungenerously refused Dr. Johnson a vote in his *emeritus* status.

Professor Vinton could be as explosively choleric as Dr. Seymour. A West Point graduate who had resigned his commission to study law, he entered the Seminary in 1836, and at the time of his election to the new professorship he was an assistant minister of Trinity Parish. Popular among the New York clergy, he had been one of the High Church candidates in 1852 when the diocese chose a "Provisional Bishop" to assume Onderdonk's duties. At that time the Evangelicals feared him even more than they did Dr. Seabury, for while the latter was "stringent in writing," Vinton was "stringent in action."[14] Mr. Strong, who admired him, noted in his *Diary* that had he been elected:

> Vinton would have bred an earthquake in the diocese . . . invaded the next meeting of the Pastoral Aid Society in person, kicked out the

13. Johnson Papers, January 12, 1867.
14. Johnson to Kemper, November 8, 1850, Johnson Papers.

members if necessary with his own episcopal foot energetically applied, locked the door, and carried off the key; would have silenced Tyng and bullied down Anthon, and ruled the flock committed to his keeping with a thick rod of red-hot iron.[15]

Strong was not enthusiastic when Wainwright was elected—"such gentleman-bishops have been and are the bane of the Anglican Churches"—but he admitted that "a milk poultice is better for the diocese than such a mustard plaster as Vinton."[16] At this juncture it might have been better for the Seminary as well, for in the autumn of 1869 the Trustees at long last brought the rotating deanship to an end, electing as the first permanent dean the Reverend John Murray Forbes. It was a sad mistake. A man less able to deal constructively with the rising Ritualism would have been hard to find.

By 1865, the years of discussion of a Pastoral Head or Executive Officer for the Seminary had come to the point of action. A revised constitution, providing among other changes a permanent deanship, was submitted to the General Convention. That body, though favorable to the establishment of such an office, amended the proposed constitution in other respects, and the Trustees refused concurrence.[17] Determined to have a dean, however, the Board provided for the office in a revised set of statutes in 1867. Unable to make the dean a member *ex officio* of the Board of Trustees without constitutional change, they devised the statutory powers they thought necessary to the office. Chapter IV of the new statutes included:

Sec. I. The academic authority of the Institution shall be vested in the Dean and Faculty.

Sec. II. The Dean shall be the chief Executive Officer. He shall be nominated and appointed in the same manner as Professors are nominated and appointed . . . The Dean shall be charged with the general superintendance of the Institution; shall take care that all the

15. *The Diary of George Templeton Strong*, ed. Allan Nevins and Milton Halsey Thomas (New York: Macmillan, 1952), II, 67.
16. *Ibid.*, p. 106.
17. *Journal of General Convention 1865*, pp. 286-302.

Statutes, Rules and Regulations be observed and the Discipline enforced . . . He shall have, under the Standing Committee, the general charge of the Buildings and premises . . .

The Dean shall attend all meetings of the Board of Trustees, and may propose Motions and Resolutions, and take part in all discussions; but shall not be entitled to vote upon any question . . .

Sec. III. The Dean and Professors shall constitute a Faculty . . . to adopt such measures . . . as they may deem expedient for securing the full benefit of the prescribed course of Theological Study . . .

Sec. IV. The Dean shall provide for the public Religious Instruction of the Students. The Professors, in rotation, or in such other order may be arranged by them, shall assist him in the duty of preaching and conducting the services of the Chapel.

Sec. V. During any vacancy, from any cause, the duties of the Dean shall be executed by the Senior Resident Professor.[18]

In June 1869, the choice of the Trustees for the new office was Theodore B. Lyman, Class of 1840, then rector of the American church in Rome and in general charge of the Episcopal chapels in Europe. Lyman declined, however, and was soon to become bishop of North Carolina. On October 12, John Murray Forbes was elected, taking up his duties at once. Forbes was not a universal favorite. Bishop Potter was unenthusiastic about the election, while Dr. Morgan Dix, rector of Trinity Parish and an ardent supporter of the Seminary, was convinced that a blunder had been made. As usual, Professor Johnson tried to find something favorable to report to Bishop Kemper about Dr. Forbes, though he could come up with little more than the observation that "our new Dean . . . seems to have no Romanizing tendencies."[19]

After considerable wrangling, the Standing Committee, with some mystified disappointment that Bishop Potter neither approved their action nor would consent to attend, arranged to install Dr. Forbes in his new office at a solemn service at the Church of the Transfiguration on February 24, 1870. In his address on this occa-

18. Tr P, June 27, 1867 (IV, 98-99).
19. Johnson Papers, January 12, 1870.

sion, Forbes made it abundantly clear that Dr. Johnson had not been guilty of exaggeration. Far from having "Romanizing tendencies," the new Dean regarded the Roman Church as the veritable "Babylon of the Apocalypse," defending Anglicanism in the manner of the older High Churchmen as "the best embodiment of Catholic truth extant."[20] Forbes' words carried weight with his audience, for he was for a time the most eminent convert to Roman Catholicism among the Episcopal clergy.

Then in his sixtieth year, and the one-time popular rector of St. Luke's, Hudson Street, Dean Forbes in the 'forties had been a strong advocate of the teachings of the Oxford *Tracts*. Disheartened by the opposition which Catholic principles encountered among Episcopalians, he joined the Roman Church in 1849, where his theological learning and effective preaching had won him by 1855 a papal doctorate from Pius IX and a conspicuous place among the Roman Catholic clergy of New York. Disenchantment with Rome finally returned him to the Episcopal Church, where he was greeted with the same enthusiastic welcome Roman Catholicism had extended to him ten years earlier. After restoration to the priesthood in 1862, he quietly assisted at his old parish, St. Luke's. A man of commanding presence and immense dignity, much respected for his learning, Dr. Forbes maintained his old-fashioned High Church principles with a doctrinaire inflexibility that was the more rigid for his personal experience of Roman Catholicism. Severe and formal in manner, ever alert for what he considered dangerous innovations in doctrine or practice, Forbes had little capacity to win the affection and confidence of his students, or to understand the spiritual vitality of new movements within the Church's life. These unfortunate limitations were increased by his conviction that the Dean's primary duty was the strict enforcement of discipline, a conclusion that was easily drawn from the wording of the new statutes. "Judging from the reports and discussions in the Board of Trustees," he said,

20. *Proceedings at the Installation of the Reverend John Murray Forbes, D.D.* (New York, 1870), pp. 28-34.

> it would seem to have been a principal design, in creating the office of Dean, to supply this defect . . . For it is a day of general lawlessness and insubordination; and this applies as well to the Church as to the family and the State . . . If, however, there is to be a reform, it must begin in the Church, and if in the Church, where more properly than in the training school of her ministers?[21]

On the evening of Forbes' installation at the Little-Church-around-the-Corner, was it possible that Dr. Houghton looked down from the rector's stall at the faces of the Faculty—Seabury and Vinton welcoming a powerful ally in their defense of the old Anglican citadel against the tide of Ritualism, Johnson betraying his misgivings, Seymour suspecting the worst? Perhaps not, but one likes to think that Houghton gave at least a momentary thought to the Seminary when he announced the selection from the Psalter: "O ever pray for Salem's peace." Chelsea Square was to have no peace for nearly three years.

Johnson and Seymour scarcely knew what to make of a dean who not only had no part in the academic enterprise, but very little share in the Seminary's common life as well. Dean Forbes came over from his house on West Twenty-third Street—he moved in 1871 to East Fifty-fourth Street—for a few hours each day, time mostly spent reprimanding students who had been absent from Seminary exercises or guilty of minor delinquencies. Forbes was a shock to the easy-going community in Chelsea Square. "Regularity in attending Chapel and the recitation room," he reported to the Standing Committee, has been "in a great degree a matter within the discretion of the student." But, he informed them firmly, "a correction has been applied."[22] It had indeed, for attendance improved speedily, but the spirit of the Seminary was unhappy and rebellious. The Dean seldom appeared at chapel services, unless he was scheduled to conduct them—usually twice a week—and his determination to regulate the services "with a single eye to bringing them into conformity with the rubrics of the Prayer Book, the decisions of

21. Tr P, June 30, 1870 (IV, 350).
22. Standing Committee Minutes, February 14, 1870.

the House of Bishops, and the established usages of the Church" aroused a natural resentment. At this very first Faculty meeting, he questioned the frequency of Communion services in the Chapel, and soon discouraged attendance at Sunday's early Eucharist. When Dr. Seabury and Dr. Vinton requested him to abandon the weekly Communion, it was temporarily discontinued.

Dean Forbes would tolerate no sign of Ritualism. Inevitably discovering one manifestation after another of what he termed "lawlessness and insubordination," he became convinced that there were "subtle influences" working against him. Undoubtedly there were. In one famous incident, the revolt of the students was encouraged by Ritualist clergy outside the Seminary. The Dean had placed the Saints' Day celebration of the Holy Communion at a late hour in the morning, only to find that a number of students attended without receiving the Sacrament, a habit which he deplored as conducive to the Catholic practice of offering a solemn noncommunicating Eucharist as an act of worship. When he remonstrated with them, the students contended that their spiritual discipline required fasting communion, and to receive at a late hour imposed a long fast injurious to their health. Dean Forbes was unwise enough to secure the passage of a Faculty regulation requiring every student to be present at celebrations of the Holy Communion unless excused by the Dean. The regulation further specified that those who did not intend to receive the Sacrament should withdraw after the prayer for the Church Militant. Disobedience would be considered a violation of Seminary discipline and treated accordingly.[23] Professor Seymour dissented vehemently from the injunction to withdraw and the threatened consequences of disobedience. Fifteen students replied with a formal declaration of open defiance, reminding the Faculty that they had no power to augment the statutes and still less to create what amounted to a new rubric. There is plenty of evidence that the students were abetted by Ferdinand C. Ewer, rector of St. Ignatius' Church, and John Henry Hopkins, Jr., who,

23. Faculty Minutes, March 21, 1872. The first form of the regulation was even more stringent (Faculty Minutes, January 26, 1872).

with the knowledge of Dr. Seymour if not his active assistance, were glad to strike a blow for an Anglo-Catholic cause.[24] The Faculty was aghast at this "willful insubordination," and the students, in order that their action might be judged on the point at issue and not on their disobedience, withdrew their protest, intending to appeal to the Board of Trustees for the right "to maintain the precious liberty wherewith Christ hath made us free, in this Reformed Branch of His Holy Catholic Church."[25] In the face of an agitation that threatened to involve the bishops and the Trustees, the Faculty on May 23 rescinded their regulation. Dean Forbes, however, would not drop the matter entirely. He offered a resolution requiring students who were "notably absent from the service, or, being present, decline to partake of the Holy Symbols" to satisfy him with an explanation. This Seymour countered with a substitute, affirming that as the reception of the Holy Communion by the students was not a subject for academic discipline and properly belonged to the spiritual and pastoral oversight of the Dean, therefore "it is inexpedient for the Faculty to make Rules and Regulations upon the subject." Dr. Seymour's substitute motion was lost, but as Dean Forbes' injunction proved to be no more than a pastoral exhortation the incident was closed.

That ecclesiastical controversy a century ago often had its melodramatic side is illustrated in another of Dr. Forbes' attempts to curb the Catholic tendencies of his students. In early June 1870, between the last recitations of the term and the annual examination, nine Seniors gathered at the rectory of E. Ferris Bishop, priest-in-charge of the Church of the Nativity in Bridgeport. The occasion was a pre-ordination retreat, conducted by Oliver S. Prescott, formerly a student of the Seminary whom Forbes described as "belonging to some religious Order in England." Prescott was one of the early Cowley Fathers in America, an associate of Charles C. Grafton, founder of the American branch of the Society of St. John the Evangelist and later bishop of Fond du Lac. The appear-

24. G.T.S. Dean's Papers, 1872.
25. Faculty Minutes, April 26, 1872; May 8, 1872.

Photograph by Peter A. Juley & Son

Dean Forbes
Seminary Portrait by
S. E. Dickinson from
an Early Photograph

Dean Seymour
Seminary Portrait

ance of Father Prescott and the students at Bishop's rectory came to the notice of Nathaniel S. Richardson, rector of the nearby St. Paul's Church. He speedily informed Dean Forbes what was afoot, and received from him a message ordering the students back to Chelsea Square at once. Mr. Richardson "sent a trusty man" to deliver the Dean's summons, only to have the door barred to his emissary by Father Prescott. Richardson himself accompanied his "trusty man" in a second attempt to see the students. They gained admission, and after cooling their heels for an hour in the rectory parlor, Richardson was allowed to read the Dean's message to the students. "They received it," he wrote Forbes, "in a manner which I was sorry to witness."[26] The students returned to the Seminary to meet the censure of the Dean and the Faculty, only to discover to their dismay that their bishops had been informed that they had

26. Standing Committee Minutes, June 13, 1870.

absented themselves from the Seminary in violation of the statutes. The students apologized and were forgiven. The real offense in Dean Forbes' eyes, as Dr. Johnson later pointed out, was not that they had left Chelsea Square, a common practice of students in the interim between the last classes and the examination, but that they had associated themselves with two priests who were thought "to be dangerous men, and disloyal to Protestantism."[27]

If the record of churchmanship quarrels in Chelsea Square at this time seems only a tedious list of exaggerated trivialities, such events were, in fact, the absorbing interest of the Episcopal Church in the decade of the 'seventies. One more incident must be recounted, for it became a *cause célèbre* that attracted wide attention and in the end was contributory to Dean Forbes' resignation. On March 23, 1870, the Dean laid before the Faculty some extracts from a student sermon that Dr. Eigenbrodt had received. For some time Eigenbrodt had been disturbed by the increasing number of sermons that presented, as he reported,

> exaggerated views of the Holy Sacraments, as if these constituted the whole of Theology and of religion . . . or to represent the use of the sacred Eucharist in particular as the chief end of the whole Christian life.[28]

The statements to which Dean Forbes objected were in a sermon by a Senior from the Diocese of Rhode Island. They appeared to embody the doctrine of transubstantiation, or what the Dean considered a close approximation of it.[29] The most alarming passage ran:

> He humbles Himself to be upon our Altars, to be handled of sinful man. As when in helpless infancy, He submitted to be wrapped in swaddling clothes, and to be treated of men as they would, whether with respect or disrespect, so now in the Blessed Sacrament, wrapped in the fine linen of the Church, or her vesture of wrought gold . . .

27. *Statement of the Rev. Samuel R. Johnson, D.D.* (New York, 1875), p. 19.
28. Tr P, June 29, 1871 (IV, 447).
29. Standing Committee Minutes, April 11, 1870.

they raise Him in their hands, the same sinful hands that raised Him in childhood when men tended the Holy Child Jesus.[30]

When the extracts were read to the professors, Seabury and Vinton proposed a "Resolution of Censure and Reference" by which the sermon would be sent to Bishop Clark of Rhode Island as containing doctrine unauthorized by the standards of the Church. Dr. Seymour, supported by Dr. Eigenbrodt, persuaded the Faculty to delay action for a week to permit more extended discussion. It did little good, however, and Dr. Seabury's motion was again offered on March 31. As the Faculty refused to divide the question, Seymour voted in the negative. He did not thereby mean to endorse all the sentiments of the sermon, but he objected to invoking a bishop's judgment upon a student's orthodoxy. Dr. Johnson agreed with him, but was powerless to support him. At this same meeting, only a few minutes earlier, the Faculty had decided that Dr. Johnson no longer possessed a vote. Professor Seymour tried vainly to put a substitute motion before his colleagues. He made it plain that while he did not personally approve the expressions in the sermon, they were not alleged to be "in conflict with any article of the Dogmatic Faith of the Church, nor in contradiction of any canon or decree of the Six Ecumenical or General Councils." He reminded the professors that the subject was "a point of divinity confessedly obscure, and in respect to which great latitude of opinion has been and is practically allowed in our Communion." He would have no part, furthermore, in putting students on trial as to their orthodoxy "while they are *learners* and not *teachers*, while they are forming and maturing their views, not proclaiming their settled and well-considered opinions."[31] As no one seconded his substitute motion, it failed to be entered upon the minutes. Dr. Seymour was simply recorded, therefore, as having opposed the motion of "Censure and Reference" with no accompanying explanation, a fact which he feared would be misunderstood when the Faculty minutes were open to the inspection of the Trustees at the end of the year. Ac-

30. Faculty Minutes, March 23, 1870.
31. Tr P, June 29, 1870 (IV, 364).

cordingly, he adopted the expedient of attaching his version of the incident, with the text of his substitute motion, to his personal report to the Trustees as Professor of Ecclesiastical History. The Board took little notice of the matter, but the professors were highly incensed to find that Seymour had contrived to put his case upon record in this unilateral fashion.

The Faculty meeting on October 25, 1870, was a stormy one. Seconded by Dr. Vinton, Professor Seabury proposed a resolution criticizing Seymour for distorting by exaggeration their statements about the sermon, and expressing the surprise and grief of the professors that he

> has publicly arrayed himself against them in their endeavor to uphold the discipline of the Seminary and to keep its teaching in harmony with the Bible and the Book of Common Prayer.

They admitted that "the Church undoubtedly allows a liberty of opinion as to the manner in which the Body and Blood of our Lord are present in the Sacrament," yet they could not believe that

> our Lord Himself, in his natural and now glorified body is personally present and united to the consecrated elements so as, for example, to be lifted up, when they are lifted up, and to suffer the indignities which may be offered to them.[32]

The affair had gone far beyond the censure of a student. That aspect of the matter had been settled months before. Dr. Morgan Dix, at the request of Professor Seymour, interceded with Bishop Clark on the student's behalf. The sensible Clark, after a talk with his candidate, decided

> to regard the discourse unguarded and unwise, as it certainly appears to be, rather as a rhetorical effusion than the deliberate expression of a dogmatic opinion.[33]

Seymour smarted under his colleagues' criticisms, and when their resolutions censuring him were not only reported to the Trustees

32. Faculty Minutes, October 25, 1870.
33. *Ibid.*, May 27, 1870.

but also printed in *The Church Journal*, to which Vinton and Seabury were editorial contributors, he regarded it as a public attack upon his integrity and loyalty to the Church's doctrinal standards. The October Trustees meeting was a disorderly session, lasting without a break from two o'clock in the afternoon until nearly eleven at night. Fifteen ballots were required to elect a successor to Dr. Johnson, and between each vote there was noisy and acrimonious debate, Bishop Coxe of Western New York leading Seymour's critics, Dr. Dix marshaling his defenders, while Bishop Whitehouse of Illinois tried vainly to secure adjournment.[34] The upshot was a vote of confidence in the Dean and Faculty.

Dr. Seymour was no man to take quietly what he was now convinced was a damaging attack upon his reputation. Public charges required a public answer. In the following spring, he published a lengthy pamphlet entitled *A Defence of the Professor of Ecclesiastical History against the Assault of the Dean and the Other Professors.* Circulated in the form of an appeal to the Board of Trustees, the tract was an indirect but scathing indictment of Dean Forbes' administration of the Seminary. It caused an immense sensation, bringing more than a hundred trustees to crowd into the West Building's Long Room for a meeting on June 29, 1871, that lasted more than ten hours. They waited impatiently through the routine business, and the excitement began when the Bishop of North Carolina proposed the appointment of a committee to investigate the charges made in Seymour's pamphlet. Dean Forbes' supporters, led by Judge William H. Bell, sprang to his defense, and amid heated arguments the Bishop's motion was tabled. At this moment, Dean Forbes presented his resignation and withdrew from the hall. Seeing this, the Reverend William Rudder forced the issue by moving that "the Board has the fullest confidence in the Dean," a resolution which, if passed, would have had the effect of condemning Sey-

34. The Reverend Philander K. Cady was finally elected at this meeting. Milo Mahan, who had previously been elected, died before he could return to the Seminary. Cady declined his election, and in the following June, the Trustees elected Samuel Buel.

mour's *Defence* and vindicating Dean Forbes without further investigation. Mr. Samuel Huntington of Connecticut quickly rose to move that the proposal of the Bishop of North Carolina be taken from the table for consideration—and pandemonium broke loose. Over the shouts of a half-dozen trustees and the impassioned voice of Judge Bell, Dr. Vinton could be heard moving that the bishops of the Church be asked to make another visitation of the Seminary. At the height of the confusion, Judge Bell, seized with a heart attack, fell dead upon the floor. Stunned into silence, the Trustees knelt in prayer and adjourned. The resignation of the Dean was not acted upon.

The professors were furious at Seymour's pamphlet. Dr. Vinton presented the Faculty with a resolution of their grievances. Professor Seymour had, he asserted, misrepresented his colleagues and defamed them in a publication that was "ungenerous in its insinuations," and as well "a breach of gentlemanly decorum and an offense against official courtesy." He implored "the Professor of Ecclesiastical History to undo, so far as he may, the injury which he has inflicted."[35] Seymour could hardly be expected to vote for Vinton's resolution, especially as it contained an expression of Faculty confidence in the Dean and his administration. The others passed it, and an apparent deadlock had been reached.

Peace was made three months later by the efforts of a committee of bishops, who visited the Seminary for a week to heal the rift in the Faculty. They drew up a formal agreement that was signed by the antagonists, each acknowledging no "intentional wrong or injustice; but of a share in that infirmity of judgment and of temper from which none of us can claim to be exempt."[36] Dean Forbes, Dr. Vinton, and Dr. Seabury solemnly averred that they had not intended to impeach Seymour's conduct or teaching; Dr. Seymour in return withdrew his pamphlet. The controversy was over. John

35. Faculty Minutes, October 5, 1871.
36. Faculty Minutes, February 29, 1872. The bishops were Atkinson of North Carolina, Whitehouse of Illinois, Lay of Easton, Bissell of Vermont, Niles of New Hampshire, and Pinkney, coadjutor of Maryland.

Murray Forbes may have had his failings, but lack of integrity was not one of them. He knew that he could not march with the changes that left the old High Churchmen isolated from the theological and ecclesiastical excitements of the times, nor would he any longer imperil the welfare of the Seminary by attempting to stem them by a discipline men chose to regard as arbitrary. He persisted, therefore, in his determination to resign, and the Trustees accepted his resignation as of November 1872. Dr. Vinton, who had been ill for some months, died on September 29, and Dr. Seabury, less than a fortnight later. As Eigenbrodt declined the request of the Standing Committee that he move into Chelsea Square, Dr. Seymour, the senior resident professor, became dean *ad interim*, a responsibility that he held until elected dean by an overwhelming majority of the Trustees in 1875.

The brief deanship of Dr. Forbes witnessed the only serious attempt to move the General Seminary out of the heart of New York City to a suburban location. The Trustees in 1869, worried lest the increasing expenses of maintenance and city assessments lead to another financial crisis, revived the project of 1859-60 and ordered the possibilities investigated afresh. In January 1870, they were assured that not only had the Seminary a legal right to dispose of its property and move, provided that the institution remained within the Diocese of New York, but also, in the best judgment of the investigating committee, it was financially expedient and desirable to do so. The Standing Committee was authorized to sell or lease the whole, or any portion, of the real estate, the intent being to sell the land west of Tenth Avenue and retain the Seminary Block as an investment.

The committee looked into a number of available sites, either by lease or gift, among them a farm at Throg's Neck, a location between 78th and 79th Streets on the East Side, a tract of land at Croton Falls, and a portion of the Van Cortlandt estate near Kingsbridge. The proposition most attractive to the committee was the offer of a gift of fifty-five acres of wild land on a low bluff in Westchester County near Mamaroneck, between the line of the

New Haven Railroad and Long Island Sound. Either the distant view of the waters of the Sound or the "salubrious atmosphere of the hills and vales of Weschester" was irresistible to the committee, for they recommended its acceptance.[37] The Standing Committee accepted a deed of October 15, 1870, together with its conditions that the property be used solely for the purpose of a theological seminary and that the Trustees erect buildings upon the premises within five years, or, in default of so doing, reconvey the land to its owner.

Financial expediency was not the sole reason some trustees were ready to move the Seminary. Chelsea had long since been engulfed in the expanding sea of traffic and the distracting turmoil of commerce. The arguments advanced a decade earlier came with renewed force to those who saw the Seminary overwhelmed by the

> business part of the City . . . surrounded by dwellings, stores, and manufacturing establishments—passed by steamboats and traversed by railroads, on either side, at all hours of the day and night, amidst the general hum of business—the excitements of pleasure and inducements to idleness.[38]

There were few moments of peace and quiet on Ninth Avenue when to the ceaseless rumble of wagons and rattle of the horse-cars was added the thundering passage of the new elevated trains with their panting locomotives. The elevated was hailed with delight in 1867, for

> by its aid the New-Yorkers fly through the air . . . in comfortable and well-appointed cars. Instead of being whirled through the darkness and monotony and poisonous air of almost continuous tunnels (as in London), the New-Yorkers are borne along, swiftly and comfortably . . . in a fresh and wholesome atmosphere.[39]

By 1873, however, when the elevated line towered over the Ninth Avenue end of the Square, the Trustees could not echo the exuber-

37. See the Report of the Committee on the Removing of the Seminary, Tr P, January 19, 1870 (IV, 278-325).
38. *Ibid.*, September 27, 1859 (III, 295).
39. *King's Handbook of New York City* (Boston, 1894), p. 138.

ance of these sentiments. Instead, they entered a damage suit for encroachment when the supports for a station platform came within a foot of the Seminary's property line.

New York was not only teeming and expanding; it was changing its character as well. The Knickerbocker city of *The Age of Innocence*, where the Newland Archers and the van der Luydens set the tone of society in the staid decorum of the old Academy of Music, was fast becoming the gaudy metropolis of *The Age of the Moguls*, in which the opulent magnificence of the Metropolitan Opera House would provide a gilded setting for Jay Gould, Commodore Vanderbilt, and the new millionaires. New York in the 'seventies was wide open. Jim Fisk, whose Grand Opera House was around the corner from the Seminary at Eighth Avenue and Twenty-third Street, systematically manipulated the finances of the Erie Railroad on his way to the fatal meeting with Edward Stokes and his pistol at the Grand Central Hotel. Boss Tweed and his gang just as systematically looted the city treasury. Newspapers were born and thrived on scandals of every sort, and thousands of citizens followed the latest reports on Victoria Woodhull or Henry Ward Beecher with avidity. New York was no place, thought many, for the pursuit of theological study. The enticing shops of Union Square, the gay theaters and luxurious hotels of Madison Square, Sixth Avenue with its notorious gaslit haunts of vice—all brought blandishments and temptations too close to Chelsea Square for the good of the students. Dean Forbes was sure that the Seminary could never do its work properly until the students could prepare for the ministry in some rural retreat "isolated from the excitement and turmoil of a great city," though equally important to him was the necessity of withdrawing the students "from the distractions of almost every kind of doctrine and every kind of practice to be found in the Church or out of the Church."[40]

Dr. Seymour, as always, disagreed with him emphatically. A retreat to Westchester would be folly. The opportunity for experience in church work was invaluable, to say nothing of the financial

40. Tr P, June 29, 1871 (IV, 441).

assistance students derived therefrom. Seymour had a real zest for the cosmopolitan experience itself. City life "broadens the mind, refines the manners, and elevates the character." He maintained that the great city, where every phase of human life is present, "is to the Seminary a Professorial Chair which teaches much, and of a kind which naught else could supply . . . Never surrender it; it is a grand point; keep it and struggle for it."[41] Fortunately, the Seminary has never surrendered it, and Chelsea Square today offers its students both challenges and advantages that surpass what Dr. Seymour could have imagined nearly a century ago.

The proposal to move the Seminary did not command enough support among the trustees to ensure its success. Dr. Dix headed an influential group determined to keep the institution in Chelsea Square, some of whom shared Mr. Strong's scornful opinion of "a malarious, sequestered bog with a defective title in Westchester County."[42] As a result, efforts to raise the half million dollars necessary to erect buildings on the Mamaroneck propery roused little enthusiasm, and in June 1872, the Trustees, with few regrets, ordered the surrender and reconveyance of the land.

Dr. Seymour's paternal administration brought to the General Seminary a peace and stability it had not known for more than thirty years. Controversy subsided, never again to be felt with the same disruptive intensity. In the new and tranquil atmosphere, Seymour commended the students "for their exemplary behavior, and their industry and attention to their studies." The professors and students alike turned with relief to "the furtherance of the objects for which the institution was organized."[43] The discipline that had troubled Dr. Forbes was no problem to Dean Seymour. He found his duties

> not only pleasant, but delightful. This gratifying result is to be attributed much more to the governed than to the governor. Indeed, but very little government . . . has been needed. The young men have

41. Tr P, June 5, 1878 (V, 161); May 9, 1883 (V, 617-619).
42. *Diary*, IV, 321.
43. Standing Committee Minutes, December 9, 1872; February 10, 1873.

been . . . a law to themselves; a kindly suggestion, a word, a look have been all that was called for, and for the most part not even these were required.[44]

In this idyllic atmosphere, the student body increased in numbers from seventy in 1872 to eighty-six in 1879, Seymour's last year as dean. He continued to be as zealous as ever in improving the fabric and the convenience of life at the Seminary. The buildings were repaired, the grounds made more attractive, and nearly all traces of neglect were removed. Nervous about kerosene lamps "in the use of which young men are proverbially reckless and careless"—it filled him with horror to find the students casually replenishing their lamps while the wicks were still alight—he persuaded the Standing Committee to introduce gas throughout the buildings. One extensive alteration that had been discussed for some years brought notable relief. In the fall of 1873, the library of nearly 15,000 volumes, wretchedly housed in the dark and badly ventilated Large Room of the East Building, was moved to the first floor Seminary Hall or Long Room in the West Building.[45] Mr. Charles C. Haight, son of Professor Haight and later the architect of the Hoffman quadrangles, planned the remodeling of the West Building. The floor of the old chapel above the Long Room was cut away to leave a balcony, reached by an iron stair, around the spacious two-story library chamber. The recitation rooms in the basement were arranged to permit their being opened into each other as an assembly hall, while the top floor, the site of the old gymnasium, was cleared of the partition that had created extra students' rooms in it, and space was provided there for the Seminary's collection of nearly 10,000 tracts and pamphlets.

The former library room in the East Building was refitted as a collegiate chapel, its altar adorned with a cross, candlesticks, and flower vases, and embellished with hangings of the colors of the

44. Tr P, June 26, 1873 (IV, 581).

45. Dr. Johnson had urged this move seven or eight years earlier (Tr P, June 29, 1865 [III, 705-708]). Seymour's alterations were more extensive than those then proposed.

church seasons. A student presented a set of five stoles, the Junior Class gave a new brass bookrest, and with the student lectors now put in cassocks and cottas, the chapel services reflected the dignified and restrained High Church usage of the time. The chapel improvements were made at a total cost of about $9000, and testimony to Dean Seymour's interest is offered by the fact that he personally raised over half that amount. Seymour, of course, revived the early Sunday celebration of the Holy Communion that had been abandoned under his predecessor, adding in 1878 a Eucharist on Thursdays as well. Thus was established the moderate Anglo-Catholic devotional tradition characteristic of the student life of the General Seminary for many years.

Dean Seymour's interest in the intellectual life of his students was as strong as his concern for their spiritual and physical well-being. A firm advocate of high academic standards, he deplored the practice of ordaining candidates inadequately trained and intellectually inferior to the professional men in their parishes. To help meet the needs of individual students, tutors were appointed to the staff to coach men in Greek, Latin, and a knowledge of the English Bible.[46] Outside lecturers were invited to give addresses or brief courses on subjects supplementary to those of the curriculum. Among others, Bishop Huntington of Central New York lectured on preaching, Dr. S. Austen Pearce on music, and Professors Henry Drisler and Charles Short of Columbia on the Septuagint and the Vulgate Bible. When Darwin's *Descent of Man*, published a year before Seymour became acting dean, stirred afresh the conflict that was presumed by some to exist between Genesis and geology, Professor Egleston of Columbia's School of Mines delivered two lectures on the first chapter of Genesis "read in the light supplied by the discoveries and developments of modern science," and "charmingly illustrated by the magic lantern."[47] Seymour resigned his deanship before one of his cherished projects came to fruition. In 1877 he urged the "estab-

46. George W. Douglas in 1876-77, and Edward H. Van Winkle from 1877 to 1880.
47. Tr P, June 5, 1878 (V, 164).

lishment and endowment of a lectureship analogous to the Bampton and the Hulsean foundations in England."[48] Three years later, Mr. George A. Jarvis established an endowment of $10,000 for a lectureship named in honor of his friend and former pastor, Benjamin Henry Paddock of the Class of 1852, then bishop of Massachusetts. The long line of distinguished scholars who have been Paddock Lecturers since 1880 would have delighted Dean Seymour.

The Statutes of 1867, following the agitation for curriculum reform in the early 'sixties, had provided for a revised "Course of Theological Learning" in seven departments, each of which was to be under the care of at least one professor: (1) *Hebrew and Greek Languages*, "comprising the linguistic knowledge necessary to the intelligent study of the Holy Scriptures," and including readings in the Septuagint and Patristic Greek as well as in the Scriptures; (2) *Biblical Learning and the Interpretation of Scripture*, for the historical and exegetical study of "the Sacred Writings in their Original Texts"; (3) *Systematic Divinity and Dogmatic Theology*, including the doctrines of Scripture, the Creeds, and the Sacraments, with special attention to the "defence of the System of Faith and Doctrine of the Protestant Episcopal Church," and knowledge of the doctrines of Rome and classical Protestantism; (4) *Ecclesiastical History*, to be studied in general and also with particular emphasis upon the history of the English Church and the Church in the United States: (5) *Ecclesiastical Polity and Law*, embracing the doctrines of the Church and the ministry as well as the principles of polity and the study of canon law; (6) *Evidences of Revealed Religion*, including Revelation, the evidences of Christianity, science and religion, and moral science in its relation to theology; and (7) *Pastoral Theology*, comprising homiletics, liturgics, religious education, pastoral care, and the "True Principles for Determining Cases of Conscience."[49]

While the resources of the Seminary in 1867 were insufficient to put this admirable scheme into effect, it was printed in the subse-

48. Tr P, May 23, 1877 (V, 102).
49. *Ibid.*, June 26, 1867 (IV, 100-101).

quent catalogues and offered guidelines for the gradual reorganization of the curriculum. In Dean Seymour's administration, further small steps were taken in the shift from the old textbook-oriented curriculum, with its monotonous recitation periods, toward the study of theological subjects by means of lectures and reading. In the catalogues after 1875, for example, the "Scheme of Studies" shows an increasing number of entries of "Lectures by the Professor" in place of a list of set books which were formerly recited upon. Though recitations still predominated, the more modern approach to theological education received an impetus from the capabilities of the new professors. Except for Dr. Eigenbrodt, the entire Faculty changed in the 'seventies, bringing to the Seminary a number of men more nearly professional scholars and teachers than their predecessors.

In 1871 the Reverend Randall Cooke Hall, a graduate in the Class of 1866, who began three years later to teach Walton's Hebrew classes, was made Clement Clarke Moore Professor. Hall, whose *Elements of Hebrew Grammar* later became a useful textbook, remained on the Faculty for twenty-eight years. Like Eigenbrodt, he was nonresident for the whole period of his service. Also living outside the Seminary until 1895 was William Jones Seabury, son of Professor Seabury, who succeeded his father as rector of the Church of the Annunciation. He was elected to Vinton's professorship of Ecclesiastical Polity and Law in 1873. William Seabury was not a professional teacher, and his ancestry was more notable than his scholarship. Great-grandson of the Bishop of Connecticut, he was the fifth and last in the direct line of Seabury clergy. Equipped by an early legal training, he taught canon law faithfully and methodically, but his greatest contributions to the life of the Seminary were made outside the classroom. The very embodiment of dignity and rectitude, possessed of a trenchant wit and a surprising ability to write charming verses, Dr. Seabury remained a professor until his death in 1916, a tenure that lasted nearly forty-four years and made him a living link between the first years of Dean Seymour and the last of Dean Robbins.

The two new resident professors, successors to Johnson and Seabury, were Samuel Buel and Andrew Oliver.[50] Both were experienced teachers. Dr. Buel, a graduate of Williams College, was a professor at the Seabury Divinity School in Faribault, Minnesota, at the time of his election to the chair of Systematic Divinity and Dogmatic Theology in 1871. Magnificently bearded, gaunt in appearance, brusque and austere in manner, Professor Buel was an accomplished lecturer and apparently the leader among his colleagues in adopting lectures in place of some of the recitations, as a method of instruction.[51]

Andrew Oliver—known affectionately to his students as "St. Andrew"—was the son of a professor at Dartmouth College, and came of Loyalist ancestry even more distinguished than that of the Seaburys. His forbears included both the Lieutenant-Governor and the Chief Justice of the Massachusetts Bay Province on the eve of the American Revolution. After graduation from Harvard, he spent some years in the law office of Rufus Choate. Turning to the ministry, he read for orders and began his priesthood in parochial work. Not only a proficient classical scholar but equally learned in Semetic languages, Dr. Oliver published a translation of the Syriac Peshito version of the Psalms in 1861. A few years later, he was made Professor of Greek and Hebrew at St. Stephen's College, and in 1873 became Professor of Biblical Learning in the Seminary, remaining on the Faculty until his death twenty-four years later. Extremely reserved, pessimistic in temperament, Dr. Oliver was endowed with a modest simplicity and a gracious manner. His strong Catholic convictions won Morgan Dix's unqualified approval, and his disciplined devotional life made him the spiritual guide of successive generations of students. Here was Seymour's Faculty—Hall, William Seabury, Buel, Oliver, and Dr. Eigenbrodt. With the addi-

50. The fact that the salaries of the resident professors were still only $2000 and a house was severely criticized in *The Church Journal*, December 26, 1872. Buel took up his residence in Johnson's quarters in the East Building, while Oliver moved into Seabury's house in the West Building.

51. After his retirement, Dr. Buel published his lectures in two volumes under the title *A Treatise of Dogmatic Theology* (New York, 1890).

tion of Thomas Richey, who became Professor of Ecclesiastical History when Dean Seymour resigned, they remained Dean Hoffman's professors for many years.

Dean Seymour had the privilege of conferring the Seminary's first degree in theology. The question of granting degrees had been raised in the Trustees forty years earlier, but despite occasional discussions, it was not until 1869 that the Standing Committee secured authority to grant degrees from the New York legislature. In 1875, a statute was enacted, largely the work of Dean Seymour and Dr. Dix, under which what were called "honorary degrees" might be conferred. The phrase meant "honors degrees," to be awarded to men whose academic achievement was of superior quality, shown either throughout their Seminary course or by a degree examination or the submission of a dissertation. The first form of the statute provided for masters' degrees, as well as bachelors' and doctors', but this provision was dropped from the amended statute of 1876. Degrees of Bachelor of Sacred Theology were to be awarded graduating Seniors, after they had been ordained priests, whose proficiency in scholarship merited the honor. In 1876 the Faculty voted to recommend ten men for the degree out of the graduating class of twenty-five, and thus began the custom familiar at the General Seminary for over seventy-five years whereby all graduates received Testimonials or Diplomas and certain of them returned as priests the following year to receive their degrees. The statute provided that the S.T.B. degree might be conferred upon an alumnus, or any other priest who was a graduate of a seminary, who successfully sustained an examination in the major theological disciplines.

The doctor's degree was to be granted to applicants who, after twelve years in the priesthood as Masters of Arts or Bachelors of Theology, gave evidence of their intellectual attainments by submitting an original essay, written in Latin or Greek, upon some theological subject, and sustaining a searching examination.[52] In 1878 the Trustees turned down a proposal that the doctoral dissertation

52. The first S.T.D. degree was awarded in 1881 to Charles Theodore Seibt of the class of 1863. He later became Professor of Moral Theology.

might be written in English. A committee reported against the change, deploring any relaxation in the standards of learning for the S.T.D. degree. Opposing the "reckless" granting of degrees, they pointed out how "deeply this vice has infected the clergy . . . every sixth Ecclesiastic in our Church has a degree of Doctor of Divinity or Doctor of Laws."[53]

The first S.T.B. degree was awarded in 1876 to Alfred Evan Johnson of the Class of 1874 who had presented himself for examination.[54] Commencement that year was held in Trinity Chapel, Bishop Clark of Rhode Island presiding. Dean Seymour conferred the degree with an appropriate Latin formula, and the festivities of the day closed with the planting of the "Class Ivy" under the windows of the East Building chapel. It was the last morning commencement with the full services of the Church as started by Bishop Onderdonk in 1843. In the next year, a new order of the final exercises was introduced in which the Holy Communion was celebrated for the Seminary community on commencement morning, coinciding in Dean Seymour's alteration of the Seminary calendar with the Whitsun Embertide. That evening, in a neighboring church, the academic ceremonies were held, including a revival of the Seminary's original commencement custom of essays read by members of the graduating class, though now limited to two or three. With a baccalaureate sermon on the previous Sunday evening, this remained the pattern of the commencement exercises until after the years of Dean Hoffman.

53. Tr P, June 5, 1878 (V, 187-189). In 1900 the requirements of an essay in the Latin or Greek language and of twelve years in the priesthood were dropped.

54. The letters S.T.B. designated the degrees until the *Catalogue* of 1885-86, when they were altered to B.D. At the same time D.D. was substituted for S.T.D. The change back to the original letters was not made until Dean Fosbroke's administration.

9
Our Most Munificent Benefactor

The troubles that beset the community in Chelsea Square before and after the Civil War had little effect upon the capacity of the Seminary to develop the potential for devoted leadership possessed by a large number of its students. Dr. Johnson's infectious enthusiasm for the Church's missionary opportunities, reinforced by the priestly ideals inculcated by Dean Seymour, turned many men toward a ministry in the Far West. One of the heroic pages of alumni history in the story of the General Seminary is that which records the labors of its graduates beyond the Mississippi during these years. The list of the Seminary's missionary bishops over the mid-century decades is a long one—William Kip in California, Ozi Whitaker in Arizona and Nevada, George Randall and John Spalding in Colorado, Daniel Sylvester Tuttle in Montana, Idaho, and Utah, Benjamin Morris in Washington and Oregon, Charles Robertson in Missouri, Thomas Vail in Kansas—these and others were accompanied by graduates who willingly embraced the hardships and discouragements that attended the gradual establishment of the Church in the prairie and mountain states. Eastward, in the Old West of Chase and Kemper, the task of building upon earlier foundations occupied a still larger number of alumni, among whose leaders were Henry Whitehouse in Illinois, William Armitage in Wisconsin, George Gillespie in western Michigan, and John Henry Hobart

Brown in Fond du Lac. When the diocese of Illinois was divided in 1877, Alexander Burgess of the Class of 1841 became bishop of Quincy, while the southern diocese of Springfield elected George Seymour its first bishop.[1]

Announcing his resignation to the Trustees in June 1878, Seymour offered to stay until the cumbersome statutory machinery for the election of a new dean could provide his successor. Accordingly, it was arranged for him to remain until the close of the academic year 1878-79. Though Dr. Seymour found the attractions of the episcopate irresistible, he was genuinely sorry to leave Chelsea Square. With all his zealous and sometimes tendentious partisanship, he had nevertheless seen the end of a period of disruptive controversy and had prepared the way for a successor who was to change the face of Chelsea Square and impart to the Seminary much of the character it possessed until very recent years.

On October 23, 1878, Eugene Augustus Hoffman was elected dean. The forty-nine-year-old rector of St. Mark's Church, Philadelphia, he had been successively rector of Christ Church, Elizabeth, and St. Mary's, Burlington, both in New Jersey, and Grace Church, Brooklyn. Dr. Hoffman was no stranger to the trustees who elected him. A graduate in the Class of 1851, after taking degrees at both Rutgers and Harvard, he had been in close contact with the Seminary throughout his twenty-seven years as a parish priest. A member of the Board of Trustees, he was on the Standing Committee before his move to Philadelphia, while his father, Mr. Samuel Verplanck Hoffman, was an active member of that committee from 1868 until his death in 1880. Nor was the new dean a stranger to New York. Family connections allied him with the Van Cortlandts, Verplancks, Storms, and other descendents of the Dutch and Huguenot clans of old New York, and the wealth and business of the Hoffmans linked him in friendship with a number of the city's affluent and influential merchants and bankers.

1. In 1874 Seymour was chosen to succeed Whitehouse in Illinois, but the strongly anti-Ritualist House of Deputies refused to confirm the election. Four years later, so rapidly had the Ritualist controversy subsided, consents to his election in Springfield were obtained with no difficulty.

It is hard for the present generation to know Dean Hoffman. His commanding presence and reticent dignity are clear from his portraits. That he possessed that dignity with no trace of pomposity, was decisive but not arbitrary, and firm without being autocratic, at least until his last years, is more difficult to grasp. One guesses rightly at his punctilious and somewhat formal courtesy, but one is likely to miss entirely the geniality and warmth of human affection that made him the best of friends and companions. Perhaps no generation fully understands its grandfathers, and particularly when in revolt against much that characterized a past age. It is often so in Chelsea Square today. The majestic marble staircase in the Hoffman refectory; the ornate Victorian elegance of his chapel, with its carved stalls, towering reredos, and alabaster statues; the professors' houses, designed for gracious living and at least two servants; the formal ceremonies that the Dean devised to mark the Seminary's great occasions—an age that views these as undesirable, even lamentable legacies, finds it hard to picture accurately and sympathetically the quality of the man with whom they were so intimately associated. The shattering effects of two world wars, with the subsequent extensive and revolutionary changes in social and moral values, separate today's generation from what Walter Lord has called "The Good Years." The days when J. P. Morgan took his friends among the bishops to general conventions in private Pullman cars, or when it could be thought a compliment to a successful clergyman to say that he might have made a great bank president are more remote from contemporary imagination than are the Dark Ages. Nor is it easy, in a day when men look to the incorporated foundation as the source of all munificence, to appreciate a Christian devotion that often prompted individual charity and philanthropy on a massive scale.

Dean Hoffman was much like many New Yorkers of his social background and education in the last part of the nineteenth century. He shared their diverse interests and often discriminating taste. Genuinely interested in the fine arts, he was an avid collector of rare books, a generous donor to the Museum of Natural History, of

Dean Hoffman
Seminary Portrait by Eastman Johnson

which he was a Fellow, and an active member of the New-York Historical Society and other similar associations. Frequent travel in Europe widened his cultural horizons and broadened his experience. What marked him off from others of his social circle was his complete devotion to the priesthood. A sturdy High Churchman, his piety was simple and sincere, strongly supported by a personal spiritual discipline that armored him against the blandishments of wealth and influence. Dean Hoffman's life was ruled by an overpowering sense of duty that at times was a hard master, for it did not always allow him to distinguish between matters of great and lesser importance. He never escaped its promptings. The more money he had, the more conscientious his sense of stewardship; the more influential he became, the more heavily the sense of responsibility weighed upon him. He gave himself freely to the Church in many capacities—in the work of the Board of Missions and in the activities of the Society for Promoting Religion and Learning, as chairman of the building committee for the Cathedral of St. John the Divine, as a deputy to five successive general conventions—but none of these obscured his fixed purpose, from first to last, to make the General Theological Seminary a place where men could receive the finest preparation that could be provided for the priesthood of the Church.

In the Seminary's annual Commemoration Service, Eugene Augustus Hoffman is remembered as "our most munificent benefactor."[2] No description could be more appropriate. The achievement of a financial security that approached affluence, the erection of a magnificent set of buildings that embodied all that was at that time most admired in ecclesiastical and collegiate architecture, the ordering of chapel, classroom, and community life so as to frame a context for the training of priests in mind and spirit—these were the aims of Dean Hoffman at the outset of his administration, and his

2. The Commemoration of Benefactors, with a Bidding Prayer including the names of departed founders and benefactors of the Seminary, was first used in 1890 on All Saints' Eve (Tr P, May 19, 1891 [VI, 547-550]). It has been an annual observance ever since.

accomplishments long before the end. So pervasive was his influence and overwhelming his achievements that there is little left in Chelsea Square today to remind men of the Old Seminary before him. One comes upon the grey stone pile of the West Building with mild surprise. It scarcely seems possible that within its walls is the faculty house in which Samuel Turner lived and died.

Today one can still see the Hoffman buildings, read the memorial plaques, gaze at his portraits, hear the music of his chimes above the discordant noise of traffic, or admire the Gutenberg Bible he counted his finest gift to the library, but he is not clothed with flesh and blood until we remember a simpler picture. Students who called at the deanery on a winter's night—he was frequently at home to them after eight o'clock—might find the Dean sitting before a blazing fire, looking over his favorite salmon flies, his collie and Irish setter stretched contentedly beside him. From the time he was eighteen and accompanied Louis Agassiz on an expedition into the forests above Lake Superior to the day of his death, Hoffman loved the woods and the wilderness. Revealing an unsuspected geniality, he would charm his callers with tales of camping and hunting trips, or recreate for them an exhilarating moment on the salmon waters of the Restigouche or the Miramachi. It is no wonder that many men, whether students or professors, friends or potential benefactors of the Seminary, found Dean Hoffman irresistible.

On the day after Bishop Seymour's deanship ended, the Hoffmans moved into a brownstone house at 426 West Twenty-third Street, and the Dean began to formulate his plans for the Seminary's expansion and improvement. He determined at once that financial security had priority over all other objectives, for the fiscal condition of the institution was discouraging, if not actually precarious. At the time the Hoffmans moved to New York, the Finance Committee reported to the Trustees that the Seminary's assets in real estate, comprising the Wharf Block and the thirty-two remaining lots of the Central Block, yielded about $11,000 a year from rents and leases. Invested funds amounted to $124,000, bringing in $7000 annually. A few donations increased the total income to $19,700. The estimated costs of maintenance and operation for 1879-80, however, were almost $25,000, leaving an anticipated deficit of over $5000. Abhoring indebtedness, Dean Hoffman was no man to rest content with deficit financing, particularly when the Seminary's liabilities in the form of endowments for specific purposes totaled nearly $27,000 more than the actual invested funds. Doubtless these were adequately protected by real estate that was optimistically valued at $300,000, but the drift toward a financial disaster similar to that of twenty years earlier was plainly evident.

Enlisting the support of a number of New York's leading clergy and influential laymen, Hoffman launched a campaign to raise at least $250,000 to close the gap between income and expenses and to provide adequate endowment for the professorships and the support of a dean. Invariably the question of moving the Seminary accompanied a threat of financial troubles. Dean Hoffman was firmly convinced that the Seminary belonged in the heart of the city.[3] His appeal for funds was issued over the signatures of Morgan Dix, an intimate and life-long friend, Hemen Dyer, assistant minister at the Church of the Ascension and a prominent Evangelical leader, Henry E. Pierrepont, Elbridge T. Gerry, Cornelius Vanderbilt, and several others.[4] More than $100,000 was raised within a year, despite some echoes of the old Evangelical opposition to the General Seminary as a "stronghold of high churchism."[5]

The Hoffman family led the way in response to the Seminary's needs. The Dean's father, a few months before his death, endowed the Eugene Augustus Hoffman Professorship of Pastoral Theology

3. Standing Committee Minutes, March 22, 1880. See his remarks on this subject, Tr P, May 9, 1883 (V, 578).
4. Tr P, June 1, 1881 (V, 430-432); see *The Churchman,* April 17, 1880.
5. *The Southern Churchman,* May 6, 1880. On June 17, the same paper reported that the Reverend Heber Newton of the Anthon Memorial Church had warned his congregation against supporting an institution in which the doctrines taught were pre-Reformation in character. Four years later, the Seminary was still called "the Seymour Theological Institute" in its columns (*The Southern Churchman,* July 10, 1884).

with a donation of $25,000. Later in the year, the Dean and his brother, the Reverend Charles F. Hoffman, joined with their mother to establish a memorial to Samuel Verplanck Hoffman in the form of an endowment of $50,000 for the support of the deanship. Dean Hoffman's bold appeal for more than a quarter of a million dollars, with its hint that this was only a beginning, attracted wide attention in the city. It was thoroughly consonant with the spirit that prompted great benefactions in the 'eighties, and the New York newspapers, commending his effort, urged wealthy Episcopalians to support him.[6] The large initial gifts of the Hoffmans stimulated the interest and generosity of others, particularly among the Dean's friends, and soon what has been called "the golden stream" began its ever-increasing and seemingly inexhaustible flow into Chelsea Square.

The Dean was blunt with the Trustees concerning their responsibility. In 1882 he warned them that

> if we are to maintain our vantage ground, and enable the Seminary to meet the demands of the Church in our day and generation, not to allude to the future, we must provide large additional endowments, and secure funds to erect buildings adequate to the demands of its growth.

The mere publication of appeals was not enough. He called for "vigorous and systematic action" in which

> no member of the Board, or friend of the Seminary, ought to rest satisfied until sufficient endowment is secured to enable it to command the services of any man in the Church, however limited his private means, for its Professorial work, and until its buildings and appliances are equal to those of any learned Institution in the land.[7]

This was the kind of plain talk that hardheaded men could respect. They were the more willing to respond when it was accompanied by changes in the Seminary's fiscal administration designed to keep the trust funds inviolate and place the financial operations under the

6. *The New York Times*, February 8, 1880; *The Evening Post*, April 9, 1880.
7. Tr P, May 24, 1882 (V, 496-497).

supervision of experienced men. Mr. Vanderbilt joined the Honorable John A. King on the Standing Committee in 1879, securing soon afterwards the election of his friend William Bayard Cutting. One or more of these men, with Dean Hoffman and Woodbury G. Langdon, who succeeded Pierrepont as treasurer in 1883, or Elihu Chauncey, who took that office in 1887, were members of the Finance Committee for many years. More capable hands could hardly have been found to manage the affairs of the Seminary in the decade of the 'eighties. As the Standing Committee also included men like Charles H. Contoit, Elbridge T. Gerry, George A. Jarvis, and John Hobart Warren, it is evident that the advancement of the Seminary's fortunes could have been as easily discussed over lunch in one of New York's clubs as at the meetings in Morgan Dix's vestry room in St. Paul's Chapel.

A comparison of the financial state of the Seminary in 1902, the year of Dean Hoffman's death, with the conditions in 1879, reveals the astounding accomplishment of his twenty-three years in Chelsea Square. The income from the real estate in 1902 was $27,000, considerably more than double its yield in 1879. Endowments had grown from $124,000 to approximately $1,375,000. The deficits had long since vanished, though the operating costs had increased to slightly more than $104,000 a year. A rough breakdown of invested funds shows that whereas in 1879 two professorships were partially endowed with their original sums of $25,000 each, by 1902 three additional chairs and the deanship were fully endowed in a total amount of more than $400,000. These endowments were chiefly due to the generosity of the Hoffmans. The Dean himself added $55,000 to his father's gift for the chair of Pastoral Theology, while the original $50,000 of the Samuel Verplanck Hoffman Foundation was so greatly augmented by the Dean that in 1902 it amounted to more than $161,000. In 1891 Dean Hoffman gave $75,000 for a professorship of the Literature and Interpretation of the New Testament in memory of his mother, Glovina Rossell Hoffman. Two years later, Mrs. Hoffman presented a similar amount, and the chair of Dogmatic Theology was designated the Mary Crooke Hoffman Professorship in her honor.[8] Wise management of these funds rapidly increased each Hoffman professorial endowment to $80,000, the sum considered necessary to endow fully a chair.[9]

Scholarship funds increased on a similar scale. The twenty-four scholarships of 1879 had grown to forty-three in 1902, with a total endowment of about $130,000, approximately double the sum so designated in the earlier year. There were no endowed fellowships when Dean Hoffman came. By 1902, five had been established: the Talman Fellowship in 1881, the three Mayo Fellowships in 1890, and the Eigenbrodt Fellowship in 1894. The endowments of these, together with the Edson Funds, created in 1882 and 1885 for instruction in elocution and church music, were about $113,000.[10] In 1879, endowments that could be used for general purposes consisted of little more than the Charles and Elizabeth Ludlow Fund of $8000. Twenty-three years later, legacies and gifts had increased this sum to well over a half million dollars. Dr. Eigenbrodt's residuary estate, for example, eventually came to more than $250,000. Mr. William H. Vanderbilt left the Seminary $50,000 in 1885, Mr. George A. Jarvis, whose other benefactions were extensive, bequeathed a similar amount in 1894, and Mr. Charles H. Contoit left $137,000 in 1899. Smaller legacies and frequent donations from the Seminary's friends brought the total endowment for general purposes to over $575,000. To complete this summary, it should be noted that in 1902 the Jarvis endowment for the Paddock Lectureship stood at $14,000, while $70,000 had been accumulated in a fund established to provide retirement pensions for the professors. Curi-

8. The words "Systematic Divinity" were dropped from the title in the Statutes of 1893.

9. Dean Hoffman had raised the salaries of the fulltime resident professors until by 1891 they stood at $4000 and a house.

10. The first Edson legacy provided for instruction in elocution "to ensure the reverent, dignified and intelligible reading of the Liturgy of the Church" (Standing Committee Minutes, December 11, 1882). Other Edson Funds provided for instruction in church music "by note (not intoning) by a competent male teacher" (Tr P, June 16, 1886 [VI, 114]).

ously enough, the library endowment in 1902 stood at $6000, exactly the same amount as in 1837.[11]

While a tabulation of these sums shows the striking contrast in the Seminary's finances between the year of Dean Hoffman's arrival and that of his death, it gives no indication of the steady flow of gifts to expand the income for operating costs or immediate special purposes. The Society for Promoting Religion and Learning made regular and sizable grants for scholarship aid and other purposes. Mr. Cornelius Vanderbilt assisted in providing a salary for the elocution instructor, and what amounted to "annual giving," as it is now called, was the habit of many friends of Dean Hoffman and the Seminary, as well as members of the Board of Trustees.

The financial achievement is the more astonishing when one remembers that these figures do not include the money raised and expended on the building program that transformed Chelsea Square. As soon as it was evident that his plea for adequate endowment was arousing an enthusiastic response, the Dean laid before the Standing Committee his plans to secure "buildings and appliances equal to those of any learned Institution in the land." The "grand design," planned for a Seminary of two hundred students by the architect Charles C. Haight, provided for a line of buildings four stories high along the north side of the Square on Twenty-first Street, turning at each end to a range along both Ninth and Tenth Avenues. Within the arms of these buildings, the open south side of the Close on Twentieth Street was to provide space for two separate units of faculty houses, replacing the original East and West Buildings, and designed in size and height to reduce as little as possible the sunny prospect on that side of the Square. The chapel was to be placed at the center of the Twenty-first Street range but at right angles to it, thus dividing the Close into East and West Quadrangles.

11. Dean Hoffman constantly appealed for an increase of the library endowment with no success, though donations were made frequently for the purchase of books. The growth of the library in the Hoffman era was largely due to the generosity of the Society for Promoting Religion and Learning which not only presented such collections as the Migne *Patrologia*, both Latin and Greek, in 1886, but made annual grants for books.

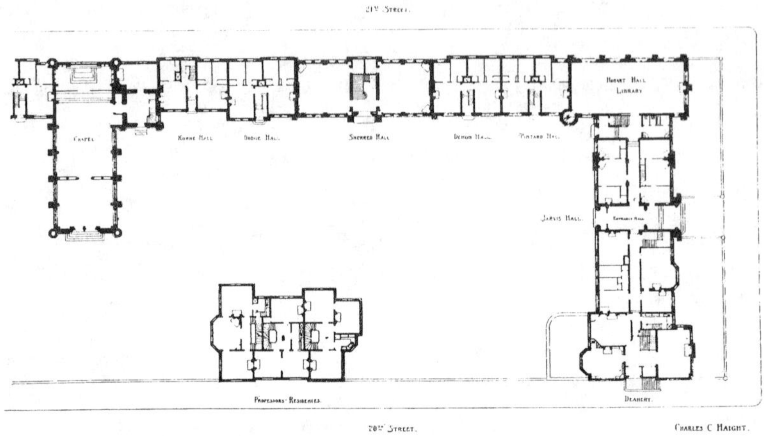

The East Quadrangle

Charles C. Haight's Plan for
the Buildings for the Eastern Half of the Close

The Chapel is at the upper left. Hobart Hall (the Library) is at the upper right, at the corner of Ninth Avenue and Twenty-first Street. Between Hobart Hall and the Deanery (lower right) is Jarvis Hall, with the new main entrance on Ninth Avenue.

An initial anonymous gift of $40,000 inaugurated the building fund, and the Standing Committee authorized work on the new buildings as soon as adequate funds were subscribed or in hand. Dean Hoffman, Dr. Dix, and Dr. Dyer, with Messrs. Pierrepont, Langdon, and Vanderbilt were named a committee of solicitation. The money came in rapidly, over $37,000 being subscribed before a year was out, and work on the East Quadrangle soon began. It was characteristic of Dean Hoffman that he erected first a building designed to implement more effectively the central purpose of the Seminary. The "depressing, stultifying atmosphere" of the basement recitation rooms in the West Building was not only intolerable to him, but in his opinion a serious handicap to the academic enterprise.[12] On May 10, 1883, therefore, the morning of Commence-

12. Tr P, May 28, 1884 (V, 669).

ment, the cornerstone was laid for a spacious classroom building, providing six large lecture rooms and to be named in honor of Jacob Sherred. Despite an early thunderstorm, it was a gala occasion.[13] In the absence of the aging Horatio Potter, Bishop Doane of Albany presided at the ceremonies, while congratulatory addresses were made by Bishop Seymour, the Honorable William M. Evarts, a distinguished lawyer who had been President Hayes' Secretary of State, Henry Codman Potter, then rector of Grace Church and four months later bishop coadjutor of New York. The construction of Sherred Hall was pursued with such dispatch that by January 1884 the new classrooms were ready for use. Today the Sherred lecture rooms appear dingy and antiquated, despite some recent renovations, but in the 'eighties they gave a new lift to the spirits and work of both students and teachers.

In the following May, the cornerstone of a library building was laid at the northeast corner of the Square. Known as Hobart Hall, it was to provide a small gymnasium in the basement, rooms for special collections on the first floor, and a large balconied reading room, three stories high, in which the Seminary's 18,000 volumes could be shelved. By Commencement 1885, not only was the library finished, but work had begun on the two residence halls, named for Theodore Dehon and John Pintard, filling the space between the library and Sherred Hall. Built in the English style of staircase dormitories, with two suites of a study and two bedrooms on each floor, the halls were ready for occupancy by thirty-two students when the new term opened in September. A few weeks later, on November 2, 1885, the whole community watched the ceremony of laying the cornerstone of a deanery at the southeast corner of the Square on Twentieth Street and Ninth Avenue. Eventually the deanery was to be connected with the library by a building containing administration offices, dormitory accommodations, and a main entrance that would reorient the Seminary from Twentieth Street to Ninth Avenue. The total cost of these first buildings was over $180,000, and before the deanery was completed, the Dean's

13. Diaries of Andrew Oliver, May 10, 1883.

mother, Mrs. Samuel Verplanck Hoffman, made her largest benefaction to the Seminary, a gift of the Chapel of the Good Shepherd in memory of her husband. Erected at a cost of $150,000, work was begun on the chapel in 1886. Mrs. Hoffman did not live to see the chapel completed two years later, but in her last months she watched its tower rise above Twenty-first Street from her sitting room in the deanery. The main body of the chapel jutted into the Close, dividing the partially completed East Quadrangle from the lawns and trees that stretched westward to Tenth Avenue. While this construction was in progress, a gift from George A. Jarvis permitted work to start on the Ninth Avenue building between the deanery and Hobart Hall. Named for Mr. Jarvis, more than half its cost of $80,000 was borne by this generous donor to the Seminary. In 1891, three years after the chapel had been completed, two additional residence halls linked it with Sherred Hall. Built at a cost of $46,000, one was named for Frederick Kohne, and the other in grateful recognition of a large legacy in the estate of Mrs. Anson G. P. Dodge, Jr.

Within eight years, the whole East Quadrangle had been finished, with the exception of the unit of professors' houses. When the books of the library were shifted to Hobart Hall during the summer of 1885, the refectory was moved from the basement of the East Building to the former site of the library in the west end of the West Building. With the refectory and old chapel gone, and its students housed in the new residence halls, the original East Building, save for Professor Oliver's house, was virtually deserted. It was closed in the fall of 1890 in preparation for its demolition. After some delays, and despite nostalgic cries from alumni and others to save the historic structure, the Standing Committee authorized its destruction in 1892, perhaps just in time to anticipate its collapse, for in the process of taking it down it was discovered that

> the floor timbers where they entered the stone walls were so badly decayed by dry rot that they could be crumbled with the hands, and it is a wonder that the floors had not fallen when they were in use.[14]

14. Tr P, June 7, 1892 (VI, 665).

However necessary, the leveling of the East Building destroyed a tangible link with the Seminary's first years in Chelsea Square, and those who regretted its disappearance found little consolation in the fact that some of its stonework could still be seen in the sunken laundry yards of the professors' houses that were erected on the site.

To reckon the cost of the East Quadrangle buildings at $350,000 is to omit other thousands spent on interior furnishings, walks, landscaping, and the wrought iron fencing. Further substantial items included Dean Hoffman's gift of a chime of fifteen tubular bells for the chapel tower in 1889, and the massive bronze doors, with their elaborate scenes, under tympana of the Resurrection and surmounted by a large vesica of Christ the Good Shepherd, which were placed in the chapel entrance arch in 1899.[15] Something over $400,000 would be a closer estimate of the amount expended on the first half of Dean Hoffman's "grand design." By the time of the Dean's death, the buildings of the West Quadrangle brought this sum to

15. Designed by J. Massey Rhind, the bronze doors were cast by John Williams of New York. They are a memorial to Eugene Augustus Hoffman, Jr., who died in 1891 at the age of twenty-eight.

The East Quadrangle upon Completion

well over $900,000. The full amount of Hoffman's personal munificence will never be known, for there are many gifts noted as coming "through the Dean" or "from a friend." Such phrases often offered modest concealment of the generosity of Eugene Augustus Hoffman.

The Trustees were dazzled by both the scale upon which the new buildings were conceived and the speed with which Chelsea Square was transformed. A new pride in the Seminary seized upon them, as well as upon the students and professors as year after year they witnessed a ground-breaking or participated in yet one more dedication ceremony. Bishop Potter, with all his resourcefulness, must have been hard put to say something new over the successive cornerstones or at the solemn opening of each building. Such was the enthusiasm of the Trustees that the hall rang with applause when they voted on May 15, 1894, that the style and title of the Dean should hereafter be "The *Very* Reverend Dean of the General Theological Seminary."

Built of brick and Belleville brownstone in a style then known as "English Collegiate Gothic," the buildings of the East Quadrangle excited universal admiration. The influence of the college courts of Cambridge and Oxford is obvious, but eighty years ago this was thought singularly appropriate for an Anglican institution. To his credit, Mr. Haight's designs incorporated a pleasing variety of line and fenestration that successfully avoided the monotonous effect which such a continuous range of massive buildings might have produced. The interiors, spaciously planned, seemed almost palatial to those who had known the inconvenient and cramped conditions in the two original buildings. Hobart, Jarvis, and the Hoffman deanery have now disappeared, replaced in 1961 by the present Ninth Avenue building that houses the same facilities, as well as two faculty apartments. The former Jarvis Hall had considerable character, and the charming vista of the lawns and trees of the Close that opened to visitors through the entrance archway has been copied in the plan of the present building. On the first floor of old Jarvis were the administrative offices, a seminar room, and a reception

The Hoffman Deanery, Looking North along Ninth Avenue

room often used as a students' common room. Inside the main door was an apartment for the mail clerk and porter, much in the fashion of the porter's lodge of an English college. Many former students will recall Ed Boise's cheery greeting from his little door as they passed in or out, or still hear the echoes of his stentorian cry as he shouted down the East Quadrangle through his megaphone for a student wanted on the telephone. Perhaps less nostalgia is evoked by the memory of the old deanery. With its imposing entrance on Twentieth Street, wide halls and enormous rooms, it was a house in the grand manner, more appropriate to the style and means of the Hoffmans than to those of its subsequent occupants. Few will regret its disappearance, though it has sometimes been warmly debated whether or not the stone structure now attached to the Ninth Avenue building as a dean's residence is an aesthetic improvement.

Consecrated on October 23, 1888, by the Presiding Bishop, John

Williams of Connecticut, and taken, according to the Instrument of Donation and Sentence of Consecration "under the spiritual jurisdiction of the Bishops of the Protestant Episcopal Church," the Chapel of the Good Shepherd was the crowning glory of Dean Hoffman's first period of building activity. The tower, rising 161 feet, was plainly inspired by Magdalen Tower in Oxford, while the high interior, with its walls of cream and red brick, arched with chestnut roof beams, is said to recall the chapel of Keble College.[16] The rows of stalls for the professors and students in the long choir were enclosed by a rood screen of quartered oak, surmounted by carved angels and equipped with a pair of ornate bronze gates. The floors of the choir and sanctuary were laid in marble and mosaic, variegated in color and decorated with elaborate interlaced quatrefoils enclosing traditional symbols and the Latin names of Christian virtues. At the east end, broad steps of gray Italian marble led up to the wide altar and intricately carved alabaster reredos, in the nine tall niches of which in 1891 were placed Rhind's marble statues of Moses and John the Baptist, the four Evangelists, St. Peter, St. Paul, and in the center, Jesus the Good Shepherd. The chapel windows, modified from a design originally prepared by John Henry Hopkins, Jr., and made in London by Lavers & Westlake, contain some fine examples of Victorian glass.

With all its elaboration, the Hoffman chapel has a dignity and beauty that is not simply due to its integrity as an architectural period piece. There is an elusive quality in its atmosphere, inseparable perhaps from the prayers and penitance, the praise and thanksgiving, which day after day, year in and year out, have been offered in this place for more than eighty years. Over the stalls around the chapel walls is incised the ordination sentence: ACCIPE SPIRITUM SANCTUM IN OFFICIUM ET OPUS SACERDOTIS IN ECCLESIA DEI . . . It is the reminder that Dean Hoffman never forgot, nor did he wish anyone else to forget, that what is now called "the formation of

16. It was much admired by English visitors; see the comments of Dean Hole, *A Little Tour of America* (New York, 1895), p. 117, on his visit to New York in 1894.

priests" was the central task of the Seminary. To this his chapel stood witness, for as he reminded the Trustees,

> in addition to and far above the education of the library and the lecture room, there is a spiritual preparation needed for the priests of the Church, and which alone can give them, in the judgment of those over whom they shall be set to teach, a moral, as well as an intellectual and official right to be heard. . . . We can scarcely over-estimate the importance of this phase of theological training. It is, as all will admit, more vital than dogmatic and pastoral instruction. Many young men enter the Seminary with devout dispositions, with fervid purpose in their hearts to serve God in His ministry, but often with as ill-defined and hazy views of their own spiritual life, and of the methods and

The Chapel of the Good Shepherd

means of its growth, as they have of the dogmatic doctrines of the faith.[17]

Dean Hoffman was determined, by precept and example, to make the chapel the vital center of the common life of Chelsea Square, and his success in establishing this tradition is where the Seminary's lasting indebtedness to him lies.

Many of the distinctive marks of student life and community custom at the General Seminary owe their origin to regulations or practices introduced by Eugene Hoffman. In the Michaelmas term of 1880, for example, the students were put into academic gowns for recitations and chapel services, a move that had been discussed for several years. In fact, in Dean Seymour's day the students had once petitioned the Faculty to be allowed to wear cassocks in the Close. The professors adopted the practice of wearing gowns at the same time, though Dean Hoffman imposed his preference that members of the Faculty at Evensong in the chapel be arrayed in surplice and black stole or scarf. This led to the custom of opening the sung service each afternoon with the vested Faculty procession that has been familiar for many years. The wearing of academic hoods by the professors naturally followed. Whether in imitation of the practice of Oxford and Cambridge, or because of his almost compulsive desire for orderliness and uniformity, the Dean persuaded the Trustees to confer the S.T.D. degree *ad eundem* upon the professors who, as Dr. Seabury put it, "had been doctored elsewhere."[18] The *ad eundem* degrees were not awarded *honoris causa*, but conferred to admit men to the same status in the General Seminary already possessed by them in another academic society, an idea which owes more to the English concept of the meaning of a degree than to the American view of it as testimony to a man's learning. At commencement in 1885, the doctorate was conferred in this fashion upon Dean Hoffman and Professors Eigenbrodt, Hall, Buel, Sea-

17. Tr P, June 15, 1886 (VI, 129-130).
18. Seabury to Robbins, January 15, 1906, G.T.S. Papers. The Statutes of 1885 made specific provision for conferring the degree "upon the Dean or any Professor of the Seminary."

bury, Oliver, and Richey.[19] The Statutes of 1885 also provided that the Trustees might award the doctor's degree without examination in recognition of "the authorship of some published theological work"—in other words, *honoris causa*, and as well upon any alumnus of the Seminary elected to the episcopate. Ethelbert Talbot of the Class of 1873, who became missionary bishop of Wyoming and Idaho in 1887, was the first to be so honored, establishing the custom familiar to the present day of conferring the honorary degree upon graduates of the Seminary who become bishops.

Dean Hoffman was meticulous in his attention to the details of academic usage. The ceremonies now surrounding the conferring of degrees at commencement derive from those first introduced by him in 1880 and 1881. In the latter year, the Standing Committee authorized the use of new Latin forms prepared by the Faculty for the degree certificates, as well as for graduation diplomas, as the old Testimonials were now called. Hoods appropriate to the degrees were adopted at the same time. Even the seal of the Seminary Corporation was changed, and in place of the Bible, Prayer Book, and mitre of 1823, there appeared an elaborate design consisting of a cross, the four equal arms of which were architecturally treated as crocketted gables, buttressed and pinnacled, containing sunken quatrefoil panels in which were depicted Saints Ambrose, Augustine, Athanasius, and Gregory Nazianzen. The central intersection bore a representation of Christ, and in a circular band around this complicated and busy example of Victorian gothic heraldry ran the Seminary's new motto: SERMO TUUS VERITAS EST.[20]

Dean Hoffman's regulations governing the students were as precise and detailed as those in which he prescribed the daily tasks of the janitor and maintenance staff. Safety probably required that students be prohibited from using "burning fluid" or kerosene in their rooms, or possessing firearms, but an injunction against throw-

19. In later years, *ad eundem* degrees were given to others who joined the Faculty. The custom did not survive Dean Robbins' administration.
20. Tr P, May 31, 1887 (VI, 192). The seal was officially adopted by the Trustees in 1888. It was modified to its present form in 1903.

ing rubbish out the windows only illustrates that the Dean's rules often anticipated the worst. Attendance at recitations was strictly enforced, and students were required to be present at daily Morning and Evening Prayer, reporting their own unavoidable absences to the Dean each month. The Holy Communion was celebrated, as it had been in Dean Seymour's time, at 7:00 A.M. on Sundays and Thursdays, Saints' Days and Holy Days. No requirement was made of attendance, but students were expected to explain any prolonged absence from the Sacrament. The rules were something of a mixed bag. Students were not allowed to marry while members of the Seminary, and though there were few formal regulations governing their general conduct, they were warned that smoking in the Close would be considered "a breach of propriety."[21]

On the whole, the students were seldom disorderly, save for occasional outbursts of complaint against bad cooking and poor service in the refectory, but these ceased when the magnificent new dining hall was erected in the West Quadrangle. Regulations against the use of "wine, beer or other alcoholic drink" at meals doubtless reduced disorder in the old refectory, and in any case the students for some time had the option of patronizing a neighboring boardinghouse. The fact that the refectory was conducted much along boardinghouse lines is clear from the provision whereby students might order "extras" if dissatisfied with the menu. Beefsteak, oysters, ham and eggs, calf's liver and bacon, for example, could be had in 1893 for an additional 25 cents, while cold meats, scrambled eggs or omelettes, or a side order of fried potatoes cost even less.

The Dean's rules were accompanied by "recommendations." Students were advised to rise at 6:30 A.M. and retire by 11:00 P.M., being careful to secure at least an hour's exercise daily in the open air. They were reminded to keep their rooms cool and airy, and even to be sure to send their clothes to the wash once a week. The

21. *Digest of the Rules and Regulations . . . Relating to Students* (New York, 1893), p. 17. The regulations of 1893 did not differ materially from those adopted by the Faculty, at the Dean's suggestion, on September 7, 1880. Student marriage was prohibited by the statutes enacted by the Trustees in 1885.

"recommendations" of the methodical Hoffman bear considerable resemblance to his own strict regimen as a seminarian thirty years before, when he trained himself to rise at 5:00 A.M. for an hour of prayer and Bible reading before breakfast, to prescribe carefully daily hours for study, exercise, and recreation, and to save time before retiring at 10:00 P.M. for his devotions.[22] *Bene orare est bene studuisse* was a favorite maxim of Hoffman, and he constantly emphasized the necessity of the steady cultivation of the spiritual life. "Theological learning," he reminded the students, "unless accompanied with real piety, is not a sufficient qualification for the Sacred Ministry."[23] Encouragement to spiritual growth was given by frequent addresses on the inner life of prayer, perhaps the most notable being those of Frederick Dan Huntington, bishop of Central New York, informal devotional meetings of students, and the introduction of an annual Lenten Quiet Day, the first one being conducted by Henry Codman Potter in 1887.

As might be expected, the enrollment increased during the Hoffman era. In the 'eighties, the average number of students was between 80 and 90, but by the academic year 1890-91, there were 116 students, and thereafter between 130 and 150. Moreover, the proportion of students from the New York dioceses declined significantly, from about one third in the Dean's early years to one fifth or less in his later years. Twenty-five dioceses were represented in the student body in 1879-80; forty dioceses in 1899-1900. Some of the increase in numbers was due to Dean Hoffman's insistence that the Seminary admit as Special Students men who were not prepared to embark upon the full prescribed course. He had no desire to lower the standards for admission to the regular classes. On the contrary, he agreed with Dr. Samuel Eliot that a proper admissions policy should include

> a scrutiny, and a close one, conducted by the Dean or the Faculty of the School, and as decisive in refusing an unworthy candidate as in welcoming a worthy one. Our schools owe it to themselves, as well as

22. E. A. H. Journals and Papers (Transcription, G.T.S. Library), p. 107.
23. *Digest*, p. 3.

to the Church, to hang a portcullis over their gates, and to be firm about letting it down.[24]

The admission of Special Students was a separate issue. Many such men, he was convinced, would

> pursue their studies in private, with such assistance as they can secure from some already overworked Parish Priest or clerical friend . . . we must make some provision in connection with our present course, by which those of the class referred to who are found incompetent to enter upon the regular course of instruction, but who evince a desire and ability to prepare for it, shall, under the care of the Faculty for six months or a year, be trained in proper habits of study.[25]

It was one of the few desires of Dean Hoffman to which the Trustees did not accede at once. Four years later, in 1884, he repeated his plea with greater emphasis, recalling the frequent occasions over the years when committees of the Trustees had urged this step. He argued with considerable cogency that it would not only benefit men who had limited ability or opportunity to prepare for holy orders but also free the Faculty from "the temptation, which now besets us, to lower our standard, lest we should lose worthy candidates who from various causes cannot conform to it."[26] The Trustees finally agreed, and provision was made in the Statutes of 1885 for the admission of Special Students who might receive a certificate for studies successfully completed under the direction of the Faculty.

Dean Hoffman established a Seminary bursary, and the first charges laid upon the students, except for the costs of Seymour's "Boarding Club," were instituted in 1881. Thirty dollars a year was charged for rooms, including fuel and light. Four years later, it was raised to $40 for accommodations in the old buildings and $60 for rooms in the new Pintard or Dehon Halls. While there was no tuition fee, in the academic year 1886-87 a charge of $225 was established for all students living within the Close, covering board as well

24. Tr P, May 24, 1882 (V, 490).
25. *Ibid.*, May 12, 1880 (V, 304-305).
26. *Ibid.*, May 28, 1884 (V, 675).

as room, though for a few years thereafter, as long as eating in the refectory remained optional, a substantial deduction was allowed to those who continued to patronize boardinghouses. Students who lived outside—and a few lived at home—were charged $25 annually. Throughout Dean Hoffman's years, save for a degree fee which began at $10 in 1889, these remained the fixed charges of the Seminary.

The Dean's ability to impress his mark upon every aspect of life within Chelsea Square was immensely strengthened by changes in the structure of Seminary authority. At long last, for example, the character and size of the Board of Trustees was significantly altered. In 1883 a committee under the chairmanship of Morgan Dix proposed amendments to the constitution that would reduce the unwieldy Board to a reasonable number of members who might be expected to take an active interest in Seminary affairs. After considerable discussion and an unsuccessful attempt to add alumni representation, the Trustees approved changes that reduced their number to the dean of the Seminary *ex officio*, every bishop who signified his willingness to serve, and 50 clerical and lay members. Of the latter, 25 were to be elected by the House of Deputies at each General Convention, and 25 chosen by certain dioceses on the basis of their former contributions to the Seminary.[27] The Convention of 1883 accepted the amendment, to become effective on October 1, 1884. The bishops on the Board dropped from 69 to the 41 who accepted positions, while the clerical and lay members were reduced from 396 to 51.[28] This welcome solution to what had become a vex-

27. Tr P, May 9, 1883 (V, 602-604). Diocesan distribution was as follows: New York, 10; Western New York, 1; Long Island, 2; Albany, 1; Central New York, 1; New Jersey, 1; Northern New Jersey, 1; Massachusetts, 1; Pennsylvania, 3; Maryland, 1; North Carolina, 1; South Carolina, 2 (*Journal of General Convention 1883*, pp. 533-535).

28. In 1913 the Board was reduced to its present composition of 42 members: the Presiding Bishop, the Bishop of New York (i.e., the diocese in which the seminary is located), and the Dean, all *ex officio;* 10 bishops, 10 priests, and 10 laymen, elected by General Convention for six-year terms; and 3 bishops, 3 priests, and 3 laymen, elected by the alumni for three-year terms. All other bishops have seat and voice without vote at Trustees' meetings.

ing problem was followed in 1885 by the thorough revision of the statutes to which reference has already been made. The most significant changes in the statutes, however, were those that defined and expanded the authority of the dean, chiefly at the expense of powers hitherto exercised by the Faculty as a whole.

The Statutes of 1867, under which Dr. Forbes had become the first permanent dean, associated the dean with the professors as "the academic authority of the Institution." With a special responsibility for the enforcement of disciplinary regulations, the dean was, in effect, the chairman or "chief Executive officer" of a faculty corporately entrusted with the governance of the internal life of the Seminary. This was not Eugene Hoffman's idea of the kind of authority appropriate to the deanship or necessary to achieve his purposes. In the revised Statutes, therefore, though the dean and professors still "constituted a Faculty" with powers to adopt measures "for securing the full benefit of the prescribed course of Theological Study and the due exercise of Discipline," the disappearance of the phrase "the academic authority" left wider scope for the interpretation of the dean's responsibility for "the general superintendance of the Institution." Numerous additional provisions clarified his extended authority. The dean alone was entrusted with the pastoral care of the students and complete charge of the chapel and its services. Professors were required to report marks and absences to him monthly, and no class or recitation might be excused, or visitor invited to address the students, without his permission. The old provision by which the duties of the dean were automatically assumed by the senior resident professor in the event of disability or a vacancy in the deanship was dropped. In such case, the Statutes of 1885 gave the Standing Committee power to designate a resident professor to assume the decanal responsibilities.[29] Professors were excluded from membership on the Board of Trustees, an eminently

29. In 1888 the office of sub-dean was established, held by a member of the Faculty elected annually by the Standing Committee, and on whom the powers of the dean would devolve in the case of sickness, absence, or a vacancy in the office. Professor Oliver was the first sub-dean.

sensible provision, but one which terminated a practice that had been common since the foundation of the Seminary. The new provision that aroused the strongest feelings, however, and made clear the virtually absolute authority of the dean, was that "the concurrence of the Dean shall be necessary to every act of the Faculty."[30] This was the famous "veto power" which a minority of the professors at once vehemently protested, and which subsequently has occasionally provoked feelings of frustration among members of the Faculty. Professor Seabury, with more than a touch of the forthrightness of his father, presented to the Faculty a memorial of vigorous opposition to a regulation which, he contended, "reduced the Professors to the position of instructors in the lecture room and ciphers at the Council Board." As he was supported only by Professor Richey and a majority of his colleagues voted down his motion, the protest was never presented to the Board of Trustees in official form.[31]

It is unfortunate that Dean Hoffman's unremitting labors for the improvement of the Seminary stopped short of the development of its intellectual life. He insisted upon the maintenance of high standards of academic work, believing that the General Seminary had

> not only the duty but the peculiar mission . . . by example and influence, to enlarge and lift the standard of clerical education throughout our whole country.[32]

High standards were maintained—an average grade of 90, for example, was required for the degree—but they were standards of accomplishment within the narrow limits of a rigidly prescribed curriculum. Except for the meager results of the agitation in 1857, the course of study had not changed substantially since the days when the Seminary first moved to Chelsea Square. Despite the cau-

30. *Constitution and Statutes* (New York, 1885), p. 21. The provisions defining the relation of the Dean to the Faculty are still part of the Seminary Statutes.
31. Faculty Minutes, May 7, 1885. Seabury's strong convictions were expressed in his *Statement in Regard to the Position of the Faculty, etc.*, printed after Dean Hoffman's death in 1902; see pp. 32 ff.
32. Tr P, May 12, 1880 (V, 304).

tious experiments of Dr. Turner and Dr. Buel, and a few changes in Seymour's time in the direction of more lectures, recitations still predominated in the classroom exercises. Hoffman was aware that the intellectual climate of the nineteenth century had changed markedly. He informed the Trustees that

> the steady development of Theological science, the progress in the cultivation of special departments, the marked advance in general culture, the great increase in the demands made upon the ministry at home and abroad, the changed conditions of pastoral work incident to the rise of large cities and the rapid development of the country, the new and strange problems continually rising which have to be met and solved, the bolder attitude which unbelief and infidelity are constantly assuming, seem imperatively to require that the studies of the Seminary course should be supplemented and enlarged.[33]

Just as one begins to believe that he is about to grasp the nettle, the Dean proposes to supplement the undergraduate course along the same lines Professor Mahan suggested thirty-five years before. He would invite guest lecturers to address the students on special topics, and introduce a fourth-year Post-Graduate Course for those able to undertake more extended study. The Post-Graduate Course was instituted in 1883, though it seldom attracted more than four or five students, while the Dean's lecturers on such topics as the Septuagint Version, the Vulgate Translation, Science and Religion, Skepticism and Belief, Dogma and Doubt, Church Architecture, Music, Dante, and the Laws of Hygiene scarcely satisfied the students' craving to share the contemporary intellectual excitements. Even the Paddock Lectures in the 'eighties, despite the opportunity offered by their more substantial courses of lectures, did not wrestle with the problems that stirred the world of biblical and theological scholarship.

Scholarship in England had felt the impact of the critical and historical work of the Germans, particularly in Old Testament studies. Wellhausen's thesis of 1878 appeared in an English edition in 1885. W. Robertson Smith at Aberdeen and Professor S. R. Driver, Pusey's

33. Tr P, May 9, 1883 (V, 576).

successor at Oxford, were influential in furthering new and challenging theories. Lightfoot's commentaries led the way to a fresh approach to New Testament studies; Westcott and Hort produced their text in 1881. Excitement of this kind in Cambridge was matched in Oxford by the effect of the work of Hatch and Sanday. On the Anglican theological side, exploration into the relation of the traditional faith to the knowledge and thought patterns of the late nineteenth century came to a head in 1889 with the publication of the essays of *Lux Mundi*, a landmark in the history of the intellectual life of the Oxford Movement.

The classrooms of Chelsea Square were virtually untouched by this ferment. They were, however, not so distant from some centers of the revolution in theological thought as to leave the students ignorant. At the Episcopal Theological School, Professors Steenstra, Henry Sylvester Nash, and A. V. G. Allen were attracting wide attention, and considerable conservative disapproval, by their willingness to make the disturbing critical and historical studies a vital part of their intellectual activity. Cambridge under Dean William Lawrence had a faculty of enthusiastic young scholars, or at least young as far as seminary professors went in those days, the oldest being no more than fifty-six and the average age under forty. Moreover, they were as freely adopting changes in methods of teaching as they were embracing the challenges of the new scholarship. They were convinced that

> the instructor's work is not the hearing of lessons so much as the inspiring and guiding the students to thought and research.[34]

Exposed to the intellectual atmosphere of the Episcopal Theological School while on a brief visit, Franklin Spencer Spalding of the Class of 1891, wrote after his return to Chelsea Square:

> The fellowship between faculty and students at Cambridge is wonderful. Silver took me into Professor Kellner's room and I talked to

34. Quoted in James Arthur Muller, *The Episcopal Theological School, 1867-1943* (Cambridge, 1943), p. 76.

SCHEME OF STUDY.

Year.	Hebrew and Greek.	Exegesis.	Eccles. History.	Systematic Divinity.	Pastoral Theology.	Eccles. Polity and Law.	Evidences of Revealed Religion.
Junior.	Tregelles' Heads of Hebrew Grammar. Readings from the Pentateuch and the Psalms. Gesenius' Hebrew Lexicon. Readings from the Septuagint.	The Four Gospels and the Acts of the Apostles. Gardiner's Harmony of the Gospels.	First Six Centuries: Mahan, Blunt, Burton and Robertson's Church Histories. Bates' Lectures on Christian Antiquities. Mosheim's Commentaries.	Theophilus Americanus. Lectures by the Professor.	Gresley's Ecclesiastes Anglicanus, Amer. edit. Brooks' Lectures on Preaching. Bishop Ellicott's Collections on Homiletics. Lectures on Homiletics, by the Professor. Four Sermons by each student.		Butler's Analogy and Sermons at the Rolls, with Lectures by the Professor. The Foundation of Ethics, as exhibited in Porter's Elements of Moral Science, with Lectures by the Professor.
Middle.	Readings from the Messianic Psalms, and Extracts from the Prophets. Gesenius' Hebrew Lexicon.	The Epistles of St. Paul, with Ellicott's and Lightfoot's Commentaries.	Seventh to Fifteenth Centuries, inclusive. Hammond on the Canons. Newman's History of the Arians. Hardwick's Middle Ages. Robertson's Church History, 3d ed. Milman's Latin Christianity.	Pearson on the Creed. Hooker on the Incarnation.	Blunt's Parish Priest. Bishop Burnet on Pastoral Care. Bishops White and Wilberforce on the Ordinal. Bishop Ellicott's Collections on Pastoral Work. Lectures on Pastoral Duties, by the Professor. Five Sermons by each student.	Abp. Potter on Church Government. Wordsworth's Outlines of the Christian Ministry. Lectures by the Professor.	Theism and Anti-Theism; Semi-weekly Lectures by the Professor. Christian Ethics, with Lectures by the Professor.
Senior.		Christological portions of the Old Testament in Hebrew, with Commentaries.	Sixteenth Century to present time. Hardwick's Reformation. Burnet's History of the English Reformation. Carwithen's and Perry's Histories of the English Church. Perry's and Wilberforce's Histories of the American Church.	Bishop Browne on the Thirty-nine Articles.	Wheatly and Procter on the Book of Common Prayer. Hooker's Eccles. Polity, Book v. Lectures on Liturgics and Pastoral Work, Conscience and Human Law, by the Professor. Six Sermons by each student.	Haddan's Apostolical Succession. Canons and other Ecclesiastical Laws. Lectures by the Professor, with Exercises on books of reference.	Nature and Need of Revelation; Inspiration of Holy Scripture; Authenticity of the Four Gospels, etc.; Direct Evidences of Christianity. Weekly Lectures by the Professor.

The Last Old Scheme of Study 1892

him about Higher Criticism for two hours. He thinks Moses wrote no more than the Decalogue, and that Leviticus is the latest book of the Five . . . We hear absolutely nothing of this here and when we ask questions the answer shows that the professor is as poorly read on the subject as we are. I don't wonder Cambridge students are fond of their Seminary.[35]

Spalding was an argumentative young man, and a harsh critic, perhaps the more so because he was not in sympathy with the prevailing Anglo-Catholicism of the Seminary's professors. Criticism of the Faculty and agitation for curriculum reform was rife among the students, supported by many of the younger alumni, by the end of the 'eighties. Men complained that ethics was not sufficiently studied, nor Old Testament adequately taught. They lamented that the books of Sanday, Westcott, and others were not assigned for New Testament study, and, perhaps most bitterly of all, complained of the inadequacy of their training in pastoral theology.

Much of this criticism was justified. The majority of Hoffman's professors in 1892 had been with him from the beginning: Dr. Oliver, Randall Hall, and William Seabury, from Dean Seymour's time; Thomas Richey, who had been elected to the History chair in 1878 when Hoffman was chosen dean; and Francis Thayer Russell, the Dean's intimate and life-long friend, who was made Instructor in Reading the Church Service and the Delivery of Sermons in 1881.[36] Dean Hoffman had the same concern for competence in public speaking and reading the liturgy as he had for professional excellence in other areas of the priest's public ministry. Russell, whose *Use of the Voice in Reading and Speaking* became a popular handbook, apparently had a genius for training students in this respect.

Dr. Richey, a graduate in the Class of 1854, after having been

35. John Howard Melish, *Franklin Spencer Spalding* (New York, 1917), p. 41.

36. Since Russell's time, the Seminary has always had a part-time Instructor in Elocution or Public Speaking. Russell was succeeded by Alfred F. Tenney, 1904-18; William Robinson, 1919-33; William Brenton, 1934-36; William F. Doscher, 1937-40; John Cathey, 1941-54; and Cornelius L. Reid, who has been Instructor in Speech from 1954 to the present time.

rector of Mt. Calvary Church, Baltimore, and, for a short time, warden of St. Stephen's College, had taught ecclesiastical history for seven years at the Seabury Divinity School at the time of his election. He was a brilliant speaker, possessed of a quick and incisive mind and armed with a pungent Irish wit. Militant in defense of his strong views and impetuous at all times, he shared Dean Seymour's devotion to the principles of Anglo-Catholicism, but he had a more profound knowledge of church history than his predecessor. Immensely popular with the students, Dr. Richey, though over sixty in 1892, was never dull. He was one of the two professors whose learning commanded the respect of as severe a critic as Franklin Spalding. The other was an Englishman, much younger, G. H. Somerset Walpole, Professor of Dogmatic Theology after Dr. Buel's retirement in 1888. A Trinity man who had achieved a First in the Theological Tripos at Cambridge, Walpole was called to the Seminary from St. Mary's Parnell, Aukland, New Zealand. A competent but conservative scholar, he lacked Buel's unusual willingness to experiment with new books and new methods, though he had acquired some experience in training ordinands at both the theological college in Truro and at St. John's College, Aukland. Walpole's stay at the Seminary was relatively brief. After he returned to England in 1896, eventually to become rector of Lambeth and bishop of Edinburgh, his term as professor was chiefly remembered because it brought his little son Hugh, later the famous novelist, to live with the family, first at 412 West Twentieth Street and later, when the new faculty houses were completed in 1892, in No. 3 Chelsea Square.

The other members of the Faculty in 1892 were Professors Jewett and Cady. Upon Dr. Eigenbrodt's retirement in 1888 at the age of seventy-five, Edward H. Jewett of the Class of 1856 was elected to the Pastoral Theology chair. Jewett had spent thirty-three years in the parish ministry, but even such extensive parochial experience scarcely equipped him to meet adequately the demands of a department of study that still included liturgics and moral theology, as well as homiletics and pastoral care. Much of the impatient criticism that had been leveled at Professor Eigenbrodt was soon transferred to Dr. Jewett.

Dr. Cady, a graduate of 1850, taught the evidences of revealed religion upon a foundation established by the alumni in 1883, when they had at last accumulated a fund of $25,000 to endow this instruction. The alumni plan was for a nonresident professor who, upon nomination by the Associate Alumni, would be elected by the Trustees for a three-year term. It was intended that he should lecture for the greater part of one semester, and not have the status of a member of the statutory Faculty. The arrangement was designed to ensure periodically a fresh approach to the Christian apologetic in the changing times. To Dean Hoffman and the Trustees, however, it was an untidy and disturbing plan, introducing an unsettling lack of continuity and the possibility of an uncontrollable personality among the professors. Nevertheless, the terms were accepted, and George Washington Dean, sometime teacher of classics at Racine College and chancellor of the Albany Cathedral, came in to lecture on evidences from 1885 until his death two years later. Philander Kinney Cady was elected in 1890, after the Trustees had twice refused to confirm the alumni nomination of John Henry Hopkins, Jr., who might indeed have fulfilled Dean Hoffman's worst apprehensions. Dr. Cady, a strong High Churchman, whose parochial ministry had included the rectorships of Grace Church, Newark, Christ Church, Poughkeepsie, and St. James', Hyde Park, was a genial personality, much admired as a preacher. Some estimate of Cady's effectiveness amid the dissatisfaction with the curriculum in the early 'nineties may be deduced from the fact that most of his favorite textbooks rose like ghosts from the Course of Ecclesiastical Study of 1804.[37] He was firmly convinced that recitations in his

37. A committee of the House of Bishops, appointed in 1856 to consider a revision of the course, did not report until 1889, and were then content to approve the original books, adding thereto a supplemental list, some of which they admitted were "not wholly approved by ourselves." Among others in this list were works by Liddon, Moberley, Westcott, Lightfoot, Trench, Dorner, Wordsworth, Browne, and Hardwick (*Journal of General Convention 1889*, pp. 753-762).

department were as essential as in those of other professors. "I may remark," he reported to the Trustees,

> that with the class of young men who come to our Theological Institutions, a system of pure lecturing, such as is the custom in great Universities, would be, as far as the students are concerned, a practical failure. Many of them are not of sufficient age, and others of them have not had sufficient mental training, to profit by mere professional lectures, unaccompanied by *viva voce* and conversational explanations, and by compulsory study with a view to immediate recitation and examination at the end of the term.[38]

Even when he lectured, Professor Cady required his students to take full and accurate notes upon which periodic recitations were based.

Whatever the shortcomings of Dean Hoffman and his professors, they were, like the students, confined in the straitjacket of a course of study minutely prescribed in the Seminary statutes and controlled by the vigilance of the Trustees' committees.[39] It was not the weight of tradition alone that inhibited change, and nothing indicates this more clearly than the response of the Standing Committee to the proposal of a close relationship with Columbia University. In 1890 Columbia offered to admit without fees students nominated by the dean to take courses in philosophy, ethics, pedagogics, political economy, and Semitic languages, as well as to grant library privileges to men enrolled in the Seminary. This arrangement led to a proposal made by the university

> to enlarge the relations of reciprocity already entered into between Columbia College and the General and Union Theological Seminaries, so as to cover whatever interchange of facilities may be thought to be desirable.[40]

38. Tr P, June 7, 1892 (VI, 661).
39. In 1883 the statutes allowed the old oral examination before the Committee on Examinations to be "partly written," and two years later examinations were permitted to be wholly in written form, though a supplementary oral exercise was often conducted. Until 1894 the Examining Committee regularly inspected the written examination questions and answers. After 1894 the committee exercised this right with sporadic bursts of activity.
40. *Ibid.*, May 19, 1891 (VI, 555).

One such enlargement, for example, was the proposal of Columbia to accept work done at the Seminary as part fulfillment of the requirements for the Ph.D.

Dean Hoffman placed the matter before the Trustees, though without enthusiasm, possibly because at that time he was more interested in a statute that would curtail the interruption of work caused when students were required to take their canonical examinations for orders during term time, a practice that annoyed him during all his years as dean. Columbia's proposal was referred to the Standing Committee, and two years later they reported unfavorably to the Board. Such an arrangement, they felt, would require a change in the constitution of the Seminary, for

> it would not be competent to this Board to enter into an alliance which would have the effect of placing our students, during a part of their training, under the charge of instructors not necessarily communicants of our Church, and in an institution not directly responsible to the General Convention . . .
>
> Moreover, it has been found by experience that the three years' course prescribed by the Statutes is already so full that none of the students have any time to pursue additional studies, without neglecting some portion of those prescribed.[41]

The members of the Standing Committee did not object to allowing Special Students, graduate students, or on rare occasions the undergraduate of exceptional ability, to take some work at Columbia when given permission by the dean. It was, however, a right of the dean to be exercised with caution and discretion.

The agitation for curriculum reform mounted to such proportions during the academic years 1890-91 and 1891-92 that it became evident to the Trustees as well as the professors that action could not be long deferred without serious consequences. Dean Hoffman, recognizing at last that change was inevitable, proposed in June 1892 that the Board of Trustees appoint a committee to meet with members of the Faculty and

41. Tr P, May 23, 1893 (VI, 743).

consider whether the recent advances in theological learning and the needs of our times do not require some modification of a course which was adopted nearly three-quarters of a century ago.[42]

Before the committee could complete its somewhat leisurely work, the impatient dissatisfaction of the students was given arresting and public expression. On February 20, 1893, Professor Oliver noted in his diary that he had received a copy of "the memorial from the students with regard to the course of study." That evening the Faculty met to speed their deliberations, while the mails carried to the Trustees a remarkable pamphlet, signed by seventy-two students and petitioning for a change in "the unsatisfactory methods of intellectual training" followed in the classrooms of the Seminary.

42. Tr P, June 7, 1892 (VI, 658).

10

The Problem of the Curriculum

The *Memorial Addressed to the Dean, Faculty and Trustees* by more than half the students was blunt and outspoken, despite its courteous language:

> We petition for a thorough change in the methods of instruction now in vogue at the Seminary. We feel that the institution does not develop, as it should, earnestness, scholarship and spirituality among the students; that there is mechanical pressure brought to bear upon them which may, it is true, keep them up to their prescribed work . . . but which militates against the development of a self-educating idea . . .
>
> What we chiefly esteem in the General Theological Seminary is that the keynote of its instruction is devotion to the Faith "once for all delivered to the saints" . . . We believe that it is owing to this feature of its training that the Seminary is to be esteemed above other institutions, where the methods of instruction are preferable. Our objection is to the methods.

The Seminary's methods of intellectual training, complained the students, were those "now abandoned at the foremost seats of learning both in this country and abroad," and their retention created a "widespread and most unfortunate impression that the Seminary is behind the times."

> We are convinced that . . . the lecture system should be very largely substituted for the system of recitations. The theory of the

latter seems to be that the professor is to make the students recite on a particular text book, in order that he may ascertain whether they are doing their work. This produces a superficial knowledge of particular books, but fails to give the student a real grasp of the subject . . . The professor should . . . teach subjects, not books.

A very important part of the lecture system is the required private reading . . . extensive and careful reading is necessary for real knowledge and mental training.

When was there time, the petitioners asked, for systematic collateral reading, "when seven or eight hours, on an average, must be consumed each day on recitations and preparations?"

Against a course of study fully prescribed they urged

that more liberty be allowed the students in the selection of the work they are to pursue . . . the modern principle of specialization would produce as good results in theology as in any branch of secular work. We therefore ask that all studies in excess of canonical requirements be made elective.

The *Memorial* appealed also for more flexibility in assigning the students to the three classes of the Seminary. Rigid placement resulted in some men being "obliged to do work for which they are not well prepared," while others were "forced to repeat work already done." In place of grades derived from monthly recitation marks, the students suggested that searching examinations be instituted at the end of each term of lectures, as affording "both the fairest and most certain test of merit and the greatest incentive to effort."

The pride of the signers in their Seminary is evident throughout the *Memorial*, mingled with the pain in which they speak so frankly. Apologizing for any appearance of brashness or impropriety, they were nevertheless constrained to put their case plainly:

Elsewhere, under the modern educational system, many of us have pursued our studies enthusiastically and profitably, while here we find our minds confused and our enthusiasm gone . . . something is wrong . . .

The question at issue is . . . whether the representative educational institution of the Church is to be below the level of secular colleges, and inferior in methods to the seminaries of the prominent sects about us.

The appearance of the *Memorial* speeded the work of curriculum revision, and by the late spring of 1893 the Faculty had drawn up a new Scheme of Study which the Trustees promptly authorized.[1] Unhappily, the revised course embodied no radical changes. A cautious recognition of the contemporary critical approach to theological studies was reflected in the descriptions of the subjects of the curriculum, and provision was made for three additional departments of study: Oriental Languages, Ecclesiastical Music, and Moral Theology and Christian Philosophy. The creation of the latter was the only change of importance in the statutory course, for it rescued moral theology from the position of a subordinate topic in pastoral theology and gave fuller scope for the study of Christian moral principles and social ethics.

The refurbished curriculum appeared in the *Catalogue* of 1893-94, and after a year or two of minor adjustments, the course of study settled into the pattern that was to last twenty-five years. The modifications made during Dean Robbins' administration, between 1903 and 1916, were comparatively slight and did not alter the basic pattern of the curriculum. It was not until 1919, after Dean Fosbroke had made his influence felt, that the course of study was modernized by radical revision.

The Scheme of Study of 1893 embodied the following curriculum, the numbers after each course indicating class hours per week:

FIRST TERM	SECOND TERM
JUNIOR YEAR	
Hebrew Grammar (4)	Hebrew Grammar (4)
Gospels & Acts in Greek (3)	Gospels & Acts in Greek (3)
Old Testament History (3)	Church History to 600 (4)
Fundamentals of Ethics (2)	Homiletics (2)

1. Tr P, May 23, 1893 (VI, 800-802).

Christian Evidences (2)
(Butler's *Analogy*)
Ecclesiastical Music (1)
(Rudiments; Individual work)

Introduction to Dogmatics (2)
(Faith, Revelation & Reason, Authority)

MIDDLE YEAR

Pauline Epistles in Greek (3)
Church History 600-1200 (4)
Hebrew Reading (2)
(Psalms & Selected Prophets)
Dogmatic Theology (4)
(Trinity & Incarnation; Man)
Pastoral Theology (2)
(Pastoral Care & the Parish)
Ecclesiastical Music (1)
(Liturgical Music & Hymnody)

Pauline Epistles in Greek (3)
Nature & Constitution of the Church (2)
Hebrew Old Testament (4)
(Historical & Poetical Books)
Christian Evidences (4)
(Theism & anti-Theism; Evolution)
Moral Theology (2)
(Individual & Social Ethics)

SENIOR YEAR

Dogmatic Theology (3)
(Soteriology; Church)
Pastoral Theology (3)
(Liturgics)
Patristic Greek (2)
(Athanasius' *De Incarnatione*)
Hebrew Old Testament (3)
(Isaiah & other Prophets; Pentateuch)
Polity and Canon Law (4)
Moral Theology (1)
(Cases of Conscience; Philosophy)

Dogmatic Theology (3)
(Sacraments; Eschatology)
Pastoral Theology (2)
(Review Pastoral Care & Homiletics)
Christian Evidences (2)
(Proofs of Christianity)
New Testament Epistles in Greek (2)
Church History 1200-1800 (4)
Ecclesiastical Music (1)
(Music in the Parish)

A number of favorite old texts and reference books, many of which dated from the Course of Ecclesiastical Studies of 1804, were dropped and more recent books substituted. Those assigned for New Testament study, for example, now included commentaries by Liddon, Westcott, Lightfoot, and Ellicott. In dogmatic theology, the basic reading shifted from the writings of Anglican divines of the seventeenth and eighteenth centuries—though Pearson on the Creed remained in use—to Browne's *Thirty-Nine Articles*, Robert Wilberforce on the Incarnation, Westcott's *Historic Faith*, Hans Martensen's *Christian Dogmatics*, with reference also to the works of Frederick Denison Maurice, R. C. Moberley, J. B. Mozley, Charles Gore, and the essays of *Lux Mundi*.

Phillips Brooks's *Lectures on Preaching* displaced Gresley, while Proctor's *History of the Prayer Book* and Blunt's *Annotated Prayer Book* became the standard texts in liturgics. Mosheim, Gieseler, and Neander in ecclesiastical history were replaced by newer books, and while Butler's *Analogy* was still prescribed for Christian evidences, the recommended list included Robert Flint's *Theism*, Alexander Bruce's *Apologetics*, and *Personality, Human and Divine* by J. R. Illingworth. The list for moral theology, still including selections from the Fathers, as well as the seventeenth-century classics of Jeremy Taylor and Robert Sanderson, was expanded to embrace Martensen's *Christian Ethics*, Richard Ely's *Social Aspects of Christianity*, John J. Elmendorf's *Elements of Moral Theology*, Samuel Harris' *Philosophical Basis of Theism*, and James Martineau's *Types of Ethical Theory*.

The reorganized course of study made no concession to the desire of the students for elective work. The normal curriculum for regular students was still inflexibly prescribed. The professors, however, were encouraged to adopt the lecture method if they wished. Most of them did so, substituting monthly tests, often called "written recitations," for the old system of reciting in the classroom. They did not all adapt themselves willingly or easily to the new method. Professors Oliver, Seabury, and Jewett, for example, found it difficult to change the habit of years. Professor Cady made little effort to lecture to the Juniors, whose course with him was devoted to a detailed examination of Butler's *Analogy*, but he employed the lecture method frequently with the upperclassmen. Dr. Theodore M. Riley, for some years a parish priest before joining the faculty of Nashotah House, and who was brought from there in 1896 to assist the elderly Jewett as Adjunct Professor of Pastoral

Theology, was not convinced that a lecture system was wholly desirable in seminary education. Lectures, he admitted, might be a useful supplement to textbook drill, for

> they may give most beautiful bird's-eye views of things; they may provide perhaps all sorts of related ideas; but as a rule they can only outline or embellish things.

He feared that a lecture system would give

> the largest scope to the idle and lazy student who wishes to escape real work and study. It is not at all an unknown thing that the indolent type of student under the lecture system does not seriously study or read during the term. He buys from some fellow student, at the end of the academic year, copies of the lectures . . . the substance of which he may transfer to his examination papers.[2]

Dr. Riley's remarks, written ten years after the adoption of the curriculum in 1893, expose the weakness of these early attempts to use the lecture method. The professors often settled for stereotyped lectures, dictated year after year with little change, and on which the students were expected to take full notes. This was far from the practice the authors of the *Memorial* had in mind when they asked for lectures that would "so lead them up to the whole subject as to enable them to make it their own."

The students accepted the Scheme of 1893, at least for a few years, with good grace. What disappointed them most was the failure to provide elective courses and easier access to the educational opportunities in other New York institutions of learning. In 1895, a number of them petitioned the Trustees to revive the matter of a closer affiliation with Columbia, but the Board tabled consideration of their request. The increase in lectures temporarily quieted most of the complaints, and the changes in the Faculty during the 'nineties brought at least the refreshment of new voices to the classrooms.

The Reverend John Charles Roper was elected to succeed Walpole in the spring of 1897. Roper had read theology at Keble Col-

2. Theodore M. Riley, *A Memorial Biography of Eugene Augustus Hoffman*, (New York, 1904), II, 669-670.

lege, Oxford, and after two years as Divinity Professor in Trinity College, Toronto, he had become rector of St. Thomas' Church there in 1888. He was typical of the additions to the Faculty since the appointment of Professors Buel and Oliver, a scholarly minded parish priest with some experience in teaching. It was an advance over the older generation of teachers who were equipped with little more than parochial experience. Dr. Roper's class work was competent, and his youth—he was under forty when he came to Chelsea Square—brought a fresh vigor that was much needed among the Hoffman professors.

Three other new professors were harbingers of a different type of seminary teacher, men whose careers had been devoted almost wholly to the academic life: Seibt, Body, and Beckwith. Charles Theodore Seibt, educated at Dresden and Leipzig, and the recipient of the Seminary's first earned doctorate in 1881, had taught at Racine College and was a professor at Bexley Hall when he was chosen by the Trustees in 1895 to fill the new chair of Moral Theology and Christian Philosophy. A year earlier, the department of Biblical Learning had been strengthened by the division of its work into separate sections of Old and New Testaments. Dr. Oliver, nearing the end of his career in the Seminary, took the newly endowed New Testament professorship, in which he was succeeded in 1898 by Isbon Thaddeus Beckwith, a Yale Ph.D. and former instructor, who had been for many years Professor of Greek Language and Literature at Trinity College, Hartford. The separate chair of Old Testament was filled by Dr. Charles W. E. Body, Provost of Trinity College, Toronto, and formerly Fellow of St. John's College, Cambridge, a distinguished Canadian priest and educator—inevitably known to the students as "Dr. Corpus."[3]

The Scheme of 1893 extended to graduate work as well as the undergraduate curriculum. The old Post-Graduate Course was

3. When Randall Hall resigned the chair of Hebrew and Greek Languages in 1898, the designation of a professorship in honor of Clement Clarke Moore was transferred to the new Old Testament chair. With two professors in the field of Biblical Learning, it was not thought necessary at the time to elect a successor to Dr. Hall.

transformed by a recommended course of study, and elective courses in advanced work were offered in the several departments. Known as the "Fourth-Year Course," students who wished a certificate of its successful completion were required to elect one or more subjects in at least three departments each term. From this Fourth-Year Course there developed in time the arrangement whereby the Seminary's graduates, holding its diploma, or graduates of other seminaries, might qualify for the S.T.B. degree by a year's further study. Perhaps the most interesting, though abortive venture in plans for graduate study in the 'nineties was the proposal of the Faculty to confer degrees in Sacred Philosophy.[4] After the Standing Committee decided in 1893 that these degrees might be conferred under the existing charter from the legislature, a program had been sufficiently formulated by 1896 to permit the requirements for the degree of Doctor of Philosophy to appear in the catalogue. Though one or two applications for candidacy were made, the degree was never awarded, and its announcement disappeared after 1899.

The interests of the students in the last decade of Hoffman's deanship were not focused wholly upon the problems of the curriculum. Athletic activity became an increasingly popular diversion, and the football team of 1890, though losing most of its games, triumphed over elevens made up of students of Columbia and New York University. By 1895 basketball had surpassed football in popularity, and a basketball team has remained a feature of Seminary life ever since. In recent years, the annual contests with other seminaries have aroused considerable spirit and enthusiasm, Union and Virginia being the Seminary's chief rivals on the court.

From 1892 until 1905, the students published an illustrated class yearbook called *The Seminarian*—revived briefly in 1931 and 1934—containing sketches of Seminary history and activities, essays on missionary and vocational topics, poetry and other literary efforts, and vignettes of class life. One of the most charming Seminary customs in the years before the First World War was begun in 1895,

4. Faculty Minutes, April 6, 1892.

The Old West Close from Tenth Avenue

when a band of students heralded the dawn of Easter Day with hymns and carols from the top of the chapel tower at 6:00 A.M., much to the delight of the occupants of the rooming houses on Twentieth and Twenty-first Streets that often advertised their accommodations as overlooking "the Hoffman theological gardens."[5] In time this custom attracted crowds to the streets below, and it continued for nearly twenty years. On one occasion, at least, the singers were accompanied by four trumpets and a trombone, and invariably the singing was concluded by a joyous peal of the chapel chimes announcing the day of Resurrection and the early Easter Communion Service that followed.

Missionary concern ran high in Chelsea Square in these years. Dean Hoffman assisted in arranging for prominent missionaries to

5. Descriptions of the singing from the tower may be read in *The Church Press*, April 20, 1895; *The Church Standard*, April 23, 1896; *The Ladies' Home Journal*, April, 1902; and *The New York Herald*, April 16, 1906.

speak at the fortnightly meetings of the Missionary Society, describing their work in the western districts, Alaska, Brazil, China, Japan, and, after the Spanish-American War, in Cuba and the Philippines, as well as challenging the students with a call to a missionary vocation. Informal associations stimulated interests in the different mission fields. In the late 'eighties, for example, the "Western Missionary Club" furthered the concern with opportunities in the Far West with such success that within a few years four men went to Colorado, seven to Wyoming, and three to Montana.

A pioneer missionary venture was launched in 1889-90, when a number of students pledged themselves to found and staff an associate mission in one of the western dioceses. When an arrangement had been concluded with Bishop Graves of Nebraska, Irving Peake Johnson of the Class of 1891, later the famous bishop of Colorado, went out to Omaha to establish a mission house. There he was soon joined by Paul Matthews of the Class of 1890, who became bishop of New Jersey in 1915, and within three years the associate mission numbered six priests who lived in community and served seven missions, a hospital, and several small congregations. So remarkable was the success of this venture that a second mission on a somewhat smaller scale was founded in Trenton, New Jersey.

The support of a particular mission continued to be an activity of the Missionary Society from the years of Dean Hoffman into those of Dean Rose. One of the most successful associate missions was begun in 1934 at Hays, Kansas, in the district of Salina, to which the Missionary Society contributed upwards of $2000 a year. In time its clergy staffed nine missions and five outstations in eleven towns. When in 1940 self-support had been achieved, the Missionary Society turned its attention overseas, undertaking to staff and support the mission of St. Francis at Upi in the Philippine Islands, a district where many graduates of the General Seminary served both in mission stations and in the Sagada Training School and its successor, St. Andrew's Seminary.

Evangelistic activity was not always distant from Chelsea Square. Near the end of the century, the work of students in the parishes of the Chelsea area expanded from the supervision of boys' clubs into an evangelistic and social program for the people of the Chelsea area. With increasing awareness of the Church's mission to the city, in 1909 the students opened a "mission room" on Twenty-eighth Street, under the direction of the Reverend Appleton Grannis, rector of the Church of the Holy Apostles. There they conducted a ministry of counseling and social service in conjunction with open air evangelistic services on the corner of Tenth Avenue. From these tentative beginnings grew the sense of community responsibility and concern that absorbed the energies of many students in the Chelsea Mission during the days of Dean Fosbroke and Dean Rose.

Dean Hoffman devoted almost all his attention during his last years to two long-cherished projects—the assembling of a unique collection of Latin Bibles in the Seminary library, and the completion of the buildings of the West Quadrangle. In 1893, with the assistance of Cornelius Vanderbilt, the Dean purchased the famous Copinger Bible Collection of 543 editions in over 1300 volumes. Assembled by Professor Walter A. Copinger of Victoria University, Manchester, England, it was believed at the time to be the largest collection of Latin Bibles in the world. Among the numerous rare items was a perfect copy of the Antwerp Polyglot, some Eggestein Bibles dating from 1466, and a dozen Cobergers printed between 1475 and 1497. One of the Cobergers, the *Postilla super totam Bibliam* of Nicholas of Lyra, Dean Hoffman informed the Trustees,

> is from the Monastery of Erfurt, and as this is a Coberger of 1481, it is more than probable that it may have been used by Martin Luther.[6]

Though the Copinger purchase was the Dean's most extensive acquisition for the library, he continued to add rare and important Latin Bibles whenever he could purchase them, seeking to fill the gaps in the library's collection. By the end of the century, the Seminary's Bible collection had become widely known among scholars and bibliophiles, its most valuable single editions being a Fust and Schoeffer Bible of 1462, and a fine copy of the Gutenberg

6. Tr P, May 8, 1894 (VII, 54-55).

Bible which Dean Hoffman purchased at auction in England in 1898 for $15,000.[7]

In 1895 the Dean's effort to complete the buildings west of the chapel began with the erection of two adjoining faculty houses at the corner of Tenth Avenue and Twentieth Street. Charles Haight's first plans for the Seminary Close had included only one faculty residence at this location, and the range originally designed for the west end of Chelsea Square was to be set nearly two hundred feet back from Tenth Avenue. Four staircase dormitories along Twenty-first Street would then join its north corner with the chapel. Alterations in the original plan, however, provided for two faculty houses and placed the west range much closer to Tenth Avenue, leaving room for more buildings along Twenty-first Street.

Gifts for the new construction came in rapidly, Trinity Church Corporation contributing $25,000 to defray the cost of one of the houses, with the stipulation that Professor Seabury be permitted to occupy it as long as he lived. In 1899, work was begun on the building at the north end of the west range; it was to contain a large gymnasium, and above that a new refectory with kitchens, domestic offices, and apartments for the dining room staff. Between the faculty houses and the refectory, the whole block was to be completed, at a total cost of about $300,000, by a dormitory named in honor of Dr. Eigenbrodt.

On Commencement Day 1900, after the graduation exercises, Eigenbrodt Hall and the new refectory-gymnasium building, Hoffman Hall, were dedicated. In many ways the magnificent dining hall was the most striking of Dean Hoffman's buildings. With its oak wainscotted walls, tall windows, lofty beamed ceiling, and a high table dais at one end lighted by the expanse of a huge oriel window and crowned above by a delicately carved gallery, the refectory had the grace and pleasing proportions characteristic of many ancient dining halls of the colleges of Oxford and Cambridge.

7. The Seminary's Gutenberg is known as the "Offenbury-Syston Park-Makellar" copy, and a description of its history is contained in a G.T.S. Library pamphlet entitled *The Gutenberg Bible of the General Theological Seminary*.

Its walls were a perfect setting for the numerous portraits of founders and benefactors, deans and professors, that the Seminary had acquired over the years.

The alumni contributed substantially to the cost of Hoffman Hall, a tribute of gratitude and affection to Eugene Augustus Hoffman, though at the same time as graduates were making their gifts to the building fund, the organization of the Associate Alumni was concluding a long altercation with the Board of Trustees by bringing legal action against them for breach of trust. The Trustees had refused to continue to elect an Alumni Professor of Christian Evidences for the originally specified three-year term. The alumni, on the other hand, declined to nominate a man to be elected for longer than three years. In this impasse, the alumni brought suit for the recovery of their endowment of the chair. When the courts ultimately decided in favor of the Associate Alumni, the Trustees paid over about $41,000, representing the initial gift of $25,000 plus accumulations of income. Two years later the Alumni, after deduct-

Buildings of the West Quadrangle: Eigenbrodt and Hoffman Halls

ing their legal fees, returned the money to the Board to be used for the support of a professorship or a lectureship with no conditions attached thereto.

Dean Hoffman's last projects included improvements in the existing buildings as well as the erection of new ones. Electricity was introduced throughout the Seminary in 1897-98. The library, numbering over 30,000 volumes and outgrowing the space in Hobart Hall, was extended into the upper floors of the north end of Jarvis Hall. There fireproof stacks were built to provide shelf space for the rapidly increasing number of books. In 1901 the Finance Committee spent $65,000 to buy back seven lots in the Central Block west of Tenth Avenue, a portion of the land Mr. Pierrepont had sold to help relieve the financial crisis forty years before. Had he lived, undoubtedly Dean Hoffman would have seen his original "grand design" for the buildings of the Close completed with

> the addition of dormitory buildings, which are expected to fill the space between Hoffman Hall and the Chapel, and the erection of two of the Professors' houses on the site of the old West Building.[8]

His death intervened, however, leaving the last dormitories unfinished and bringing the West Building a reprieve from the sentence of demolition.

After the turn of the century, the Dean showed signs of advancing age, as well as symptoms of the heart disease that afflicted him. His beard had turned snow-white, his brisk step became slower and more measured, and the drowsiness of illness frequently overtook him, even in the chapel. Often he roused himself with a conscious effort at the end of Evensong to take the final prayers, his voice frequently fading with weakness as he concluded the service with the collect he had devised for the Seminary:

> ALMIGHTY and most merciful God, we make our humble supplications unto Thee for all Thy servants in this Seminary: that Thy Fatherly hand may ever be over them; that Thy Holy Spirit may ever be with them; and that with one heart they may desire the prosperity

8. Tr P, May 29, 1900 (VII, 535).

of Thy Holy Apostolic Church, and with one mouth profess the Faith once delivered unto the Saints: to the glory of Thy name, through Jesus Christ our Lord. Amen.[9]

The burdens of age and illness separated Dean Hoffman from the intimate contact with the Seminary's daily life and routine he had so long maintained. In his last years, the student body became restless under an administration that seemed unbearably paternalistic and often equally distant and authoritarian. Dissatisfaction with the intellectual life of the Seminary increased, and the curriculum came under fire, not only for its inflexibility, but also for "holding men responsible for little or nothing except the facts contained in the lectures, or even in the dictated notes of lectures."[10] Protests against the disproportionate amount of time devoted to Hebrew language study were loud and long. "À bas l'Hebraique" was the cry raised among the students.[11] Even the members of the Committee on Examinations shared the conviction that not enough was required of the students intellectually, and they sharply criticized the practice of accepting the feeding back of lecture notes on examination papers as evidence of satisfactory work.

Dean Hoffman was beyond the reach of this restlessness. His last days were singularly appropriate to the interests and activities of his whole life. On Commencement Day 1902, the cornerstone was to be laid for three new dormitories—Lorillard, White, and Edson—adjoining Hoffman Hall along Twenty-first Street. The graduation ceremonies began without the Dean. To husband his failing strength, he entered the chapel only when the moment came to confer the degrees. For the last time, he took his seat before the altar, robed in the scarlet of Oxford's doctorate which had been conferred upon him in 1896, and recited the Latin formulae of the ceremony. As the procession left the chapel to proceed down the

9. Hoffman's collect replaced earlier Seminary prayers composed by Bishop Hobart and Professor Samuel Seabury (G.T.S. Clippings, January, 1910); see also Tr P, June 1853, App. A., and *Occasional Prayers and Services . . . of the General Theological Seminary* (New York, 1861).

10. G.T.S. *Seminarian* (1903), pp. 40-42.

11. *Ibid.* (1899), pp. 13-14.

Close to the site of the new buildings, the Dean supported his faltering steps with hands on the shoulders of the priests in front of him. He finished his task at the cornerstone—his final official act—and when the Seminary closed for the summer vacation he left with Mrs. Hoffman for his favorite fishing camp on the banks of the Restigouche in the Canadian woods. There for a while he seemed stronger. A last salmon rose to his fly and he landed it successfully, but within a few days it was plain that the end was near and a return to New York imperative. On June 17, Dean Hoffman died in his sleeping car on the Delaware & Hudson train en route home. His final benefaction to the Seminary for which he had done so much was a legacy of $100,000 to establish a fund for the support and increase of the library.

The floodtide of dissatisfaction came hard on the heels of the Dean's death, and the outburst in 1902 was similar to that which accompanied the student *Memorial* ten years earlier, though tinged with greater bitterness:

> This Seminary does not offer a course that will fit a man to be ordered deacon in those of our dioceses that have a high standard of scholarship; and many men have a far greater need of work in preparing for their canonical examinations than for their Seminary examinations . . . What is the spirit of the student body? Enthusiastic and loyal? No, but dissatisfied, irritated and rebellious . . .
>
> One shudders at the memory of dreary hours of dictated lectures, when hand and brain were wearied in taking down matter which could have been mastered in five minutes on the printed page of a syllabus . . .
>
> We are not taught how to use books . . . All our theories and arguments are given to us in nicely assorted and numbered bundles . . . we take them on authority.[12]

An exaggerated criticism perhaps, but such complaints made it plain that curriculum revision would be the imperative task of Dean Hoffman's successor. From every side, letters and articles flooded the church press, calling for the election of a professional scholar

12. G.T.S. *Seminarian* (1902), pp. 44-45.

and educator whose knowledge and experience would equip him to raise the level of the Seminary's intellectual life. The Trustees of the General Seminary, however, have seldom been easily influenced by sentiment within the institution or opinion throughout the Church. Some undoubtedly feared that aggressive academic reform might alter the traditional curriculum too radically. Others were possibly swayed by the notion, frequently prevalent at the end of a long regime, that what was needed was a dean whose pastoral experience and close touch with the practical affairs of the Church and the world could be relied upon to bring the Seminary out of some fancied isolation. At all events, the Board of Trustees ignored the clamor for a scholar or experienced educator, and on April 16, 1903, they elected a successful parish priest, Wilford Lash Robbins, a graduate of Amherst and the Episcopal Theological School, who since 1887 had been dean of All Saints' Cathedral in Albany.

Forty-three years old, Dr. Robbins, if not a scholar, was a thoughtful and gifted priest, enjoying a well-deserved reputation as a stimulating preacher, a skillful pastor and spiritual guide, and an efficient administrator. Endowed with an attractive and engaging personality, his warmth of spirit and ready friendliness brought him an intimacy with the students that strengthened his influence upon their preparation for the priesthood.

The morale of the Seminary community ran high with an enthusiastic expectancy in Dean Robbins' first years. With all the veneration paid to Dean Hoffman's memory, and it was very great, no one expected or wanted his successor to be like him. All that was desired was progress in those areas he had left unchanged. The student body continued to be large, averaging over 100 in the three regular classes, with 8 to 10 Special Students and a similar number of graduates enrolled each year. There were no financial worries, for the Seminary enjoyed an "Indian summer" of Hoffman prosperity. The endowment actually increased, passing the two million mark in 1908, chiefly due to the realization of substantial sums from the remaining real estate west of Tenth Avenue. In 1902 the city began the apropriation of the Wharf Block for dockage facilities,

Dean Robbins
Seminary Portrait by S. E. Dickinson

compensating the Seminary in 1906 with more than $400,000 plus four years of accumulated interest. In 1907 most of the interior lots of the Central Block were sold in a favorable market for $355,000.[13] Lorillard, White, and Edson Halls were completed, their cost being almost entirely borne by members of the Hoffman family.[14] In 1910 the interior of the West Building was completely remodeled, with the exception of the original professor's house on the east end, and the apartments familiar today were created. Dean Robbins was able to inaugurate a new building fund in which nearly $60,000 in cash

13. In 1932 another segment of the Central Block was sold to the New York Central Railroad for $100,000 to provide for the elevation of its tracks, leaving the Seminary in possession of the strip of lots along Tenth Avenue which it still owns.

14. Dean Hoffman had given $16,500 for this purpose before his death. Mrs. Hoffman and their children gave $92,000 toward the completion of the buildings.

and pledges had accumulated by the time of his resignation in 1916. His hope was to erect a building adjacent to Edson Hall which would contain four additional classrooms and an assembly hall or auditorium to seat 300 persons. The gymnasium was the only place the Seminary community could be assembled for special meetings or lectures, and Dean Robbins made constant use of it, but a gymnasium equipped with folding chairs was a temporary and uncomfortable substitute for an attractive auditorium.[15]

The Dean responded to the expectancy that greeted him with assiduous attention to a number of aspects of Seminary life. The function of the institution, as he saw it, was to train "faithful and intelligent parish priests," a phrase repeatedly occurring in his reports and addresses. He was convinced that the tendency of a seminary community to become ingrown and sheltered from the world must be constantly combated. "Theological seminaries," he said,

> have rather a bad name. They stand more or less, in the popular mind, for what is doctrinaire and unpractical, out of touch with everyday doings and real life . . . the Seminary must itself be brought into close touch with life. Every department must, by one path or another, arrive at a practical goal, and teach, directly or indirectly, the application of its theories to the crying needs of men.[16]

To bring the students into touch with the affairs of the world's everyday life, the Dean persuaded laymen from different businesses and professions to speak at frequent informal assemblies in the gymnasium—"smokers," as they were then called—on subjects as varied as business methods in church affairs, religious philanthropy, the newspaper world, the Church and social problems, and what the laity expect of their clergy. President Woodrow Wilson of Princeton was perhaps the most distinguished of these visitors, though many others were scarcely less prominent. The Dean constantly stimulated the missionary zeal of the students. Informal mission

15. Dean Robbins' hope was eventually realized in the erection of Seabury Hall during Dean Fosbroke's administration.
16. *Installation Address of the Very Reverend Wilford L. Robbins, D.D.* (New York, 1903), pp. 11-12.

study classes and voluntary seminars were provided, and in some terms as many as six separate missionary study groups were holding regular meetings. The Missionary Society maintained a reading room in Hobart Hall where missionary books and periodicals were available, while on the walls were plaques bearing the names of graduates serving in the several mission fields of the Church.

Dean Robbins had a genuine pastoral concern for his students, and encouraged the development of a strong spiritual life in Chelsea Square. The chapel schedule was augmented by more frequent celebrations of the Holy Communion, until by the academic year 1906-07 there was a daily Eucharist at 7:00 A.M. Morning Prayer was scheduled at 8:30 A.M., and Evening Prayer was moved from 5:30 to 6:00 P.M. This remained the pattern of the daily chapel services until the last months of the First World War when Dean Fosbroke placed Morning Prayer at 7:00 A.M., followed by the Holy Communion.

In the choice of outside lecturers, the Dean sought earnestly to secure the finest exponents of Anglican scholarship in the early years of the century. The Paddock Lecturers, for example, between 1903 and 1916 were all men of distinction, and some, either then or later, of considerable fame. Among them were Bishop Brent of the Philippines in 1904; William Ralph Inge, then vicar of All Saints', Knightsbridge, and later the famous dean of St. Paul's, whose lectures of 1907 were published as his *Personal Idealism and Mysticism;* Professor William Porcher DuBose, the distinguished theologian of the School of Theology of the University of the South in 1908; Dr. Francis J. Hall, Professor of Dogmatic Theology in the Western Theological Seminary, and Professor Dickinson Miller of Columbia, both later to become members of the Seminary Faculty, who lectured in 1909 and 1910; John Neville Figgis of the Community of the Resurrection whose *Fellowship of the Mystery* constituted the Paddock Lectures of 1913; and in 1915 William Temple, then rector of St. James' Church, Picadilly, and later the outstanding Anglican philosopher, theologian, and churchman of the first half of the twentieth century.

In the midst of this activity, however, curriculum revision remained the central problem. Neither Dean Robbins nor his early professors had yet gained the professional academic experience necessary to a bold and constructive reform. Like his predecessor, the Dean desired high standards of achievement in the classroom, but the Faculty found it difficult to break with the traditional prescribed curriculum and the conviction that the Church's official seminary was bound to provide amply for all the subjects required by the canons. Moreover, there were conservative pressures applied by those who feared that the critical scholarship of the day was too often negative, stopping short of positive reconstruction. Radical change might admit radical views. Dean Robbins admitted the

supreme need of a thorough-going critical scholarship in our Seminary training, and a manly facing of every difficulty raised by modern thought.

But, he said, with less clarity than one might desire:

If Seminary training beguiles a man into the belief that he can feed the flock committed to him on critical theories, or that the congregation is thirsting for the latest results of German scholarship, it has done him an irreparable injury. But it remains true that until a man has himself faced a difficulty, he cannot help his brother who has fallen into the same difficulty.

The Dean clung to his conviction that

the safeguard of Theological education, under the strain of this great task of criticism, which is laid upon it, consists in the dogmatic stability of the Catholic Church—the Faith once for all delivered to the Saints . . . That this body of doctrine should become the most intimate possession of mind and heart is of the first importance in fitting a priest for his work. This is what he must minister to men, would he truly serve them . . .

But the intellect plays but a subsidiary part in any true and adequate Theological education . . . pre-eminent above all other factors in preparation for priestly work rises the activity of the spirit . . .

The priestly life—this is what we are here to cultivate in ourselves. and in the students committed to our charge.[17]

17. *Installation Address*, pp. 14-19.

Those were his sentiments in 1903. Five years later, he informed the Trustees that he had not altered them, nor would he be stampeded by demands for change or novelty. "There are," he said,

> two tendencies evident in the educational world of America today . . . one stands for radicalism, exceeding boldness in experiment, big and quick returns. The other is predominantly conservative, lays emphasis upon quality rather than quantity, prefers slow but well-assured progress to novelties which may or may not prove of value. There is little question as to which of these is most in accord with the spirit of the times, and which is the most widely popular. As to which gives greater promise for the future of our educational system there may be more room for discussion.[18]

Dean Robbins refused to yield his major point. In 1914 he was still reminding critics that

> amidst voices which from time to time urge ambitious scholastic experiment, we must remember that the prime task of the Seminary is to train efficient parish priests.[19]

The Robbins Faculty made constant minor adjustments to the curriculum, struggling to make the best of both worlds. Given a freer hand by a revision of the statutes in 1906 which eliminated detailed requirements of topics to be taught in each department, they shifted courses about from term to term, changing the emphasis within them and altering the number of class hours for some subjects. In the Scheme of 1906-07, for example, Hebrew, New Testament, Old Testament, and polity and canon law were reduced in hours to allow additional time to be given to dogmatic theology, liturgics, and social ethics.

Hebrew, of course, was required for those seeking to qualify for the degree, but statutory revision now permitted the increasing number of men whose bishops granted them canonical dispensations from Hebrew to receive the Seminary's diploma of graduation.[20]

18. Tr P, June 2, 1908 (VIII, 623).
19. *G.T.S. Bulletin* (November 1914), p. 2.
20. In the Statutes of 1906, the degree was still "held to represent a scholarly acquaintance with the three languages, Hebrew, Greek, and Latin" (Tr P, May 29, 1906 [VIII, 449]).

For such men the Old Testament courses were given on the English text, and additional courses in the exegesis of the Greek New Testament were prescribed in place of the required work in Hebrew grammar. By 1906-07 nearly one third of the students were normally dispensed from Hebrew, and by 1914-15 the number had risen to more than half the student body. Curriculum revision was further complicated by the fact that men were now appearing with little or no preparation in Greek.[21] By 1905-06 a course in elementary New Testament Greek had been introduced; in 1914-15 it was made an additional required subject for those who had no Greek or had failed the Greek entrance examination.

The adjustments in the curriculum made no provision for electives among the prescribed courses of study. Instead, students were permitted to take electives as "voluntary courses" in addition to the regular schedule, or "substitute courses" if prescribed subjects were passed off by special examination. A small number of electives were offered in each department that might be taken under this scheme. Electives could also be taken at Columbia, for in 1903 Dean Robbins established the long-desired affiliation by agreement with President Nicholas Murray Butler.[22] Students approved by the dean were accepted into university courses without fees, while Columbia seniors and graduate students were admitted to Seminary classes. The university further agreed to accept work done in certain departments of the Seminary in part fulfillment of graduate credit. This limited elective program, though often involving considerable extra work, offered some relief from the straitjacket of the prescribed course. In most years, about eighteen or twenty men added "voluntary courses," or passed off prescribed subjects and enrolled in "substitute courses," though shortly before the First World War, the number occasionally rose to thirty-five a year. Close perusal of the Faculty minutes indicates that the courses passed off by examination were frequently the same few, and one is led to suspect that the requirements in these subjects could be readily fulfilled by reading a textbook or two, or borrowing the class notes of previous years.

21. Tr P, May 14, 1907 (VIII, 522).
22. Faculty Minutes, December 3, 1903.

The Scheme of 1906-07 was rearranged in 1914-15, again by shifting courses and altering the proportion of class hours to make room for a new emphasis on pedagogy (religious education) and American church history. For a time the Faculty experimented with terms of different lengths and a "block system," allowing concentration on fewer subjects at one time. The opportunity to read off prescribed courses was extended to the summer after the Junior year, while "advanced sections" were formed in classes of the Middle and Senior years to permit men of exceptional academic ability to work on a different level from that of some of their classmates. For the most part, these patchwork experiments only nibbled around the edges of the problem of radical revision of the curriculum, nor did they quiet the criticism of the Seminary's intellectual life. In 1907, for example, the General Convention established a Joint Committee "to consider the affairs of the General Theological Seminary, and to report such measures as in its judgment would lead to the greater efficiency of the Seminary."[23] The committee's original task was to explore methods whereby the composition of the Board of Trustees might be altered in the interests of greater effectiveness, and its recommendations led to the changes in 1913 that established the present composition of the Board.[24] The members of the committee, however, interpreted their mandate on a wider scale, proposing in 1908 to discuss the condition of the Seminary with the dean and the professors. The Faculty declined to cooperate with what they feared would be a formal visitation by the committee. They were willing to confer with committee members unofficially, but reminded them that by the constitution visitatorial powers were lodged with bishops who were members of the Board.[25]

The professors were somewhat on the defensive, for much of the criticism was aimed at their lack of public recognition as scholars of distinction. By this time there was a wide expectation that seminary professors, no matter how well-read or gifted as teachers, should

23. *Journal of General Convention 1907*, p. 127.
24. See above, page 269.
25. Faculty Minutes, March 10, 1908.

possess such technical and professional attainments of scholarship as might enable them to make contributions to the intellectual life of the Church. Dean Robbins resented this criticism:

> I feel moved to advert very briefly to certain comments on our lack of distinction in the wider world of learning and literature . . . It were a sorry commentary on our educational ideal if we were unconditionally to gauge scholastic attainment by the degree of popular recognition it receives. Other things being equal, it would be well doubtless for the Seminary to number as many famous men as possible on its Faculty. When the famous men appear who satisfy other requisites, probably the Seminary will seek to obtain their services . . . A famous scholar, on a Theological Faculty, said to me recently: "You may have spent too much of your energy on trying to meet the needs of the average man and to turn out faithful and intelligent parish priests. But if you have erred on one side, we have erred on another, and in trying to promote higher learning we have failed where you have succeeded." And a writer of somewhat wide repute said to me on another occasion, "The members of our Faculty have been writing too much for publication; it begins to tell detrimentally in class-room work."[26]

Some of the professors were undoubtedly vulnerable to the criticism they received. The Dean and the Trustees had missed an unusual opportunity to assemble a large group of experienced teachers and scholars in a short time, for few of the Hoffman professors remained long after the old Dean's death, the notable exception being Dr. Seabury who outlasted Dean Robbins himself. Six men—Jewett, Riley, Richey, Russell, Seibt, and Cady—were all gone within a few years after Dean Hoffman's administration ended. By 1906 Dr. Body's long illness and Dr. Beckwith's retirement removed them from active service. Dr. Roper remained until 1912, when he returned to Canada to become bishop of British Columbia.

The professors who replaced them were generally men whose preparation for seminary teaching had been considered adequate a generation earlier—a parochial ministry with some experience in teaching, but with few of the academic qualifications beginning to

26. Tr P, June 2, 1908 (VIII, 621-622).

The Old Ninth Avenue Front in the Days of the Elevated Trains

be expected of faculty members. In the case of Herbert McKenzie Denslow, however, elected in 1902 to the chair of Pastoral Theology, the qualifications for that professorship were adequately met. He was an experienced parish priest who had broken his parochial ministry with an interlude as chaplain at Kenyon College and Instructor in Liturgics at Bexley Hall from 1893 to 1896. To the vacancy in Ecclesiastical History, the Trustees elected in 1903 Frederick J. Kinsman, who, after a few years in a parish and as a master at St. Paul's School, had become Professor of Church History at the Berkeley Divinity School in 1900. The professorship of Christian Evidences was filled in 1902 by Charles Harris Hayes of the Class of 1894, a scholarly priest who, like Dr. Kinsman, had taught for a few years after an initial parochial ministry.[27] At the

27. In 1906 the name of the department became Christian Apologetics.

time of his election he was Professor of Ecclesiastical History and Liturgics at Trinity College, Hartford. Dr. Seibt's work was taken by Arthur Prince Hunt of the Class of 1900, a brilliant student who had been four years on the staff of the Albany Cathedral. He came to the Seminary as Instructor in Ethics in 1904 and was elected Professor of Christian Ethics four years later. Dr. Beckwith was succeeded in the New Testament professorship in 1906 by Charles Carroll Edmunds of the Class of 1880, whose ministry had been entirely parochial, for some years in the Diocese of Albany. In the same year, some of Professor Body's responsibilities in Old Testament were assumed by Francis Branch Blodgett, who was appointed instructor in that department. A graduate of the Episcopal Theological School in 1902 and a canon of the Albany Cathedral from 1904 to 1906, Blodgett was made adjunct professor in 1908 and full professor in 1912. As the vacancy caused by Randall Hall's resignation in 1899 had not been filled, the teaching of Hebrew was undertaken by Charles Norman Shepard of the Class of 1894, who had remained at the Seminary as a fellow. Successively an instructor and adjunct professor, he was elected to the chair of Hebrew and Cognate Languages in 1906. In time, Dr. Shepard's service to the Seminary matched that of Dr. William Seabury, for Shepard retired in 1940 after forty-three years of teaching.

However limited their experience, the new professors had no lack of zealous devotion to their tasks. Moreover, most of them possessed the vitality and enthusiasm of youth. Dr. Denslow at fifty was the oldest, Dr. Edmunds being slightly younger. The rest were thirty-five or under. Youth, however, did not wholly compensate for the lack of wide academic experience, and until such experience had been acquired, the Faculty wrestled with the problem of curriculum revision less successfully than might otherwise have been.

There were two men, however, of exceptional academic qualifications: William Henry Paine Hatch and Loring Woart Batten. Dr. Hatch, a Harvard Ph.D. and a graduate of the Episcopal Theological School, came to the Seminary as Instructor in New Testament and was made professor in that department in 1913. A profound scholar, he later rose to a place of eminence in the field of New Testament textual criticism. Most of Dr. Hatch's work on Greek and Syrian manuscripts was done after he left Chelsea Square in 1917 to join the faculty of the Episcopal Theological School, but the Seminary enjoyed his influence and teaching for nine years.

Dr. Batten, who received his Ph.D. from the University of Pennsylvania, taught Old Testament at the Philadelphia Divinity School for ten years before coming to New York as rector of St. Mark's Church in 1899. During Professor Body's illness, Dr. Batten served as acting professor, and in 1908 he was elected Clement Clarke Moore Professor of the Literature and Interpretation of Old Testament. A creative scholar who embraced the new biblical scholarship with courage and constructive insight, Professor Batten was an inspiring teacher. His commentaries on Ezra, Nehemiah, and First Samuel, as well as his writings on Hebrew prophecy and Old Testament theology extended his influence far beyond the classroom. Dr. Batten's interests were not confined to the Old Testament. He was a pioneer among those exploring the relation between psychiatry and religion, and he began at the Seminary the first formal study of psychotherapy in its relation to pastoral care.

By 1910 Dean Robbins had come to share the view that however valuable it was to have men of wide parochial experience on the Faculty,

> we must also have teachers of more distinctively academic experience, original investigators, recognized experts in some special department of learning.[28]

He made every effort, and with considerable success, to make subsequent appointments to the Faculty from the ranks of scholars and teachers of that description. When Dr. Kinsman resigned in 1908 to become bishop of Delaware, his place was taken two years later by Arthur Whipple Jenks, a Seminary graduate in the Class of 1892 with fifteen years' experience of teaching church history at Nashotah and Trinity College, Toronto. The vacancy in Christian Apolo-

28. Tr P, May 30, 1911 (IX, 278).

getics caused by the sudden death of Professor Hayes in 1910 was filled by the election of Dr. Dickinson S. Miller, Professor of Philosophy at Columbia. With doctorates in both philosophy and science, Miller had studied at Harvard, Berlin, and Halle. Brilliant, somewhat erratic, and nearly always provocative, Professor Miller often propounded his views with a lack of restraint that nettled his colleagues, but his intellectual demands made the study of apologetics an exacting discipline. When Professor Roper resigned in 1912, the chair of Dogmatic Theology was given to Francis Joseph Hall, who had been teaching at the Western Theological Seminary for more than twenty-five years. Dr. Hall's three volumes of *Theological Outlines*, published in the mid-nineties, had established his reputation as a scholar, and the appearance of his massive ten-volume *Dogmatic Theology*, between 1907 and 1922, provided students with an exhaustive and systematic exposition of traditional Catholic doctrine. In 1909 the Pastoral Theology department was strengthened when Dr. Charles H. Boynton was appointed to assist in homiletics and teach the new courses in pedagogy. A Ph.D. of New York University and a pioneer in the development of the study of religious education, Dr. Boynton had taught for some years at the DeLancey Divinity School. In 1914 he was made Professor of Homiletics and Pedagogy.

The new professors represented a wide range of thought and churchmanship within the Episcopal Church, for with all his ardent devotion to Catholic principles, Dean Robbins was free of any narrow or partisan spirit. He strove earnestly to make the Seminary truly "general" in the welcome it extended to men and ideas over the whole spectrum of Anglicanism. His effort was occasionally marred by divisions in Chelsea Square, both within the Faculty and among the students, the inevitable reflections of the periodic churchmanship controversies that disturbed the Church in the first decades of this century. These were the years when the General Convention's "open-pulpit canon" of 1907 roused Anglo-Catholic fears and led to the conversion of a number of Episcopal clergy to the Roman Church. The excitement on an intellectual level was kept alive by the publication of *Foundations* in 1912 and the struggle between Bishop Gore and Hastings Rashdall, Dr. H. D. A. Major, J. M. Thompson, J. F. Bethune-Baker, and other English Modernists—all of which had its echo in the American seminary classrooms.

Despite his ebullient spirit, Dean Robbins was seldom in robust health, and the continuing strain of Seminary administration laid a heavy burden on his strength. Incapacitated by severe illness in 1911, he was on leave of absence until December 1912. He never fully recovered and, convinced that he was unable to bear the burdens of his office effectively, resigned the deanship in the spring of 1916. He was succeeded in January 1917 by the most distinguished of all the deans of the General Seminary, Hughell Edgar Woodall Fosbroke, a man whose spiritual and intellectual capacities placed him in the category of true greatness. Born in England and educated at Harvard and Nashotah House, Dr. Fosbroke had taught Old Testament for sixteen years at Nashotah and at the Episcopal Theological School, where, at the time of his election, he was Professor of the History and Religion of Israel. Equipped with a penetrating and incisive grasp upon the principles of an effective theological curriculum, and endowed with the capacity to lead the Faculty in the steps of revision, Dean Fosbroke at once attacked the problem of reform in the Seminary's course of study. Designing a new curriculum, he informed the Trustees, required

> a clear conviction as to the right relation to each other of the two functions of the Seminary, that of preparing men for the practical ministry and that of conserving and promoting theological scholarship in the more formal sense of the term. Each has its claims which must not be ignored, but the order in which these claims are recognized is all important. Our primary task must surely be that of training men for the work of the ministry.[29]

This, however, implied no neglect of the encouragement of scholarship:

29. Tr P, May 28, 1918 (X, 376).

The Seminary must not only prepare men for an efficient ministry, but it must also keep in mind the necessity of developing those who may by their further studies and by the use of the method acquired here deepen the intellectual life of the Church . . .[30]

Early in the course men of distinctly scholarly bent of mind would be discovered. These . . . would be encouraged to take more advanced and more highly specialized courses for which the Faculty is abundantly able to make provision . . .

In brief, the principle for which I am contending is that of a primary emphasis on simple, concrete, practical knowledge, necessary alike for the equipment of an efficient ministry and as the foundation of a scholarship which shall be rich and productive.[31]

Dean Fosbroke never ceased to make plain his conviction that

scholarship to be rich and fruitful must understand the needs of the practical ministry, and the men whose bent is in the direction of the practical must have at least some glimpse of the worth and meaning of scholarship.[32]

Intellectual effort and spiritual discipline were inseparably bound together in the vocation to the priesthood:

The Church needs thinking men in its ministry. To say this is not to forget for one moment the indispensable necessity of prayer and love. Indeed, the Seminary is seeking continually ways of deepening men's devotion and quickening eager interest in all that gives practical expression to Christian love and service. But the emphasis on scholarship simply means that there can be no true devotion that does not involve the consecration of all one's powers of thought, no genuine loving service that does not enlist the mind's best energy.[33]

Assisted by Professors Denslow, Shepard, Miller, and Blodgett, Dean Fosbroke concluded in 1918 a thorough and revolutionary revision of the course of study that would implement his principles, providing for

the preservation of the traditional and proved elements of a funda-

30. Tr P, May 24, 1917 (X, 289).
31. *Ibid.*, May 28, 1918 (X, 377).
32. Fosbroke to Miller, March 7, 1918 (Draft), Fosbroke Papers, G.T.S. Library.
33. Tr P, May 24, 1927 (XII, 147).

mental theological discipline, the increase and standardization of elective courses, and the extension of time devoted to instruction. The revision attempts to meet two pressing demands of seminary education, to ground the student in the fundamentals of theological training and at the same time give an opportunity for more detailed study in certain departments; both are quite essential; neither can be ignored.[34]

The new curriculum which went into effect in 1919 involved a complexity imposed by the language requirements. Students were assigned to three groups according to their linguistic studies. Men who passed the Greek entrance examination and enrolled in Hebrew courses were assigned to Group A. In Group B were those who had fulfilled the Greek requirements but were dispensed by their bishops from the study of Hebrew. Group C included those dispensed from Hebrew who were unable to qualify as sufficiently prepared in Greek and, therefore, were required to begin its study in the Seminary. All students who completed their course successfully were awarded the diploma of graduation, but only those in group A who attained an average of 90 per cent were eligible for the degree. Fourth-year students holding a seminary diploma might qualify for the degree by taking four courses each term for two terms, achieving an average of 85 per cent and submitting an acceptable thesis.

The curriculum for each of the three groups was as follows, all courses being three hours per week:

GROUP A

JUNIOR YEAR

FIRST TERM	SECOND TERM
Pastoral Theology (Religious Education)	Pastoral Theology (Sermon Construction)
Christian Missions	Church History to 1400
Old Testament (Historical Books: English text)	Old Testament (Prophetical Books: English text)

34. *G.T.S. Bulletin* (October 1920), p. 2.

Hebrew Language	Hebrew Language
Synoptic Gospels (Greek text)	Synoptic Gospels (Greek text)

MIDDLE YEAR

Old Testament (Pentateuch: Hebrew text)	Old Testament (Psalms: Hebrew text)
Church History 1400-1900	Apologetics
Dogmatic Theology	Dogmatic Theology
Christian Ethics	Christian Ethics
Pauline Epistles (Greek text)	An Elective

GROUP B

JUNIOR YEAR

The courses were the same as for Group A, except that in place of two terms of Hebrew, students took the year of Dogmatic Theology.

MIDDLE YEAR

Each term an elective was taken in place of Dogmatic Theology. In the first term, an elective was taken instead of the course on the Pentateuch. In the second term, the study of the Old Testament Poetical Books and Wisdom Literature replaced the Psalms course.

GROUP C

JUNIOR YEAR

Elementary Greek was substituted for Hebrew, and in place of the year course on the Synoptic Gospels, two terms were devoted to a general introduction to the New Testament.

MIDDLE YEAR

The Pauline Epistles were taken in an English section, and an elective course was substituted for that on the Pentateuch. In the second term, the students joined those of Group B in the Old Testament course on the Poetical Books and Wisdom Literature.

ALL GROUPS

SENIOR YEAR

The Senior Year was the same for all groups, except that in New Testament men in Groups A and B studied Romans and Hebrews on the Greek text, while those in Group C did the Synoptic Gospels.

FIRST TERM	SECOND TERM
Church History (American)	Polity and Law (Constitution & Canons)
Liturgics	Pastoral Theology (Pastoral Care & the Parish)
New Testament (See above)	An Elective
An Elective	An Elective
An Elective	An Elective

This scheme of thirty courses, divided between prescribed and elective work, made a bold and decisive break with the old course of study, and remained the basic pattern of the Seminary's curriculum until 1968.[35] Its remarkable feature was the liberal allowance for electives, the students in Group A having six, those in Group C seven, and those in Group B nine. Additional electives could be taken as "sixth courses." The *Catalogue* of 1919-20 carried forty elective courses, and students might also take advantage of an arrangement with New York University somewhat similar to that with Columbia.

In the fifty years that followed, minor changes were constant. New courses were introduced, the work in the several departments expanded and contracted, the study of Greek made elective, and courses shifted about, especially in the nineteen thirties when it was felt that the studies of the first year should be chiefly historical,

35. A change in the total number of courses was made in the academic year 1926-27 when Hebrew became an elective subject. Thereafter until 1943 two extra courses, thirty-two in all, were required to qualify for the degree without Hebrew. In 1926 the average grade required for the degree was changed to B.

those of the second year speculative and theological, and those of the last year largely practical. Amid these changes, the original liberal number of electives was curtailed to four in the late 'thirties, gradually increasing again to six by the time of the last years of Dean Rose. Yet the basic structure of the first Fosbroke curriculum endured. The drastic revision of 1968 which reduced the whole course of study from five subjects each term to four, returned more closely to Dean Fosbroke's principles of 1919 than any of the intervening experiments. Its establishment of a minimum core of required work embodied what he had called "the traditional and proved elements of a fundamental theological discipline," while its generous expansion of the proportion of elective to required work was in accord with his original design for seminary education.

II
The Seminary of Yesterday

In the thirty years of his deanship, Hughell Fosbroke reoriented the life of Chelsea Square, opening to men a broader conception of the scope of theological education and a deeper understanding of the vocation of the Seminary in the Church. The intellectual activity of the community revealed the impress of his own relentless standards of scholarship and his refusal to isolate theological study from the widest range of man's learning. The Dean was preeminently a teacher, and one who taught both students and teachers. His clarity of insight and incisiveness of mind, breadth of learning and depth of appreciation were matched by few of his contemporaries. Yet, however accurate, this description of Hughell Fosbroke will be inadequate to many who knew and admired him. To men who penetrated his shield of reticence and found behind it the deep springs of Christian affection, or to those who braved his forbidding manner to meet the redemptive outreach of a wise priest and pastor, perhaps no description can be adequate. Dean Fosbroke had no superficial charm of personality. Tall, craggy, and Lincolnesque in appearance, he often seemed to be aloof, concealing his warmth of spirit and genuine human concern under the abruptness of his shy reserve. Nothing, however, could conceal his dedication to the will and purposes of God, the commitment of his whole heart and mind to the demands of his vocation. Through this he ministered the reality of God's presence and power to those about him. To listen to his lectures on the Prophets was to experience the moment of truth of God's reign over history and creation, and His demand for man's obedience in each decision and every responsibility. To hear him read the Holy Week gospels was to encounter Christ in his passion, and to feel the inescapable Christian tension of embracing the pain of God's judgment and the recreative power of God's love at one and the same time. The Dean had little talent for drama and no shred of sentimentality in these things. He revealed only what was in him, a profound understanding of what it meant to love and to obey the living God. From this rose his capacity for leadership, the compelling personality that drew from men their best efforts, and the unflinching courage with which he assumed responsibility for decisions that affected not only the welfare of the Seminary but the lives and vocations of generations of students as well.

Dean Fosbroke did not suffer fools patiently, nor did he withhold his ready rebuke of all that was trivial and superficial. He asked of students "that high seriousness which will not stop short of giving the best that is in one to the task at hand."[1] He knew too well that

> there exists, along with the desire to serve, a strange unwillingness to admit in practice that service involves the acceptance of discipline. This displays itself in a tendency to sit rather lightly to the responsibility of seminary life. The Candidate for Orders too often seems to think of himself as a privileged person. Obligations must not interfere with his personal liberty. Accustomed to having his own way, he goes out into the Ministry impatient of difficulty and opposition, but little prepared to endure hardness . . . the Seminary should in all kindness help the student to learn the value of the disciplined life and of the frank and dutiful acceptance of the obligations of his calling.[2]

Nor did he shrink from the painful duty his convictions laid upon him. Students whose failure in seriousness of purpose was conspic-

1. Tr P, May 24, 1921 (XI, 73-74).
2. *Ibid.*, May 24, 1917 (X, 288-289).

Photograph by Blackstone Studios
Courtesy of *The Living Church*

Dean Fosbroke

uous met a firm insistence that they "continue their studies elsewhere if their Bishops desire to continue them as Candidates."[3]

The "high seriousness" the Dean demanded was revealed when students worked and prayed to the limit of their capacities. He did not expect them all to be scholars:

> It cannot be too often insisted that the intellectual life of the Seminary is of the first importance. This involves no failure to recognize the absolute necessity of a full and rich devotional life. In a theological school there can be no progress unless men are giving themselves to prayer and have in their hearts a great longing to be used in the service of others. But it is sometimes forgotten that a man who is preparing himself for the teaching work that the ministry involves, cannot attain full measure of consecration unless he is dedicating his mind to the service of God. I need hardly say that this does not mean that there is room only for men of brilliant intellectual gifts. Indeed, I have seen many students fail in their examinations and yet evince a sturdy sincerity of mind and persistance of endeavor which testify to an honest use of their limited powers such as gives promise of great usefulness in the ministry.[4]

He emphasized the point some years later to Professor Hall. "I quite agree with you," he wrote,

> that it is neither necessary nor possible to make every minister a scholar. This Seminary must always put first the need of the average plain man. But it must help him to think clearly and honestly up to the very limit of his powers. In my thirty years' observation of Seminary life I have learned at least this, that there can be no wholesome spiritual growth unless men are using honestly such intellectual activity as God has given them.[5]

Never for a moment would Dean Fosbroke allow a sundering of the academic and spiritual aspects of a man's preparation for the priesthood. He explained to the Trustees:

3. Tr P, May 24, 1921 (XI, 75).
4. *Ibid.*, 73.
5. Fosbroke to Hall (Draft), October 25, 1927, Fosbroke Papers, G.T.S. Library.

It is often supposed that the balance and proportion of our work can be fairly estimated by simply considering the time allotted to the various phases of our activity, intellectual, practical, spiritual. In reality it is the unity of these which we must continually seek. The teaching of the classroom ought to be so informed with the spirit of reverence that every fact and every truth is felt to stand in relation to that revealing love of God which is the source of all our knowledge; our devotions ought to breathe that sincerity which is the soul of scholarship, and both in the classroom and in the Chapel we can never forget the needs of men, women, and children for whom we are learning to be God's ministers.[6]

Such was the mind and spirit of the man whose influence brought the Seminary to its finest achievements and continued to shape the intellectual aspirations and spiritual life of the community in Chelsea Square for more than a decade after his retirement.

One of Dean Fosbroke's well-known accomplishments was the assembling of a group of colleagues whose learning was of exceptional distinction and who, at least during the decade from 1925 to 1935, had an influence upon the intellectual life of the Church unsurpassed by the scholars in any of the seminaries. Changes in the Faculty began on the eve of the Dean's arrival. Professor Seabury died in 1916, bequeathing to the Seminary the bulk of his library, including a number of his great-grandfather's books as well as Bishop Seabury's letters of orders, certificate of consecration, and the concordat he made with the bishops of the Scottish Episcopal Church—priceless documents of the heritage of the American Episcopal Church. Ralph B. Pomeroy of the Class of 1901 took over William Seabury's work, and was elected professor in 1919. When he resigned six years later, polity and canon law was taught by John A. Richardson, a graduate of the Episcopal Theological School. The Ludlow Professorship was not filled after Pomeroy's resignation, and in later adjustments to the curriculum, the study of polity was absorbed into the church history courses, while the Church's canon law in its pastoral aspects was made a topic in the course on pastoral care and parochial administration.

6. Tr P, May 15, 1930 (XII, 367).

When Professor Blodgett resigned in 1921 to become dean of St. Paul's Cathedral in Erie, Pennsylvania, Dean Fosbroke took a larger share of the Old Testament instruction. Upon Dr. Batten's retirement in 1930, the Dean assumed charge of that department, thus identifying himself more closely with the academic activity of the Seminary than had any dean since Professor Seymour. Administrative responsibilities, however important, were never allowed priority over Dean Fosbroke's study or classroom work, and it was this intimate involvement with the academic enterprise and the daily experience of his professors that assisted him in assembling around him the kind of faculty he wanted. Hebrew was still in Professor Shepard's capable hands, and to assist the Dean in Old Testament, Cuthbert Aikman Simpson, a graduate of King's College, Halifax, and a former Rhodes Scholar, was made instructor in 1930 and assistant professor in 1934.[7] For New Testament, Professor Burton Scott Easton was brought from the Western Theological Seminary in 1919, after fourteen years of teaching there and at Nashotah House. He succeeded to the Glorvina Russell Hoffman Professorship upon Dr. Edmunds' retirement in 1929, and in the same year, Donald Fraser Forrester, a teaching fellow who had graduated in 1918, was made assistant professor.

In quick succession others were added to the Faculty. Frank Stanton Burns Gavin of the Class of 1915, whose brilliant researches had earned him doctorates at both Columbia and Harvard, was elected to Dr. Jenks' chair of Ecclesiastical History in 1923. To succeed Dickinson Miller, who resigned in 1924 to become Professor of Philosophy at Smith College, Dean Fosbroke brought from England Leonard Hodgson, then one of the most promising young scholars in the Anglican world. In 1928 Marshall Bowyer Stewart of the Class of 1905, who, like Dr. Easton, had taught at both the Western Seminary and Nashotah, was elected Professor of Dogmatic Theology.

7. Dr. Simpson was made Professor of Old Testament Literature and Interpretation in 1940. At that time, the designation of the professorship by the name of Clement Clarke Moore was abandoned. In 1950, in recognition of an annual grant from Trinity Parish, the Old Testament chair became known as the Trinity Church Professorship.

Few will challenge the brilliance of this galaxy of scholars. Every alumnus of that time cherishes his own recollections of the intellectual excitements of the Seminary. Dr. Easton's crisp and emphatic lectures opened his inexhaustible store of learning to class after class, while a stream of articles, books, and technical monographs poured from his pen. Easton became a New Testament scholar of international repute with his commentary on *The Gospel of St. Luke* (1926). Two years later, *The Gospel Before the Gospels*, an account of Synoptic study since 1900, contained a searching examination of the new form criticism, and it was followed shortly by a contribution to New Testament theology in *Christ in the Gospels.* Among his other writings were *The Purpose of Acts* and a commentary on *The Pastoral Epistles*, the latter published in 1947, the year before his retirement from the Seminary. Dr. Easton's amazing versatility of interest and learning was revealed on the one hand in a translation and edition of *The Apostolic Tradition of Hippolytus*, and, on the other, by his collaboration with Howard Chandler Robbins in the publication of *The Eternal Word in the Modern World*, an exposition of the Prayer Book epistles and gospels for liturgical preaching.

Dr. Gavin's *Seven Centuries of the Problem of Church and State* is his only book now in frequent use, though *Some Aspects of Contemporary Greek Orthodox Thought* and *The Jewish Antecedents of the Christian Sacraments*, a significant contribution to knowledge in this area, were widely read in the 'forties. His impact upon the students was marked by the same enthusiastic and arresting presentation of the history and tradition of the Church that Mahan, Seymour, and Richey had possessed before him. In the ecumenical scene of the 'thirties, particularly on the side of Orthodox-Anglican relations, Professor Gavin made a lasting contribution to the advance of ecumenical understanding in the Episcopal Church. For many, though, the memory of Frank Gavin is inseparable from the unswerving devotion to the Catholic faith in all its fulness that made him both a beloved pastor and an energetic apologist to the day of his untimely death in 1938 at the age of forty-eight.

Compared with his colleagues, Dean Fosbroke wrote little for publication. He could never overcome a reluctance to commit his restless and meticulous scholarship to the finality of the printed page. He contributed articles on the Prophetic Literature and the Book of Amos to *The Interpreter's Bible*, gave the Winslow Lectures at Seabury-Western in 1950 on "Divine Transcendence in the Old Testament," and was persuaded to publish some of his most penetrating Good Friday meditations in *By Means of Death*. That was about all.[8] But he constantly encouraged his professors to the research he knew was essential to the refreshment of their scholarship, and there were few men on the teaching staff who did not respond to the Dean's confidence and encouragement. This was the experience of Cuthbert Simpson when he came to the Seminary as a fellow and tutor in 1928. Later the Dean's associate in Old Testament, he remained in Chelsea Square as professor and subdean until he accepted the Regius Professorship of Hebrew at Oxford in 1954. Dr. Simpson's *Revelation and Response in the Old Testament* brought the thesis of his magisterial analysis of *The Early Traditions of Israel* within the grasp of his undergraduate students, and in his lectures, the history and literature of the Israelites became subjects of living interest and immediate relevance. Few professors in the Seminary's history won the affection of the students to the degree that Dr. Simpson enjoyed it. They relished the informality of his hospitality, accepted contritely his occasional vehement rebukes, and turned to him constantly for help and guidance that was unfailingly given.

When seeking a successor to Professor Miller, Dean Fosbroke resisted all pressures to appoint a man whose specialty was the popular presentation of the Christian faith. He wanted a scholar of the stature of C. C. J. Webb or A. E. Taylor, both of whom he admired, a teacher who combined a profound grasp of Christian the-

8. He also contributed a chapter to *Preaching the Christian Year*, ed. H. A. Johnson (New York, 1957), in 1957. A number of his lectures and short essays were published in 1962 in *God in the Heart of Things*, edited by Edward A. French, and including a memoir of Dean Fosbroke by Stephen F. Bayne, Jr.

Marshall B. Stewart

Burton S. Easton

A Galaxy of Scholars in the Fosbroke Era

Frank S. B. Gavin

Leonard Hodgson

Cuthbert A. Simpson
Seminary Portrait by J. C. Johansen

Charles N. Shepard
Seminary Portrait by S. E. Dickinson

ology with a sympathetic understanding of the world to which the Church's apologetic was addressed. He found him in Leonard Hodgson, then the thirty-six-year-old Dean of Divinity in Magdalen College, Oxford, whose learning was attested by a distinguished degree in both classical schools and theology. Hodgson's *And Was Made Man* and his *Essays in Christian Philosophy* belong to his six years in Chelsea Square, before his return to England in 1931 to become canon of Winchester and later Regius Professor at Oxford, achieving fame as a philosopher and theologian by his writings on the Trinity and the Atonement and by *For Faith and Freedom*, his Gifford Lectures of 1956.[9]

The other member of this band of scholars was Marshall Bowyer Stewart. His Paddock Lectures of 1925, *God and Reality*, reveal the perceptiveness that characterized his teaching of theology for more than twenty years in Chelsea Square. Patient with his students, gentle in all things, and possessed of a transparent simplicity of life

9. Canon Hodgson returned to the Seminary in 1936 to give the Paddock Lectures, published under the title *The Grace of God in Faith and Philosophy*.

and devotion, Professor Stewart's quiet and unostentatious influence was far-reaching. Few who knew him will forget his love of art and nature, audible in the enthusiastic musical evenings at his house, and visible in the care he lavished upon the flower beds of the Close. He carried a heavy schedule of Seminary teaching, for after Professor Hunt died in 1925 and the basic courses in the Department of Ethics and Moral Theology had been given for a few years by Howard H. Hassinger and Haven Palmer Perkins, both teaching fellows, Dr. Stewart assumed charge of this instruction, offering courses in ascetical theology as well.

Around the central body of scholars were assembled competent instructors in other fields. The demands on the department of Pastoral Theology, for example, had expanded so widely that they could no longer be met by one or two professors. Dr. Denslow resigned the professorship in 1924, though he remained sub-dean and lecturer in Liturgics for some years thereafter. After an experiment in which Thomas Sparks Cline, an able and experienced parish priest, combined the rectorship of St. Peter's Church with the chair of Pastoral Theology, in 1929 Dr. Howard Chandler Robbins, then dean of the Cathedral of St. John the Divine, accepted the professorship with the understanding that he would concentrate his attention upon instruction in preaching. To assist in the courses in pastoral care and parochial administration, Frederick Curtiss Lauderburn of the Class of 1897, who had been at one time Professor of Pastoral Theology at the Berkeley Divinity School, was made instructor in 1927, and clergy of the city were employed as visiting lectures on special topics. Lauderburn was appointed chaplain in 1930, with responsibility for the chapel and much of the pastoral care of the students, taking over as well the direction of their fieldwork which Professor Cline had organized. The growing interest in the technical and pastoral aspects of social work led to an arrangement whereby lecturers from the New York School of Social Work conducted a new required course for Seniors until Miss Mary Swan Brisley of the Church Mission of Help was made lecturer in this field in 1937. From the beginning, Dean Fosbroke had constantly directed the students' attention to "the problems of our social order," seeking ways to increase

> that familiarity with the actual conditions under which most men and women get a living, of which students for the most part remain sadly ignorant.[10]

Drawing upon the resources of New York's School of Social Work and other similar institutions; introducing the required study of social work and elective courses in rural and urban sociology; encouraging the activities of the Christian Guild for Social Action, an organization that flourished among the students in the 'thirties to implement the "prayer, study and work of those who seek to apply the principles of Christ to the economic and industrial society"; endeavoring to make the students' fieldwork a program of broad experience—all these helped to inform and sharpen the social conscience of the community in Chelsea Square.

When Professor Boynton resigned in 1929, courses in religious education were undertaken by various members of the Faculty, as well as by visiting experts in this field, among whom were Charles H. Ricker, John W. Suter, Miss Adelaide T. Case, and Otis R. Rice, the latter also offering courses in pastoral psychology in succession to the study of psychotherapy and pastoral care that Professor Batten had introduced. The mounting interest in Christian education was assisted by the residence in the Close of Dr. Daniel A. McGregor, at that time executive secretary of the Department of Religious Education in the National Council. Sometime Professor of Dogmatic Theology in the Western Seminary, Dr. McGregor taught the required course in apologetics for ten years after Professor Hodgson returned to England.

Mr. Clement R. Gale, one of the founders of the American Guild of Organists and Instructor in Ecclesiastical Music since the last year of Dean Hoffman, was succeeded in 1934 by Dr. Ray Francis Brown, a graduate of Oberlin College and its Conservatory of Music. After some years as director of the Music School at Fiske

10. Tr P, May 28, 1918 (X, 377).

University, Dr. Brown had studied in England with Sir Sydney Nicholson at the College of St. Nicolas. An accomplished musician and an inspiring teacher, Ray Brown's love for all that was best in church music, as well as his exacting standards of performance, made the Seminary's chapel music widely known. He was a member of General Convention's Joint Commission on Church Music, an active participant in the production of the Hymnal of 1940, and his publication of Anglican settings for the psalms and canticles in *The Oxford American Psalter* was an invaluable service to many church choirs.[11]

However competent were his professors and their assistants in the lecture hall, Dean Fosbroke was convinced that the process of theological education at its best required more than lectures, for

> the lecture system by itself assumes on the part of the student a much greater ability to read and to think than is actually his. Every lecturer refers his class to a large number of books, and for the most part the students . . . read with little discrimination and their power to understand conflicting theories . . . is sadly limited. Valuable conferences are held in some of the courses, but something more is needed . . . If means could be found for a closer supervision of the reading combined with free discussion of the subject matter of the lectures . . . the gain would be very great.[12]

This was in 1917, and though the curriculum revision of 1919 provided opportunity for group discussion in its elective seminars, the Dean felt strongly that this same advantage should be extended to the prescribed studies. The lectures should be supplemented by

> full opportunity for discussion in small groups. For this work we need men as preceptors or tutors, for to ask a Professor to carry the whole of this additional burden is to forbid that study and research which are essential to the vitality of his teaching. In our definitely established graduate work we are now happily making a beginning of training men who will be qualified for such preceptorial functions.[13]

11. Dr. Brown died in 1964. His successor as Associate Professor and Director of Music was Dr. Leonard Raver, formerly Associate Professor of Music at Pennsylvania State University.
12. Tr P, May 24, 1917 (X, 289-290).
13. *Ibid.*, May 29, 1923 (XI, 244).

Three years earlier, the graduate program had been expanded by the provisions of 1920 for awarding the degree of Master of Sacred Theology after at least one full year of advanced study. As fellowship endowments for the support of full-time graduate students had increased from the five in Dean Hoffman's time to nine, it was decided to request the holders of fellowships to give perceptorial or tutorial assistance.[14] The influence of Leonard Hodgson largely determined the decision to adopt a modification of the English totorial system as the supplement to the lectures. Beginning in the fall of 1926, each Junior met his tutor weekly, the basis of their discussion being the student's brief essay on an assigned topic related to his reading and the material of the lectures. In the next year, the system was extended to the Middle Class, the students then meeting their tutors in pairs. As an adjunct to the tutorial system, in the Senior year the students were divided into four or five groups, each meeting weekly with one of the senior professors for a less structured discussion.[15]

An immediate success, the tutorial system altered the whole dynamic of the Seminary's curriculum and provided, as Dean Fosbroke reported to the Trustees,

> that personal guidance which enables a student of good will to come to close grips with the problems . . . and to do his own sustained and honest thinking.[16]

Dean Fosbroke always remained firm in the conviction that the work of the tutors had peculiar importance in theological education:

14. The George Williamson Smith Fellowship and the John Alsop King Fellowship were founded in 1910; the Ethel H. Cotheal Fellowship in 1912; and in 1918 the Mary Louise Styles Foundation was established with an endowment of more than $70,000 to provide grants to graduate students and teaching fellows. The Samuel Roosevelt Johnson Fellowship was added to these in 1939.
15. The groups were abandoned in 1947 when Dean Rose began the Dean's weekly conference with the Seniors. The best description of the tutorial system in its early days is given by Professor Hodgson in the G.T.S. *Seminarian* (1931), pp. 28-36.
16. Tr P, January 18, 1928 (XII, 213).

In other departments of learning it may be enough that a man secure mastery of the subject; in theology the subject must penetrate and master the man if his knowledge is to enable him to help others. Intensive work with the individual is therefore indispensable.[17]

The tutorial system remained an essential part of the Seminary's academic enterprise for forty years. For the greater part of that time, the results fulfilled Dean Fosbroke's confident expectations. At best, men received from their tutors a rigorous training in disciplined habits of study, and were challenged to full use of their intellectual capacities. At the same time, they were drawn into a close personal and pastoral relation with a young priest, but a few years older, who gave himself readily to his students as "guide, philosopher and friend." The demands upon the Seminary tutors were severe. They had to resist the temptation to indoctrinate their students or coach them in their courses—particularly difficult with students of limited academic ability—and they were called upon to acquire a sound grasp of a wide range of theological learning. The tutorial experience was one of inestimable value to those preparing themselves to fulfill a vocation to an academic ministry in the Church.

Many an older graduate of the Seminary will recall the tutorial sessions of the late 'twenties and 'thirties. In them, he was led to explore the profundities of Taylor's *Faith of a Moralist*, Hocking's *Meaning of God in Human Experience*, Thornton's *Incarnate Lord*, and discussed with his mentor William Temple's *Nature, Man and God* or Rawlinson's *Essays on the Trinity and the Incarnation*. He was introduced to Quick's *Christian Sacraments*, Moberley's *Ministerial Priesthood*, and Evelyn Underhill's *Worship*; learned to appreciate the writings of Baron von Hügel and Kenneth Kirk; and perhaps argued with his tutor the merits of Bethune-Baker's *Early History of Christian Doctrine*. The prevailing theological tone of the Seminary thirty years ago was the "Liberal Catholicism" of *Essays Catholic and Critical*, though Dean Fosbroke was never con-

17. Tr P, May 21, 1935 (XIII, 233).

tent with any "prevailing tone," uncritically adopted. He saw to it that the students came into contact with as many distinguished minds as possible, and the list of occasional speakers invited to Chelsea Square included Bishop Gore and Bishop Headlam, Arthur Darby Nock, Alfred Deissman, Rudolph Otto, Johannes Hempel, Allison Peers, Lindsay Dewar, Adolph Keller, Sergius Bulgakov, and Paul Elmer More. Among the students, several associations for intellectual stimulation flourished, the best known being the Origen Society, formed in the academic year 1934-35 by ten members of the Union Theological Seminary and ten from the General Seminary, and which has continued its meetings to the present time.

Between the two World Wars the enrollment in the Seminary surpassed that of any previous period in its history. There was a sharp drop in the number of students from 1916 to 1919, only 68 men being registered at the end of the First World War. More than 20 students had enlisted in the armed forces, as well as a number of graduates, while nearly 100 alumni served as chaplains, most of them overseas with the A. E. F. or the Red Cross in France. Eleven men gave their lives in the service of their country. The recovery in enrollment was rapid after 1919. By 1922 there were 101 students, and in 1933 the total number had risen to 192, its peak in Dean Fosbroke's administration. Of these, 125 were in the undergraduate classes, 22 were Special Students, and the rest graduates. Thereafter, during the years of the depression, there was some decline, the average number in the decade of the 'thirties being about 150.

Rigorous as they were, the academic pressures did not inhibit student activity in other aspects of Seminary life. The Missionary Society, its budget of pledges increased by the proceeds of the students' annual dramatic performances, continued to support the Philippine Mission at Upi among its projects, and expanded the neighborhood work into the Chelsea Mission that continued well into the time of Dean Rose. After 1934, a number of men began work under the Council for Clinical Training or entered the Summer Training Program begun in 1937 under the auspices of the

New York City Mission Society. The social life of the Seminary community was strong in those years. Students enjoyed the hospitality of the members of the Faculty and their families, and immense quantities of tea and cakes were consumed at the tables of Mrs. Easton, Mrs. Simpson, Mrs. Forrester, and other women of the Close. The erection of Seabury Hall in the academic year 1931-32, in accordance with the designs of Alfred Morton Githens, provided a spacious common room as a student social center, as well as a small auxiliary refectory, apartments for the tutorial staff, a Faculty common room, and the auditorium that Dean Robbins had wanted more than twenty years before. The original building fund had grown slowly over the years, and by 1931, chiefly through the efforts of Paul Matthews, then bishop of New Jersey, sufficient funds were in hand for the cornerstone to be laid on May 26 of that year. The building was a memorial not only of the first Bishop of Connecticut, but also of his descendants who had served so many years on the Faculty, and the crowded ceremony of dedication on January 20, 1932 was enhanced by the presence of Judge Samuel Seabury, son of Professor William Seabury, and then in the midst of his famous campaign against corruption in the affairs of New York City.[18] Seabury Hall was completed at a cost of $155,000. Appeals for its building fund were part of a wider effort, launched in 1925, to raise over a million dollars to increase the Seminary's endowment, provide higher salaries for the Faculty and staff, and enable the modernization of some of the buildings and facilities. Operating expenses had risen sharply after the First World War, and despite the constant assistance of the Society for Promoting Religion and Learning, as well as other friends of the Seminary, the income was no longer adequate to meet them. For four years, Dean Fosbroke devoted a large amount of his time to the uncongenial task of raising money, and the strains of this labor were so severe as to

18. Judge Seabury married a daughter of Professor Richey. There is a pleasant description of social life among the faculty families in the 'nineties in Herbert Mitgang's *Man Who Rode the Tiger* (New York, 1963), a biography of Judge Seabury.

send him on a leave of absence in 1929. The assistance of Professor Batten and a loyal response of the alumni, however, saw nearly $700,000 raised before the campaign ceased. The endowment was increased significantly, salaries were raised, buildings received at least some essential repairs, central heating was everywhere installed, and the library fund augmented—all just on the eve of the great depression, a disaster that threatened the Seminary with a return of the precarious financial situation that existed before the coming of Dean Hoffman.

Soon after the financial crash of 1929, the Seminary's income dropped at an alarming rate. Only the most stringent economies could contain the annual deficits within manageable proportions. After 1932, when no credit balance would appear for fourteen years, even the herculean efforts of Admiral Reginald R. Belknap, who became treasurer in 1930, were of little avail. The gap between income and expenses widened with inexorable regularity as costs rose and the value of investments depreciated. From 1934 to 1941, the annual deficits ran between $30,000 and $40,000. With the outbreak of the Second World War and the further increase in costs of maintenance, the situation became critical. Fortunately, the oldest supporters of the Seminary rallied to its relief. Trinity Parish made substantial annual grants, and the Society for Promoting Religion and Learning, unfailingly responsive to the Seminary's distress, increased its contributions to nearly $30,000 a year.

In these severe straits, the Associate Alumni rose magnificently to the Seminary's need. In 1938 a group of graduates, led by Gregory Mabry of the Class of 1915 asked the alumni to observe "Seminary Sunday" in their parishes, appealing for a special offering on the Second Sunday after Easter. Sixty-three of them responded with a total offering of $1208.50. The next year the offering for the Seminary was over $4500, and in 1940 nearly $8000 was raised. In that year the General Convention, acting upon a motion offered by Dr. Roelif H. Brooks, rector of St. Thomas Church, New York, and a trustee of the Seminary, adopted the plan for a special seminary offering throughout the whole Church on a Sunday appointed by the Presiding Bishop.[19] Theological Education Sunday soon became the occasion of a church-wide appeal by the graduates of the several seminaries in support of their respective institutions. A movement had been launched which, though it did not affect materially the critical situation at the end of the depression or in the early years of the war, gradually gained such momentum as to be of immense assistance to the Seminary in the period of recovery after 1944.[20]

The Second World War again drastically reduced the student body. In the academic year 1944-45, for example, though more than 30 graduates and Special Students were registered, there were only 8 Juniors and a total of 33 in the three undergraduate classes. The following year was much the same, 36 men in the regular classes. Though the demand for men in the armed forces and the operation of the Selective Service Act were the chief causes of this diminished enrollment, Dean Fosbroke's admissions policy did not encourage men to take advantage of the draft exemption extended to theological students. He was reluctant to accept applicants until they had confronted their duty conscientiously and were prepared to believe that vocation to the ministry laid upon them "a degree of self-sacrifice fully equal to anything that military service demands."[21] It would be unfortunate, he felt, if men in the ministry of the postwar world had not shared in the experience of their generation. He therefore accepted only those men who in his judgment "faced fairly all that is involved in asking for deferment from the national service."[22] The Dean's own personal convictions were made plain in his answer to an inquiry about theological students and the draft. "I cannot feel," he wrote,

> that it is desirable that theological students should be exempt. No one can doubt the importance of the ministry to the morale of the country, but that importance will be greatly diminished if the ranks of the min-

19. *Journal of General Convention 1940*, p. 378.
20. The annual offering for the Seminary was more than $50,000 in 1950. By 1961 it had passed the $100,000 mark, and five years later it was nearly $150,000.
21. Tr P, May 26, 1942 (XIV, 15).
22. *Ibid.*, May 25, 1943 (XIV, 24).

istry of tomorrow should be filled with men who have had no part in the disciplined service of their country. There is this difference between the minister and the doctor, that the year in service may well be a very valuable element in a man's preparation for the ministry.[23]

The war depleted the Seminary staff as well as the student body, as employees and members of the administrative force were called up for service. Indeed, at times it seemed as though only the devoted efforts of Admiral Belknap, Mr. Frank Strup, and Miss Helen B. Chapman kept the routine operation of the institution from grinding to a halt. Mr. Strup came to the Seminary as an office boy in 1906 to begin a period of faithful service that lasted more than fifty-five years. He was invaluable in the operations of both the business and the academic offices, serving in turn through the years as custodian, bursar, and registrar, all the while a devoted guardian of the Seminary's traditions and customs as well as its property. Miss Chapman, the dietitian and mistress of the refectory from 1931 to 1968, rose to meet every new emergency with characteristic cheerfulness and competence, taking upon herself a multitude of domestic responsibilities when the war curtailed her staff. The dining hall in Hoffman Hall was closed, as were a number of the dormitories, and the Seminary community was accommodated during these years in the auxiliary refectory in the basement of Seabury Hall.

As the country emerged from the Second World War, Dean Fosbroke faced the same urgent task that had confronted him nearly thirty years before, the assembling of a faculty of competent scholars and teachers. Five professorships had gradually become vacant between 1925 and 1941—Ecclesiastical History, Hebrew and Cognate Languages, Apologetics, Pastoral Theology, and Moral Theology. The necessity of strict economy during the depression had made the election of new professors impossible, a situation that inspired one of the trustees to remark that in these lean years the Faculty of the Seminary resembled a square of British infantry

23. Fosbroke to Roberts (Draft), June 24, 1941, Fosbroke Papers; see also Tr P, May 27, 1941 (XIV, 14).

Dean Fosbroke Leaving the Chapel after
His Last Commencement 1947

under fire in one of the Victorian campaigns: when a man dropped, his comrades just stood closer. While some of the work was in the hands of lecturers from outside the Seminary, a large part of the instruction was carried on by members of the tutorial staff in addition to their own duties. The situation was far better than might be inferred, however, for the Seminary was fortunate in possessing the tutorial services of three graduates of unusual capabilities: Thomas J. Bigham, who took much of the instruction in ethics and moral theology; W. Norman Pittenger, who after 1944 carried the entire Department of Apologetics as well as considerable elective work in theology; and Edward Rochie Hardy, Jr., whose wide range of theological learning and encyclopedic knowledge equipped him to teach Hebrew, Greek, history, missions, liturgics—indeed, he had extraordinary competence in nearly all the subjects of the curriculum. Dr. Hardy bore a heavy burden of classroom work for many years before he was called to a professorship at the Berkeley Divinity School in 1945. There was, moreover, one new appointment to the Faculty in 1940. Miles Lowell Yates of the Class of 1914, formerly a professor at Bard College, was made chaplain after Frederick Lauderburn's death. A priest of wide pastoral experience, counselor and confessor to students and Faculty alike, Miles Yates communicated to those about him a large measure of his serenity of spirit and self-abnegating devotion. For many years he taught an introduction to preaching and the course popularly known as "Baby Greek."

Dean Fosbroke refused to be discouraged by the combination of circumstances that threatened ruin to much of his work. He was confident that the Seminary would emerge from its trials stronger than before, and, indeed, by 1945 signs of financial recovery had appeared. There was no deficit in that year. A group of laymen from the Trustees were meeting with modest success soliciting gifts for the Seminary, and the Theological Education Sunday offering was steadily mounting. The Dean warned the Trustees against delay in filling the vacancies in the ranks of the Faculty:

> The Seminary owes it to these men who have wholeheartedly committed themselves to the unwearying service of theology to strengthen their hands by adding to their number, thus relieving them of the strain under which they have been working for some years past . . . It must mean the provision of a very considerable addition to our income, but . . . to make ample provision for those who are to mould the thought of the coming generation, to assure them of that margin of comfort and of opportunity for the realization of the ideals of scholarship upon which the heart of every good teacher is set, ought to be the unquestioned priority in every institution of learning.[24]

Dean Fosbroke made a start upon the task which he knew would be the first duty of his successor when the chair of Ecclesiastical

24. Tr P, May 22, 1945 (XV, 17).

History was filled by the election of Powel Mills Dawley. A graduate of the Episcopal Theological School who had received his doctorate at the University of Cambridge and was then dean of St. Luke's Cathedral in Portland, Maine, Dr. Dawley was the first of the new group of professors who came to Chelsea Square in the early years of the Seminary's recovery.

At the end of the academic year 1946-47, Hughell Fosbroke retired from the office he had held for thirty years, and Lawrence Rose, dean of the Berkeley Divinity School, was unanimously elected his successor. A graduate of Harvard, and of the Seminary in the Class of 1926, Dean Rose had been among the first group of fellows entrusted with the tutorial responsibilities instituted in the year of his graduation. After a short period of parochial work in Montana, he was a member of the faculty at the Central Theological College in Tokyo until the expulsion of foreign missionary personnel from Japan in 1941 brought him back to teach for a year at Bexley Hall before becoming dean of Berkeley. No successor could have pleased Dean Fosbroke more. Lawrence Rose was a thoughtful and perceptive scholar, trained at the Seminary in the days of its most brilliant teachers. Sharing fully Dean Fosbroke's conception of the nature and scope of theological education, Dean Rose was yet aware that the reinvigoration of the activities of the Seminary could not be achieved by an attempt to turn the clock back to the late 'twenties or early 'thirties, however halcyon those days had been. The effects of the war had been far-reaching, and the task was not only one of conserving ideals and values that had a permanent place in theological education but also of finding ways to give them new vigor and expression in the postwar generation.

A formidable array of tasks confronted Dean Rose: the expansion of the Faculty and tutorial staff, as well as new provisions for their housing and more adequate salaries for the support of their families; the extensive rehabilitation of the Seminary's physical plant; and the augmentation of the endowment to sustain a program of expanded operation and keep pace with the rising costs of maintenance. A note of urgency was imparted to them all by the unprecedented influx of students, many of them returning from battle experience

Dean Rose

in the Pacific or on the Normandy beaches. There were 78 students in the three regular classes by the academic year 1947-48, but a Junior Class of 52 appeared in September 1948, 54 in the next year, and 60 in 1950. This steep acceleration brought the number of undergraduates to 165, while Special Students and graduates raised the total to over 200, the highest point reached in the Seminary's long history. Numbers of undergraduates leveled off at approximately 150 after this first abrupt increase, with an additional 25 to 30 graduates and 15 to 20 Special Students enrolled each year.[25]

The increased enrollment taxed the Seminary's existing facilities to the utmost, both in classrooms and in dormitories. Crowding in

25. The enrollment declined in the nineteen sixties to between 130 and 140 in the three regular classes.

the latter was eased when larger numbers of married students appeared, yet this only posed the more difficult problem of making provision for the housing of married students and their integration into the community life of Chelsea Square. The pastoral care and spiritual guidance of such a large body of postwar students, now far more diverse in character and experience than before, was a ministry that made incessant demands upon the time and attention of the Dean. On his own list of priorities, this claim stood first, however urgently other duties pressed upon him. Like Fosbroke, he sought to maintain high standards of scholarship and set the same example of a disciplined devotional life before Seminary community; like Hoffman, he was engulfed by financial responsibilities and building programs in Chelsea Square. Yet among all his predecessors, Dean Rose's closest kinship of vocation was perhaps with the spirituality and pastoral concern of Samuel Roosevelt Johnson. Yielding his time freely and himself fully to the needs of others, it is as priest, friend, and counselor that Dean Rose is best remembered by those who knew him.

Supported by the Trustees, the Dean began the expansion of the Faculty without delay. The election of Dr. Dawley in 1945 had filled one of the vacant professorships, and when Dr. Easton retired in 1948, Pierson Parker took his place as Professor of New Testament. Two years later, when Dr. Forrester concluded thirty years of teaching at the Seminary, O. Sydner Barr joined Professor Parker in the department, and in 1953 Chaplain Yates was made Associate Professor of Greek. Dr. Simpson took over Dean Fosbroke's work in Old Testament, assisted in turn by R. Norman Whybray and R. Rhys Williams of the Class of 1947. In 1953 Harvey H. Guthrie, Jr., a graduate in the same class, was appointed Instructor in Old Testament, remaining at the Seminary until he became a professor at the Episcopal Theological School in 1958. When Professor Simpson left for Oxford in 1954, eventually to occupy the distinguished post of dean of Christ Church, Dr. Robert C. Dentan of the faculty of the Berkeley Divinity School was elected Trinity Church Professor of Old Testament Literature and Interpretation.

Like Hughell Fosbroke, Dean Rose identified himself as closely as possible with the Seminary's academic life, chiefly by relieving Professor Stewart of the extra burden of instruction in moral theology. Dr. Bigham was made Instructor in Ethics, and later Professor of Moral Theology. The Department of Ecclesiastical History was strengthened by the appointment of C. Kilmer Myers, later to be bishop of California, as instructor in 1946. For three years, before Kilmer Myers left Chelsea Square to establish a center of the Church's new urban work at Grace Church, Jersey City, the students responded to the influence of a man who, with Paul Moore, Jr., of the Class of 1949 and Robert B. Pegram, a former fellow and tutor, became a pioneer in the attempt to arouse the Church to its mission in the inner city and, in Myers' own phrase, to "light the dark streets." In his place, Robert S. Bosher of the Class of 1936, a former fellow and tutor, joined the Faculty in 1949, upon his return from graduate study at the University of Cambridge, to assist Professor Dawley in church history. Elected a professor in the department in 1951 and named Director of Graduate Studies three years later, Dr. Bosher shouldered the responsibility of supervising the expanding graduate program which the Dean constantly encouraged. Some estimate of the increase in graduate students during Dean Rose's administration may be gained from the fact that of the 111 S.T.M. degrees awarded before 1967, no less than 72 were earned after 1947. Similarly, since Dr. Seibt was granted the first doctor's degree in 1881, 27 other doctorates have been earned, the great majority since 1954.[26] Dean Fosbroke's hope that the graduate program of the General Seminary would make a significant contribution to the intellectual life of the Church has been amply fulfilled.[27]

26. The letters designating the earned doctorate were changed in 1933 from S.T.D. to Th.D. to mark the difference between an honorary degree and one received in course.

27. The majority of the resident students who have taken advanced degrees were members of the tutorial staff. A glance at the list of tutors in the Appendix will reveal the large number of men who later occupied places on the faculties of seminaries and universities.

In 1951 Dr. Pittenger was elected to the professorship of Christian Apologetics, bringing to that position the experience of fourteen years of teaching in Chelsea Square.[28] Until his resignation in 1966 when he took up residence in England in association with King's College, Cambridge, and continued there the research and writing through which he has made a significant contribution to Anglican theological scholarship, Professor Pittenger gave his classes the benefit of consistently superlative instruction. He possessed to a high degree the rare gift of stimulating students of superior academic abilities while at the same time reaching effectively those of more modest intellectual capacities.

Two English scholars held the professorship of Dogmatic Theology after Dr. Stewart's retirement: J. W. Langmead Casserley and Kenneth John Woollcombe. Professor Casserley's scintillating and provocative lectures enlivened the theological scene in the Close from 1952 until 1959, and among the graduates attracted to advanced study under his guidance was Eugene E. Crommett of the Class of 1954, a fellow and tutor. After Professor Casserley left Chelsea Square to join the faculty of the Seabury-Western Theological Seminary, Dr. Crommett became Instructor in Dogmatic Theology for a year, until he was chosen first dean of the new Episcopal Seminary of the Caribbean, to which he took several of the Seminary's tutorial staff as members of the original faculty there. Professor Woollcombe, formerly Fellow and chaplain of St. John's College, Oxford, succeeded to Dr. Casserley's professorship in 1960, returning to Great Britain three years later to become Principal of the Edinburgh Theological College. Dr. James A. Carpenter then came to the Seminary as assistant professor, and was elected to the Mary Crooke Hoffman Professorship in 1965.

Three professors have occupied the chair of Pastoral Theology since 1949. The first was Arthur C. Lichtenberger, who in 1951 accepted his election as bishop coadjutor of Missouri, later becom-

28. In 1952 the chair of Apologetics was endowed by legacies from Charles L. Gomph of the Class of 1903, and his sister Ida R. Gomph, as the Charles Lewis Gomph Professorship.

ing Presiding Bishop of the Church. His successor was George W. Barrett, who resigned in 1955 to become rector of Christ Church, Bronxville, and afterward bishop of Rochester. In 1956 Wood Bowyer Carper, then rector of the Church of the Holy Spirit, Lake Forest, Illinois, was appointed to the professorship, and a year later, Dora Phyllis Chaplin, a lecturer in the department since 1953, was made assistant professor, the first woman to occupy a place on the statutory Faculty of the Seminary. Dr. Chaplin rapidly developed the courses in Christian education in the Seminary's curriculum, and in 1964 she was elected by the Trustees to the professorship of a new Department of Christian Education.

The enlargement of the Faculty did not stop with the filling of the vacant professorships. Dean Rose and his colleagues hoped to add to the staff of each department younger men who could share the increased burdens of instruction brought by the enlarged student body. In 1960 Richard W. Corney, a graduate of 1957, was made Instructor in Old Testament, and a year later William G. Weinhauer of the Class of 1951 was appointed to assist in the Greek and New Testament courses. Both men were elected assistant professors in 1964. Three years later, shortly after Dean Rose's retirement, Dr. Charles Don Keyes was made Assistant Professor of Dogmatic Theology.[29] Meanwhile, the Dean and other members of the Faculty matured plans to establish a professorship of Liturgics, enabling the Seminary thereby to offer a program of graduate research to meet the greatly heightened interest in this field of study stimulated by the modern Liturgical Movement. Since Professor Denslow's resignation in 1931, undergraduate instruction in liturgics had been provided by men who gave their time to it amid other responsibilities: Professor Easton, Kilmer Myers, Dr. Stanley Brown-Sermon, Michael G. Mayer, a former fellow and tutor, and Canon Edward N. West of the Cathedral of St. John the Divine. The new

29. These appointments have continued. In 1968 Dr. J. Robert Wright of the Class of 1963, formerly on the faculty of the Episcopal Theological School, was elected Assistant Professor of Ecclesiastical History, and Boyce M. Bennett of the Class of 1953, a former fellow and tutor, was appointed instructor in the Bible departments.

professorship was established and filled in 1960 when H. Boone Porter, Jr., a fellow and tutor from 1950 to 1952, who had received his doctorate for his liturgical research at Oxford, was called to the Seminary from the faculty of Nashotah House.

The expansion of the Faculty to full strength was made possible by the success of a simultaneous effort by Dean Rose and members of the Board of Trustees to augment the Seminary's financial resources, providing among other things new housing and adequate support for the enlarged teaching staff. A group of lay trustees under the leadership of Mr. William B. Given, assisted by Professors Dawley and Lichtenberger, undertook the solicitation of special gifts to the Seminary, raising nearly $130,000 by 1950. This was the beginning of an assiduous effort, carried on by Dean Rose, Benjamin M. Washburn of the Class of 1912, then bishop of Newark and chairman of the Board, members of the Standing Committee, and other trustees, to widen the circle of the Seminary's contributing friends and supporters. At the same time, the appeals of the Theological Education Sunday Committee continued to be met by an enthusiastic response from the Associate Alumni, and each year the offering climbed to a new record. Other sources of income to meet the annual expenses of operation and maintenance were further large increases in the grants from Trinity Parish and the Society for Promoting Religion and Learning, gifts for special purposes from a number of foundations whose interest Dean Rose had aroused, and the rise in student fees that narrowed to some degree the wide gap between the cost of educating a candidate for holy orders and the amount he was charged by the Seminary. Meanwhile, legacies and gifts to the capital funds, some of them unexpectedly large, steadily increased the endowments. The Seminary received, for example, a bequest of well over a million dollars from the estate of Mrs. H. Sylvia Wilks, and nearly another million from several other gifts and legacies within a few years. The gradual appreciation of invested funds in the postwar years resulted in higher returns of income, bringing a measure of financial security that enabled the Seminary to operate without significant deficits until the end of Dean Rose's time in Chelsea Square. The summary financial statistics of the nineteen years of the Dean's administration are reminiscent of those of Dean Hoffman's days. The endowments of the Seminary stood at a little over $2,700,000 when Dean Rose came in 1947. In 1966, the year of his retirement, these funds had risen to more than $8,800,000. This extraordinary increase was not entirely due to gifts and legacies. Some of it derived from the inflationary trend during these years, but much of it was due to the efforts of the Dean, the responsible stewardship exercised by the Standing and Finance Committees, and the careful administration of the treasurers who succeeded Admiral Belknap: Mr. John D. Plant, Mr. Samuel S. Hall, Jr., and particularly Mr. Allen B. McGowan, who served the Seminary from 1955 to 1966.[30] The phenomenal rise in endowment, however, brought none of the affluence that had been known in the Hoffman administration. Over a similar nineteen year period, the costs of operation and maintenance in New York City spiraled incredibly. Annual expenditures in 1947 were about $220,000; in 1966 they had risen to nearly $900,000. The Seminary had become almost a million-dollar operation.

The increase in resources permitted a number of improvements in the physical plant. Some of the Hoffman faculty houses were modernized as much as their design allowed, Nos. 8 and 9 being completely remodeled into a unit with three apartments. In 1955 the construction of a building was begun, filling the last gap in Dean Hoffman's West Quadrangle between Edson and Seabury Halls. Named for Clement Clarke Moore, to whose memory, curiously enough, no earlier building had been dedicated, the functional structure was designed by the architects Robert B. O'Connor and Walter H. Kilham, Jr. Containing eight faculty apartments of varying sizes, Moore Hall was completed at the end of the summer of 1956, at a cost of approximately $370,000, and was immediately occupied by members of the teaching staff, for some of whom the Seminary had been providing apartments outside the Close. A grant

30. Mr. McGowan's successor as treasurer was Mr. Donald F. Bush.

of about $132,000 toward the construction of Moore Hall was received from the national Church's "Builders-for-Christ Campaign," and contributions added nearly $100,000. The remainder of the cost was appropriated by the Trustees from unrestricted endowments.

The total list of Dean Rose's accomplishments on the physical and administrative side of the Seminary's life is a long one. The older dormitory buildings of the East Quadrangle were improved to conform with the city's modern building code—to the expense of which Trinity Parish contributed a very substantial sum; a new four-bed infirmary in the West Building replaced the inadequate facilities in Hoffman Hall; the classrooms of Sherred Hall were refurnished; the old, dusty clay tennis courts were turned into a modern all-weather court; and the chapel organ, in use since 1888, was replaced in 1957 by a magnificent Holtkamp organ of neoclassic tonal design as a memorial to Miles Lowell Yates. Amid this extensive work of rehabilitation, the Dean never lost sight of the needs of both Faculty and student families. Not only were the salaries of the professors raised in the attempt to keep pace with the rising living costs but also a children's allowance was instituted to assist Faculty members with growing families to meet their educational expenses. A workable system of sabbaticals was put into operation, giving opportunity for the research and intellectual refreshment necessary if members of the Faculty were to maintain a high level of competence in their teaching.

The families of married students were a constant concern to the Dean and the professors. By the mid-'fifties married men numbered approximately one third of each entering Class, and save for a few basement apartments created when the old faculty houses were remodeled, the Seminary had no facilities for their housing. They were scattered with their families in apartments and dwelling houses, at their own expense, throughout the Chelsea area. Often isolated from each other and only tenuously related to the Seminary community in the Close, these conditions laid upon them an almost insupportable burden of sacrifice and hardship. Steps were taken to alleviate this situation in March 1957 when the Trustees purchased

Photograph by Bartlett A. McCarthy

The Married Students' Apartments

a three-entry apartment building opposite the chapel at Nos. 420, 422, and 424 West Twentieth Street. By 1959 its previous tenants had moved, and all forty-five apartments were available for students. Their families were given the opportunity to enjoy a common life adjacent to the Close, and every attempt was made to integrate the two communities of married and unmarried students as far as possible in the activities of the Seminary. Inevitably the provision of housing for married students intensified the pressure to change the regulation forbidding the marriage of undergraduate students while members of the Seminary. Though the Dean was by no means convinced that this step was wholly judicious, he joined the Faculty in petitioning the Trustees to rescind the statutory prohibition. The Trustees refused to accede to the request when first made, but in January 1964 the statute of 1885 was altered to permit students to marry. Since then a number of men in each class have enlarged the ranks of married students by marriage during the summer.

The proximity of nearly fifty student families altered the character of life in the Seminary quadrangles, and since the mid-'fifties, the Close has rung with alternate cries of joy, frustration, and mischief from the small fry of both faculty and student families. At times there have been nearly a hundred children in all, and the dangers of being overwhelmed by a band of roller skaters, run down by an avalanche of tricycles, or threatened by a posse hunting Indians around the West Building were a daily hazard. Mrs. Rose was the chief architect of an organization known as the Women of General, or "Wogs" for short. Under her guidance, both student and faculty wives met regularly for companionship, attended special lectures given them by the professors, or joined sewing classes, prayer and study groups, or other activities according to their individual tastes. Her concern reached out beyond the organization of the Women of General to meet the problems and needs of the women with affection and counsel, and every student's wife left Chelsea Square better prepared by Mrs. Rose's example and tutelage to enter upon the duties of a priest's wife.

The pastoral care of a large number of married students and their families added to the spiritual responsibilities of the Dean and the professors, though a large share of this ministry naturally fell to the chaplain. Arthur Corson Kelsey of the Class of 1939 succeeded to this office upon the death of Professor Yates in 1956, and he at once extended the chaplain's care to the members of the new and growing married community and their children. The second Sunday Eucharist at 8:30 A.M. in the chapel became for some years a popular family service. The chaplain's informal classes in the Christian life of prayer filled a need felt by many students, supplementing the instruction given by visiting lecturers in ascetical theology upon a lectureship established in the academic year 1955-56.[31]

Dean Rose was never free from the pressures and responsibilities of a building program. Scarcely had Moore Hall been finished when it became evident that a far more extensive addition to the Semi-

31. After Chaplain Kelsey's death in 1965, the chaplaincy was vacant until the appointment in 1968 of Rowland J. Cox of the Class of 1953.

nary's facilities was long overdue. Dean Fosbroke had warned the Trustees in his last report that Hobart Hall, built in 1885 to hold a library of 35,000 volumes was totally inadequate to contain the 106,000 volumes of 1947. Dean Rose reminded the Trustees of this serious condition again in 1950, and by 1956, when the library had grown to over 118,000 volumes, his appeals to the Board were insistent. Severe overcrowding had forced the dispersion of some collections to other buildings, and lack of study space both restricted the ordinary use of the old library and made research a discouraging and time-consuming chore. The Seminary's greatest resource for its central purpose was becoming increasingly less useful. On January 16, 1957, after a thorough investigation of the problem, the Board of Trustees voted to raze the Ninth Avenue block front and erect a building to contain not only a library but also a new deanery, some additional faculty apartments, rooms for graduate students, modern administrative offices, and recreational facilities for the students. A venture on this scale necessitated a drive for funds conducted with the skilled assistance of professional campaign counsel. The appeal was launched in October 1957, and by the following April over a million dollars had been subscribed, chiefly by donors of large special gifts. During the next two years, the response widened as numerous contributions, memorial gifts, and foundation grants increased the mounting total. Meanwhile, the demolition preceeding construction was begun in the summer of 1959, accompanied by a dislocation in Chelsea Square that imposed considerable strain and curtailed a number of Seminary activities for two academic years.

The campaign was conducted under the supervision of a central committee that included both trustees and alumni, Mr. Kempton Dunn of the Board of Trustees assuming its active chairmanship. The task of raising a large sum proved to be a difficult one, discouraging at times, and exhausting to those who bore the brunt of work and responsibility. The fact was again discovered, as it had been in the early years of the nineteenth century, that the General Seminary, seeking to be true to its foundation to serve the whole Church,

The New Ninth Avenue Building

lacked that close regional or diocesan identification which has often provided ample support for some other seminaries. The same story was again learned—the Seminary that belongs somewhat vaguely to everybody is not likely to have first claim on anybody outside the circle of its friends and graduates. Yet the hard and continuous work of a host of trustees, professors, alumni, and friends of the institution, sustained by the faith that churchmen would respond to the Seminary's need, was rewarded by 1961 with pledges of nearly $2,900,000, virtually all of which were paid. The construction of the new building, the campaign costs, the expenses of dislocation, and the purchase of the married students' apartment building totaled about $3,000,000, leaving a relatively small amount to be financed from unrestricted endowments.

On no one did the campaign pressures fall more heavily than on the Dean. The earlier responsibilities of building and expansion were now capped by some years of concentrated effort during which his time and energy were demanded by the daily tasks incidental to the raising of funds and progress of construction. If anyone else worked as long and hard on the whole project, it was Dr. Niels H. Sonne, librarian of the Seminary since 1947. His participation in the task of designing the new library was a decisive factor in its excellence. In consultation with the firm of O'Connor & Kilham—the same architects who designed Moore Hall—Dr. Sonne planned many of the details that now assist its efficient operation and make for a remarkable ease of use for study and research.

The new deanery was occupied by Dean and Mrs. Rose in December 1960, and in the following summer the books were returned to what was now called St. Mark's Library, a name bestowed by two of the most generous donors to the building.[32] Today the building possesses all the accommodations planned at the outset, and the library is unsurpassed by any of its size and character. Ample space for shelving its 150,000 volumes is provided, and the unusually generous reading room facilities are supplemented by over fifty individual study carrels for students. Special stacks are provided for the large rare book and manuscript collections, including both the historic Bible Collection and the eight thousand volumes of sixteenth- and seventeenth-century English theology and history. Seminar rooms are located adjacent to collections often in use by graduate classes, special study rooms are available for scholars engaged upon research and writing, and areas of the library are devoted to modern microfilm and audio-visual equipment. Many of these are memorials of donors or those in whose names gifts were made.[33] Statistics are of interest only for what they reveal, and the best indication of the value which the Dean, the professors, and the Trustees have placed upon the library as a vital center of the Seminary's academic enterprise is that whereas in 1947 about $1200 was expended annually for the purchase of books and periodicals, by 1967 the annual expenditure was nearly $29,000.

32. In 1961 the top floor of the library was left roughly finished to be completed at some future date when expansion warranted it. In the last few months before his retirement in 1966, Dean Rose almost single-handedly secured gifts from individuals, foundations, and Trinity Parish sufficient to finish the floor, and in 1967 the library was extended into this additional space.

33. The old name Jarvis Hall has disappeared, and Mr. Jarvis' memory is perpetuated in the Jarvis Seminar Room. With the loss of Hobart Hall, the Seminary now has no building named for one of its chief founders.

In its essential structure, the curriculum of the Seminary remained unaltered during Dean Rose's administration. Minor changes transferred courses from one term or year to another, and the main thrust of some of them, particularly in apologetics, pastoral theology, and missions was given considerable redirection in accordance with the changing patterns of thought of the time. The Departments of Religious Education and Liturgics were expanded, and students were encouraged to make fuller use of the resources of other institutions, especially those of the Union Seminary and the New School for Social Research. Among other changes, Greek was finally made elective, a Degree Examination covering the major theological disciplines was substituted for the older type of comprehensive examination, and the Seminary's traditional requirement that a man be in priest's orders before receiving his S.T.B. degree was altered to allow the degrees to be conferred at graduation. The Dean and members of the Faculty were well aware of the pressures for curriculum change that rose from the ferment over the character and methods of theological education that seized upon the Church in the 'sixties. Nor was the Dean insensible of the care that should attend such change. In his last report to the General Convention on behalf of the Trustees, he said:

> To chart a sound course for theological education through this immensely difficult field, avoiding a sterile subservience to formulae framed in forgotten terms on one hand, and simple capitulation to contemporary fashions in communication on the other, is an awesome responsibility.[34]

The last curriculum changes in Dean Rose's time, those appearing in the *Catalogue* of 1964-65, not only made shifts in the distribution and content of some prescribed courses but also provided for as much elective work as possible without altering the basic structure of the curriculum.[35] Whatever changes might be made, Dean Rose was convinced that

34. *Journal of General Convention 1964*, p. 548.
35. See Tr P, May 26, 1964 (XVIII, 24-26).

for those called to leadership in promoting the reconciling work of our Lord in his Church, there is no substitute for the hard concentrated discipline of historical and theological study . . . There is a vast accumulated deficit in our society, and among Christian people, in that knowledge of historic origins and developments that constitutes the Church's corporate memory and its assurance of its identity as participating in the saving work of Christ.

Formal theological education, in the short span of time allotted to it, and dealing with those who are heirs to the general deficit, must perforce concern itself largely with history, the past, tradition. If nostalgia or antiquarianism are main interests in that concern, there is at once a betrayal of the Gospel . . . Proper orientation of theological education toward the needs of the contemporary world requires solid grounding in the classical theological disciplines.

This means that there are strict limits to what can be done by way of additions to the curriculum of a seminary to guarantee our students' acquaintance with the sociological, psychological, and technological dynamisms of a world in revolution . . . But much can be done and must be done, too, if not by way of additions to, certainly by way of orientation of, all theological instruction towards "revelance" and "involvement," and towards the sensitizing of the clergy to the "deep and God-given secularities of our day." That Christianity is an historical religion means both that its faith is in the God who has entered the historic process in specific times and places, and that all history, even ours, is under his Lordship. That he is not just interested in religion and what happens in churches ought not to surprise any but the biblically and theologically illiterate. But that he does will to draw men to conscious union with himself, through prayer, sacrament, worship, and the devout teaching and learning of the truth of his manifestations in saving power, must never cease to constitute the prime ground of the Church's mission.[36]

The Dean and Faculty felt that further and drastic curriculum revision would come more wisely and surely after careful study, and particularly when opportunity was had to receive the report of the Presiding Bishop's Special Committee on Theological Education, then in preparation, under the chairmanship of President Nathan M. Pusey of Harvard and the direction of Dr. Charles L. Taylor, for presentation to the General Convention of 1967.

36. *Journal of General Convention 1964*, pp. 546-548.

To all the duties and responsibilities that accompanied his achievements during the years of change that coincided with his deanship, Lawrence Rose gave himself without rest or sabbatical break, and so prodigally that by the early spring of 1965 the drain had taken a serious toll of his health. Yet he did not abandon a single duty. On March 25, 1965, for example, just a month before the first sign of the illness that impaired his physical health and vigor, he joined a large number of students and Faculty members in the chapel at 4:00 A.M. to celebrate the Eucharist for the delegation leaving at daybreak to join the historic Selma March. In April the Dean was ordered to a complete rest until mid-summer, and Professor Dawley, the sub-dean, carried on temporarily for him. He returned in the fall, but it was not long before he realized that his reduced strength dictated that he lay down the burden of his office. Dean Rose retired shortly after the Commencement of 1966, with the affectionate good wishes of the entire Seminary community, and on the testimonial occasions in his honor during commencement week, hundreds of graduates in the Associate Alumni bore witness to their gratitude for his ministry in Chelsea Square.

On May 24, 1966, the Trustees unanimously elected as the seventh dean of the General Seminary Samuel Joseph Wylie, a graduate of Wheaton College and the Biblical Seminary, Master of Sacred Theology of Union Seminary, a priest of wide experience as a college chaplain and counselor of students, who was at that time rector of the Church of the Advent in Boston.

Epilogue

The restless revolution that has swept through Christendom, manifesting itself in impatience with the traditional structures of the Church, seeking means of renewal, exploring avenues of drastic liturgical reform, radical theological reorientation, heightened participation in social action, and solid ecumenical achievement, has had far-reaching effects upon theological education and the seminaries. Change and renewal are the contemporary watchwords, and the Sesquicentennial Year 1967 saw the General Theological Seminary well launched upon a new chapter in its long history. Said Dean Wylie at his installation on December 12, 1966:

> In the gap between yesterday's climate of thought and way of life and those that will emerge tomorrow we find the vocation of today's seminary and seminarians . . . To affirm the Gospel in simplicity requires a sophistication beyond that of our fathers. Because our witness is challenged on many fronts, it requires spiritual toughness and intellectual depth in order to be effective.

"Enthusiasm," he continued,

> is not a substitute for scholarship. Neither is uncritical solidarity with one's own generation . . . We cannot make an intelligent decision whether to be men of our times or to deplore them without a profound knowledge of history. We cannot responsibly accept or condemn the "new theology" unless we know the thought of the Scriptures and the Fathers and something of the unfolding of theological thought both in the East and in the West since the division of Christendom. We cannot

challenge the spirit of the age or evaluate it if we know no other spirit.

The graduate of this Seminary who can speak to his own age with power and in radically new symbols will be a man who recognizes the authenticity of all former expressions of the Faith, not excluding the Victorian era, but who speaks the new idiom or creates one because he is a man of his times with something to say. In such a man intellectual comprehension and devotional response will be united.[1]

Something of the changing scene was reflected in the spirit of the Seminary's sesquicentennial observances themselves, designed as they were, not only "to remember with joy and thanksgiving to Almighty God a century and a half of life, work and service," but also

to identify with the continuing and new tasks which face the contemporary Church; to seek rededication and renewal for future service to the Church in a new age; these are the broad objectives.[2]

Accordingly, the convocation in Hoffman Hall on January 11, 1967, with which the anniversary year began, was devoted to a recognition of the enlarged and significant role played by the laity in the life and witness of the Church. A doctorate in theology was conferred upon Clifford P. Morehouse, well-known churchman and author, formerly president of the House of Deputies of the General Convention, and the first layman to be awarded an honorary degree in the Seminary's history. Citations were presented to others of the laity for their outstanding service in Christian causes that included the defense and extension of the civil rights of all citizens, and a courageous witness to the demands of the Gospel in other areas of moral, social, and humanitarian concern. Recipients were the Honorable Thurgood Marshall, associate justice of the Supreme Court of the United States and a member of the Seminary's Board of Trustees; the Honorable John V. Lindsay, mayor of New York, a speaker on the occasion; Mary Parkman Peabody, a lifelong leader

1. *G.T.S. Bulletin* (February 1967), pp. 5-6.
2. The Rt. Rev. Robert R. Spears, Jr., chairman of the Sesquicentennial Committee in the *G.T.S. Bulletin* (November 1966), p. 2.

Photograph by *Bachrach*

Dean Wylie

in areas of Christian social and racial concern; and Jackson A. Dykman, noted canonist and counselor of many general conventions.

The academic convocation in the Cathedral of St. John the Divine with which the observances of the Sesquicentennial Year closed on November 8, 1967, as well as the symposium that followed the ceremonies, directed attention to another contemporary Christian activity and future challenge, the ecumenism that has transformed relations among the separated Churches of Christendom. Honorary degrees were conferred upon a distinguished group of Christian leaders who have devoted their energies to the furtherance of unity: Lakdasa de Mel, bishop of Calcutta and metropolitan of the Anglican Church of India, Pakistan, Burma, and Ceylon; Archbishop Iakovos of the Greek Archdiocese of North and South America; John J. Wright, bishop of the Roman Catholic Diocese of Pittsburgh; Eugene Carson Blake, general secretary of the World Council of Churches; the late Franklin Clark Fry, leading American

Lutheran churchman; Monsignor Charles Moeller of the University of Louvain; Professor Albert C. Outler of the Perkins School of Theology; Dean Alexander Schmemann of St. Vladimir's Orthodox Theological Seminary; Brother Roger Schutz, prior of the Community of Taizé in France; and Douglas Van Steere, former professor in Haverford College.[3]

The changes upon which the Seminary was launched by the end of 1967 rapidly altered some of its traditional structures and much of the face of life in Chelsea Square. The new free-standing altar in the Hoffman chapel, for example, stands as a symbol of identification with the modern liturgical renewal, while the experiments and changes in the community's chapel services and other devotional exercises seek to provide a viable pattern for the spiritual formation of priests who will minister in a rapidly changing world. A sweeping reform of the Field Education program secured to the students an effective and closely supervised practical experience of the setting in which the Church's mission to the world is now placed, as well as opening men to the possibilities of special vocations amid the ever-widening diversity of today's Christian ministry. Increased ecumenical contacts with Roman Catholic, Orthodox, and Protestant seminaries in the New York area have drawn both institutions and their members into a closer fellowship. The Seminary is an active participant in the Metropolitan Association of Theological Schools, a cooperative venture of a number of seminaries, seeking not only to implement theological dialogue and the joint exploration of the tasks common to all Christian ministry today but also by interseminary curriculum planning to share their academic resources and personnel.

A process of curriculum reform has been instituted at the Seminary, conceived as a continuing effort rather than the rigid substitution of one fixed curriculum for another. The curriculum revision introduced in the academic year 1968-69 was frankly experimental,

3. A detailed report of the activities of the Sesquicentennial Year, events, speakers, citations, etc., may be found in the *G.T.S. Bulletin* for November 1966, and February, May, June, and November 1967.

its main thrust being the establishment of a scheme of study incorporating a large measure of flexibility and seeking to provide sharper stimulation of the student's own intellectual resources. In it the traditional pattern of five units of work per term was reduced to four, enabling concentration upon fewer subjects and their exploration in greater depth. A "core course" of required subjects offers a basic introduction—and no more than that—to the major theological disciplines, while a generous proportion of elective courses permits the pursuit of special interests or a particular field of concentration. Students who show exceptional academic achievement in their first year are given the option of an entirely elective program thereafter.

Accompanying this scheme were changes in methods of instruction, some of which had been tested previously. Individual "reading courses," for example, had been arranged to meet the needs of particular students for some years, and permission for qualified students to complete units of work as "independent study" was introduced in Dean Rose's time. The chief new experiment was the abandonment of the old system of formal two-hour lectures supplemented by tutorial sessions. In its place was substituted a flexible combination of shorter lectures and small discussion groups, involving the lecturers and professors in a preceptorial process. Many of the values of the seminar method employed in the elective courses were thus extended to the "core course" of required work.

The curriculum of 1968 was designed to incorporate perhaps only one permanent feature—flexibility. In both structure and detail, it is open to alteration as new experience and need dictate. At least one of its objectives, however, is as old as the early years of the Seminary, when the "band of brothers" read for orders under the guidance of Samuel Turner in New Haven. This is the development of study which is increasingly independent, directed and interpreted by lectures, stimulated by preceptorial sessions and conference hours, and leading to the engagement of a student with methods and habits of study that might be his lifelong possession as a priest.

As this book goes to press, it is almost a hundred and fifty years to the day since Dr. Turner and Dr. Jarvis met their first students in the little room in St. Paul's Chapel, launching the Church upon a venture in theological education that led to the shaping of seminaries as they have been known in the past. Now, a century and a half later, the Church again faces the challenge of experiment in theological education, and, in Dean Wylie's words, it is precisely "this one hundred and fifty years of equity in theological education which gives us the freedom to experiment and to change."[4] The General Theological Seminary, like all institutions for the training and formation of Christian ministers and priests, is embarked today upon a course largely uncharted, and if its legacy from the past is an equity in long experience, it is equity as well in the steadfast Christian commitment of faith, courage, and devotion that marked the long procession of men who have responded to the call of God in their generations in Chelsea Square. The path of the future may be uncharted, but its direction is clear, and nowhere more plainly put than in a report Dean Fosbroke made to the Trustees twenty-five years ago:

> On two things we shall continue to insist without reservation; we shall seek ever to keep before our students the wholeness of God's revelation of Himself, in nature, in history, in the discipline of a people, in the ministry and teaching, the death, and the resurrection of Jesus Christ, in the work of the Holy Spirit in the life of the Church down through the centuries. It is in the unity and proportion of the Christian faith that there is to be found the true conservation of all the values that have made human life worth living, and, indeed, invested it with rich splendor wherever consciously or unconsciously it has been lived in the service of God.
>
> And then we shall try to bring men to understand that this Catholic faith in all its unity and proportion, not simply known, but lived and loved, as it has had its extraordinary relevancy to every aspect of human life in the past, again and again disclosing fresh sources for the renewing of the face of the earth, so has unsuspected wealth of meaning for the changing conditions of our own day. In a sentence, we shall try to make them see and feel all that is implicit in the fact that

4. From a "Report to the American Association of Theological Schools" embodying the results of a Faculty study of the Seminary in 1967-68.

the God and Father of Our Lord Jesus Christ is ceaselessly at work in this disordered world, and that to his redeeming power the life of every child of man may be related.[5]

5. Tr P, May 26, 1942 (XIV, 18).

Appendix

DEANS, PROFESSORS, AND OTHER MEMBERS OF THE TEACHING STAFF 1817–1967

DEANS

The office of Dean was created in 1832 to be held by the resident professors in annual rotation. The Statutes of 1867 established a separate deanship, and the powers of the office were augmented in 1885.

John Murray Forbes 1869-72
George Franklin Seymour 1875-79 (Acting 1872-75)
Eugene Augustus Hoffman 1879-1902
Wilford Lash Robbins 1903-16
Hughell Edgar Woodall Fosbroke 1917-47
Lawrence Rose 1947-66
Samuel Joseph Wylie 1966-

SUB-DEANS

The office of Sub-Dean was established by the Statutes of 1888.

Andrew Oliver 1889-97
Philander Kinney Cady 1898-1904
John Charles Roper 1904-07
Herbert McKenzie Denslow 1907-31
Charles Norman Shepard 1931-40
Burton Scott Easton 1940-48
Cuthbert Aikman Simpson 1948-54
Powel Mills Dawley 1954-

PROFESSORS AND INSTRUCTORS

Samuel Farmar Jarvis, Professor of Biblical Learning 1819-20, and Samuel Hulbeart Turner, Professor of Historic Theology 1819-21, were the original professors. In New Haven, Thomas Church Brownell assisted Professor Turner by teaching Pastoral Theology in 1820-21. The following lists begin with the union of the General Seminary and the New York Diocesan School in 1821.

BIBLICAL LEARNING

Samuel Hulbeart Turner (Professor 1821-61)
Samuel Seabury (Professor 1862-71)
Andrew Oliver (Professor 1873-94)

In 1894 the Department of Biblical Learning was provided with separate professorships of Old and New Testament. Professor Oliver became Professor of New Testament.

OLD TESTAMENT

Charles William Edmond Body (Professor 1894-1906)
Loring Woart Batten (Acting 1904; Professor 1908-30)
Francis Branch Blodgett (Instructor 1906; Adjunct Professor 1908; Professor 1912-21)
Hughell Edgar Woodall Fosbroke (Dean and Professor 1917-47)
Cuthbert Aikman Simpson (Instructor 1930; Assistant Professor 1934; Professor 1940-54)
Roger Norman Whybray (Instructor 1948-50)
Richard Rhys Williams (Instructor 1950-53)
Harvey Henry Guthrie, Jr. (Instructor 1953-58)
Robert Claude Dentan (Professor 1954-)
Richard Warren Corney (Instructor 1957; Assistant Professor 1964-)
Boyce M. Bennett, Jr. (Instructor 1968-)

NEW TESTAMENT

Andrew Oliver (Professor 1894-97)
Isbon Thaddeus Beckwith (Professor 1898-1906)
Charles Carroll Edmunds (Professor 1906-29)
William Henry Paine Hatch (Instructor 1908; Adjunct Professor 1909; Professor 1913-17)
Burton Scott Easton (Professor 1919-48)
Donald Fraser Forrester (Assistant Professor 1929; Associate Professor 1944; Professor 1948-49)
Pierson Parker (Professor 1949-)
Orlando Sydney Barr (Instructor 1954; Assistant Professor 1958; Associate Professor 1961; Professor 1965-)

Billy Wilson Rodgers (Instructor 1960-61)
William Gillette Weinhauer (Instructor 1961; Assistant Professor 1964-)

ECCLESIASTICAL HISTORY

Benjamin Tredwell Onderdonk (Professor 1821-22)
Francis Lister Hawks (Acting 1834)
William Rollinson Whittingham (Professor 1836-40)
John David Ogilby (Professor 1840-51)
Milo Mahan (Professor 1851-64)
George Franklin Seymour (Professor 1865-79)
Thomas Richey (Professor 1879-1902)
Frederick Joseph Kinsman (Professor 1903-08)
Marshall Bowyer Stewart (Instructor 1907-09)
Henry Peter Scratchley (Acting 1908-10)
Arthur Whipple Jenks (Professor 1910-23)
Ralph Brouwer Pomeroy (Instructor 1917-19)
Frank Stanton Burns Gavin (Professor 1923-38)
Harold Neil Renfrew (Instructor 1929-31)
Powel Mills Dawley (Professor 1945-)
Chauncie Kilmer Myers (Instructor 1946-49)
Robert Semple Bosher (Instructor 1949; Associate Professor 1951; Professor 1954-)
John Robert Wright (Assistant Professor 1968-)

DOGMATIC THEOLOGY

The professorship was first known as that of Systematic Divinity. In 1871 Dogmatic Theology was added to the designation, and in 1893 Systematic Divinity was dropped.

Bird Wilson (Professor 1821-50)
Samuel Roosevelt Johnson (Professor 1850-69)
Samuel Buel (Professor 1871-88)
George Henry Somerset Walpole (Professor 1889-96)
John Charles Roper (1897-1912)
Thomas Davies (Instructor 1909-11)
Francis Joseph Hall (Professor 1913-28)
Marshall Bowyer Stewart (Professor 1928-51)
Julian Victor Langmead Casserley (Professor 1951-59)
Eugene Earl Crommett (Instructor 1959-60)
Kenneth John Woollcombe (Professor 1960-63)

James Anderson Carpenter (Assistant Professor 1963; Professor 1965-)
Charles Don Keyes (Assistant Professor 1967-)

CHRISTIAN APOLOGETICS

The professorship was originally known as that of the Evidences of Revealed Religion and of Moral Science. It soon became shortened to Christian Evidences, and in 1906 it was designated as Christian Apologetics.

Gulian Crommelin Verplanck (Professor 1821-25)
George Washington Dean (Professor 1885-88)
Philander Kinney Cady (Professor 1889-1902)
Charles Harris Hayes (Professor 1902-10)
Dickinson Sergeant Miller (Professor 1911-24)
Leonard Hodgson (Professor 1925-31)
Albert Arthur Cock (Visiting Professor 1932-33)
William Norman Pittenger (Instructor 1949; Professor 1951-66)
Robert Elwin Terwilliger (Adjunct Professor 1967-)

PASTORAL THEOLOGY

Pastoral Theology and Pulpit Eloquence was the term used for the professorship until 1864 when the second part of the title was dropped. Homiletics and pastoral care were the main subjects of the department, though until 1893, moral theology was a topic under Pastoral Theology, as was liturgics until 1924. Pedagogy (Religious Education) became a topic in 1901, and Christian Education was made a separate department in 1964.

John Henry Hobart (Professor 1821-30)
Henry Anthon (Acting 1834-35)
Hugh Smith (Acting 1836-37)
Benjamin Isaac Haight (Acting 1837-38; Professor 1841-55)
William Ernest Eigenbrodt (Professor 1862-89)
Edward Hurtt Jewett (Professor 1889-1901)
Theodore Myers Riley (Adjunct Professor 1894-1902)
Rudolph Michael Binder (Instructor 1901-03)
Herbert McKenzie Denslow (Professor 1902-24)
Thomas Davies (Instructor 1908-09)
Charles Homer Boynton (Instructor 1909; Adjunct Professor 1910; Professor 1914-29)
Thomas Sparks Cline (Professor 1925-28)

Frederick Curtiss Lauderburn (Instructor 1927-40)
Howard Chandler Robbins (Professor 1929-41)
Otis Radcliffe Rice (Instructor 1937-58)
Arthur Carl Lichtenberger (Professor 1949-51)
George West Barrett (Professor 1951-55)
Wood Bowyer Carper (Professor 1956-)
Dora Phyllis Chaplin (Assistant Professor 1957; Associate Professor 1961-64)

CHRISTIAN EDUCATION

Created as a department separate from that of Pastoral Theology in 1964.

Dora Phyllis Chaplin (Professor 1964-)

ECCLESIASTICAL POLITY AND LAW

Benjamin Tredwell Onderdonk (Professor 1821-61)
Francis Vinton (Professor 1869-72)
William Jones Seabury (Professor 1873-1916)
Ralph Brouwer Pomeroy (Professor 1919-25)
John Alexander Richardson (Instructor 1927; Assistant Professor 1929-45)

CHRISTIAN ETHICS AND MORAL THEOLOGY

Charles Theodore Seibt (Professor 1895-1903)
Arthur Prince Hunt (Professor 1908-25)
Lawrence Rose (in charge of the Department 1948-66)
Thomas James Bigham, Jr. (Instructor 1945; Associate Professor 1956; Professor 1959-)

BIBLICAL LANGUAGES

The professorship and instructorships have been known by a variety of designations: Hebrew and Greek Literature, Hebrew and Cognate Languages, Greek, etc.

Clement Clarke Moore (Professor 1821-50)
George H. Houghton (Instructor 1850-63)
William Walton (Instructor 1863; Professor 1868-69)
Randall Cooke Hall (Instructor 1869; Professor 1871-99)

Abraham Yohannan (Instructor 1901-03)
Charles Norman Shepard (Instructor 1897; Adjunct Professor 1902; Professor 1906-40)
Francis Branch Blodgett (Instructor 1905-06)
Harold Francis Hamilton (Instructor 1906-07)
Marshall Bowyer Stewart (Instructor 1907-08)
Edward Rochie Hardy, Jr. (Instructor 1940-45)
Miles Lowell Yates (Instructor 1940; Associate Professor 1953-56)

LITURGICS

Harold Neil Renfrew (Instructor 1931-36)
Harry Boone Porter, Jr. (Professor 1960-)

ECCLESIASTICAL MUSIC

John Henry Hopkins, Jr. (Instructor 1855-57)
George J. Tattam (Instructor, 1887-89)
George Edward Stubbs (Instructor, 1890-1901)
Clement R. Gale (Instructor 1901-34)
Ray Francis Brown (Instructor 1934; Director of Music 1957-64)
Stuart M. Gardner (Acting Director 1964-66)
Leonard Raver (Associate Professor and Director of Music 1966-)

ELOCUTION AND PUBLIC SPEAKING

Francis Thayer Russell (Instructor 1881-1903)
Albert Francis Tenney (Instructor 1904-18)
William Robinson (Instructor 1919-33)
William Brenton (Instructor 1934-36)
William Frederick Doscher (Instructor 1937-40)
John Cathey (Instructor 1941-54)
Cornelius Lawrence Reid (Instructor 1954-)

CHAPLAINS

Frederick Curtiss Lauderburn 1930-40
Miles Lowell Yates 1940-56
Arthur Corson Kelsey 1956-65
Lewis Wilson Towler (Acting 1965-66)
Paul Bauchman Clayton (Acting 1966-68)
Rowland Johns Cox 1968-

DIRECTORS OF FIELD EDUCATION

The Chaplains acted as directors of Field Work until the introduction of a new Field Education Program in 1967-68.

Lewis Wilson Towler 1967-

ASSISTANTS AND TEACHING FELLOWS

George W. Douglas 1876-77
Edward H. Van Winkle 1877-82
Charles Norman Shepard 1894-97
Maurice Picard 1918-20
Donald Fraser Forrester 1920-29
Arthur Turner Reasoner 1924-25
Pryor McNeil Grant 1924-25
Howard Henry Hassinger 1925-28
George Arthur Meyer 1925-28
Haven Palmer Perkins 1928-34
Edward Rochie Hardy, Jr. 1931-40
Thaddeus Hoyt Ames 1932-33
Charles Rudolph Feilding 1932-35
William Wilson Manross 1933-39
Lauriston Livingston Scaife 1934-36
Theodore Parker Ferris 1935-37
Thomas S. K. Scott-Craig 1937-38
W. Norman Pittenger 1937-45
Thomas James Bigham, Jr. 1938-45
Louis A. Haselmayer, Jr. 1938-41
John Atherton Bell 1939-40
Frank S. North 1942-43
Shunji Forrest Nishi 1948-50
Robert Baker Pegram 1948-49
Edward Chandler 1949-51
Robert Elwin Terwilliger 1949-50
Charles Pratt Berger 1950-51
Edward Townsend Look 1950-58
Arthur Corson Kelsey 1951-52
Eugene Earl Crommett 1958-59

LECTURERS

OLD TESTAMENT

Hughell E. W. Fosbroke 1954-57
Samuel Lucien Terrien 1956-57

NEW TESTAMENT

Robert Pierce Casey 1942-43
Robert Baker Pegram 1949-53
Orlando Sydney Barr 1952-54
William Henry Paine Hatch 1955-56

ECCLESIASTICAL HISTORY

James Arthur Muller 1922-23
Edward Clowes Chorley 1922-23
F. J. Foakes-Jackson 1925-27
John Alexander Richardson 1926-27
George Petrovitch Fedotov 1943-45
Charles Wesley Lowry, Jr. 1950-52
Angus Dun 1966-67

DOGMATIC THEOLOGY

John Loftus Scully 1912-13
Philip N. Waggett 1923-24
Michael H. Murray 1967-68

CHRISTIAN APOLOGETICS

Samuel Seabury 1835-38
Dickinson Sergeant Miller 1909-10
J. Lewis Parks 1910-11
William Romaine Newbold 1923-25

Byron Edward Underwood 1931-32
Daniel Arthur McGregor 1934-45
Thomas S. K. Scott-Craig 1951-52
Robert Elwin Terwilliger 1966-67
James Alfred Martin 1966-67
John MacQuarrie 1966-67

PASTORAL THEOLOGY

Horatio Potter 1857-65
Philip N. Waggett 1923-24; 1926-27
Paul B. Bull, C. R. 1924-25; 1926-27
Joseph Wilson Sutton 1924-26
Pryor McNeil Grant 1925-27
G. A. Johnston Ross 1925-26
Adelaide Teague Case 1928-29
Edmund deSchweinitz Brunner 1930-46; 1955-56
Leonard Withington Mayo 1931-35
Thaddeus Hoyt Ames 1932-33
George Arthur Buttrick 1934-35; 1936-39
Otis Radcliffe Rice 1934-37
John Wallace Sutter 1934-36
Mary Swan Brisley 1935-45
Thomas S. K. Scott-Craig 1937-38
Harold Frederick Hohly 1940-49
John Gass 1940-41
John Atherton Bell 1940-52
Gordon Butler Wadhams 1940-49
John Henry Keene 1941-44; 1946-49
Howard Chandler Robbins (Honorary) 1941-50
Elise de la Fontaine 1945-48
Walter Russell Bowie 1945-50
Helen Brougden Turnbull 1945-46
Evelyn Spickard 1946-52
Thomas Alfred Tripp 1946-54
Samuel Moore Shoemaker 1950-52
Leonora Harris 1950-52
Chester Burge Emerson 1951-52
Robert Elwin Terwilliger 1951-52
Dora Phyllis Chaplin 1953-57
James Stewart Wetmore 1954-55
George West Barrett 1955-56
Will Herberg 1967-68

ECCLESIASTICAL POLITY AND LAW

Edwin A. White 1917-18
Walter Herbert Stowe 1945-46

CHRISTIAN ETHICS AND MORAL THEOLOGY

John M. S. McDonald 1922-23
John Andrews Fitch 1926-27
Friedrich Wilhelm Foerster 1941-42

LITURGICS

Herbert McKenzie Denslow 1924-31
C. Kilmer Myers 1949-53
Stanley Brown-Sermon 1952-54
Michael George Mayer 1954-57
Edward Nason West 1957-60
Alexander Schmemann 1967-68

CHRISTIAN MISSIONS

J. Lewis Parks 1911-12
William Codman Sturgis 1925-27
Artley Beeber Parson 1928-29
Robert Frederick Lau 1929-31
Arthur Mason Sherman 1931-32
Andrew Y. Y. Tsu 1932-33
James Thayer Addison 1940-42

ECCLESIASTICAL LATIN

Eugen Kullmann 1958-60; 1963-67
Harry Ellsworth Chandlee 1961-62
A. Dean Calcote 1962-63

COMPARATIVE RELIGION

Abraham V. W. Jackson 1909-11
Samuel Lucas Joshi 1923-24

LECTURES IN ASCETICAL THEOLOGY

A lectureship providing for the annual appointment of a visiting lecturer was established in 1955.

Visiting Lecturers

1955-56	Kenneth Riches
1956-57	H. Theodore Smith, S.S.M.
1957-58	Cyril Patrick Hankey
1958-59	Reginald Edward Cant
1959-60	Martin S. F. Thornton
1960-61	Edmund Robert Morgan
1961-62	Kenneth Riches
1962-63	Kenneth Needham Ross
1963-64	Herbert Montague Wadhams
1964-65	Martin S. F. Thornton
1965-66	Reginald Edward Cant
1966-67	Arthur MacDonald Allchin
1967-68	Arthur MacDonald Allchin

PADDOCK LECTURERS

A lectureship founded by George A. Jarvis in 1880 and named for Benjamin Henry Paddock of the Class of 1852.

1880-81	John Williams
1882-83	William Dexter Wilson
1883-84	Abram Newkirk Littlejohn
1884-85	Henry Champlain Lay
1885-86	William Henry Platt
1886-87	John Hodson Egar
1887-88	Hugh Miller Thompson
1888-89	Edward Hurtt Jewett
1889-90	Hollingworth Tully Kingdon
1891-92	Morgan Dix
1892-93	Arthur Cleveland Coxe
1893-94	Charles W. E. Body
1894-95	Robert Brinkerhoff Fairbairn
1895-96	Arthur James Mason
1896-97	John Dowden
1898-99	James Dow Morrison
1899-1900	Charles Woodruff Shields
1901-02	Alfred Magill Randolph
1902-03	Arthur C. A. Hall
1903-04	Alexander Charles Garrett
1904-05	Charles Henry Brent
1905-06	James Haughton Woods
1906-07	William Ralph Inge
1907-08	William Porcher DuBose
1908-09	George H. S. Walpole
1909-10	Francis Joseph Hall
1910-11	Dickinson Sergeant Miller
1911-12	Charles Lewis Slattery
1912-13	John Neville Figgis, C.R.
1913-14	Philip Mercer Rhinelander
1914-15	William Temple
1915-16	Samuel Hart
1916-17	Thomas Alexander Lacey
1917-18	Loring Woart Batten
1918-19	Lucius Waterman
1919-20	John Punnett Peters
1921-22	Oliver Chase Quick
1923-24	A. E. J. Rawlinson
1925-26	Marshall Bowyer Stewart
1927-28	Burton Scott Easton
1929-30	Wilbur Cosby Bell
1931-32	Alfred Leslie Lilley

1933-34	Henry St. George Tucker	1955-56	Eugene Rathbone Fairweather
1935-36	Leonard Hodgson	1958-59	William Grosvenor Pollard
1945-46	Cuthbert Aikman Simpson	1962-63	John N. D. Kelly
1949-50	Edward Rochie Hardy, Jr.	1967-68	William Norman Pittenger
1951-52	Stephen Fielding Bayne, Jr.		
1953-54	Charles H. E. Smyth		

WINSLOW LECTURERS

A lectureship on archaeology and the Bible established in 1943 by a bequest from William Copley Winslow of the Class of 1865.

1949-50	Millar Burrows	1961-62	Alfred Denis Baly
1952-53	Carl H. Kraeling	1964-65	Sherman Elbridge Johnson
1955-56	John Lowe	1966-67	David Noel Freedman
1957-58	Robert Claude Dentan	1968-69	Pierre Benoit, O.P.
1959-60	James Bennett Pritchard		

LIBRARIANS

Henry James Feltus 1821-23
William Rollinson Whittingham 1825-29
Charles W. Bradley 1829-30
Robert William Harris 1830
Benjamin Isaac Haight 1831-34
Thomas Pyne 1835-36
Professor Whittingham 1836-40
Professor Ogilby 1841-51
Christian Frederick Crusé 1851-65
Professor Johnson 1865-71
Professor Buel 1872-88
Professor Hall 1889
Professor Jewett 1890-1901
Professor Cady 1902-04
Edward Harmon Virgin 1905-16
Grace Amelia Littell 1916-17
George Dobbin Brown 1917-23
Professor Easton 1923-48
Niels Henry Sonne 1948-

TUTORS

Members of the tutorial staff since its inception in 1926. Dates indicate the year of appointment.

1926	William Lamson Griffin, Jr.	1927	Felix Lossing Cirlot
1926	John Lowe	1928	William Henry Cole
1926	George Arthur Meyer	1928	Richard Spink Martin
1926	Harold Neil Renfrew	1928	Cuthbert Aikman Simpson
1926	Lawrence Rose	1929	Charles Rudolph Feilding

1929 Edward Rochie Hardy, Jr.
1929 William Wilson Manross
1930 Haven Palmer Perkins
1930 John Alexander Richardson
1930 Robert Denison Smith
1930 Harold Merritt Wilson
1931 Robert Jennings Gibson
1932 Henry Matrau Eller
1933 Stephen Fielding Bayne, Jr.
1933 Theodore Parker Ferris
1933 Jonathan Goodhue Sherman
1934 Robert Noel Rodenmayer
1935 William Norman Pittenger
1937 John Atherton Bell
1937 Thomas James Bigham, Jr.
1939 George Albert Heald
1939 Robert Leslie Clayton
1940 Frederick Quentin Shafer
1941 John Oscar Bruce
1945 John Durham Wing, Jr.
1946 Robert Semple Bosher
1946 James Albert Pike
1946 Robert Baker Pegram
1947 Robert Elwin Terwilliger
1947 Shunji Forrest Nishi
1948 Charles Pratt Berger, Jr.
1948 Edward Chandler
1948 John Bernard Hibbitts
1949 Christopher Morley, Jr.
1949 James Leland Jones, Jr.
1949 Alvin Van Pelt Hart
1950 Charles Kane Cobb Lawrence
1950 Harvey Henry Guthrie, Jr.
1950 Harry Boone Porter, Jr.
1950 Herman Karl Lutge
1951 John William Pyle
1951 Gordon David Griffith
1951 John Arnold Cranston, Jr.
1951 Steele Wade Martin
1951 Thomas Carleton Lee
1952 Michael George Mayer
1952 Maurice Allen Martin Garrison
1952 Charles Layfaette Winters, Jr.
1952 Percy Linwood Urban, Jr.
1953 Wilbur Emory Hogg, Jr.
1953 Charles Wheeler Scott
1953 Hugh Martin Jansen, Jr.
1953 William Andrew Norgren, Jr.
1953 Lloyd George Patterson
1953 Richard Nelson Bolles
1954 John Charles Vockler
1954 John Pairman Brown
1954 Eugene Van Ness Goetchius
1954 William Henry Ralston, Jr.
1955 Maurice Stanton Donovan
1955 Anthony Jefferson Morley
1955 Richard Alfred Norris, Jr.
1956 Eugene Earl Crommett
1956 Edward Gideon Holtam, III
1956 Robert Bernard Hybel
1956 Lewis Roper Shamhart
1956 Richard Morisse Spielmann
1956 Christopher Lawrence Webber
1957 George Phelps Mellick Belshaw
1957 Richard Warren Corney
1957 John Marshall Roberts, III
1957 Francis Xavier Walter
1958 William Paul Haugaard
1958 Morley Edward Pinkney
1958 Sheldon Flory
1958 Billy Wilson Rodgers
1959 Maxwell McNee Thomas
1959 Richard Carl Adams
1959 James Edward Griffiss, Jr.
1959 Daniel Wayne Hardy
1959 William Alan Sadler, Jr.
1959 William David Jones
1959 Richard Tuttle Loring
1960 David Rhinelander King

1960 Richard Franklin Tombaugh
1960 George Duncan Buchanan
1961 James Edward Gardner
1961 William Brown Patterson, III
1961 Alan Condie Tull
1962 Donald Lynn Rogan
1962 Gehret David Deppen
1962 Frederick Hardman Shriver, Jr.
1963 Robert Avon Bennett
1963 Boyce McLean Bennett, Jr.
1963 Charles Wilson Patterson
1963 Lewis Wilson Towler
1964 Ronald Lee Woodruff
1964 Grahame Gordon Butler-Nixon
1964 Richard Cassels Nevius
1964 Richard John Bowman
1964 James Henry Brennan
1965 James Cooper Wattley
1965 Eric Freidus
1965 Robert Lewis Meaney
1966 Jeremy John Bunting
1966 Paul Tyler Coke
1966 Paul Bauchman Clayton, Jr.
1966 Thomas George Peterson
1966 Alan William Jones
1966 Marion Josiah Hatchett

Index

Academic gowns, 264
Adams, William, 119
An Address to the Episcopalians of the United States, 62, 63
Admission requirements, 92, 267, 268, 334
A.E.F., 331
Agassiz, Louis, 250
All Saints' Cathedral, Albany, N.Y., 277, 297, 307
All Saints' Church, New York, 84, 143
Allen, A. V. G., 273
Alumni, 119-20, 245, 265, 269, 277, 290, 293, 322, 331, 354
Alumni Association (Associate Alumni), 120, 277, 293, 333, 344, 354
Alumni professorship, 277, 293, 294
American Bible Society, 89
Amherst College, 131, 297
Anderson, Abel T., 197, 199, 201, 203, 206n
Andover Theological Seminary, 30
Anglo-Catholicism, 213, 215, 216, 220, 227, 239, 275, 276
Anthon, Charles, 142
Anthon, Henry, 142, 143, 144, 146, 152, 154-57, 174, 183; his *True Issue for the True Churchman*, 155
Antwerp Polyglot Bible, 291
Apologetics, the study of, 19, 87, 88, 90, 137, 192, 240, 277, 284, 285, 306, 308, 309, 323, 325, 336, 342
Armitage, William Edmond, 245
Assistants in instruction, a list of, *see* Appendix
Associate missions, 290
Atkinson, Thomas, 232, 233n

Bachelor of Sacred Theology, requirements for the degree of, 243, 244, 271, 283-84, 288, 302, 303, 312-15, 352, 358-59
Banner of the Cross, 157
Baptists, 7, 12
Bard College, 337
Barnwell, William, 165
Barr, Orlando Sydney, 340
Barrett, George West, 343
Barrow, Isaac, *A Treatise on the Pope's Supremacy*, 21, 90
Bartlett, C., 162
Basketball team, 288
Batten, Loring Woart, 307, 308, 321, 327, 333
Bayne, Stephen F., Jr., 323n
Beach, Abraham, 15
Beckwith, Isbon Thaddeus, 287, 305
Beecher, Henry Ward, 236
Belknap, Reginald R., 333, 335, 345
Bell, William H., 232, 233
Bennett, Boyce M., 343n
Berkeley Divinity School, 306, 326, 337, 338, 340
Berrian, William, 145, 154, 156
Bethune-Baker, J. F., 310; his *Early History of Christian Doctrine*, 330

Bexley Hall, 287, 306, 338
Bible Collection, 291-92, 351
Biblical Learning, the professorship of, 43, 44, 79, 240, 242, 287, 364
Biblical Seminary, 354
Bigham, Thomas James, Jr., 336, 341
Bishop E. Ferris, 227, 228
Bishops, *see* House of Bishops
Bishops' *Declaration of 1820*, 57-58
Blackman, George L., *Faith and Freedom*, 193n
Blair, James, 15
Blake, Eugene Carson, 357
Blodgett, Francis Branch, 307, 311, 321
Blunt, John Henry, *The Annotated Book of Common Prayer*, 285
Board of Trustees, 86, 90, 92, 95, 97, 106, 107, 110, 113, 114, 115, 121, 122, 126, 127, 128, 129, 131, 166, 177, 178, 179, 189, 192, 193, 198, 199, 200, 202, 203, 205-206, 222, 223, 231-34, 235, 237, 243, 246, 252-53, 260, 264, 268, 270, 278, 279, 293, 297, 304, 305, 340, 344, 346, 347, 349; in New Haven, 58-59, 60; at the union with the New York Diocesan School, 76-77, 79; size and composition of, 76-77, 99, 269; influence of New York in, 78-79, 100-101, 182-83; investigation of the Seminary by, 160-64; *Memorial* to General Convention by some members of, 165; *Memorial* of students to, 281-83
Boarding Club, 134, 216-17, 268
Body, Charles W. E., 287, 305, 307, 308
Boise, Edward, 261
Bosher, Robert Semple, 341
Bowen, Nathaniel, 9, 12, 15, 24, 28, 41, 42, 57, 75, 77 106
Boynton, Charles Homer, 309, 327
Branch School at Geneva, 71-72, 73, 79, 101-102
Breck, James Lloyd, 118, 119, 153
Brenton, William, 275n
Brisley, Mary Swan, 326
British Critic, 153
Brooklyn property, 201-202, 206
Brooks, Phillips, *Lectures on Preaching*, 285
Brooks, Roelif H., 333
Brown, John Henry Hobart, 245-46
Brown, Ray Francis, 327, 328; his *Oxford American Psalter*, 328
Brown-Sermon, Stanley, 343
Brown University, 131
Browne, Edward Harold, *Exposition of the Thirty-Nine Articles*, 90, 137, 285
Brownell, Thomas Church, 9, 62, 97, 98, 106; solicits for the Seminary, 41-42; supervises the Seminary in New Haven, 55, 57, 60-61, 66; furthers the union with the New York Diocesan School, 74-75, 76n, 77
Bruce, Alexander, *Apologetics*, 285
Bruton Parish Church, Williamsburg, Va., 3
Buel, Samuel, 232n, 242, 264, 276
Builders-for-Christ campaign, 346
Bulgakov, Sergius, 331
Burgess, Alexander, 246
Burhans, Daniel, 41
Burnet, Gilbert, *Exposition of the XXXIX Articles*, 21, 90, 137; *Discourse on Pastoral Care*, 22
Bush, Donald F., 345n
Butler, Joseph, *Analogy of Religion*, 19, 21, 90, 285
Butler, Nicholas Murray, 303

Cady, Philander Kinney, 232n, 276, 277, 278, 285, 305
Calhoun, John C., 27
Calvary Church, New York, 194
Cambridge University, 260, 264, 276, 287, 292, 338, 341, 342
Cameron, Duncan, 56, 59, 63, 76, 77, 78
Canon law and polity, the study of, 20, 61, 86, 87, 137, 192, 220, 240, 241, 284, 302, 314, 320
Canons: of *1789*, 17; of *1792*, 17-18; of *1808*, 18
Carey, Arthur, 146, 147, 148, 152-56, 158, 177
Carey ordination, 145-46, 152, 154-57, 177
Carpenter, James A., 342
Carper, Wood Bowyer, 343
Carter, Lawson, 49, 51
Case, Adelaide Teague, 327
Casserley, J. V. Langmead, 342
Catalogue of the Seminary, the first, 131-32, 134
Cathedral of St. John the Divine, New York, 249, 326, 343
Cathey, John, 275n
Catholic heritage of Anglicanism, 99, 147, 148, 153, 154, 212, 213
Cave, William, *Lives of the Apostles; Lives of the Most Eminent Fathers*, 19

Central Block, 199, 206, 207, 250, 294, 298
Central Theological College, Tokyo, 338
Chandler, Thomas Bradbury, 15, 26
Chapel: in the East Building, 116, 124, 125n, 238, 239, 244; in the West Building, 124-26, 217, 218, 219, 225, 226
Chapel of the Good Shepherd, 98, 247, 255, 256, 258, 259, 261-64, 289, 292, 294, 295, 358
Chapel services 94, 116-17, 124, 126-27, 217-19, 225, 226, 239, 266, 300
Chaplain, the office of, 130-31, 326, 337, 348
Chaplains, a list of, *see* Appendix
Chaplin, Dora Phyllis, 343
Chapman, Helen Beatrice, 335
Chase, Carlton, 182, 206
Chase, Philander, 9, 57, 78, 148, 157, 165, 166, 183, 184, 245
Chauncey, Elihu, 253
Chelsea, 104-105; student activity in, 119, 290, 291
Chelsea Mission, 291, 331
Chelsea Square, use of the name of, 111; Moore's gift of the land in, 46, 68, 104, 106, 112-15, 198, 203
Chillingworth, William, *The Religion of Protestants*, 21
Christ Church, Bronxville, N.Y., 343
Christ Church, Elizabeth, N.J., 246
Christ Church, Fairfield, N.Y., 72
Christ Church, New York, 83-84, 97, 98
Christ Church, Oxford, 340
Christ Church, Philadelphia, Pa., 16
Christ Church, Poughkeepsie, N.Y., 72, 277
Christian apologetics, *see* Apologetics
Christian Apologetics, the Charles Lewis Gomph professorship of, 342n
Christian education, the study of, 304, 309, 312, 327, 343, 352
Christian evidences, see *Apologetics*
Christian Evidences, the Alumni professorship of, 277, 293-94
Christian Guild for Social Action, 327
Christian Herald, 62
Christian Journal, 38
Christian Witness and Church Advocate, 157
Church history, the study of, 18, 19, 21, 43-44, 61, 86, 87, 90, 136, 137, 185-86, 240, 283-85, 304, 312, 313, 322, 337
Church Journal, 180, 187, 206n, 232
Church Mission of Help, 326
Church of the Advent, Boston, Mass., 181, 213, 354
Church of the Annunciation, New York, 177, 185, 194, 241
Church of the Ascension, New York, 84, 251
Church of England, 4, 10, 147
Church of the Holy Apostles, New York 119, 291
Church of the Holy Spirit, Lake Forest, Ill., 343
Church of the Nativity, Bridgeport, Conn., 227
Church of St. Esprit, New York, 83
Church of St. Mary the Virgin, New York, 213
Church of the Transfiguration, New York, 185, 208, 213, 223, 225
Church Register, 109
Churchman, 98, 146n, 147, 149, 154, 157, 166, 169, 183
Churchmanship controversy: over the Oxford Movement, 145-79; its effects upon the Seminary, 177-79, 180-82, 199; during the Ritualistic Movement, 185, 212-15; further effects upon the Seminary, 217-22, 225-29; in the twentieth century, 309-10
Civil War, 123, 134, 144, 195-97, 206, 207, 212, 245
Claggett, Thomas John, 10, 11
Clark, Orin, 72
Clark, Thomas March, 230, 231, 244
Clarke, Charity, 104
Clarke, James P. F., 49
Clarke, Thomas, 104
Claude, Jean, *Essay on the Composition of a Sermon*, 143
Cline, Thomas Sparks, 326
Clinton, DeWitt, 84, 103
Coberger Bibles, 291
Collier, Jeremy, *Ecclesiastical History of Great Britain*, 21, 90
Columbia College, 40, 69, 82, 98, 103, 120, 132, 207
Columbia University, 83, 215, 239, 309, 321; relation of the Seminary with, 278-79, 286, 303
Commemoration of Benefactors, 249
Commencement ceremonies, 97, 98-99, 265
Commencement exercises, 92, 97-99, 244

Complutension Polyglot Bible, 102
Congregationalists, 8, 30
Connecticut, the Church in, 13
Constitution of the Seminary, 76-77; attempted revision in *1865*, 222; in *1883*, 269-70
Contoit, Charles H., 253
Contoit legacy, 254
Copinger, Walter A., 291
Copinger Bible Collection, 291
Corney, Richard Warren, 343
Cotheal fellowship, 329n
Council for Clinical Training, 331
Council of Trent, 154, 155, 160, 167, 169, 170
Course of Ecclesiastical Studies of *1804*, 18-23, 48, 87, 90, 134, 168, 187, 277, 284
Course of study, *see* Curriculum; Scheme of study
Cox, Rowland J., 348n
Coxe, Arthur Cleveland, 232
Creed of Pius IV, 152, 155
Croes, John, 11, 40, 57, 80, 121
Croes, Robert, 80
Crommett, Eugene E., 342
Curriculum: as planned by the Theological Committee, 43-44; in New Haven, 60-61; before *1867*, 86-90, 134-38; as revised in *1867*, 240-41; in *1893*, 283-85; under Dean Robbins, 302-304; in *1919*, 312-15; in *1968*, 358-59. *See also* Scheme of Study; Course of Ecclesiastical Studies of *1804*
Curriculum revision: proposals for, 187-94; student agitation for, 271-75, 278-83, 295; made in *1893*, 283 ff; under Dean Robbins, 296-97, 302-304; made in *1919*, 312-15; under Dean Rose, 315, 352-53; made in *1968*, 315, 358-59. *See also* Methods of study
Cutler, Timothy, 15
Cutting, William Bayard, 253

Daily Offices, 116-17, 218, 264, 266, 300
Dartmouth College, 131, 242
Darwin, Charles, *The Descent of Man*, 239
Daubeny, Charles, 20, 54
Dawley, Powel Mills, 338, 340, 341, 344, 354
Dean, George Washington, 277
Dean, the office of, 95; held by the professors in rotation, 127-31; made permanent, 131, 222; powers and authority of, 222-23, 224-25, 270-71
Dean, styled "the Very Reverend," 260
Deanery, 257, 258, 260, 261, 351
Deans, a list of, *see* Appendix
Degrees *ad eundem*, 264-65; *honoris causa*, 265, 356, 357-58
Degrees in philosophy, proposals for, 288
Degrees in theology, 90, 243-44, 287-88, 329, 341, 352; *see also* Bachelor of Sacred Theology; Master of Sacred Theology; Doctor of Sacred Theology
Dehon, Theodore, 9, 10, 12, 14, 15, 29, 33, 41, 178; his concern for theological education, 15, 28; advocates a general theological seminary, 30-31, 57; persuades the House of Bishops, 35-36; author of the resolutions to establish the Seminary, 39-40, 43; death of, 42
Dehon Hall, 257, 268
Deissman, Alfred, 331
DeKoven, James, 215
DeLancey, William Heathcote, 160, 173, 177-79, 202
DeLancey Divinity School, 309
Delaware, the Church in, 12
DeMel, Jacob Lakdasa, 357
Denslow, Herbert McKenzie, 306, 307, 311, 326, 343
Dentan, Robert Claude, 340
Depression of the *1930*'s, 333-34, 335
Deputies, *see* House of Deputies
Dewar, Lindsay, 331
Dickinson, S. E., 228, 298, 325
Diplomas, 243, 265, 288, 302
Director of Graduate Studies, the office of, 341
Dix, Morgan, 223, 231, 237, 243, 251, 256, 269
Doane, George Washington, 49, 51, 121, 129, 150, 166, 173
Doane, William Croswell, 257
Doctor of Sacred Theology, requirements for the degree of, 243-44; number granted, 341
Doctor of Theology, made the designation of earned doctorates, 341n
Dodge, Mrs. Anson G. P., Jr., 258
Dodge Hall, 258
Dodge legacy, 258
Dogmatic theology, *see* Theology

Dogmatic Theology, the Mary Crooke Hoffman professorship of, 253-54
Dorr, Benjamin, 49
Doscher, William F., 275n
Drisler, Henry, 239
Driver, S. R., 272
DuBose, William Porcher, 300
Duer, John, 152, 157
Dunn, Kempton, 349
Dyer, Hemen, 251, 256
Dykman, Jackson A., 357

East Building 106-13, 115-16, 123, 124, 131, 132, 133, 162, 194, 197, 204, 214, 216, 217, 238, 255, 258-59
East Quadrangle, 255-59, 260, 261
Eastburn, Manton, 49, 66, 67, 96, 143, 159, 160, 161, 177
Easter, caroling at dawn on, 289
Eastern Diocese, 10, 150
Easton, Burton Scott, 321, 322, 324, 343; his *Gospel of St. Luke*, *Gospel before the Gospels*, *Purpose of Acts*, *Pastoral Epistles*, *Christ in the Gospels*, *Apostolic Tradition of Hippolytus*, and *Eternal Word in the Modern World*, 322
Easton, Mrs. Burton Scott, 332
Ecclesiastical history, *see* Church history
Ecclesiastical History, the St. Mark's-Church-in-the-Bowery professorship of, 139-40
Ecclesiastical Music, department of, 283; *see also* Music in the Seminary
Ecclesiastical Polity and Law, the Ludlow professorship of, 220
Ecclesiologist, 153
Ecumenical activity, 358
Edinburgh Theological College, 342
Edmunds, Charles Carroll, 307, 321
Edson Funds, 254
Edson Hall, 295, 298, 345
Edson legacies, 254n
Eggestein Bibles, 291
Eigenbrodt, William Ernest, 194-95, 220, 229, 230, 234, 241, 242, 254, 264, 276, 277
Eigenbrodt fellowship, 254
Eigenbrodt Hall, 292, 293
Eigenbrodt legacy, 195, 254
Elective courses, 282, 285, 286, 303, 313-15, 327, 352, 359
Eliot, Samuel, 267
Ellicott, Charles J., 284
Elliott, Stephen, 165
Elmendorf, John J., *Elements of Moral Theology*, 285
Ely, Richard, *Social Aspects of Christianity*, 285
Endowments, 120, 139, 195, 197-203, 205-207, 220, 240, 250-55, 296, 297-98, 332-33, 344-46
Enrollment, *see* Students, numbers of
Episcopal Church, after the American Revolution, 3-5, 8-15
Episcopal Recorder, 157
Episcopal Seminary of the Caribbean, 342
Episcopal Society of New Jersey for the Promotion of Christian Knowledge and Piety, 13, 24
Episcopal Theological School, 273, 275, 297, 307, 308, 310, 320, 338, 340, 343n
Erie Canal, 103
Essays Catholic and Critical, 330
Ethics, the study of, 192, 283-84, 285, 313
Evangelicalism, 9, 151, 157, 213-14
Evangelicals, 9, 16, 142, 143, 147-51, 152, 154, 155, 157, 159, 173, 177, 179, 183, 199, 213, 216, 221
Evarts, William M., 257
Evening Prayer, *see* Daily Offices
Everett, William, 153
Evidences, the study of, *see* Apologetics
Ewer, Ferdinand C., 226
Examination, the annual, 90, 135-37, 181, 278n
Examination Committee, 90, 101, 128, 135, 152, 181, 187, 278n

Faculty: powers of, 94-95, 270; investigation of by the Trustees, 159-63; investigation of by the House of Bishops, 165-71; quarrels among under Dean Forbes, 225-33; actions subject to the Dean's veto, 270-71. *See also* Professors
Fairfield Academy, 72
Fellowships, 254, 329
Feltus, Henry, 84, 140
Field education, 358
Field work, 102, 119, 290-91, 326-27
Figgis, John Neville, 300
Finance Committee, 197, 201, 203, 250, 253, 294, 345
Financial campaign of *1957*, 349-51

Financial crisis of the mid-nineteenth century, 197-207

Financial troubles during the depression, 333-37

First World War, 303, 331

Fiske University, 327

Flint, Robert, *Theism*, 285

Flushing Institute, 131

Forbes, John Murray, 222, 223-25, 237, 270; elected Dean, 223; disciplinary measures of, 225-26; his opposition to Ritualism, 226-30; quarrels with Professor Seymour, 230-33; favors removing the Seminary from New York, 234, 236; resignation of, 234

Forrester, Donald Fraser, 321, 340

Forrester, Mrs. Donald Fraser, 332

Fosbroke, Hughell Edgar Woodall, 283, 291, 321, 323, 331, 332, 335, 336, 337, 340, 341, 360; elected Dean, 310; his views on theological education, 310-12, 328, 360-61; undertakes curriculum revision in *1919*, 312-15; character and personality of, 316-20; his influence in the Seminary, 316-17; insists on high intellectual standards and spiritual discipline, 319-20; his professors, 321-28, 336-38; his writings, 323; establishes the tutorial system, 329-30; wartime admissions policy of, 334-35; retirement of, 338

Foundations, 310

Fourth-Year course, 288, 312

French, Edward A., 323n

Froude, Hurrell, 153

Fry, Franklin Clark, 357

Fust and Schoeffer Bible of *1462*, 291

Gadsden, Christopher Edwards, 4, 9, 15, 34, 35, 45, 56, 106, 159, 160, 173, 178; his concern for the establishment of a general theological seminary, 27-28, 30-31; urges support of the Seminary, 42-43, 62; his *Reasons in Favour of the General Theological Seminary*, 62

Gadsden, Philip, 80

Gale, Clement R., 327

Gavin, Frank Stanton Burns, 321, 324; his *Seven Centuries of the Problem of Church and State, Some Aspects of Contemporary Greek Orthodox Thought*, and *Jewish Antecedents of the Christian Sacraments*, 322

General Convention, *see* House of Bishops; House of Deputies

General Convention: of *1789*, 4, 17; of *1792*, 17; of *1804*, 18; of *1808*, 18n; of *1811*, 3, 10, 12, 14; of *1814*, 8, 28, 29, 30-31, 33, 34, 35; of *1817*, 8, 11, 26, 36, 39-40; of *1820*, 40, 44, 46, 55, 56; of *1821*, 74-77; of *1844*, 163-66; of *1865*, 222; of *1868*, 213; of *1874*, 213; of *1883*, 269; of *1889*, 19n; of *1907*, 304; of *1940*, 333; of *1967*, 353

General Theological Seminary: sentiment for the foundation of, 26-31, 33-38; established by resolutions of General Convention, 39; work of the Theological Committee on behalf of, 40-41, 43-46; its opening in New York, 48; its difficulties with Bishop Hobart, 48-54; in New Haven, 56-57, 60-62, 64-69; competes with Bishop Hobart's Diocesan School, 59-60, 68-72; its claim to the Sherred legacy, 72-75; unites with the New York Diocesan School, 75-80; reopens in New York, 80-81; located at St. John's Chapel and Park, 82-110; in Chelsea Square in the early nineteenth century, 111-44; churchmanship controversy in, 145-59; investigated by its Board of Trustees, 159-64; subjected to a visitation by the House of Bishops, 165-72; mid-century troubles of, 180-85; proposals for curriculum change in, 187-94; its financial crisis, 197-207; proposals to move from New York, 202-203, 234-237; influence of Ritualism in, 215, 217, 219-21; Forbes becomes Dean of, 222-25; quarrels in its Faculty, 226-34; its prosperity and expansion in the Hoffman era, 245-71, 288-95; clamor for curriculum reform in, 271-83; its Scheme of Study of *1893*, 283-86; problems of the curriculum, 296-97, 300-305; under Dean Fosbroke, 310-38; since the Second World War, 334-54; sesquicentennial year of, 355-58

Geneva (Hobart) College, 102, 131

Gerry, Elbridge T., 251, 253

Gieseler, Johann K. L., 285

Gillespie, George deN., 245

Githens, Alfred Morton, 332

Given, William B., 344

Gomph, Charles Lewis, 342n; the Charles Lewis Gomph professorship, 342n

Gomph, Ida R., 342n
Gore, Charles, 285, 310, 331
Gospel Messenger, 157
Grace Church, Brooklyn, N.Y., 246
Grace Church, Jersey City, N.J., 341
Grace Church, New York, 49, 83, 184, 257
Grace Church, Newark, N.J., 277
Graduate program, 272, 287-88, 312, 329, 341
Graduate students, 272, 279, 312, 331, 334, 339, 341
Graduate study, 191, 272, 287-88, 312, 329, 341
Graduation, requirements for, 90-92, 192-93, 271, 283-84, 302-304, 312-15, 352, 358-59
Grafton, Charles C., 227
Grannis, Appleton, 291
Graves, Anson Rogers, 290
Greek, the study of, 18, 86, 136-37, 240, 283-84, 303, 312-14, 352
Gresley, William, *Ecclesiasticus Anglicanus,* 143-44, 285
Griswold, Alexander Viets, 9, 10, 12, 16, 35, 57, 75, 78, 150
Grotius, Hugo, *The Truth of the Christian Religion,* 19
Gutenberg Bible, 250, 291-92
Guthrie, Harvey Henry, Jr., 340
Gymnasium, 125n, 238, 292, 299

Haight, Benjamin Isaac, 143-44, 145, 154, 158, 160, 161, 161n, 163, 169, 182, 194, 238
Haight, Charles C., 238, 255, 260, 292
Hall, Francis Joseph, 300, 309; his *Theological Outlines* and *Dogmatic Theology,* 309
Hall, Randall Cooke, 241, 242, 264, 275, 287n; his *Elements of Hebrew Grammar,* 241
Hall, Samuel S., Jr., 345
Hardy, Edward Rochie, Jr., 336-37
Harison, William H., 197
Harris, Samuel, *The Philosophical Basis of Theism,* 285
Harris, William, 40
Harvard College, 131, 246, 307, 309, 310, 321, 338, 353
Hassinger, Howard H., 326
Hatch, Edwin, 273
Hatch, William Henry Paine, 307-308
Hawks, Francis Lister, 139, 140, 144, 185
Hayes, Charles Harris, 306, 309
Hayes, Rutherford B., 257
Headlam, Arthur Cayley, 331
Hebrew, the Clement Clarke Moore professorship of, 115, 321n
Hebrew, the study of, 18, 87, 136-37, 185, 189, 192, 240, 283-84, 295, 302, 303, 312-13, 335, 337
Hempel, Johannes, 331
Henshaw, John P. K., 9, 16
Herbert, George, 211
Herring, F. W., 186
Higbee, Edward Y., 154
High churchmanship, 9, 25, 26, 147, 148, 194, 212, 214; in the Seminary, 99, 100-101, 121, 126, 141, 143, 152-53, 158-61, 185-87, 220, 224, 249, 251, 275, 276, 277, 309. *See also* Ritualist movement
High churchmen, 10, 29, 145, 147, 150, 153, 154, 161, 165, 173, 177, 185, 213, 214, 220, 249, 277
Historic Theology, the professorship of, 43, 44, 363
Hobart, John Henry, 9, 10, 12, 16, 20, 29, 31, 38, 40, 42, 46, 57, 58, 62, 64, 73, 80, 87, 95, 99, 100-102, 108, 109, 117, 138, 139, 141, 147, 184, 185, 191, 295n; character and personality of, 10, 25-26; his concern for theological education, 14, 26, 31-33, 79; his views on a seminary, 31-35; his *Grammar School and Theological Seminary,* 33-34; a member of the Theological Committee of the General Convention, 40, 42; devises a curriculum for the Seminary, 43-44; relations with the Seminary in *1819-20,* 48-51, 53; his quarrel with Professor Jarvis, 51-54; his *Pastoral Letter of 1820,* 59-60, 64, 68; establishes the New York Diocesan School, 59-60, 68-72; supports the union of the Seminary and the New York School, 75-77; his influence in the Seminary, 76, 95, 100-101, 185; becomes Professor of Pastoral Theology, 79, 87
Hobart, John Henry, Jr., 119
Hobart College, 102, 131
Hobart Hall, 257, 258, 260, 294, 300, 349, 351n
Hocking, William Ernest, *The Meaning of God in Human Experience,* 330
Hodgson, Leonard, 321, 324; his *And Was Made Man, Essays in Christian*

Philosophy, and *For Faith and Freedom*, 325
Hoffman, Charles F., 252
Hoffman, Eugene Augustus, 110, 123, 134, 244, 264-65, 268, 269, 278, 279, 288, 289, 290, 294, 297, 305, 327, 333, 340, 345; building program of, 125, 255-64, 292-94, 295; as a student, 134-35; his professors, 243, 275-78, 286-87; elected Dean, 246; character and personality of, 247-50; financial achievements of, 250-55; the Eugene Augustus Hoffman professorship, 251-52, 253; his personal gifts to the Seminary, 251-52, 253, 259-60, 296, 298n; rules and regulations of, 265-67; his concern for the spiritual life, 262-64, 266; his views of the academic enterprise, 267, 271-72; augments the authority of the Dean, 270-71; faces agitation for curriculum reform, 273-75, 280-86, 295-96; his interest in the Bible Collection, 291-92; last years and death of, 294-96
Hoffman, Eugene Augustus, Jr., 259n
Hoffman, Glorvina Rossell, 252, 253, 258; the Glorvina Rossell Hoffman professorship, 253, 321
Hoffman, Mary Crooke, 253, 296, 298n; the Mary Crooke Hoffman professorship, 254
Hoffman, Samuel Verplanck, 246, 252; the Samuel Verplanck Hoffman Foundation, 252, 253
Hoffman buildings, 250, 255-64, 292-94, 295, 296
Hoffman deanery, 257, 258, 260, 261
Hoffman Hall, 292, 293, 295, 335, 346, 356
Hoffman legacy, 296
Holtkamp organ, 346
Holy Communion, services of, 94, 99, 117, 126-27, 217-18, 226, 227, 239, 244, 266, 300
Homiletics, the study of, 22, 44, 142-44, 188, 189, 193, 283, 284, 285, 312
Hone, Philip, 88
Hooker, Richard, *The Laws of Ecclesiastical Polity*, 20, 22, 54, 90
Hopkins, John Henry, 78, 97, 98, 157, 165, 173, 174, 179, 214; his *Law of Ritualism*, 214
Hopkins, John Henry, Jr., 209-10, 226, 262, 277
Hort, F. J. A., 273
Houghton, George H., 185, 204, 208, 213, 220n, 225
House of Bishops, 8, 10, 11, 14, 15, 18, 38-39, 57-58, 59, 163, 164, 165, 166, 172, 173, 174, 188; *Pastoral Letter of 1811*, 14; *Pastoral Letter of 1817*, 8; visitation of the Seminary by, 166-72
House of Deputies, 12, 30-31, 34, 35, 36, 39, 40, 56, 57, 58, 76, 164, 165, 356
How, Thomas Y., 31, 40
Hunt, Arthur Prince, 307, 326
Huntington, Daniel, 47, 88, 105, 172
Huntington, Frederick Dan, 267
Huntington, Samuel, 233
Hurd, Richard, 90, 137

Iakovas, Archbishop, 357
Illingworth, J. R., *Personality, Human and Divine*, 285
Incorporation of the Seminary, 86
Infirmary, 123, 346
Inge, William Ralph, 300
Inman, Henry, 11
Instructors, a list of, *see* Appendix.
Interior School, *see* Branch School
Ives, Levi Silliman, 80, 145, 147, 150, 166, 173

Jarvis, Abraham, 10, 15, 45
Jarvis, George A., 240, 253, 254, 258, 351n
Jarvis, Samuel Farmar, 59, 63, 65, 80, 83, 96, 100, 101, 108, 140, 191, 360; made professor, 44-46; classes of, 48-51; his quarrels with Bishop Hobart, 48, 51-54; resignation of, 52-53, 59
Jarvis Hall, 258, 260, 294, 351n
Jarvis legacy, 254
Jefferson College, 131
Jenks, Arthur Whipple, 308, 321
Jewett, Edward Hurtt, 276-77, 285, 305
Johansen, J. C., 325
Johnson, Alfred Evan, 244
Johnson, Eastman, 248
Johnson, Irving Peake, 290
Johnson, Samuel, 15
Johnson, Samuel Roosevelt, 68, 80, 186, 191, 194, 196, 197, 206, 207, 215, 217, 219, 223, 224, 225, 229, 230, 232, 242, 340; made professor, 185; hardships of, 204-205; character and influence of, 207-11; his opinions on Ritualism, 219-221; resignation of, 221
Johnson, William A., 188-89

Johnson, William Lupton, 74, 80, 207
Johnson fellowship, 329n
Joint Commission of General Convention on Church Music, 328
Joint Committee of General Convention on the General Theological Seminary, 304
Jones, William, *The Scholar Armed against the Errors of the Time*, 21

Keble, John, 147, 153, 167, 211
Keble College, Oxford, 262, 286
Keller, Adolph, 331
Kelsey, Arthur Corson, 348
Kemp, James, 11, 57, 75, 76, 78
Kemper, Jackson, 9, 16, 45, 49, 51, 55, 58, 59, 62, 64, 65, 69, 75, 106, 118, 173, 187, 207-208, 210, 245
Kenyon College, 306
Keyes, Charles Don, 343
Kilham, William H., Jr., 345, 351
King, John A., 253
King, Rufus, 40, 53, 70-71
King fellowship, 329n
King's College, Cambridge, 342
King's College (Columbia), 15
King's College, Halifax, 321
Kinsman, Frederick J., 306, 308
Kip, William Ingraham, 245
Kohne, Frederick, 110, 258
Kohne Hall, 258
Kohne legacy, 110, 122, 200, 201-202, 206n

LaFayette, Marquis de, 103
Langdon, Woodbury G., 253, 256
Lauderburn, Frederick Curtiss, 326, 337
Lawrence, Isaac, 59, 63, 64
Lawrence, William, 273
Lectures, *see* Methods of study
Lecturers, a list of, *see* Appendix
Lecturers in Ascetical Theology, a list of, *see* Appendix
Lectureships: the Ascetical Theology lectureship, 348, 371; the Paddock lectureship, 240, 371; the Winslow lectureship, 372
Lee, Francis Praileux, 136
LeJay Polyglot Bible, 102
Leslie, Charles, 90, 137
Liberal Catholicism, 330
Librarians, a list of, *see* Appendix
Library, 63, 64-65, 102, 115, 120-21, 125n, 198, 238, 250, 255, 257, 258, 291, 294, 296, 349-51
Lichtenberger, Arthur Carl, 342
Liddon, Henry Parry, 284
Lightfoot, Joseph B., 273, 284
Lindsay, John V., 356
Liturgical movement, 343
Liturgical renewal, 358
Liturgics, the study of, 22, 44, 61, 284, 285, 314, 343, 344, 352
Locke, Clinton, 135
London Polyglot Bible, 102
Lord, Walter, 247
Lorillard, George, 122
Lorillard Hall, 295, 298
Lorillard legacy, 122, 199
Low churchmen, 9, 25, 47, 214
Ludlow, Elizabeth, 220; the Charles and Elizabeth Ludlow professorship, 220, 320
Luther, Martin, 291
Lux Mundi, 285
Lyell, Thomas, 84, 102
Lyman, Theodore B., 223

Mabry, Gregory, 333
McDonald, Daniel, 72
McGowan, Allen B., 345
McGregor, Daniel A., 327
McIlvaine, Charles Pettit, 73, 148, 149-50, 157, 158, 166, 170, 171; his *Oxford Divinity*, 149
McMaster, Benjamin, 153, 158
McVickar, Henry, 153
McVickar, John, 16, 23, 35, 120, 121, 154, 156, 215
Madison, Dolly, 5
Madison, James, 4, 10, 11, 12, 13
Magdalen College, Oxford, 325
Magee, J. A. V., 90
Mahan, Milo, 185-87, 189, 190, 191-92, 194, 196, 204, 215, 217, 232n, 272, 322
Major, H. D. A., 310
Marriage of students, statute on, 266n, 347
Married students, 340, 346-48
Married students' apartments, 347
Marshall, Thurgood, 356
Martensen, Hans, *Christian Dogmatics*, 285; *Christian Ethics*, 285
Martineau, James, *Types of Ethical Theory*, 285
Maryland, the Church in, 12

Massachusetts, the Church in, 13
Massachusetts Diocesan Convention, of *1831*, 78; of *1843*, 159
Massingberd, F. C., 167
Master of Sacred Theology, the degree of, 243, 329, 341; requirements for, 329
Matriculation, 92-94, 96
Matriculation Book, 93-94
Matriculation vow, 94
Matthews, Paul, 290, 332
Maurice, Frederick Denison, 285
Mayer, Michael G., 343
Mayo fellowships, the, 254
Meade, William, 3-4, 6, 9, 11, 13, 77, 78, 149, 157, 165, 185
Memorial Addressed to the Dean, Faculty and Trustees, 280-83, 286, 296
Mercer, Charles F., 40
Meredith, William, 36, 37, 40, 59, 63; his *Brief Remarks*, 36-38
Methodists, 7
Methods of study, 54, 68, 87-89, 138, 189-92, 193, 241, 272, 280-83, 328; before the establishment of theological seminaries, 15-17, 18-23; recitations *vs.* lectures, 87-89, 134, 192, 241, 272, 281-82, 285-86, 295, 296; the lecture-preceptorial, 328, 359; the lecture-tutorial, 329-31
Metropolitan Association of Theological Schools, 358
Middlebrook's Almanac, 67
Miller, Dickinson Sergeant, 300, 309, 311, 321, 323
Milman, Henry Hart, 90
Milnor, James, 64, 65, 69, 73, 74, 80, 83, 129, 148, 151, 157
Missionaries in the West, 119, 245-46, 290
Missionary concern in the Seminary, 118-19, 211, 289-90, 299-300
Missionary Society, 118, 290, 331
Missionary work: overseas, 290; in Chelsea, 291, 331
Mitchell, William H., 49
Moberley, R. C., *Ministerial Priesthood*, 330
Moeller, Charles, 358
Moore, Benjamin, 10, 46, 104
Moore, Clement Clarke, 84, 101, 104, 105, 117, 136, 138, 144, 161, 162, 168, 345; his gifts to the Seminary, 46, 63, 68, 104-105, 112-15, 203; made professor, 71, 79; his *Hebrew Lexicon*, 72; author of *A Visit from St. Nicholas*, 105; the Clement Clarke Moore professorship, 115, 287n, 321n; retirement of, 144, 185
Moore, Paul, Jr., 341
Moore, Richard Channing, 9, 11, 35, 41, 57, 75, 84
Moore Hall 345, 346, 348, 351
Moral theology, the study of, 240, 283, 284, 313
More, Paul Elmer, 331
Morehouse, Clifford P., 356
Morgan, J. Pierpont, 247
Morning Prayer, *see* Daily Offices
Morris, Benjamin Wister, 245
Mosheim, Johann Lorentz von, 20, 22, 54, 90, 285
Mount, W. S., 148
Mt. Calvary Church, Baltimore, Md., 276
Mozley, J. B., 285
Muhlenberg, William Augustus, 9, 16, 62, 185, 188
Muhlenberg Memorial, 188
Music in the Seminary, 209-10, 254, 283, 284, 327-28, 346
Myers, Chauncie Kilmer, 341, 343

Nash, Henry Sylvester, 273
Nashotah House, 119, 210, 285, 308, 310, 321, 344
Neale, John Mason, 90
Neander, Johann A. W., 90, 285
Neufville, Edward, 165
New Hampshire, the Church in, 13
New Haven, the Seminary in, 55-59, 60-68, 73-77
New Haven Plan, 60-62, 94
New Jersey, the Church in, 13, 24
New School for Social Research, 352
New Testament, the Glorvina Rossell Hoffman professorship of, 253
New Testament, the study of, 19, 43, 61, 86-87, 137, 240, 273, 275, 283-84, 302-303, 308, 312-14, 322
New York, the Church in, 13, 25-26, 32
New-York American, 107
New York Bible and Common Prayer Book Society, 25
New York churches, 83-86
New York City, in the *1820*'s, 82-86; in the *1870's*, 235-37
New York City Mission Society, 332
New York Diocesan Convention, of

1813, 33; of *1814*, 33, 34-35; of *1817*, 42, 49; of *1818*, 49; of *1819*, 49; of *1820*, 68-70; of *1821*, 75-76; of *1841*, 150; of *1843*, 157
New York Diocesan School, 31-35, 59-60, 64, 68-73, 75-79; proposals for the re-establishment of, 177-79
New-York Evening Post, 73
New-York Historical Society, 63, 249
New York Protestant Episcopal Theological Society, 25
New York School of Social Work, 326
New York trustees, 76-77, 79, 99-100, 182-83
New York University, 132, 288, 309
Newman, John Henry, 147, 153, 167
Newton, Heber, 251n
Nicholas of Lyra, 291
Nicholson, Sydney, 328
The Night before Christmas, see *A Visit from St. Nicholas*
Ninth Avenue building, 349-51
Nock, Arthur Darby, 331

Oberlin College, 327
O'Connor, Robert B., 345, 351
Odenheimer, William Henry, 206
Ogilby, John D., 141, 144, 161, 163, 170-72, 175, 185
Ohio Diocesan Convention, of *1840*, 149; of *1843*, 158
Old Testament, the Clement Clarke Moore professorship of, 115, 287n, 321n
Old Testament, the study of, 19, 43, 61, 86-87, 89, 137, 240, 272-75, 283-84, 302-303, 308, 312-14, 323
Old Testament, the Trinity Church professorship of, 321n, 340
Oliver, Andrew, 242, 258, 265, 270n, 275, 280, 285, 287
Onderdonk, Benjamin, 51, 74, 95, 121, 136, 141, 142, 144, 152, 164, 165, 185, 211, 221, 244; made professor, 71, 79; devoted to Catholic principles, 99, 121, 147-51; character and ability of, 138-39, 173; his influence in the Seminary, 139, 183-84; trial and suspension of, 139, 144, 172-74, 183; and the Carey ordination, 145-47, 154-58; his replies to the Trustees' queries, 160-63; his answers to the Bishops' questions, 169-70
Onderdonk, Henry Ustick, 164
Oriental languages, 283
Origen Society, 331
Ormsby, W. L., 172
Otey, James Hervey, 165
Otto, Rudolph, 331
Outler, Albert C., 358
Oxford Movement, 139, 147, 150, 212; its influence in the Seminary, 126, 141, 144, 152-54, 158-61, 162-64, 169-72, 174-77, 180, 181
Oxford University, 147, 260, 262, 264, 278, 292, 295, 323, 325, 340, 342, 344

Paddock, Benjamin Henry, 240
Paddock lecturers, 240, 272, 300, 326n; a list of, *see* Appendix
Paddock lectureship, 240, 254
Paine, Thomas, *The Age of Reason*, 6
Paley, William, *Christian Evidences*, 19, 22, 90, 137
Palmer, William, 167
Paradise, John, 32
Parker, Pierson, 340
Parker, Samuel, 13, 15, 28
Pastoral Theology, the Eugene Augustus Hoffman professorship of, 251, 253
Pastoral theology, the study of, 61, 66, 86, 87, 137, 141-44, 189-90, 192, 195, 240, 275, 276, 283-84, 308, 312-14, 326
Pastoral Theology and Pulpit Eloquence, the professorship of, 79, 194, 194n, 251
Peale, Rembrandt, 74
Pearce, S. Austen, 239
Pearson, John, *Exposition of the Creed*, 21, 68, 89, 90, 285
Pegram, Robert B., 341
Pendelton, Margaret, 120
Pennsylvania, the Church in, 13
Pennsylvania Diocesan Convention, of *1816*, 36; of *1817*, 36; of *1820*, 55
Perceval, Arthur Philip, 137
Perkins, Haven Palmer, 326
Philadelphia Divinity School, 308
Philippine mission, 290, 331
Pierrepont, Henry E., 203-204, 206-207, 251, 256, 294
Pinckney, Charles, 5
Pintard, John, 63-66, 67, 72, 73, 80, 100, 101, 102, 121, 138, 139, 140, 257
Pintard Hall, 257, 258
Pittenger, William Norman, 342
Pius IX, 181, 224
Plainsong, the controversy over, 209-210
Plant, John D., 345

Pomeroy, Ralph Brouwer, 320
Porter, Harry Boone, Jr., 344
Post-Graduate Course, 272, 287-88
Potter, Alonzo, 129
Potter, Henry Codman, 257, 260
Potter, Horatio, 184, 194, 205, 206, 211, 215, 223, 257
Potter, John, *Defence of Church Government*, 20, 54, 90, 137
Prayer for the Seminary, 80-81, 294-95, 295n
Preceptorial system, 359
Presbyterians, 8, 12, 30
Prescott, Oliver S., 227, 228
Price, Joseph, 145, 154
Princeton Theological Seminary, 30
Princeton University, 25
Proctor, Francis, *The History of the Prayer Book*, 285
Professors: in the early years, 44-48; in the New York Diocesan School, 71-72; at the union, 79; before *1850*, 138-44; during the mid-century years, 185-87, 194-95, 203-204, 207-11, 215-16, 221-22, 224-26; in the Hoffman era, 241-43, 275-78, 285-87; before the First World War, 305-309; under Dean Fosbroke, 310-11, 316-28; in recent years, 335-38, 340-44, 348; a list of, *see* Appendix
Protestant Churchman, 157, 181, 186
Protestant Episcopal Society for the Advancement of Christianity in South Carolina, 12, 24
Protestant Episcopal Society for Promoting Religion and Learning, 25, 101, 205, 207, 216, 249, 255, 255n, 332, 333, 344
Protestant Episcopal Theological Education Society of the State of New York, 60, 68, 69, 70
Protestant Episcopal Tract Society, 25
Provoost, Samuel, 4, 10
Psychotherapy and pastoral care, 308
Pusey, Edward Bouverie, 147, 167, 272
Pusey, Nathan M., 353

Quick, Oliver Chase, *The Christian Sacraments*, 330

Racine College, 215, 277, 287
Randall, George Maxwell, 245
Randel, John, 83
Rashdall, Hastings, 310
Raver, Leonard, 328n
Rawlinson, A. E. J., *Essays on the Trinity and the Incarnation*, 330
Reading for orders, 15-25, 96
Recitations, *see* Methods of study
Red Cross, the, 331
Reed, John, 72
Reeves, John, 22
Refectory, 133-34, 216-17, 247, 258, 266, 292-93, 335
Reid, Cornelius L., 275n
Religious education, *see* Christian education
Removal of the Seminary from New York, proposals for, 202-203, 234-37, 251
Rhetorical Association, 118
Rhetorical Society, 193
Rhind, J. Massey, 259n, 262
Rhinelander, William C., 84, 133; the William C. Rhinelander scholarship, 133
Rhode Island, the Church in, 13
Rice, Otis R., 327
Richardson, John Alexander, 320
Richardson, Nathaniel S., 228
Richey, Thomas, 243, 265, 271, 275, 276, 305, 322, 332n
Ricker, Charles H., 327
Riley, Theodore M., 285-86, 305
Ritualist movement, 185, 212-15, 219-21, 246n; its effects in the Seminary, 217-21, 225, 226-29
Robbins, Howard Chandler, 322, 326
Robbins, Wilford Lash, 241, 265, 283, 332; elected Dean, 297; activity of, 297-300; his efforts at curriculum revision, 300-304; his professors, 304-310; resignation of, 310
Robertson, Charles Franklin, 245
Robinson, William, 275n
Roman Catholicism, conversions to, 80, 176, 181-82, 224
Roper, John Charles, 286-87, 305, 309
Rose, Lawrence, 290, 291, 315, 329n, 331, 338, 339, 340, 341, 343, 347; elected Dean, 338; his views on theological education, 338, 352-53; his pastoral concern, 340, 348; financial achievements of, 344-46; building program of, 345-46, 348-51; his curriculum changes, 352-53; retirement of, 354
Rose, Mrs. Lawrence, 348, 351
Rudd, John Churchill, 62

Rudder, William, 232
Russell, Francis Thayer, 275, 305; his *Use of the Voice in Reading and Speaking*, 275
Rutgers University, 141, 246

Sagada Training School, 290
St. Alban's Church, New York, 213
St. Ambrose, 265
St. Andrew's Seminary, Manila, P.I., 290
St. Athanasius, 265
St. Augustine, 265
St. Clement's Church, Philadelphia, Pa., 213
St. Francis' Mission, Upi, P.I., 290, 331
St. George's Church, Flushing, N.Y., 207
St. George's Church, New York, 16, 64, 83, 148
St. Gregory Nazianzen, 265
St. Ignatius' Church, New York, 213, 226
St. James' Church, Hyde Park, N.Y., 207, 277
St. James' Church, New York, 45, 53, 83
St. John Chrysostom, *Christian Priesthood*, 22
St. John's Chapel of Trinity Parish, New York, 50, 51, 84-86, 94, 95, 96, 98, 102, 104, 118
St. John's Church, Brooklyn, N.Y., 208, 215
St. John's Church, Elizabeth, N.J., 62
St. John's College, 132
St. John's College, Aukland, N.Z., 276
St. John's College, Cambridge, 287
St. John's College, Oxford, 342
St. John's Lane, 84
St. John's Park, 82, 85-86, 117, 127, 197; the Seminary located at, 84-109
St. Luke's Cathedral, Portland, Me., 338
St. Luke's Chapel of Trinity Parish, New York, 84
St. Luke's Church, New York, 84, 140, 224
St. Mark's Church, Philadelphia, Pa., 246
St. Mark's Church-in-the-Bowery, New York, 84, 139, 142, 146, 152, 308
St. Mark's Library of the Seminary, 351, *see also* Library
St. Mary's Church, Burlington, N.J., 246
St. Mary's College, 131
St. Mary's Parnell, Aukland, N.Z., 276
St. Michael's Church, Bristol, R.I., 16
St. Michael's Church, Charleston, S.C., 27, 28
St. Michael's Church, New York, 45, 83
St. Paul's Cathedral, Boston, Mass., 52
St. Paul's Cathedral, Erie, Pa., 52
St. Paul's Chapel of Trinity Parish, New York, 48, 50, 83, 85, 253
St. Paul's Church, Baltimore, Md., 215
St. Paul's Church, Bridgeport, Conn., 228
St. Paul's College, 185
St. Paul's School, 306
St. Peter's Chapel, New York, 98, 119, 124
St. Peter's Church, New York, 48, 98, 119, 143, 145, 156, 326
St. Philip's Church, Charleston, S.C., 27, 28
St. Philip's Church, New York, 84
St. Stephen's Church, New York, 84, 145, 156
St. Stephen's College, 215, 242, 276
St. Thomas' Church, New York, 84, 139, 333
St. Thomas' Church, Toronto, Ont., 287
Samuel Verplanck Hoffman Foundation (for the support of the deanship), 252, 253
Sanday, William, 273, 275
Sanderson, Robert, 285
Scheme of study: as framed in *1818*, 43-44; in the New Haven Plan, 60-61; at St. John's Park, 86-89; in the early *Catalogues*, 134-38; in *1867*, 240-41; in *1892*, 274; in *1893*, 283-86, 287-88; in *1906*, 302-303; in *1914*, 304; in *1919*, 312-15; in *1968*, 315, 358-59. *See also* Curriculum
Schmemann, Alexander, 358
Scholarships, 101, 133, 198, 205, 254
Schroeder, Frederick, 66
Schutz, Brother Roger, 358
Schuyler, Cornelius, 84
Scott, Sir Walter, 136
Scottish Episcopal Church, 4, 320
Seabury, Samuel (Bishop), 4, 147, 241, 320, 332
Seabury, Samuel (Judge), 332, 332n
Seabury, Samuel (Professor), 72, 166, 169, 185, 194, 196, 204, 215, 221, 225, 226, 241, 242; editor of *The Churchman*, 147-48; advocate of the *Tracts* and defender of Bishop Onderdonk, 149, 156-57; supports Arthur Carey,

154-56, 177; made professor, 194; quarrels with Professor Seymour, 230-31, 233-34; death of, 234
Seabury, William Jones, 241, 242, 264-65, 271, 271n, 275, 285, 292, 305, 307, 320, 332
Seabury Divinity School, 242, 276
Seabury documents, 320
Seabury Hall, 299n, 332, 335, 345
Seabury-Western Theological Seminary, 342
Seal of the Seminary, 92, 295
Second World War, 333, 334-35, 338
Seibt, Charles Theodore, 243n, 287, 305, 307, 341
Selective Service Act, 334
Selma march, 354
Seminarian, 288
Sesquicentennial year, 356-58
Seymour, George Franklin, 211, 217, 221, 225, 241, 250, 257, 266, 268, 272, 275, 321, 322; a champion of Ritualism 185, 215, 217-20; made professor, 215; character and ability of, 215-16; influence of, 216-19, 236-39, 241; his quarrels with Seabury and Vinton, 220, 231-33; his difficulties with Dean Forbes, 225-28, 230-34; his *Defence of the Professor of Ecclesiastical History, etc.*, 232; elected Dean, 234; confers the first degrees, 243-44; resignation of, 246
Shelton, William, 219, 220
Shepard, Charles Norman, 307, 311, 321, 325
Sherlock, Thomas, 143
Sherred, Jacob, 63, 72, 73, 74, 86, 199, 257
Sherred Hall, 257, 258, 346
Sherred legacy, 72-74, 199
Short, Charles, 239
Simpson, Cuthbert Aikman, 321, 323, 325, 340; his *Revelation and Response in the Old Testament* and *The Early Traditions of Israel*, 323
Simpson, Mrs. Cuthbert Aikman, 332
Smedes, Aldert, 195
Smith, Benjamin Bosworth, 79, 151
Smith, Hugh, 143, 144, 145-46, 152, 153, 154, 156, 157; his *True Issue for the True Churchman*, 157
Smith, John Augustine, 41
Smith, Robert, 11
Smith, W. Robertson, 272
Smith College, 321
Smith fellowship, 329n
Social action, 327
Social work, 291, 327
Society for the Advancement of Christianity in Pennsylvania, 25
Society for the Advancement of Christianity in South Carolina, 12, 24
Society for the Education of Pious Young Men for the Ministry, 41, 54
Society of Inquiry, 118
Society for Promoting Religion and Learning, *see* Protestant Episcopal Society, etc.
Society for the Promotion of Christian Knowledge, 24
Society for the Propagation of the Gospel, 4, 16, 24
Sonne, Niels Henry, 350-51
South Carolina, the Church in, 11, 12, 13, 24, 27, 29
South Carolina College, 132
South Carolina Diocesan Convention, of *1814*, 26, 27-28, 30; of *1815*, 36; of *1817*, 36; of *1819*, 43
South Carolina trustees, 106, 140, 160
Southern Churchman, 251n
Spalding, Franklin Spencer, 273, 275
Spalding, John Franklin, 245
Sparrow, William, 174, 175
Spears, Robert R., Jr., 356n
Special students, 267-68, 331, 334, 339
Stackhouse, Thomas, *A Complete Body of Divinity*, 21, 22, 89
Standing Committee, 95, 100, 106, 108, 193, 203, 204, 223, 234, 246, 253, 255, 278, 279, 288, 344, 345
Statutes of the Seminary, 86-87, 90, 92, 94, 95, 226, 266n, 278n, 347; revision of *1867*, 193, 222-23, 240, 270; revision of *1885*, 265, 270-71
Steenstra, Peter Henry, 273
Stewart, Marshall Bowyer, 321, 324, 325-26, 342; his *God and Reality*, 325
Stokes, Edward, 236
Strong, George Templeton, 121, 143, 202, 221, 222, 237
Strup, Frank, 335
Students, numbers of, 48-49, 68, 96, 122, 123, 180, 196, 238, 267, 331, 334, 339-40
Student fees and expenses, 133-34, 216, 268-89, 344
Student life: in the earliest days, 48-51; in New Haven, 66-68; at St. John's Park, 86-94, 96-99, 102-104; in the East Building, 115-16; in the eighteen-thir-

ties and 'forties, 116-121, 126-27, 133-34; 135-38; under Dean Seymour, 217-220; in the Hoffman era, 264-67, 288-91; in recent years, 297-300, 331-32, 338-40, 346-48
Stuyvesant, Peter G., 139, 140, 141, 165
Styles Foundation, 329n
Sub-Dean, the office of, 270n
Sub-Deans, a list of, *see* Appendix
Suter, John W., 327
Systematic divinity, *see* Theology
Systematic Divinity, the professorship of, 71, 79, 185, 240, 242, 254n, *see also* Dogmatic Theology, the Mary Crooke Hoffman professorship of

Talbot, Ethelbert, 265
Tallman fellowship, 254
Taylor, A. E., 323; his *Faith of a Moralist,* 330
Taylor, Charles Lincoln, 353
Taylor, Jeremy, 285
Teaching Fellows, a list of, *see* Appendix
Temple, William, 300; his *Nature, Man and God,* 330
Tenny, Alfred F., 275n
Testimonials, 90-92, 96, 97, 120, 243, 265
Theological Committee of the General Convention of *1817*, 40-41, 43-46, 48, 49, 54, 55, 56; its *Address to the Members of the Church,* 43
Theological education: before the establishment of seminaries, 15-26; canons governing, 17-19; the societies' aid to, 24-25; proposals for reform of, 187-93; Dean Fosbroke on, 310-12, 319-20, 360-61; Dean Rose on, 352-53; today, 355-56
Theological Education Sunday, 198-99, 333-34, 337, 344
Theological Seminary of the Protestant Episcopal Church in the Diocese of Ohio, 78
Theological Society, 89, 193
Theology, the study of, 21, 61, 86, 87, 90, 137, 240, 273, 283-85, 302, 312-14
Thirty-Nine Articles, 149, 152, 154-55, 163, 167, 170
Thompson, J. M., 310
Thornton, Lionel, *The Incarnate Lord,* 330
Tomline, George Pretyman, *Elements of Christian Theology,* 21
Tract 90, 147, 149, 151, 154, 169
Tracts for the Times, 147, 148, 149, 150, 151, 152, 153, 160, 162, 163, 164, 167, 168, 169, 170, 180, 185, 212, 213, 224
Trapier, Paul, 160, 164, 165, 183
Trench, Richard C., 90, 137
Trinity Chapel of Trinity Parish, New York, 244
Trinity Church, Boston, Mass., 15, 28, 45
Trinity Church, Geneva, N.Y., 72
Trinity Church, New Haven, Conn., 65
Trinity Church, New York, 10, 38, 80, 83, 143, 145, 174, 202, 211, *see* Trinity Parish
Trinity Church, Newport, R.I., 28
Trinity Church professorship, 321n
Trinity College, Cambridge, 276
Trinity College, Hartford, 287, 307
Trinity College, Toronto, 287, 308
Trinity corporation, 120, 205, 292
Trinity Parish, New York, 16, 25, 31, 40, 48, 51, 71, 85, 120, 143, 156, 205, 221, 223, 333, 344, *see* Trinity Church
Trinity School, 80, 85, 95, 195
True Catholic, 153
Trumbull, John, 66
Trustees of the Seminary, *see* Board of Trustees
Turner, Samuel Hulbeart, 15, 16, 23, 53, 54, 55, 59, 62, 75, 79, 80, 82, 88, 95, 96, 100, 101, 108, 109, 117, 124, 137, 138, 139, 140, 141, 144, 176, 177, 183, 203, 250, 272, 359, 360; made professor, 44-46, 79; character and personality of, 46-48; his first classes, 48-51, 54; death of, 48, 194, 204; in New Haven, 57, 64-68; moves into the East Building, 111-12; takes his turn as Dean, 128, 129-31, 158-59; replies to the Trustees' queries, 161-62; attitude toward the Bishops' visitation, 166, 169, 171-72; his proposals for curriculum revision, 189, 191; objects to the use of Plainsong, 209-10
Tutorial sessions, 330-31
Tutorial system, 329-30, 359
Tutors, a list of, *see* Appendix
Tuttle, Daniel Sylvester, 245
Tweed, Boss, 236
Tyng, Stephen H., 9, 16, 22

Underhill, Evelyn, *Worship,* 330
Union College, 41, 57, 132

Union Theological Seminary, 278, 288, 352
University of Pennsylvania, 44, 132, 308
Upi, P.I., St. Francis' Mission at, 290, 331

Vail, Thomas Hubbard, 245
Vanderbilt, Cornelius, 85, 251, 253, 255, 256, 291
Vanderbilt, William H., 254
Vanderbilt legacy, 254
Van Steere, Douglas, 358
Vermont, the Church in, 13
Verplanck, Gulian Crommelin, 72, 79, 87, 88, 138; his *Essay on the Nature and Uses of the Various Evidences of Revealed Religion*, 87
Veto power of the dean, 271
Vinton, Francis, 220, 221-22, 225, 226, 230, 231, 232, 233, 234, 241
Virginia, the Church in, 3, 6-7, 12-13, 14, 15
Virginia Diocesan Convention of *1813*, 13; of *1815*, 41; of *1821*, 78; of *1824*, 78n
Virginia Theological Seminary, 41, 78, 134-35, 182, 208, 288
A Visit from St. Nicholas, 105
von Hügel, Baron, 330

Wadhams, Edgar, 153
Wainright, Jonathan Mayhew, 9, 184, 222
Waldo, Samuel, 74
Walpole, G. H. Somerset, 276, 286
Walpole, Hugh, 276
Walton, William, 220n, 241
Walworth, Clarence, 146, 153, 154, 159
War of 1812, 5, 34
Ward, William G., 167
Warren, John Hobart, 253
Washburn, Benjamin M., 344
Washington (Trinity) College, 132
Waterland, Daniel, 90, 137
Webb, C. C. J., 323
Weinhauer, William Gillette, 343
Wellhausen, Julius, 272
Wentworth, Samuel, *Ode for the Canal Celebration*, 103
West, Edward N., 343
West Building, 122-25, 158, 162, 171, 217, 218, 238, 250, 255, 256, 258, 294, 298, 346, 348
West Close, 289
West Point Military Academy, 131, 221
West Quadrangle, 255, 259, 266, 291, 293, 345
Westcott, B. F., 284; his *Historic Faith*, 285
Western Theological Seminary, 300, 309, 321, 327
Western University of Pennsylvania, 131
Wharf Block, 200, 201, 207, 297
Wharton, Charles H., 39, 40, 44, 58
Wheatly, Charles, *Rational Illustration of the Book of Common Prayer*, 22
Wheaton College, 354
Whitaker, Ozi William, 245
White, William, 4, 10, 11, 15, 16, 17, 18, 23, 25, 35, 36, 40, 41, 47, 50, 52, 53, 57, 75, 77, 97, 107, 134, 138
White Hall, 295, 298
Whitehouse, Henry John, 80, 232, 245, 246n
Whittingham, William Rollinson, 140-41, 143, 144, 173, 174, 179, 188, 215n
Whybray, R. Norman, 340
Wilberforce, Robert, 285
Wilks legacy, 344
William and Mary College, 6, 13, 15, 41, 58
Williams, John, 261-62
Williams, Richard Rhys, 340
Williams College, 242
Wilmer, William H., 9, 41, 54, 55, 58, 70
Wilson, Bird, 15, 79, 87, 88, 89, 112, 117, 128, 136, 138, 139, 141, 144, 161, 162, 168, 175, 176, 185
Wilson James, 79
Wilson, Thomas, *Parochialia*, 22
Wilson, Woodrow, 299
Winslow lecturers, a list of, *see* Appendix
Women of General, the, 348
Woodhull, Victoria, 236
Woollcombe, Kenneth John, 342
Wright, J. Robert, 343n
Wright, John J., 357
Wylie, Samuel Joseph, 354, 355, 357, 360

Yale University, 27, 45, 62, 69, 77, 132, 287
Yates, Miles Lowell, 337, 340, 346, 348

Zion Church, New York, 84